Chief Justice
Fred M. Vinson
of Kentucky

A Political Biography

James E. St. Clair
and
Linda C. Gugin

UNIVERSITY PRESS OF KENTUCKY

Publication of this volume was made possible in part by a grant
from the National Endowment for the Humanities.

Scholarly publisher for the Commonwealth,
serving Bellarmine University, Berea College, Centre
College of Kentucky, Eastern Kentucky University,
The Filson Historical Society, Georgetown College,
Kentucky Historical Society, Kentucky State University,
Morehead State University, Murray State University,
Northern Kentucky University, Transylvania University,
University of Kentucky, University of Louisville,
and Western Kentucky University.
All rights reserved.

Editorial and Sales Offices: The University Press of Kentucky
663 South Limestone Street, Lexington, Kentucky 40508-4008

06 05 04 03 02   5 4 3 2 1

Frontispiece: Portrait of Vinson as Chief Justice. (Courtesy of
Special Collections, University of Kentucky Library.)

Library of Congress Cataloging-in-Publication Data

St. Clair, James E.
    Chief Justice Fred M. Vinson of Kentucky : a political biography /
James St. Clair and Linda Gugin
        p. cm.
    Includes bibliographical references and index.
    ISBN 0-8131-2247-3 (cloth : alk. paper)
    1. Vinson, Fred M., 1890-1953. 2. Judges—United States—Biography.
3. United States. Supreme Court—Biography. I. Gugin, Linda C. II. Title.
KF8745.V55 S7 2002
347.73'2634—dc21   2001007628

This book is printed on acid-free recycled paper meeting
the requirements of the American National Standard
for Permanence of Paper for Printed Library Materials.

Manufactured in the United States of America

To my mother, Mary Reiss St. Clair
And the memory of my father,
Robert Wilson St. Clair

J.E.S.

To my mother, Kathryn Corr Carstarphen
And the memory of my father,
Taylor Townsend Carstarphen, Jr.

L.C.G.

Contents

Acknowledgments

The start and completion of this biography would not have been possible without the generous assistance from numerous individuals and institutions. The staff and resources of the Special Collections Department at the Margaret I. King Library, University of Kentucky, were indispensable. Without fail, the Special Collections staff treated us like family during the countless hours we spent poring over the some four hundred boxes of Vinson papers as well as other archival materials. The staffs at four other libraries deserve special recognition. They are the Harry S. Truman Presidential Library, the Library of Congress, the Filson Historical Society, and our own library at Indiana University Southeast.

We readily acknowledge the important financial support from IU Southeast that was so instrumental during critical periods of the project. We received summer faculty fellowships as well as sabbatical leaves that gave us the time to devote our full energies to research and writing. In addition, the grant money IU Southeast provided enabled us to hire these very able research assistants—Kim Pelle, Fred Hecht, Lee Bruce, Megan Renwick, and Kurt Fetz—and to help with associated publication costs, including the purchase of photographs and copyright permissions. Special thanks go to Margaret Fukunaga, who assisted with research and securing copyright permissions and tackled the job of indexing with her usual dedication and efficiency.

The expert advice, the editing skills, and the wise counsel of James W. Ely Jr., professor of law and history at Vanderbilt University, were invaluable. Although extremely busy with his own work, Ely unselfishly gave of his time to help guide and shape the chapters dealing with Vinson's judicial service.

We gained valuable insight into how the Supreme Court operated under Vinson from three of his former law clerks, Newton Minow, Howard Trienens, and Justice Byron White. They provided helpful information on particular cases, shared stories about Vinson the man, and revealed fascinating behind-the-scenes information.

We also appreciate the contributions of the two anonymous reviewers of the manuscript, whose comments and suggestions helped us add perspective and depth to this work.

Introduction

In the almost fifty years since his death, the name Fred M. Vinson has all but disappeared from public awareness and consciousness. This work is intended to bring the life and times of a dedicated public servant back to the surface for examination and study by present and future generations of Americans. He was, above all, a true believer in government and public service. Vinson never doubted for a moment that the highest calling for an American was serving in government—federal, state, county, or municipal. For more than thirty years, he demonstrated that conviction, starting out as a part-time city attorney for his tiny hometown of Louisa, Kentucky, and rising to the top levels of all three branches of national government, a feat that few have equaled. He obviously enjoyed the fame and acclaim he received from public service, but more pleasing to him than any personal glory was the good that government could do for the "folks back home." From his first day in Congress to his last day on the Supreme Court, Vinson never lost sight of the fact that he had been entrusted with the high privilege and responsibility of serving the people. Sometimes he excelled at it and sometimes he fell short of expectations, but never did he shrink from his duties or give them less than, as he might put it, his dead-level best.

The values and beliefs he maintained for a lifetime were those he inherited as a child of the rugged but nurturing hills and valleys of eastern Kentucky. The legacy of tenacious but kind and considerate forebears instilled in Vinson a burning desire to succeed—but not at all costs. He played by the rules and expected others to do the same, and he accepted defeat, not willingly but nonetheless with grace and without rancor. The praise and best wishes from both sides of the aisle that greeted Vinson upon his departure from the House of Representatives were fitting tributes to a politician who paid more than just lip service to the spirit of bipartisanship. He was a Democrat with a capital *D* and also a democrat with a small *d*. Although Vinson believed deeply that the principles and policies of his party best served the interests of the common citizen, he believed even more strongly that government was required to act and move ahead. He was a pragmatist who focused on the problem at hand with no fixed ideological or philosophical position but rather with a belief that solutions would present themselves after a thorough study of the matter and after open, honest, and harmonious debate. He was fond of saying, "Things go better when you don't get hot and bothered."

Vinson's calm and steady hand helped steer the country through such monumental crises as the Great Depression, World War II, the postwar economy, and the Cold War. Although a fiscal conservative and orthodox in his economic thinking, Vinson recognized that the desperation of the Depression required the bold measures initiated by Roosevelt and his New Deal. He dutifully enlisted for the front lines, shouldering much of the responsibility for finding the financial muscle for programs that powered people out of despair and destitution. His most enduring legislative achievement was his work on the Social Security Act of 1935. Vinson's unselfishness and willingness to serve were apparent during the war years when he readily gave up lifetime tenure on the federal bench to take on a number of difficult and demanding assignments for Roosevelt and Truman. As the country's economic czar during the war, Vinson's decisions on prices and wages touched every American. He used his power wisely and judiciously, winning the respect of even those he ruled against. The reputation he earned as a skilled negotiator and reconciler of conflicting views led President Truman to turn to him in the mid-1940s when the Supreme Court was bitterly divided by intense infighting that had become public and was hampering the court's ability to function. It was Vinson's final call to duty, one that was a work in progress when he died.

The record book is replete with Vinson's imprint as legislator, administrator, and jurist. The laws and decisions that he crafted are given the extensive treatment they deserve in this work, but—because the measure of a person is more than what can be recorded in the archives of official proceedings—here too are the personal and human sides of Fred Vinson. Experts can quibble about and debate the lasting value of the public side of the Vinson ledger, but there can be little argument that the personal side is one that stands the test of time and one that offers sound guidance to those who choose to enter public service.

Although he could command the ear of presidents, foreign leaders and dignitaries, and captains of business and commerce, Vinson never lost connection with the man on the street, even after moving into the cloistered and rarefied chambers of the Supreme Court. He gladly welcomed old friends from Ashland, Morehead, and other Kentucky towns who would drop by for a visit. And his guests did not feel they had committed a serious breach of protocol if they addressed him as Fred instead of Mr. Chief Justice. A photographer assigned by *Parade* magazine to take the chief justice's picture for the cover recalled that he was nervous to be photographing such a prominent official but that Vinson immediately put him at ease. "It's comforting to know that the man you are waiting to photograph is a 'down home' sort who makes plain people feel at home," he said of his encounter.[1]

Vinson would have considered unseemly the practice that is so common today of public officials who use their service in government as a gateway to riches in the private sector. When presented with his one opportunity to cash in, he turned it down because he thought it would tarnish the image of the Court. He essentially lived paycheck to paycheck, just like millions of his fellow citizens. In fact, he was in debt much of the time while he was in Congress because he paid for his primary and election campaigns largely out of his own pocket. He even fell behind on mortgage payments a time or two when he was in the executive branch.

Obviously, then, in the way of tangible assets, Vinson left little behind. On a broader scale, his heritage is immensely rich, though impossible to measure. How do you assess the impact of the time, attention, and wise counsel that he dispensed so freely to family, friends, and strangers engaged on a street corner or through the mail? Whenever he had the opportunity, Vinson extolled the virtues of a career in public service, and his exhortations may have caused a thousand Vinsons to bloom in city halls, state houses, and federal offices throughout the land.

A father wrote Vinson shortly after the end of World War II seeking his advice about what his son and his nephews should do after being discharged from the military. Vinson, not surprisingly, suggested public service. "Government service—elective and appointive—holds many satisfactions," he wrote. Foremost, Vinson said, was "the all-important feeling of accomplishment in the public interest."[2] When the teenage boys of the Brooklyn-Queens Political Society wrote Vinson in 1947 while he was chief justice to praise his work and let him know that they were "really interested in politics and government," Vinson responded that the letter "touched [him] deeply." "[It is] truly a great thing," he continued, "for the boys and girls of today to take an active interest in good government, because it is to you that we must look for the future of America and our democratic system of government. I know that you will do everything in your power to preserve and protect it."[3]

Vinson did his part to preserve and protect. Asked to summarize Vinson's career, Willard Pedrick, who had worked for him as a law clerk on the circuit court and as an assistant in the economic stabilization office, said a fair assessment required going beyond just viewing his tenure as chief justice, which tends to get disproportionate attention and low marks. "He was so much more than that," Pedrick said, citing his extensive and significant service in the House, in two administrations, and on the lower court. "I don't think that we can expect the man who was one of the greatest decathlon performers to also be the world's greatest pole vaulter. In terms of the public servant, this was a great man, a man devoted to his country, a man who gave everything he had to the country and who served with distinction in every branch of federal government."[4]

CHAPTER 1

A Long Journey from "Jail"

In the fall of 1948, President Truman confronted gloomy prospects both at home and abroad. He was all but counted out in his race against Republican Thomas E. Dewey to retain the White House, and Cold War tensions had escalated because of the Soviet Union's blockade of Berlin. Seizing on a suggestion by two young campaign aides, Truman decided the time was ripe for bold action on the international front, action that, if it was successful in easing the tension, might also reverberate to his advantage in the election. So on October 3 the president called his good friend Fred M. Vinson, then chief justice of the United States, and asked him to undertake a peace mission to Moscow. Truman believed the deep-seated suspicion and distrust that existed between the two nations were caused in part by poor communications. He hoped that Vinson, who had a well-deserved reputation for being able to calm troubled waters, could, in a face-to-face meeting with Joseph Stalin, open a channel of constructive and ongoing dialogue. Truman wanted Vinson to give the Soviet leader "a better understanding of our attitude as a people and of our nation's peaceful aspirations for the whole world." He said, "I had a feeling that Stalin might get over some of his inhibitions if he were to talk with our own Chief Justice."[1]

During World War II and the turbulent postwar period, turning to Vinson had become a habit in Washington. So much so that he became known as "Available Vinson" because of his willingness to tackle difficult assignments for President Roosevelt and then for President Truman. He was, according to one pundit, "the trouble shooter who could be relied upon to step into a sticky situation and, by a blend of shrewdness, geniality and a talent for stressing areas of agreement, resolve a conflict or at least smooth the ruffled feathers of the antagonists."[2] Vinson's remarkable string of troubleshooting assignments began in 1943 when Roosevelt asked him to take the position of economic stabilizer and lead the administration's effort to hold down inflation during World War II. Even though Vinson had to relinquish his lifetime appointment as a judge on the U.S. Court of Appeals for the District of Columbia, he readily agreed to accept, saying to Roosevelt simply, "You're the commander in chief."[3] Later, the president put Vinson in charge of planning for the country's postwar years by naming him director of the War Mobilization and Reconversion Office. Shortly after Truman became president, he made Vinson his secretary of the Treasury, a position that not only kept Vinson at work on the knotty problems of the U.S. economy but also required him to map out strategies for dealing with economic recovery on a global scale. Truman again sought Vinson's steady hand in 1946 when he appointed him chief justice in the hope that he could unify a feuding and fractured Supreme Court.

Obviously, saying yes came naturally to Vinson, especially when summoned to duty by the president. When Truman proposed the Moscow venture, however, Vinson's inclination was otherwise. He told Truman, "As Chief Justice I must decline. But if you make it as a presidential request, I shall have a clear duty to comply." Truman did just that, saying, "I am sorry Fred, to do this to you, but in the interest of the country and the peace of the world I am compelled to request you to go." Vinson responded, "I'll be ready in a few days."[4] Because of his strongly held belief that justices should refrain from activities outside their duties on the Court, especially in an election year, Vinson insisted that if he undertook the assignment he would have to resign from the Supreme Court and not be reappointed.

In the end, the Vinson mission was scrapped because of the forceful opposition to it by Secretary of State George C. Marshall, who feared that such unilateral action would undermine the Western unity that had been forged to contend with the Berlin blockade. Nonetheless, once again Vinson had demonstrated his willingness to answer the call, even if it would, as in this case, mean stepping down from one of the highest and most powerful positions in government.

Acceding to a president's plea during a national crisis is understandably all but inevitable, but Vinson found it difficult to turn aside any request for help, regardless of its nature or who sought it. Vinson's generosity and unfailing kindness were traits he inherited as a son of the rugged hill country of eastern Kentucky, and he never shed them even as he scaled lofty heights in all three spheres of national government. The

Vinson is honored in his hometown of Louisa on July 11, 1951. (Courtesy of Special Collections, University of Kentucky Library.)

Vinson clan long had a reputation for being "ready to do a kind act or charitable deed to any who might stand in need."[5]

When Frederick Moore Vinson was born on January 22, 1890, in the small, neighborly town of Louisa on the banks of the Big Sandy River, his roots in the region were already well established by his Anglo-Saxon ancestors on both branches of the family tree.[6] On the maternal side his lineage extended back to the venerable Samuel Ferguson Sr., who settled in Tazewell County in southwestern Virginia in 1772 and moved north into the Big Sandy Valley in the early 1800s. The early Fergusons were farmers, merchants, timbermen, and owners of large tracts of land, but in subsequent generations Fergusons increasingly turned to law and politics. The Vinsons would follow a remarkably similar path to prominence.

Fred Vinson's paternal great-grandfather, James, made his way into the Big Sandy Valley at the turn of the nineteenth century from his native South Carolina. James Vinson was part of the great westward migration of pioneers who crossed mountains and navigated rivers to stake out their places in the rich bottomland of the river valleys in the foothills of Kentucky and present-day West Virginia.

Carving a new life out of the forbidding terrain and the raw wilderness embedded in pioneers like the Vinsons distinctive characteristics and values that were to be part of an enduring legacy to their descendants. Because they lived on isolated homesteads, families in the Big Sandy were by necessity close-knit and self-sufficient. Their rugged existence also made them resourceful, disciplined, and determined.

James and Rhoda (Sperry) Vinson, settling on the Virginia side of the Big Sandy River around 1812, laid claim to several hundred acres of dense forest and began the arduous task of clearing the land for farming. They were soon helped in their labors by their eight sons and two daughters. This second generation of Vinsons—Democrat in politics and Christian in their faith—firmly planted the family as one of the region's most prominent and influential. One son, Lazarus, who was Fred Vinson's grandfather, went into the timber business after acquiring large tracts of land on both the Kentucky and the then-Virginia sides of the Tug Fork near what is now Louisa. Other brothers, most notably William, Samuel, and Lafayette, also became entrepreneurs and owners of much land in the Big Sandy Valley.

The next generation of Vinsons, while continuing to be involved in business activities, also branched out into the legal profession, banking, and politics. The second James Vinson, Lazarus's son and Fred's father, fittingly was one of the family's political pioneers. He had followed his father into the timber business, but his interest in the enterprise eventually waned, and he looked for a way out of the rigors of rural life; he found it for a time through politics. In 1885, at the age of twenty-nine, Jim Vinson was elected jailer of Lawrence County, Kentucky, and he moved his wife, Virginia, and their three children—daughters Lourissa and Georgia and son Robert—from the farm into the town of Louisa.

Five years after the move, the couple's fourth and last child, Frederick Moore, was born. In later years, Vinson, who spent a lifetime associated with the law—either arguing it, making it, or interpreting it—liked to startle people by claiming that he was "born in jail." His actual birthplace, however, was the jailer's newly built eight-room, two-story, red brick home on the courthouse square, not the jail, which was a small separate building in the back.

Nevertheless, life in Louisa for the spirited, inquisitive, and impressionable young Vinson took on added luster and meaning because of the environment in which he was raised. The courthouse square in the small,

Although he liked to joke that he was "born in jail," his birth actually took place in the family's residence, not the jail, which was a small separate building in the back. Vinson's father was the jailer in Louisa at the time. (Courtesy of Special Collections, University of Kentucky Library.)

quaint southern river town was the locus of activity at the turn of the twentieth century, and it was Fred's playground. He romped under the sycamores and maples in the courthouse yard, experienced the pageantry of the traveling circuit court judge, lawyers, and others trooping to the county seat for trials, and listened to the drama unfolding before the bench from his perch in a courthouse window. As a son of the county jailer, Fred also was able to get even closer to the action. The circuit judge at the time, Stephen Gerard Kinner of Catlettsburg, a friend of Jim Vinson's, occasionally let Fred sit beside him on the bench while court was in session.[7] In addition, the judge, as well as the commonwealth attorney and other lawyers, boarded at the Vinson home, and they allowed him to listen in to their conversations, which naturally were liberally sprinkled with discussions of the law and politics. Although this youthful experience did not necessarily foreordain Vinson's career, it clearly planted a seed.

Fred's courthouse surroundings also provided him with an early opportunity to demonstrate the kindness that would come to be such an indelible trait. Fred and his older brother Bob roamed freely through the jailhouse and frequently befriended the inmates. When aunts and uncles visited the Vinsons, the boys would plead for money to buy tobacco for the men in jail. In one instance, young Fred's sympathy for one inmate got carried away, even in the eyes of the would-be beneficiary. It happened when he was four years old. Fred, recalling the incident years later, said, "There was a prisoner to whom I took a liking. I decided he didn't belong in jail. He hadn't told me he wanted out, but I made up my mind I'd help him escape. I got hold of my father's hatchet, and one day when no one was looking, I walked up to his cell and slipped it through the bars to him." The prisoner, though, was an unwilling participant in the plot. Calling out to Fred's father after the youngster had departed, he said, "Jim, here is a little present your boy just gave me. I figured you would like to have it back" (172).

The man's reaction was in part an indication of the respect prisoners held for Jim Vinson, who treated his wards fairly but ran the jail with an iron hand. Bob Vinson said his father "could be a tough man to cross. He was as strong as an ox; he'd take no guff from anybody" (182).

Firm but fair also described the Vinson home. "I was reared in a rather disciplinarian household—justice, but discipline," Fred Vinson said. "My parents were serious folk. They both considered life as an obligation toward God, country and family." Vinson thought his mother in particular had a profound effect on his life: "She was an omnivorous reader and well-informed. She believed in duty and service. She planted in me a deep regard for religion, respect for law, and faith in a good cause." Vinson said his mother taught her family "to do the proper thing without expecting any reward save the knowledge that we had done the right thing" (186).

Virginia Vinson's great influence with the children—especially with Fred, the youngest—may be traced to 1895, when she was forced to assume increased responsibility for raising the family because of a tragedy that shattered the rhythm of the Vinson household. Jim's father, Lazarus, or Uncle Lace as he was widely known, was found robbed and murdered under a bridge near Catlettsburg, where he had traveled to collect money due his timber business. By this time Jim was town marshal and had moved his family from the jailer's residence to a frame house close to the banks of the Big Sandy. He resigned that position and devoted most of the next three years to searching for the killers, leaving the affairs of the family in Virginia's hands. Once the suspects were apprehended, their trial in Catlettsburg and convictions took another three years, and during this period Jim was again away from home much of the time.

Fred, who had gone through the formative years of age five through age eleven in the near-absence of his father, was well on his way to maturity. He started school the year of his grandfather's murder and quickly established himself as a star pupil, an eager learner with an almost photographic memory and unusual powers of concentration. His first teacher, Margaret Hatcher, said she recognized his brilliance and ambition from the beginning, adding that he "couldn't bear to let anybody get ahead of him."[8] Older brother Bob recalled that at home Fred would sprawl out on the floor, poring over his school work while whistling softly through his teeth. At night he studied by the glow of an oil-burning lamp because the Vinson house was without gas, and electricity did not arrive in Louisa until 1923.

Fred excelled in school and spent hours at the public library devouring books, magazines, and newspapers, but he was far from being just a bookworm. Though spindly and asthmatic as a child, he nonetheless tackled sports on the sandlots—football and baseball in particular—as energetically and effectively as he did homework. According to his brother, he was "noisy as hell in a ball game" and a stickler for the rules. A shortstop in baseball and quarterback in football, Fred was "a natural leader—scrappy, aggressive and sure of himself."[9]

His youthful zeal and consciousness carried over to the odd jobs he held to help out the family, whose finances were naturally strained by Jim Vinson's absence. Fred did his part by selling and delivering the Sunday edition of the *St. Louis Post Dispatch,* the *Saturday Evening Post,* and a weekly newspaper called *Pennsylvania Grit.* He was especially attentive to his job of peddling *Grit,* and it was an experience that he long remembered.

Upon receiving his stack of *Grit*s each week, Fred eagerly read the current issue cover to cover, which enabled him to discuss its contents with prospective buyers. When a judge boarding at the Vinson home chided him that he should not be selling a publication filled with "damned old Yankee nonsense," Fred won the judge over as a subscriber by persuading him that the paper contained news and information that he would find interesting. Years later, another young paper-peddler won over then-congressman Vinson by triggering his fond memories of selling *Grit.* A young boy named Billy Bagby, of Grayson, wrote asking if Vinson would buy a subscription to the *Ashland Independent* to help him win a prize in a sales contest. Vinson already subscribed to the Ashland newspaper, but he sent seven dollars to the youngster for an additional subscription. When he got the request, Vinson explained in a letter to Bagby, "my

mind turned back thru the years when I was a little boy selling newspapers and I can remember now every regular subscriber. I sold the
Pennsylvania Grit and made 2 cents on each sale, so I made up my
mind that I wasn't going to let you miss getting a subscription from
me, even tho' it did cost a few dollars and even tho' I already had
subscribed to it."[10]

Fred's budding entrepreneurial activities in Louisa were interrupted
in 1902 shortly after he turned twelve years old, when his family moved
about twenty-five miles north to Catlettsburg; there Kentucky, West Virginia, and Ohio meet where the Big Sandy empties into the Ohio River.
Jim Vinson, having spent a great deal of time in Catlettsburg during the
trial of the men charged with his father's murder, became attracted to
the city and decided it was the best place to live and raise a family.[11]
Thus the lively river town was the Vinsons' home for two years while
Jim tried his hand at yet another venture.

Jim Vinson was not without resources, even though his six-year crusade to avenge his father's death naturally was costly. He owned the
family farm and timber business, which had continued generating income. Jim was therefore able to purchase a ten-room hotel called the
Price House in Catlettsburg, which he remodeled into a boardinghouse
and renamed the Vinson House; he and Virginia operated the facility
until they sold it and returned to Louisa in 1904.

Although Fred had to start high school in new surroundings, he
adapted quickly, becoming, in the words of one of his teachers, "very
popular here."[12] In later years, Vinson, warmly recalling attending school
in Catlettsburg, credited his English teacher there with awakening "in
me the real pleasure that is incident to school work. I always liked con-
tests and the spirit of interest created in the diagram work in your gram-
mar class did much to awaken me."[13] Vinson's settling in was effortless
in part because being in Catlettsburg, county seat of Boyd County, was
in at least one sense like being back in Louisa. The Vinson House ca-
tered mainly to the same sort of courthouse clientele that had boarded
with the Vinsons in Louisa when the circuit court came to town, including Judge Kinner. The judge, as he had done earlier, frequently let Fred
sit beside him on the bench while he presided. And again, Fred listened
with fascination when nightly conversation at the Vinson House turned,
as it invariably did, to discussions of lawsuits, court proceedings, and all
kinds of other legal matters. In later years, discussing the effect of this
atmosphere on his decision to pursue law, Vinson said, "I suspect that it
may have been the challenge of the subject and the deep enjoyment

these men seemed to derive from the law, that might have had some influence upon me."[14]

The dominant force for Fred in his career decision, however, and in most things, for that matter, was his mother. "Her influence in my life was very great," he said. "In the first place, her deep love and confidence in me are known to everyone. She believed in me, and fought my battles and desires to secure an education" (185).

Back in his hometown in 1904, Fred completed his secondary education at Louisa High School and was quarterback of the 1906 football team that crowned its undefeated season with a 12-0 win over arch rival Ashland High School. After graduating from high school, he enrolled for two years of study at Kentucky Normal College, a nonaccredited teacher training school that had relocated in Louisa after its facility in Prestonsburg had been destroyed by fire. Although Fred had no desire to be a schoolteacher, attending Kentucky Normal was a convenient and inexpensive way for him to continue his education. The school, which charged a dollar a week for tuition, emphasized learning by rote and reasoning. Students were drilled repeatedly in such core subjects as English, Latin, German, mathematics, history, philosophy, and biology.[15] Fred, with his drive and nearly photographic memory, flourished at Kentucky Normal, graduating valedictorian in the class of 1908.

Vinson was quarterback of the Louisa High School football team that went undefeated in 1906. (Courtesy of Special Collections, University of Kentucky Library.)

Vinson, third from right, was valedictorian of his 1908 graduating class at Kentucky Normal College. (Courtesy of Special Collections, University of Kentucky Library.)

The president and founder of Kentucky-Normal, Walter M. Byington, recognizing that his school was limited in what it could do for this gifted student, was eager to have Fred attend a university, where his full intellectual promise might be reached. He was able to persuade Centre College in Danville, Kentucky, a private liberal arts college known for its academic excellence, to accept Fred as a senior on a probationary basis (84). Even so, Vinson had to come up with money for tuition and living expenses to take advantage of this opportunity, a prospect made more difficult by the economic depression that wracked the country in 1908.

This financial hurdle was cleared when Dr. Morton G. Watson, a Louisa physician, banker, and local Democratic Party stalwart, arranged a loan of four hundred dollars for Fred. His oldest sister, Lourissa, who was insistent that Fred attend college, took in washing so she could help with his expenses. Miss Lou, as she was generally known, sent him five dollars a week; in return, Fred, ever the stickler for detail, mailed back a weekly report on how the money was being used.[16] Dr. Watson's crucial intervention in his behalf was something Vinson long cherished. While in Congress, Vinson wrote in a letter to Dr. Watson's brother, "Were I to live beyond my allotted space, I could not repay him for the help he gave me in the formative years of my life." Vinson was not referring only to the monetary assistance, as he made clear in this passage: "It was to your brother that I turned for counsel and advice in the early days of my school life and it was he who strengthened my purpose to arrive at an honorable position in life."[17]

When Fred arrived at Centre College, located in the stately Kentucky Bluegrass, in September 1908, he made his first impression on fellow students by his appearance. It was still vivid nearly forty years later to classmate George L. Alley, who described Vinson as a "tall, slender, beak-nosed, black-haired, taciturn mountaineer."[18] Once the young man from the foothills of eastern Kentucky settled in, though, he made just as unforgettable impressions through his academic achievements and athletic prowess. Another classmate, John Diederich, who became an Ashland attorney and Republican national committeeman, said Vinson "entered into practically all the various college activities; he studied and played hard; in fact he was most aggressive in everything."[19] Lawrence Hager, later editor and publisher of the *Owensboro Messenger and Inquirer* and a Vinson confidant, recalled that Fred "always sat up on the edge of his seat, anxiously awaiting and seeming to invite questions. I was in practically all of Fred Vinson's classes at Centre and don't recall that he missed a single question asked him."[20]

It is not surprising, then, that by the end of his senior year at Centre, Vinson was at the head of his class, compiling a 97 percent average in course work that consisted of astronomy, constitutional law, economics, English, Greek, Greek literature, history, mathematics, physics, and Spanish.[21] At that time his grade average was the highest ever attained by a student since the college's founding in 1819, and it earned Vinson the coveted Ormond Beatty Alumni Prize of fifty dollars. The 1909 college yearbook, *Cardinal and Blue,* attesting to Vinson's scholarship, noted alongside his class picture, "Vins knows all his books off by heart. He can recite any lesson he's had since the beginning of the year, word for word as it is in the book. Just tell him the page and line you want him to begin on, and that's all you have to do except stop him (and that's the hardest part)."[22]

To Vinson, college was "a test by fire" and an opportunity to demonstrate one's true measure, a latter-day challenge of the sort his ancestors confronted in taming the thick frontier woodlands a century before. Vinson's prescription for success in college was to remain true to oneself and not go along with the crowd. "When a young man enters college he is thrown, to a large degree, upon his own resources and ofttimes one with a weak character considers it is necessary for him to do things in order to be one of the boys and not show that he is unaccustomed to such things," he wrote to a young man going off to Centre in the 1920s." The "weakling succumbs to temptations because it is the course of least resistance," but those who resist construct "a stronger character with which to wage the battle of life." He closed by advising, "Don't do anything that you would not do if you were at home."[23]

Vinson was also determined to prove, in the course of his "test by fire" at Centre, that his talents transcended the classroom. Playing baseball, a passion of his since childhood, was a natural extracurricular activity; he also played varsity basketball. But trying to be what in today's parlance is called a student athlete did cause Vinson anguish over whether he should divert attention from his studies. In fact, his friend Hager said he had difficulty persuading Fred to return to the 1909 Centre baseball team after he quit to devote more time to his courses. He did return, and for three seasons was Centre's star shortstop—two as team captain. Diederich, who played on the 1909 and 1910 teams, said what Vinson "lacked in weight, he made up in spirit and fight; he pulled many a game out of the fire by his superb fielding and timely hitting."[24]

Vinson believed that a decision forced upon him in the spring of 1909 while a member of the Praying Colonels baseball team marked the transition from boyhood to manhood for him. The team was scheduled for a week's trip to Virginia and North Carolina ending on the eve of

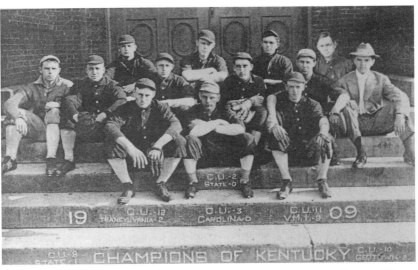

Vinson (second row, third from right) on Centre College's 1909 baseball team. (Centre College yearbook.)

Vinson family portrait. In the front row, from left to right, are his brother Robert, his mother Virginia, and father James. Vinson is flanked by sisters Lourissa, left, and Georgia, right.

final examinations. Vinson said he "wanted to go so bad I could taste it," but he had also promised his mother that he would win the aforementioned Ormond Beatty Prize. Another student was close to him in class ranking, and any misstep during finals would cost him top honors. "I finally decided to make the trip and win the prize as well or break a hamstring," Vinson said. He took his books with him, studying on the train and between games; he passed the finals as fluidly as he had fielded and batted the ball during the road trip and, of course, kept his promise to his mother.

After obtaining his undergraduate degree in 1909, Fred entered Centre's law school in accordance with his mother's wishes, but he continued playing baseball and even flirted for a time with the idea of making it a career.[25] During the summers he earned money to help pay for his education by playing throughout Kentucky and West Virginia, and in the spring of 1911, just before graduating from law school, he actually signed a contract to play professionally for Lexington in the Blue Grass League.

In the end, however, the influence of Virginia Vinson prevailed. As Fred put it, "I loved baseball, but I did not continue in that field." He said he loved his mother more and that he "had confidence in her judgment that I ought not get side-tracked from the legal profession."[26]

As might be expected, Vinson stayed on track during law school,

Vinson, upper right, on the 1911 Centre College basketball team. (Centre College yearbook.)

finishing the two-year program as the leader of his class with a grade average of 98.5 percent. He won both the Jacobs Junior and Senior Law Prizes for his top grades and the Bobbs-Merrill Prize in his senior year for preparing the best legal brief. His achievements are even more remarkable considering that he held various part-time jobs and continued to be heavily involved in extracurricular activities. He worked as a teaching assistant in history and mathematics at the college, as law librarian, as a special tutor, and as a teacher in the college preparatory school in Danville. In addition, he was an editor of the law school's journal, the *Basilisk;* president of the Deinologian Literary Society; president of Ye Round Table, a discussion group; an officer in the Proctor Knott Debating Society; and a member of Phi Delta Theta fraternity. He was on the baseball team both of his years in law school and on the basketball team his last year.

Fred had packed in all he could in the tight space of three years at Centre because it was his nature, as he explained in a letter to a friend, "to speed up things. I have been hurrying all my life. In school I felt I had to get out in a hurry and, as a matter of fact, on account of the money situation did have to speed it up." After college, Vinson added, he was in debt and "had to hurry in order to get that paid off, but more particularly because of wanting to ripen into a lawyer quickly."[27]

At the age of twenty-one, his formal education completed, Fred M. Vinson returned to Louisa to practice law. His time at Centre, Vinson readily acknowledged, had been crucial in building a foundation for what was to come. When he arrived at Centre, Vinson said, "I was painfully shy and suspicious of anyone who wasn't kin to me." However, the people of Danville and the faculty and students at Centre "treated me like a person, wooed me out of myself, and taught me to let go and try my wings in varied activities. Above all, I learned to love and enjoy people. Without that life is pretty empty and vain."[28]

In the ten-year period from 1911 to 1921, Vinson continued spreading his wings, but his pace was less frenzied than it had been at Centre when he was driven by the need to prove his mettle in that "test by fire." Now it was time to settle in and enjoy the fruits of such arduous efforts. In his law practice—first in partnership with Forrest Lee Stewart, an older, well-established Louisa lawyer, and then on his own—Vinson built a reputation as an honest, hard-working attorney, handling the typical small-town workload of deeds, negligence cases, and wills. He also acquired a reputation as the town's best checker player, according to W.E. "Snooks" Crutcher, a towheaded youth in Louisa at the time. Crutcher, who later became publisher of the *Morehead News* and several other eastern Kentucky papers, noted that throughout his life Vinson was determined to be the best at whatever he tried, even if it was just checkers. He reigned as the king of the checkerboard at John Justice's barber shop, where he waged many hard-fought duels with the shop's shoeshine man, also an accomplished player. The matches, of which Vinson generally won two out of three, always drew a crowd because they were considered "the best game in town," Crutcher recalled.[29]

Besides checkers, Vinson also frequented the barber shop to indulge in the twenty-five-cent special, which consisted of a hot bath, a haircut, hair tonic, a shave, and a massage. Crutcher said it was the usual practice of Vinson and other "sporty men in Louisa" to bring fresh clothes to the barber shop and then change into them after being treated to "the works."

Vinson's sole try for public office during the decade came in 1913 when he persuaded the Louisa city council to make him city attorney. An older attorney in town, Henry Sullivan, also wanted the position, but Vinson, who was dogged in every pursuit, made the council an offer it could not refuse. He promised to forgo the fifty-dollar-a-month stipend the job paid and instead be compensated by collecting the five-dollar attorney fee levied in criminal cases in police court.[30] By a margin of one vote, Vinson was elected city attorney, a position he held for only one year. During this period Vinson also tried his hand in commerce, becoming a silent partner in a short-lived wholesale grocery business concern, and he played shortstop for Louisa's semiprofessional team. Crutcher, who was batboy and water boy for the team, noted that Vinson "played baseball with his brain as much as with his physical body." He studied opposing pitchers so he could advise his teammates "whether the other pitcher had a curve ball, fast ball or so forth and whether he was wild and should be waited out."[31] Vinson's semipro playing days lasted until 1916.

For the next five years, with the exception of the war years, Vinson mainly concentrated on his law practice. When the United States entered the war in Europe in 1917, Vinson registered for the draft but was rejected twice for being underweight. He then became active on the home front, giving public speeches to promote government bond drives and Red Cross appeals as well as donating liberally from his own modest earnings to such causes.[32] By August of 1918, he was judged suitable for service and was sent to Camp Zachary Taylor south of Louisville for basic training. In late October Vinson was assigned to officer training school at Camp Pike in Arkansas, but before he was able to complete the course, the war ended; he was discharged in early December and returned to Louisa. Although his stay in the military was brief, the impression Vinson made on at least one fellow trainee at Camp Taylor was long-lasting. "The short session of army life was enjoyable . . . and I have always counted myself fortunate in having had the pleasure of knowing you," Harry E. Ritter of Cincinnati wrote to Vinson nine years later. "Notwithstanding the fact that I have not seen you since the day I was transferred from the old 9th Company Depot Brigade, you very often play prominently in my periods of reminiscence."[33]

When he launched his political career in earnest three years after his discharge, Vinson demonstrated that he could captivate voters in much the same way as he had his fellow soldier. In 1921 he was elected commonwealth attorney for the thirty-second judicial district of Kentucky, an area comprising Lawrence, Elliott, and Carter counties. In winning in this nominally Republican district, Fred had help from someone he and his brother Bob had befriended during their youthful days as jailhouse patrons. "Our kindness to those men wasn't always bread cast upon the waters," Bob said. He explained that he and Fred used to slip tobacco to an inmate named Bob Neace, who had been charged with murder but was acquitted during his trial by reason of self-defense. "He told me he'd never forget us," Bob recalled. By the time Fred ran for commonwealth attorney as a Democrat, Neace had become an influential figure in local Republican politics. Bob went to him to remind him of his pledge. "I told him that Fred—no question about it—was the best possible candidate, and would make us all proud of him some day. And I asked Neace if he'd vote for Fred and ask his friends to do so. Neace did so."[34] The intervention apparently helped. Fred won by a margin of 857 in a race that had gone to the Republican candidate in the previous election by more than 1,250 votes.

At the time, commonwealth attorneys could hold office and continue practicing law, so Vinson conducted the state's business and his private practice from the same offices in a Louisa bank building. "Snooks" Crutcher, who had been batboy for the town's baseball team, became Vinson's office boy and protégé. It was one of the most exciting experiences of his life, said Crutcher. His main task was to clean the offices every day, but he also had the opportunity to witness the parade of local and state politicians filing in to see Vinson and was able to soak in Vinson's discussions of cases and courtroom strategies.[35]

As the state's prosecutor for the three-county district, Vinson became known as a hard worker with a good legal mind and an advocate who argued his cases "with bulldog tenacity." Occasionally, though, his fervency got the best of him. For example, an argument between Vinson and another lawyer before Judge Allen N. Cisco of Ashland got so personal and vindictive that the judge imposed a five-dollar fine on each and even threatened to lock them up. As he was lecturing the two young attorneys, the judge noticed tears streaming down Vinson's face. A few minutes later Vinson arose, paid his fine, and humbly apologized to the court.[36]

Vinson liked to use humor and ridicule when defendants in the assault and homicide cases he prosecuted pleaded self-defense. In his summations, he told juries a story about two drunkards taking a dead man to a bar, propping him up between them, and ordering drinks. When their binge was over, they left and told the bartender their friend would pay the bill. When the bartender asked the dead man to pay and got no response, he hurled a bottle at his head. The police arrived, found the dead man and the broken bottle, and arrested the bartender for murder. "And," Vinson would tell juries, "the bartender pleaded self-defense, loudly protesting that the deceased, with rage in his eyes, had rushed towards him with a bottle."[37]

It was obvious at the time, according to Crutcher, that Vinson was destined for higher political office. He recalled political leaders "from all over the county and neighboring counties" visiting Vinson to urge him to run for Congress. When he was ready to pursue that next political plateau, two trials in particular proved beneficial, because they made his name more widely known in the region. The most publicized proceeding Vinson prosecuted during his two-year tenure as commonwealth attorney was the Duvall-Biggs murder case of 1922. Several relatives of a Grayson, Kentucky, physician, who had been murdered, were charged with seeking revenge on the alleged killer by hiring a professional hit man named Dominique Guerdini from the Chicago Black Hand gang to settle the score. The target of the plot was fired on from an ambush but was not killed. Thereafter, Guerdini and four members of the Biggs family were arrested and charged with attempted murder. As a result of Vinson's prosecution, both Guerdini and Jack Biggs, the slain man's brother, were sentenced to eight years in prison. The court of appeals reversed Jack Biggs's conviction and in doing so delivered a stinging critique of Vinson's closing statement to the jury in the Biggs trial. In his summation, Vinson had said the Biggs family had threatened him and Guerdini. The appeals court, however, asserted that there was no evidence in the record to support such a claim and concluded that Vinson "was . . . flagrant in abusing the license allowed to attorneys in arguing their cases."[38]

The other celebrated trial was also a murder case, but Vinson handled this one as part of his private practice. It involved two West Virginia state policemen who were charged with murdering a Louisa man. The man's father, a prominent and wealthy Louisa businessman, wanted his hometown lawyer to help with the prosecution because of his confidence that Vinson could win convictions. According to Crutcher, the financial arrangement was especially enticing. Vinson was paid $5,000 for just agreeing to take the case, and he was to receive $1,000 for each year of imprisonment he could get the jury to award, $25,000 if the policemen got life, and $50,000 if they got the death sentence. The father's faith in Vinson was well placed, since he won guilty verdicts and the two men were sentenced to twenty-one years each in prison; as a result Vinson received $21,000 in addition to the up-front payment.

With a measure of financial stability and some fame as well, Vinson was now in a good position to cash in by seeking a higher elective office. But before he embarked on such a course, he had a more personal ambition in mind. Vinson was one of several suitors competing for the affection of attractive, bright, and lively Roberta Dixon, the only daughter of prominent Louisa businessman Robert Porter Dixon. Although Fred grew up playing with the four Dixon boys, his relationship with Roberta, eight years younger than he, was sometimes rocky. Once when he was home from Centre College, he saw her riding in her pony carriage that she was about to outgrow, and Fred teased her by suggesting that she get out and let the pony ride. Her reaction, she said later, was one of indignation toward "that fresh college boy."[39]

Frosty relations had also existed between Fred and his future father-in-law, because they belonged to rival factions in local Democratic politics. Dixon, who had been Lawrence County clerk for three terms and chairman of the county Democratic Party, had attempted to block Fred's election as city attorney; likewise, Vinson opposed Dixon when he was up for Louisa postmaster.

Past clashes notwithstanding, Fred ultimately won Roberta's heart and her father's blessings. The wedding, which took place on January 24, 1923, in a private ceremony in the Dixon home, "was a case of a boy and a girl wiping out a non-shooting feud," Vinson said.[40] It was front-page news in the local newspaper, the *Big Sandy News,* which noted that after an extended honeymoon on the East Coast, the couple would return to live in Louisa.

The couple's stay in their apartment on Main Street, however, would be brief. Before the year 1923 was out, Fred M. Vinson began a journey that would propel him from the shores of the Big Sandy to seats of power and influence in Washington, D.C.—first in Congress, then in the executive branch, and finally at the summit of the nation's judiciary.

Although he spent much of the rest of his life in the nation's capital, Vinson never strayed far from the values and traits of his eastern Kentucky roots. He was fiercely proud of being a son of the Big Sandy and credited whatever success he attained to his upbringing there and to the legacy of the region's settlers. In a welcoming speech at the 1927 county fair and homecoming in Louisa, Vinson said the greatness of the Big Sandy "lies in the character of the people who felled the forests and populated its territory." It was these God-fearing, law-abiding pioneers, "of strong, sturdy stock, with minds clear and visions unimpaired," who opened the way for future generations to take "their proper places in the sun."[41]

CHAPTER 2

The Capitol as His Oyster

"It's right amusing to think about Vinson when we went to Washington," recalled the wife of Vinson's chief aide, Hubert Hutton, in an interview more than fifty years after she and her husband rode with Congressman-elect Fred M. Vinson and his wife, Roberta, aboard the Chesapeake and Ohio number two train from Louisa to the nation's capital. "We were like four little lost ducks or something up there on the Hill. We went up to tour around, to see where the Capitol was," Althea Hutton said. "I suppose Mr. Vinson thought it looked like an oyster and he would take it."[1]

As was his wont, Vinson did try to take Congress by storm, but his ambitions were throttled by the hard realities of the day: Republicans controlled both houses of Congress and the White House; he was a Democrat from a small state; he was assigned to three relatively minor committees (pensions, public lands, and flood control); and the prevailing political mood of complacency in the country, ushered in by Harding's return to normalcy and continued under Coolidge's presidency, was a restraint on legislative activism. The period after World War I and before the depression has been called "a comparatively quiet time" in national politics as a passive president "made no effort to get his legislative program adopted by Congress, being content merely to submit it in the traditional messages and let the legislature take it or leave it."[2]

Although presidential quiescence might have been the order of the day at the White House, it was not in Vinson's nature, as he had demonstrated during his days at Centre College, to be a shrinking violet, even when he found himself in unfamiliar surroundings. He felt comfortable being in Congress from the outset of his service there in 1924. In a sense it was like being back on campus, in that Congress resembled the all-male, clannish, and competitive atmosphere that had brought out the best in Vinson. In Congress, as at Centre, Vinson studied hard to master mounds of details on a wide assortment of subjects, and he amazed colleagues with his uncanny ability to recite complex and detailed information on the spot. This genius for mathematics and statistics eventually won him recognition as the foremost expert on taxation in the House.

The clubbiness of Congress was reinforced for Vinson by his residence at the Congress Hall Hotel, located across the street from the House office building. Home to about one hundred members of Congress and their families, the hotel had two dining rooms with reserved tables for residents and a large ballroom where dances were held every Wednesday and Saturday night.[3] Vinson's favorite form of entertainment at Congress Hall, though, was playing bridge. Writing to old friends from Louisa about his resumption of the game after arriving in Washington, Vinson said, "I was green at it, to some extent, but finally refreshed my memory."[4] For a time Vinson even continued playing baseball, holding down his old position of shortstop during the annual game between Democratic and Republican members of the House.

Vinson's chance to advance through the ranks, as is often the case in politics, was the result of happenstance. The sudden turn in his career, which propelled him from his position as a state prosecutor in a pocket of eastern Kentucky to the halls of Congress, had its genesis in the 1923 Democratic gubernatorial primary. Ostensibly, the race was between J. Campbell Cantrill and Alben W. Barkley, both congressmen at the time, but the real contest was the struggle for power between the two main factions of the state Democratic Party, divided in part by the issue of pari-mutuel betting. Barkley, who opposed racetrack gambling, had the support of the faction that included *Louisville Courier-Journal* owner Robert Worth Bingham. The wing of the party backing Cantrill, a pari-mutuel supporter, included Bingham rivals James B. Brown, who owned the *Louisville Herald-Post,* and Desha Breckinridge, owner of the *Lexington Herald.* Cantrill won the nomination, but he died within a month after the primary, leaving the party without a candidate for governor. The subsequent selection of a replacement by the Democratic State Central and Executive Committees, controlled by forces opposed to Barkley, was virtually dictated by Brown. "That fact meant that factionalism would remain an issue and that the nominee would be an anathema to Brown's enemy, Bingham."[5] Vinson, who cast his lot with the Brown-Breckinridge wing of the party, by extension also became anathema to Bingham and the *Courier-Journal.*

The party's candidate for governor now was William J. Fields, a veteran congressman whose nineteen-county Ninth District included Vinson's home county of Lawrence and several neighboring ones in the Big Sandy Valley. When Fields vacated his seat after decisively winning the 1923 governor's race, Vinson seized the opportunity to move up to a bigger political playing field with characteristic zeal. He was ambitious, and he savored an electoral battle in much the same way that he had relished competition on the athletic field. Vinson often compared politics with sports, believing that each required careful preparation, hard work, and a will to win. He also felt that the fight must be clean and that contestants had to play by the rules. "There is always consoling reward in defeat when the battle waged was clean fought," he said.[6] Vinson, of course, never intended to lose. He remarked to a friend about his campaign to succeed Fields, "I am in this fight with both feet, and while I have not been making a great lot of noise, I have been working the situation out as thoroughly as I can."[7] His diligence paid off: he was the unanimous choice of a district committee to be the party's candidate in a special election being held to fill Fields's unexpired term. He then crushed Republican W.S. Yazell of Maysville on January 12, 1924, by a vote of 15,681 to 5,822, or about 73 percent of the total vote cast.[8] Vinson won every county in the district, but the results from his community were the most gratifying of all. "No matter what the future may hold in store for me, success or failure, I will always have the vote of Louisa and Lawrence County in the Special Election to visualize and warm my heart," he wrote to a supporter.[9]

Less than three weeks after his victory in the special election, Vinson's small entourage, which also included his mother, Virginia, and Eva Price, who had worked for Roberta's family and was to be the live-in housekeeper for the Vinsons, was bound for Washington. Over the next thirty years, Vinson rode the rails countless times between Washington and the Big Sandy, but doubtless no journey ever matched the thrill of the one that began on that morning of January 29, 1924. Two days later, with wife and mother at his side, Fred M. Vinson, who had just turned thirty-four years old, was sworn in as the newest member of the Sixty-eighth Congress.

The day after his swearing in, Vinson was on the job, busily replying to stacks of mail from constituents, writing friends to report on his activities since his arrival, and poring over documents and reports to get up to speed on issues before the House. In a letter to Louisa hardware dealer and friend Ernest Shannon, he wrote, "I have been working pretty keen and don't know whether I can go quite as strong as I have been going or not. Didn't get supper last night until 8:15."[10] Vinson was in a hurry, as usual. In part, his haste to harness the details of his new responsibilities was in keeping with his need to speed things up. But he was also under pressure to make a mark quickly, because he would have to face voters again later in the year. Anticipating opposition in the party's August primary, he set about lining up his campaign structure after being in Washington less than a month. In a letter to one county official, Vinson wrote, "I am making preparations for the fight in August and would like to know whether or not you would be my Campaign Manager in Bracken County." Explaining his strategy, Vinson said, "While it is thought by many that Mr. [Ryland] Musick will not run I want to start early on the organization so that we can put him on the shelf if he does attempt it."[11]

Vinson's need to establish a political identity for himself quickly was aided by the decline of strict party discipline, which by the time he entered Congress had given way to the "force of localism in American politics," a change that "reflected the growing diversity of interests in a pluralistic society."[12] Thus, rather than being bound to vote for measures designed to carry out platform pledges, members could instead give more weight to how their votes would play back home. This development, which House Speaker Tip O'Neill would encapsulate years later in his famous maxim that "all politics is local," was of particular importance to Vinson because of the strong Republican nature of his district and because it coincided with his own belief that he should vote in accordance with the majority views of those in his district. Explaining his view of his role in Congress to a constituent, Vinson wrote, "As long as I am permitted to represent the great people of the Ninth District it will be my purpose to accurately interpret the prevailing sentiment and register their wishes with respect to legislation by the votes which I cast in Congress."[13]

Vinson got a taste of what was in store for him as a member of the minority party after casting his first vote on the floor of the House. He voted against a proposal to reinstate some jobs in federal land offices in several states, "but as usual, it carried," he wrote in another letter to Shannon.[14] But Vinson, bursting with ambition and ability, was not deterred. He was determined to make his presence known, and he chose to do so by positioning himself as a staunch defender of the "little" people against the privileged. It was a sure-fire strategy given the tenor of the times. The Teapot Dome scandal over the secret leasing of oil reserves on public land to private companies, which was first revealed to the general public during Vinson's freshman year in Congress, had become a symbol of power, influence, and corruption. There were also "revelations of the distribution of some $250 million in graft in the Veterans Bureau and of corruption in the Office of the Alien Property Custodian."[15] By staking his claim to populism, Vinson was not merely engaging in political expediency; rather, he was acting on long-held beliefs. He enunciated his political philosophy in a stump speech: "I am a Democrat saturated with the idea that the party of Jefferson is the party of the people, thoroughly imbued with the notion that the Democratic Party and the principles upon which it stands represent the best interests of the people." He added, "Since I arrived at the age of accountability—and even before—I was told that the Republican Party sponsored laws that legisled money into the pockets of the few, whereas the Democratic Party had for its foundation rock—equal rights for all and special privileges for none. I am a Democrat by birth, family, and of choice."[16]

Once in Congress, Vinson saw Andrew Mellon, Coolidge's secretary of the Treasury, and his tax reduction plan for the wealthy as ample evidence that his descriptions of the two major political parties were exact. Mellon, the third-richest man in America, was consumed by the pursuit of wealth and constituted "the dominant symbol of the marriage of high finance and government."[17] Vinson had been in Congress only two weeks when, ignoring the time-honored tradition that new members should remain on the sidelines until they are more seasoned, he rose to make a twenty-minute speech concerning the tax reduction plan, which was at the time the biggest item on the legislative agenda. Mellon, in much the same vein as modern-day "trickle-down" economic theorists, sought to reduce taxes on the rich as a way of stimulating the economy. Vinson, however, characterized Mellon's proposal as a scheme for the "ultrarich" that would only "create more wealth for themselves and their posterity." He urged Congress to adopt an alternative tax reduction plan submitted by John Nance Garner, Democratic representative from Texas, which Vinson said would benefit "the people."

The speech was well crafted and an early demonstration of the ease with which Vinson discussed and deciphered complicated tax issues. His presentation even included tax tables that he had devised based on Garner's plan showing the tax savings for those with incomes under $50,000 and the extra taxes paid by those whose incomes exceeded $50,000. Vinson also laced his address with humor and ridicule, and he managed to get in an aside about Teapot Dome. In a pointed reference to the clumsy explanations being offered for the sudden wealth of Interior

Secretary Albert Fall after he granted leases on public lands to big oil companies, Vinson said that people often got confused when talking about large sums of money. For example, Vinson said, $68,000 became "in the minds of some to be six or eight cows." This was the yarn spun by the manager of Fall's ranch, who insisted he was misunderstood when he told someone about a gift from oil magnate Harry Sinclair. It was not $68,000 (sixty-eight thou), but "six or eight cows." Vinson also turned the tables on Republican congressman John Tilson of Connecticut, who, in presenting the Mellon proposal to the House, had belittled those in the lower income tax brackets as "squawkers." Vinson delighted in pointing out that in Kentucky there were only 45 people who were not "squawkers," or those benefitting from Mellon's plan, but there were 69,451 "squawkers" in the state who would gain under the Garner proposal. Then, noting the political import of this imbalance, Vinson said that if the Coolidge administration continued its "reactionary work in the interests of 'big money,' all of the good Republicans in Kentucky will be squawking under the 'rooster,'" a symbol of the Democratic Party.[18]

Turning to Mellon, Vinson likened the Treasury secretary to the cartoon character Andy Gump, whose mood fluctuated between despair and mirth depending on his shifting financial fortunes. "Andrew of the Treasury," Vinson said, could be just as mercurial in assessing the country's financial condition. He said when the bonus bill for veterans was up for passage, Mellon pleaded with Congress not to pass it because "the Treasury was depleted." But then "the magician of the Treasury waves his wand, and it is full to overflowing" when there is legislation "to reduce the taxes of the ultrarich" (2619).

Vinson's speech might not have made much of a dent in the tax reduction debate, but it did foreshadow Vinson's legislative career in several ways. The speech signaled that he intended to make tax issues a main focus of his time in Congress; that he would diligently do his homework; and that he was prepared to play hardball, using wit and sarcasm when it suited his purpose. Perhaps most important, the speech won him the notice of Garner, who had long made taxation his specialty. He welcomed having a confederate with Vinson's grasp of complicated tax matters as well as someone who could ridicule Mellon, something that Garner himself delighted in doing. When he became Democratic floor leader later in the 1920s, Garner included Vinson as part of a small inside group "which planned party strategy and tactics in the House."[19] It was an impressive group considering that three of its members, including Garner himself, would eventually become Speakers of the House. The other two future Speakers that Garner included in his small circle were fellow Texan Sam Rayburn and John W. McCormack of Massachusetts. Over the years, they too formed close professional and personal relationships with Vinson.

To make sure that his Ninth District constituency was fully informed about his efforts to defend the "little people," Vinson had fifty-five thousand copies of his maiden speech reprinted and mailed throughout the district. One recipient of the mailing, J.H. Testor of Gilmore, Kentucky, praising the speech in a letter to Vinson, said that it was "so clear and convincing and of such force of logic that it clearly demonstrates and exposes the primary object of the Mellon tax bill and at the same time fully illustrates the wisdom and soundness of the Democratic tax bill."[20]

Vinson had little trouble in gauging the direction of political winds back home when another prominent issue came before Congress in early 1924. This was a bill to restrict immigration from all regions of the globe except western Europe. In his speech on the subject, Vinson no doubt reflected the racial bigotry that permeated the country and his district, which was overwhelmingly populated by Anglo-Saxon descendants. He asserted the superiority of the "old" immigrants of English, Irish, Scottish, and French stock to the new wave of "undesirable foreign hordes, fleeing from an overpopulated Orient, or war-ridden eastern and southern Europe." Vinson said that whereas the early immigrants, because of their shared beliefs and values, were able to forge America into "the greatest nation on the globe," the "new" immigrants were having a divisive effect. "In the vast centers of population we have a Chinatown; we have a Ghetto; a Japanese settlement; the Czechoslovakia, Lithuania, Greek, and Polish colonies and so on ad infinitum," Vinson said, adding, "Water will not mix with oil, neither will peoples of diverse habits, traits and characteristics."[21]

The House debate on restrictive immigration gave Vinson an opportunity to score even more points with constituents when he and Republican representative Fiorello LaGuardia of New York squared off in a caustic exchange. LaGuardia, fiercely proud of his Italian ancestry and resentful at the suggestion of Anglo-Saxon supremacy, responded to Vinson by disparaging the mountains of Kentucky as a place lacking in schools and job opportunities. He added that an immigrant living in the mountains of Kentucky would have no chance of being assimilated "because he will have no opportunity there to learn much of our institutions. He would certainly have no opportunity there to learn and see a good example of law and order and law enforcement" (6130).

Vinson, naturally, leaped to defend his state's reputation, saying that "no finer American type can be found in these United States than those who populate Kentucky.... From the attitude of the gentleman I am led to believe that he has never visited our state; that he is ignorant of the real conditions in Kentucky; that he does not understand the worth of her great people." He continued, "I challenge the statement of the gentleman in respect of the illiteracy of the mountain folk in our state; and if the gentleman would come with me among my mountain people I feel sure that he would retract and strike from the Record the maligning remarks in respect of her great citizenship" (6135–36).

Predictably, Vinson's ardent defense was roundly praised by fellow Kentuckians and widely reported in newspapers back home. One supporter wrote, "I sincerely believe it strengthened your support wonderfully in the Ninth, and heard a great many of the voters in Fleming, Rowan, and Montgomery counties express themselves as being behind you, owing to the fact that you made the extemporaneous speech."[22] It was a "masterful reply to Mr. LaGuardia," the chairman of the Democratic Party in Fleming County said in his letter. "I am exceedingly proud of the way you are representing the Old 9th."[23] In his reply to one correspondent, Vinson said, "It certainly makes me tired to hear people talk about Kentucky when it is shown that they know nothing about her and her people." He said such people "think we wear horns, and when I run across a fellow with that attitude, I want him to know mine are sharp, at least as sharp as I can make them."[24]

In addition to standing up for "the people" against the ultrarich and for Kentucky against haughty New Yorkers, Vinson took up the cause of veterans, a constituency he was to champion throughout his legislative career. The first opportunity for him to show his allegiance to this group came during the spring of 1924 when Congress debated measures to reward World War I soldiers with a bonus to make up for the skimpy pay they had received and to increase the pensions for veterans of earlier wars. President Coolidge opposed these measures on the grounds that many states had already granted bonuses to veterans and that the nation's budget could not withstand such a drain on the treasury. Coolidge was not alone in his opposition. A group known as the Ex-Service Men's Anti-Bonus League lobbied Congress to reject the compensation bill, saying that "good business and steady employment will get us more than any possible bonus." The Anti-Bonus League also claimed that "the noise for the bonus comes from a very small minority. The vast majority of ex-service men are practically indifferent."[25]

Vinson dismissed the Anti-Bonus League as a tool of the moneyed interests in New York City and the East. In response to one pleading from the group, he wrote, "Instead of protesting against this measure, it occurs to me that your masters should grovel in the dust, if need be, in petition to the ex-service men in the world war for them to receive this small token of esteem in which they should always be held."[26] Taking to the House floor on March 15, 1924, Vinson urged that the bonus proposal, known as the Adjusted Compensation Act, be changed so that veterans could receive a cash award instead of getting paid-up insurance policies that permitted recipients to borrow up to one-quarter of the value of their insurance. Claiming that the amount to be paid out was infinitesimal compared with the country's financial resources, Vinson said a cash bonus would be "a symbol of appreciation of the wealthiest country in the world to its defenders."[27] His efforts on this occasion failed, but Vinson, so sure of the merit of this cause, persevered, and his view ultimately prevailed twelve years later.[28]

In yet another display of populist sentiment, Vinson sided with labor in the debate over legislation that would have changed the way disputes between railroads and their workers were handled. Responding to a letter he received about bills sponsored by Republican Sen. Robert B. Howell of Nebraska and Kentucky's Alben Barkley, then a member of the House, Vinson said, "It will be a pleasure to support any legislation looking toward the securing of fair and reasonable rights for the 'men in overalls.'"[29]

Howell and Barkley proposed replacing a nine-member labor board, established by the 1920 Transportation Act to settle worker complaints, with four so-called adjustment boards, which would attempt to resolve minor labor disputes, and a five-member board of mediation and conciliation, which would hear appeals of adjustment-board decisions and handle major work-related disagreements. Railroads opposed the Howell-Barkley bill because they felt it gave unions too much power by allowing them to nominate one-half of the members to the four adjustment boards. Vinson, rejecting that objection, noted that railroads had equal representation on these boards and that any decision of an adjustment panel could be appealed to the superior board, composed of five members from the public nominated by the president.

Vinson conceded that Howell-Barkley favored labor more than it did the railroads, but he felt such a tilt was justified because he considered the 1920 act as prorailroad. He also backed the measure because, he said, the industry officials with whom he discussed the bill "admit that the present Act with the present Labor Board is not functioning. They further admit that in scores of instances railroad companies have refused to obey the findings of the Labor Board."[30] An old friend from Louisa who was a railroad union official wrote to express his "fondness for you for voting right on, the Howell-Barkley Bill." The writer, who addressed his letter to "My Dear Friend Freddy," also chided Vinson about the hapless Washington Senators baseball team. "Guess you and yours are always in the grand stand when your 3rd raters play at home. If it was not for Walter Johnson I do not know whether I would spare the time or not to see them."[31]

Although Vinson's committee assignments—pensions, public lands, and flood control—were not the sort of plums that normally yielded great notice, he nonetheless was pleased with his assignments given the fact that he had come into Congress after composition of the committees had already been determined. Vinson was especially happy with his assignment to the Public Lands Committee, which at the time was examining the claim of the Northern Pacific Railroad that it was entitled to nearly 3 million acres of wilderness in the Pacific Northwest under an 1870 federal land grant. Coming as it did in the wake of Teapot Dome, the investigation appeared to have the makings of another scandal involving corporate exploitation of public property. Vinson saw it this way. Writing to a constituent about the Northern Pacific land grant, he said, "Its history since 1864 is a long trail of influenced legislation always inuring to its [Northern Pacific Railroad's] benefit."[32] In a letter to hometown friend Ernest Shannon about the issue, he said, "I am in love with my work upon the Public Lands Committee, as it's a real law-suit; no doubt about that."[33] The Northern Pacific matter was finally resolved in 1929 when legislation was enacted that removed the disputed land from the grant and placed it under the protection of the Forest Service.

As important as speeches on the House floor and committee work were in establishing his credentials as a worthy public servant, Vinson knew that the primary barometer of his job performance would be how well he attended to the needs, little and large, of the people back home. He left no doubt that he intended to perform this duty as diligently as his others. To one constituent Vinson wrote, "It has been my purpose to give thorough consideration to the wishes of my people in the Departmental work [casework] and I am very glad that in most instances I have been able to secure the result sought."[34] Responding to a letter from a friend in Louisa, Vinson wrote, "[I] noticed your statement 'keep your sleeves rolled up to help us.' I was pleased to know that you realized that they were always rolled up and didn't have to be rolled up."[35] Although the era of big government, ushered in by Roosevelt's New Deal, was still nearly a decade away, people in the early 1920s nevertheless looked to Washington and their congressmen to help solve problems. As fellow Kentuckian and future Supreme Court colleague Stanley Reed wrote to Vinson when requesting information about changes in the bankruptcy law, "the wants of constituents flow on forever."[36]

If the flow ever bothered Vinson, it did not show; keeping with up the steady stream of letters from constituents and other correspondents was such a high priority for him that he spent five thousand dollars of his own money to supplement his secretarial staff with additional stenographic and clerical help. Requests flowing into Vinson's office ranged from the routine to the complex, from the trivial to the traumatic: county agents requesting farmers' bulletins published by the government; the unemployed wanting government jobs; government workers dismissed for various reasons trying to get reinstated; ex-servicemen seeking to have dishonorable discharges reversed; parents of an asthmatic boy wanting weather information for the southwestern states; school children asking for the names of Cabinet members; and a woman seeking compensation for damages Union soldiers caused to a hotel she and her husband owned in Louisa during the Civil War.

Supplicants also frequently sought personal donations from Vinson for various purposes, and he tried to comply even if he could only afford a few dollars. Many of these requests were from churches seeking money for new pews, church repairs and additions, and even to supplement a minister's annual salary of $3,000. Vinson gave $25 for the minister's salary. He also pledged $50 to fund-raising efforts to build a dormitory at what was then Lees Collegiate Institute in Jackson and another $50 to help fund a campaign to get Mammoth Cave designated a national park. Beginning in 1924, Vinson received annual requests from octogenarian Henry M. Hutchinson of Elkfork for a birthday present. For his eighty-first birthday in 1924, Vinson sent a knife as requested and then checks for $2 in following years. He was asked for a $50 loan by one correspondent, though Vinson could only send a check for $25 "in view of the present status of my bank account."[37] On another occasion, Vinson was unable to help a woman seeking to raise $100 to buy her daughter a piano. In his typical gentle way, Vinson responded that he had "found it necessary to deny myself the pleasure of making contributions of this character, much as I would like to do so were I financially able to do it."[38]

Vinson's benevolence also was evident in his correspondence to individuals whose troubles he had seen reported in the local press. For example, he wrote to a pastor in Louisa, "I notice in the News that you have been confined to your home several days by illness. I trust . . . your condition is materially improved and that you will soon be restored to your normal condition."[39] To a woman in Mt. Sterling, Vinson wrote, "I saw in the Sentinel-Democrat where you had suffered a painful burn," adding that he hoped "no serious results will ensue therefrom."[40] Vinson was also solicitous when a colleague in the Kentucky House delegation, Tenth District Republican John W. Langley, encountered difficulties. Besides contracting an illness, he had been found guilty of selling and transporting whisky illegally. Writing to thank Vinson for his expressions of concern and good will, Langley said he had known members of the Vinson family since boyhood, and "while they have practically all been on the other side from me politically, they have been my warm personal friends, and I have always held the memory of our friendship in the highest esteem, just as I do now the knowledge of yours."[41]

Naturally, letters also flowed between Vinson and his family. He was eager for news from home and could never get enough letters from his parents, in-laws, and friends. "Roberta got a letter from her mother today which was full of a lot of news, and I certainly wish we would receive letters more frequently," he wrote to his mother.[42] The correspondence with family included the usual tidbits about sickness and health, work, travel, and the weather, as well as the expression of joy and sorrow that are inevitable in the cycle of life. Vinson was ecstatic with the birth of Frederick junior on April 3, 1925. He wrote to a friend about his newborn son, "That boy of mine is a hum-dinger. I have given up all notion of practicing law, attending Congress, or attempting to realize any ambition that may be smoldering within my heart. That boy has buffaloed me. Honestly, I just love him to death. I can sit and hold him by the hour or watch his every movement with real genuine joy."[43]

As the health of his father started to deteriorate in early 1927, Vinson wrote his mother that a visit to Hot Springs, Arkansas, "would be a great trip for him. The question of diet would help, the change of scenery, etc., and moderate baths would be of great benefit to him." Vinson told his mother not to worry about costs, because he "would be more than glad to meet all of the expenses incident to his trip."[44] Jim Vinson did seem to respond to the therapy at Hot Springs, but back in Louisa in early June of 1927 he suffered a stroke while at the post office, lapsed into unconsciousness, and died a few days later at age seventy-one.

On occasion, Vinson's letters home contained items of a more practical or political nature. Vinson's father-in-law, Robert Dixon, told him in a letter of a land purchase he was making with Ernest Shannon and offered to let Vinson in on the investment. "Of course, I want in on that deal if you boys are good enough to let me in," Vinson replied.[45] In one letter to his mother, Vinson advised her how best to handle the sale of some property. In another he asked her to do some spadework in case he was opposed for renomination: "Go to my office and look in the big drawer on the right-hand side of the chair usually occupied by me and get the pencil tablet sheets upon which appear the names of all those persons who voted at my special election," he requested.[46] Vinson was upset at the prospect of opposition in the party's August 1924 primary, because he felt his freshman performance in Congress had been strong enough at least to ward off a challenge from within. His pique is obvious in an exchange of letters with his friend Dick Chiles, a Mt. Sterling attorney, about the probable primary race against Ryland C. Musick of Breathitt County. "At times I get thoroughly disgusted with the political game," Vinson said in one letter.[47] And when Chiles wrote that in his candid opinion Musick "will make a strong candidate,"[48] Vinson responded with self-pity: "I have worked mighty hard to serve the district. . . . Most of the work not being of a legislative nature. I find that my friends misunderstand me, and that hurts."[49]

But Vinson was not one to brood for long. Regardless of the challenge or difficulty he faced, he did what he had to do. Writing to his father-in-law, Vinson said, "I have bought a mimeograph machine and we intend to turn out the stuff here enough to beat Mr. Musick. It will be our aim to spread more ink than his blotters can absorb."[50] He certainly made good on that claim. In a letter to a supporter, Vinson noted that his office was sending out "sixty thousand Immigration speeches within the next few weeks and also same number of speeches on Kentucky. Ten thousand letters will go out next week to the veterans of the World War."[51] He also blanketed the district with a "My dear friend" form letter that outlined the reasons he should be the party's choice in the primary. Vinson noted his electoral prowess in the special election by sweeping the district, carrying even the traditionally Republican counties of Lawrence, Boyd, Carter, Greenup, and Lewis. Furthermore, he wrote, "I have tried hard to perform true service. Hundreds of people who have made requests of me know that this statement is true." Vinson also reminded voters that when the good name of Kentucky "was attacked in the slanders of the New Yorkers, I faced them on the floor of the House, and did my best to put them to shame." He said the main question to be answered in the primary was, "Are you satisfied with my record in Congress?"[52]

When the first session of the Sixty-eighth Congress adjourned in early June, Vinson was free to return home to discuss that record face-to-face with voters. He hit the campaign trail that summer in a Model T Ford loaded down with campaign posters and three-by-five candidate cards, which carried his picture and election information on one side and a laudatory editorial from the *Big Sandy News* on the other. Happily by his side on these electioneering jaunts was "Snooks" Crutcher, his loyal office boy when he was commonwealth attorney. Crutcher called the experience "the greatest thing that ever happened to me in my boyhood. I sat on back porches and listened to him discuss the race with the leading politicians of each county. Of course, all of this was fascinating and I guess my only regret then was that I wasn't old enough to vote for Fred Vinson."

Crutcher's recollections of his travels provide an instructive view of Vinson the campaigner. He recalled that Vinson "had a great ability to get his point over whether he was talking to a farmer, a miner, a storekeeper or one of the county or courthouse political leaders." Vinson's "memory for names and faces was perhaps his greatest asset in politics throughout his life." It was an asset that Vinson worked hard to perfect, Crutcher said, noting that as they traveled between stops he would hear Vinson "mumbling to himself in his assimilation of faces and names." He described how Vinson schooled himself: "Say a fellow was named George Wilson, he would say to himself, 'George Wilson, he's a farmer and usually votes Republican, wears overalls, almost bald, wife's name Mary, two daughters in grade school, one little boy.'" Crutcher said Vinson repeated the facts until they were embedded in his memory. "And you could just bet your last dollar that if Fred Vinson saw George Wilson or Mrs. George Wilson again that he would remember them and he would call him or her by their first name."

Vinson stopped at every crossroads store in the district, "sort of the meeting place of the community" and "of course the best place to campaign," Crutcher recalled. While the candidate was busy politicking at these stops, Crutcher made sure campaign material was displayed and distributed. He always asked store owners for permission to put up some Vinson posters and was never refused. "I always put the posters in the

Vinson campaign poster for Congress. (Courtesy of Special Collections, University of Kentucky Library.)

best places and I secured them real good as Mr. Vinson had instructed me to do," Crutcher said. He also passed out candidate cards to everyone in the store and left a stack of thirty or forty beside the cash drawer. In addition, Crutcher was responsible for getting posters nailed to roadside trees and poles. "I would jump out of the car and scramble up the bank and tack up a poster," he said. "I generally tacked up one on each side of the tree or the post so that you could see them both ways."

Crutcher noted that Vinson made "at least one speech in every courthouse in the district and sometimes we'd return to one county four or five times, particularly if he thought he was having trouble or if he could strengthen his position." Most of the campaign trips were daylong excursions, but when it was not possible to get back to Louisa, Vinson insisted on paying for rooms at a boardinghouse or hotel instead of accepting the invitations he received to stay at someone's home. He felt that if he accepted the hospitality of one family, others whose offers he could not then accept might feel slighted. "That was one of his campaign rules," Crutcher said.[53]

The long, hot summer of campaigning paid off. Vinson won more than 70 percent of the primary balloting and outpolled Musick in every county but three—Musick's home county of Breathitt and Montgomery and Robertson. In the fall Vinson was elected to his first full two-year term in Congress by defeating his Republican challenger, George Osborne. He had a vote total of 45,899, or 54.5 percent of the total cast, compared with Osborne's 38,295, or 45.5 percent. Although this race was considerably closer than the special election earlier in the year, Vinson nonetheless was gratified because he had bucked the Republican tide that returned President Coolidge to the White House and increased the GOP majorities in both houses of Congress. Coolidge carried Kentucky over Democratic challenger John W. Davis, and the state would now have two Republican senators for the first time in history when political newcomer Frederic M. Sackett of Louisville defeated incumbent Democratic senator A.O. Stanley. "Things certainly went to rack," was Vinson's blunt assessment about the election. "It is remarkable that the Republicans did not make greater gains in Congress in view of the landslide," he wrote to a friend. "We are hoping to gain control in 1926. As you know, they only captured twenty-three seats from us in the House."[54]

The chairman of the Fleming County Democratic Party, writing to congratulate Vinson, said he had not written sooner "on account of being depressed" with the election results. He listed several factors that he thought contributed to Coolidge's victory in Kentucky and the overall poor showing of Democrats: "We had no money. The Republicans had all that they could use. I had only $60.00 at my disposal to finance our Campaign. On account of the KKK we had the assurance of the support of the colored voters, which they did not deliver, but voted the straight Republican ticket as usual. The KKK also supported the Republican Ticket."[55]

Although the election had been a disaster for Kentucky Democrats, Vinson, by bucking the GOP tide, had again demonstrated his potency at the polls. In less than a year's time, he had faced voters of Kentucky's Ninth Congressional District on three occasions—in a special election, a primary, and a general election—and each time he had won by decisive margins. This achievement did not go unnoticed. In early January 1925, a commentary in a newspaper published in Mt. Sterling called *People and Politics* included Vinson in its list of up-and-coming Democratic politicians in Kentucky who might be ripe for picking as the party's nominee for governor. Though flattered by the suggestion, Vinson, as the year 1925 began, was more than happy to be returning to his duties as Ninth District congressman and to continue building on his budding reputation as an earnest and effective member of the House.

His efforts in that regard suffered a minor setback in early 1925, however, when he took to the floor to recite a bit of doggerel he composed after reading a newspaper account about President Coolidge's use of a mechanical hobbyhorse in the White House for exercise. As Vinson started to read his poem, entitled "Cal's Hobby Horse," Republican Rep. Robert Luce of Massachusetts objected, contending that it was a breach of House rules for a member to ridicule the president. Democrats, including Alben Barkley of Kentucky, responded that there was no precedent for denying Vinson the floor. After more heated debate, Republican Rep. Bert Snell of New York, the presiding officer, ruled that Vinson could continue. Here are samples of Vinson's poetic effort:

> The "hobby horse," 'tis easily seen,
> Is as silent as its master;
> It trots and canters in one spot,
> The "jockey" urging it faster.
> But, unlike the horses of old Kaintuck,
> Unexcelled for their vim and vigor,
> The White House steed will never buck,
> And mar the President's "figger."

The reaction to Vinson's poetry was swift and scornful. "It was a very ill considered effort on your part, one committed in the poorest possible taste," one person wrote.[56] From another critic Vinson heard, "Shame on a chosen representative of a people, to so far forget the dignity of his position, as to stoop to such a level as you have exhibited in this."[57] Vinson's friend Howard Gumm of Ashland wrote that "a number of your Republican admirers and constituents are miffed at your comic stuff. Personally I think your poem had poor meter and again it didn't mean anything. I am still for you but be yourself Freddie, be yourself."[58] Chiles B. Van Antwerp, a constituent from Farmers, Kentucky, wrote, "I cannot see how such behavior can either increase your own prestige or that of the state, and district you represent. Such extraneous utterances have no rightful place in our supposedly dignified legislative halls."[59] In his reply to Van Antwerp, Vinson said he did not think he should be judged too harshly "for poking a little fun" at the president. After all, he wrote, "in our little town, the town-folks cuss the Mayor and the City Council. They, together with the folks who live in the rural districts, cuss the county Judge and the Fiscal Court. Everybody cusses the State Legislature, the Governor of the State, and the Congress of the United States." He also noted that in Woodrow Wilson's last days "the Congressional Record is filled with bitter, caustic communication of him; statements that he was feigning illness, which held him up to the country as a liar and a hypocrite."[60]

The fallout from this incident, though, was brief and inconsequential. In fact, Vinson's first-year performance in Congress so impressed party leaders in the House that they tapped him for assignments to larger and more powerful committees. In the Sixty-ninth Congress he was assigned to Military Affairs, a major committee, and in the Seventieth Congress he won appointment to the Appropriations Committee, one of the big four in the House. These assignments gave Vinson the opportunity to deal with the more important and complex issues before the House, and he soon demonstrated that he was clearly up to the task. The "Hobby Horse" episode notwithstanding, Vinson proved that he did have a seriousness of purpose. He put in long hours of study on the issues before his committees, crafted legislative proposals, and worked in harmony with Republicans to get bills passed.

Vinson's assignment on Military Affairs put him in the thick of the raging national debate in the mid-1920s—precipitated by Gen. William Mitchell—over the role and future of military aviation. Mitchell, the controversial champion of air power, had openly accused military leaders of incompetency, criminal negligence, and almost treasonable conduct by failing to develop aviation adequately for national defense. He was court-martialed, found guilty of insubordination, and resigned from the service. Nevertheless, Mitchell was in a sense vindicated, because his case spurred the Coolidge administration and Congress to action. The president, reacting to heightened public concern over the state of American aviation, appointed a board to investigate Mitchell's charges and to plot a course for the orderly development of the nation's air transportation, both military and commercial. The recommendations of this panel, known as the Morrow Board for its chairman Dwight Morrow, essentially became the blueprint for the congressional debate that followed. Legislation, which eventually was enacted in July 1926, mapped out a five-year, $150 million expansion program for army and navy aircraft and personnel and created new assistant secretaries for aviation in the Departments of War, Navy, and Commerce.

Vinson's work on this legislation drew effusive praise from Republican W. Frank James of Michigan, chairman of the House Military Affairs Committee. He said, "No gentleman on this committee has spent more hours in the study of the problems than has he. No member has missed fewer hearings than he; no member has made any harder effort to get to the bottom of every problem." In drafting the five-year program, James continued, Vinson "showed again and again his good judgment and mental keenness. His speech on the bill was one of the best made on the subject. It certainly was evidence of his mastery of the subject, which could come only by untiring efforts."

James had such respect for Vinson's knowledge and skills that he went against the political grain when he named five members from Military Affairs to a joint subcommittee with Naval Affairs to study the issue of aircraft procurement. Custom called for James to name three Republicans and two Democrats, but he felt so strongly that Vinson should be on the joint panel that the delegation from Military Affairs became three Democrats and two Republicans. "I am proud that I selected Vinson," James said. "Not only from other members of the committee have I heard most laudable statements, but I sat . . . in the closing two weeks of deliberations, and I know that no person had a stronger grasp upon this situation and the work before them than did he."[61]

Because of his acumen on the subject, Vinson drafted and introduced legislation creating an Aircraft Procurement Board consisting of assistant secretaries of the War, Navy, Commerce, and Post Office Departments to plan and coordinate all aircraft purchases by the federal government. James, calling Vinson's bill "a most important piece of legislation," said the measure would save money, but more important, it would prevent a repeat of what happened at the beginning of World War I when the United States was unable to expand aviation production quickly enough to satisfy wartime demands. Continuing his salute to Vinson, James noted that when discussing Vinson's proposal "with a most distinguished gentleman of this House, he remarked to me that this bill was one of the most sensible pieces of legislation that he had seen in many a day." Howard E. Coffin, who was a member of the Morrow Board, also praised the legislation. "It's a fine job," he wrote to Vinson, noting that the heretofore haphazard ways aviation matters were handled prevented Congress from obtaining dependable information and often engendered distrust and misunderstandings. The creation of a centralized purchasing board, Coffin said, "will provide the Congress with a definite and authoritative point of contact with all phases of aviation, both governmental and civil."[62]

During this period Vinson was also interested in military purchases of a more down-to-earth nature, namely horses. Even at the dawn of the air age, the old-fashioned cavalry and horse-drawn artillery were still important components of the army in the 1920s. When he realized that no permanent legislation existed for the War Department to purchase the animals for its Remount Service, Vinson, representing a state renowned for its thoroughbreds and other desirable breeds, gladly offered a remedy.

His bill, which became law, not only gave the War Department authority to buy horses to be used in training cadets at West Point and in ceremonies; it also permitted purchases for breeding purposes. This feature of the legislation resulted in a successful partnership between government and the public. The Remount Service loaned out high-quality stallions—thoroughbreds were used extensively—to farmers and small breeders, giving them an opportunity to improve their stocks. The program ensured that the military had a ready supply of horses that met its rigid requirements and that horsemen had a way of increasing their earnings by producing a better grade of livestock. The popularity of this arrangement was evident: by early 1927 there were more than fifteen hundred requests on a waiting list for stallions.

The cause of veterans, an issue Vinson had staked out as one of his prime concerns in his first year in Washington, continued to occupy a great deal of his time and efforts during the 1925–1929 period. In the Sixty-ninth Congress, he assisted in writing legislation, which Coolidge signed, adding $19 million to the budget to increase the pensions of Spanish-American War veterans. His most involved and protracted work on veteran-related legislation in the middle to late 1920s involved trying to get a veterans' hospital located in Kentucky. Writing to the commander of the American Legion of Kentucky, Dr. S.C. Smith of Ashland, Vinson reported, "I have been appearing before the Committee and the Sub-Committee handling this measure, and will leave no stone unturned to get Kentucky included."[63] Vinson and other Kentucky congressmen prevailed only after fighting for the facility in four sessions of Congress and overcoming the opposition of the chairman of the House Veterans' Affairs Committee and the indifference of Gen. Frank T. Hines, director of the Veterans Bureau, forerunner of today's Department of Veterans Affairs. "A united delegation made it possible for this work to have been accomplished," Vinson said. "It was secured without the approval of General Hines and without the O.K. of the Budget. Congress responded to the needs of our soldiery."[64]

Naturally, when projects of this type are proposed, communities in the state designated for the federal largess—a $2.5 million, 250-bed complex in this instance—lobby hard to have it land on their turf. Thus, Vinson received correspondence from representatives of chambers of commerce, veterans' groups, and other organizations throughout Kentucky pleading their case for the new hospital. In response to one petitioner, a director of the Carrollton chamber, Vinson said that although he would be pleased if the hospital was located somewhere in his Ninth District, he felt "that politics and influence should not play any part in the selection of the site." He said the facility "should be located at the point where it will best serve the afflicted veterans of our country."[65] As it turned out, the veterans' hospital was built in 1931 on a 290-acre expanse of farmland outside Lexington. The facility, serving patients from throughout Kentucky and several surrounding states, originally treated war veterans suffering from all types of maladies but eventually confined its work to the treatment of nervous and mental disorders.

Dr. Smith, head of the American Legion in Kentucky, wholeheartedly supported Vinson's efforts to get the veterans' hospital for the state, but he was opposed to a provision in the legislation that required the Veterans Bureau to provide free hospitalization and treatment to veterans of any war. "I think it very commendable to make it mandatory that any indigent ex-service men be treated, but feel that it would be class legislation of a very vicious type, to make it mandatory to hospitalize those who are able to pay, regardless of the nature or type of disability."[66]

In response, Vinson wrote, "I do not like to disagree with my friends . . . but I think there is an obligation on the part of the Government to its veterans." He felt the provision was needed because he knew of "hundreds of cases that are actually service connected, but are unable to be proved to the satisfaction of the Bureau." Furthermore, Vinson was not worried that the system would be abused or overloaded. Writing to Smith, he said, "I don't know how you Doctors feel about hospitalization, but we fellows on the out-side want to stay away from them as long as we can." In closing, Vinson wrote, "I may be wrong about it, but I would rather the Government hospitalize several times as many who are not entitled to it, than to refuse those who are in fact entitled."[67]

As proud as he was of his work on behalf of veterans, Vinson felt that the greatest accomplishment of his first stint in Congress was his effort to provide federal assistance to Kentucky after spring rains devastated a large area of the state in 1927. At the time there was no precedent for the federal government to appropriate money to rebuild roads and bridges damaged in a natural disaster. Vinson helped establish that precedent. Along with congressional colleagues from Kentucky and Governor Fields, Vinson argued forcefully and successfully that the devastation in the state caused by the deluge in late May of 1927 merited federal assistance. Flooding in twenty-seven counties, including eight in Vinson's Ninth District, caused the deaths of nearly one hundred people, left several thousand others homeless, and forced nearly twenty thousand workers out of their jobs. Damage to homes, coal mines, business property, railroads, roads, and bridges was estimated at $57 million. More than four hundred bridges and twenty-five hundred miles of highway in the affected counties were destroyed or greatly damaged. These counties, Vinson noted, having already reached their constitutional limits on bonded indebtedness, lacked the financial wherewithal to repair their infrastructure. Ultimately, Congress was persuaded to appropriate nearly $2 million to Kentucky, an amount that was matched by a state appropriation. "This fight occupied several months, and I can say with pardonable modesty that I was in the forefront of the battle," Vinson said. "My heart runs over with the warmth of joy when I anticipate the benefits that will come to those now living in the flood area and to persons yet unborn resulting from this effort."[68]

Vinson was also gratified by his work in Congress on matters affecting water transportation and the coal industry, obvious interests to him because of his district's location along the Big Sandy and Ohio Rivers and the economic importance of mining in eastern Kentucky. He was especially pleased about his role in getting Congress to adopt the "recapture clause" when it authorized private companies or individuals to build bridges over navigable waters. This provision meant that ownership of privately constructed bridges was transferred to the public after construction costs were recaptured and investors received a fair return. "It was a far-reaching step, protective of the public," Vinson said (5133). The first use of the recapture clause was in a bill Vinson introduced that authorized a bridge crossing the Big Sandy at Catlettsburg. An attorney in Huntington, West Virginia, writing to a friend about this development, said, "I feel that our getting this Bridge Bill through the House was almost entirely due to the efforts of Mr. Vinson." He added that although he knew Vinson was a man of ability, "I was somewhat surprised to find how much standing and influence he has gained in Congress in such a short time."[69] In rapid succession Vinson also steered through Congress legislation for six other bridges in his district: two at Ashland, two at Maysville, one at Augusta, and one at South Portsmouth.

Vinson was also instrumental in preventing the Corps of Engineers from carrying through on its plan to abandon improvements to locks and dams on the Big Sandy River and on the Tug and Levisa Forks near Louisa. The corps felt the project was not worth the cost, citing the limited volume of commercial traffic on these waterways and the fact that railroads paralleled both the Tug and Levisa Forks. Vinson responded by publishing an eight-page pamphlet in the fall of 1925 entitled "Protest against the Abandonment of the Big Sandy River Improvement." In it he argued that repairs and enhancements to the area's system of locks and dams would spur increased use of water transportation not only by the large coal fields nearby but also by an oil refinery at Catlettsburg and by the area's nascent brick and tile industry. Noting the vast savings possible in shipping commodities by river compared with rail, Vinson said, "The people of the Big Sandy valley are entitled to benefits which would accrue to them in the cheapened transportation of its products in virtue of water transportation."[70] Vinson and his supporters won this round, but by 1950 the corps once again claimed modernization of the Big Sandy uneconomical and subsequently suspended locking services on the river.[71]

In yet another show of support for water transportation and the coal industry, Vinson, in a speech on the House floor, advocated approval of a $2 million appropriation to recondition coal-carrying boats for use in export trade. Calling such an investment a "tremendous benefit to all coal-producing sections," he said the renovations to the vessels would increase trade to the East Indies, the Mediterranean, and South American ports by many million tons of coal.[72]

As the election season of 1928 dawned, Vinson should have had every reason to feel confident in being returned to the House for what would be his third two-year term. During his time in Washington, he had compiled a solid record of service and achievement by conscientiously attending to the demands of his position. Vinson, though, was looking beyond just winning another term in Congress. Another victory at the polls would solidify his rising-star status in the party and make him a strong contender for higher office, most likely a run for governor. Such an eventuality, of course, assumed that he would win his race and that he could gain the support of both wings of the fragmented state party. On both scores, Vinson had reason to be both optimistic and concerned.

He knew that the party could unite in the interest of winning. Vinson saw it firsthand as campaign manager for Alben Barkley's successful race for the U.S. Senate in 1926 against incumbent Republican Richard P. Ernst when the two factions put aside their differences. This temporary truce apparently resulted from Barkley's pledge not to push the contentious pari-mutuel issue if elected.[73] The deep divisions resurfaced a year later during the party's gubernatorial primary. Democrats once again were split by the issue of pari-mutuel betting, and again rival newspaper publishers supported different candidates. Former governor J.C.W. Beckham, a foe of racetrack gambling, had the backing of the Bingham faction; pari-mutuel supporters, including newspaper publishers Breckinridge and Brown, lined up behind Robert T. Crowe, who was state auditor and former speaker of the Kentucky House. Vinson also supported Crowe, but he said it was out of friendship, not because of the pari-mutuel issue, which he dismissed as not being all that important. When Beckham defeated Crowe, Vinson, who placed a high premium on party loyalty, made a number of speeches in behalf of Beckham's candidacy against the Republican nominee, Flem Sampson. "It is no effort for me to whole-heartedly support the nominee of my party," Vinson said in one speech. "I am a Democrat. I believe in party unity. Loyalty and gratitude are part of my religion."[74] Other Crowe supporters, most notably Breckinridge of the *Lexington Herald* and Brown of the *Louisville Herald-Post,* were not so willing to bury the hatchet, choosing instead to oppose their party's nominee.[75] With the Democratic party again so divided, it was hardly surprising that Sampson won by a comfortable margin.

Vinson's attempt at peacemaking drew only scorn from the other side, according to Clay Wade Bailey, a reporter who covered the state capital for the *Kentucky Post*. He informed Vinson that Percy Haly, a leader in the Bingham faction, had said that "your speeches in the recent campaign for J.C.W.B. were only speeches for yourself and really hurt Beckham. He seemed to credit you with having higher political ambitions, and his whole tenor seems to be that of an obstructionist." For his part, though, Bailey assured Vinson that "anything I hear said about you will be reported to you, as I hope to be counted as your friend."[76]

With party paralysis apparently still in the offing, Vinson shifted his attention to a more pressing matter—his own reelection. Here, the prospects certainly appeared to be more favorable. He had, after all, captured nearly 60 percent of the vote in 1926 while devoting much of his attention to managing Barkley's campaign for the Senate. He had also easily dispatched two primary opponents, and his Republican challenger in the fall, Elva R. Kendall, a farmer and public accountant from Carlisle, was little known and had never held elective office. His friend newspaperman Bailey confidently wrote after the primary that "the District is sure to roll up a good, big, Democratic majority for both yourself and Al Smith."[77] The political ground had shifted swiftly under Vinson in two years' time, however, and he lost his seat to Kendall by nearly six thousand votes. Vinson, so dominant in previous elections, lost in twelve Ninth District counties, including his home county of Lawrence. His defeat may have been inevitable, because he had to run on a ticket headed by the Democratic nominee for president, New York governor Alfred E. Smith, a man reviled in many sections of the country, the South in particular, for his ties to the Tammany Hall bosses, his opposition to prohibition, and above all his Roman Catholic religion.

Vinson, usually so cautious when it came to his election campaigns, assumed an uncharacteristically blithe attitude in the fall of 1928. He might have had a better chance of escaping the Smith albatross had he devoted more time to his own reelection effort instead of working on Smith's campaign as a vice chairman in the party's regional office in St. Louis. Besides keeping him out of the state for long periods of time, this position also had the effect of indelibly linking him to a figure that so many of his constituents considered anathema. Vinson had ample warning that Smith's candidacy might cause Republicans in his district to vote the straight party ticket instead of splitting it to vote for him, as many typically did, and might also cost him among Democratic voters.

Thomas R. Underwood, managing editor of the *Lexington Herald,* wrote Vinson in early September with a gloomy assessment of his prospects in Montgomery County, a county he had easily carried in 1926. He told Vinson that one hundred Democrats in one church in Mt. Sterling "are going to bolt against Smith on the dry question and may vote against you also." He added that "the argument that they are using against you is that you have turned wet or you would not be so strong for Smith."[78] In a letter a few days later, the party chairman in Boyd County, Davis M. Howerton, gave another pessimistic report, about his county and neighboring Greenup County, again counties that had gone for Vinson two years earlier. He told Vinson that "400 members of the South Methodist Church at Ashland had signed the pledge to vote for Hoover. The *Ashland Daily Independent* has come out editorially for Hoover and its news columns are being colored so as to advertise and promote his candidacy in every way." He added that the "Hoover Women's Club in Greenup . . . has as many Democratic women as Republican." Although Howerton was still confident that Vinson could win, he nonetheless appealed to him to return to Kentucky to campaign on his own behalf. He reminded Vinson "that in accordance with your policy of safety first your race must not be overlooked."[79] The pastor of the First Baptist Church in Catlettsburg, W.C. Pierce, wrote to scold Vinson on the issue of prohibition, saying, "It is a matter of deep regret to me and to hosts of others that have supported you in the past that you are standing in the present campaign as you are. I have supported you in the past with the conviction that you were dry and could be depended on as true to the dry principle." He closed with, "Why did you desert us?"[80]

Vinson had not deserted the prohibitionists, but his position on this white-hot issue was clouded not only by his allegiance to Smith but also by some erroneous reporting in the *New York World* and reprinted in the *Western Recorder,* a publication of the Kentucky Baptists. The comments in the article attributed to Vinson scoffed at the notion that religious leaders held such sway over their flocks that they could lead them into voting against Democrats on the issue of prohibition alone. Vinson denied ever making such comments, a claim supported by others present during Vinson's brief conversation with Charles Michelson of the *World.* Michelson wrote to Vinson, "I am deeply distressed that I appear to have misquoted you, but of course on your recital of the matter that must be the case."[81]

In a letter to the *Western Recorder* to set the record straight, Vinson said, "I have always been, am now, and will continue to be, an ardent, active advocate of prohibition. I am not just politically dry; I was dry before I entered the political arena." He noted that he had led the fight in his home county for statewide prohibition and had never failed to vote dry in Congress. Vinson added, "Not only am I dry in theory, but I am dry in practice."

Turning to his support of Smith, the antiprohibitionist, Vinson explained that as a member of the Democratic party "because of birth, tradition and choice" and as a "commissioned officer in its ranks," he was duty-bound to support the party's nominee and platform. He said, however, that he would not be persuaded by Smith's views to change his position: "I will never vote to repeal the 18th Amendment nor to weaken the Volstead or any Prohibition Enforcement Statutes."[82] Four years later, when Franklin Roosevelt was the party's nominee and the Democratic platform called for repeal of prohibition, Vinson would backpedal from that Shermanesque declaration.

Vinson's protestations in 1928 notwithstanding, he could not withstand the Hoover juggernaut. The Republican nominee carried 94 of the state's 120 counties, and five Democratic congressmen, including Vinson, were defeated. On election night, Vinson was in his law office in Louisa when he was called to the telephone for news from a neighboring county. "Looks bad, eh?" Vinson asked. He hung up, turned to those gathered in his office and calmly remarked, "I'll be damned if I'm not beat."[83]

And so he was, for the first and only time in his political career.

CHAPTER 3

Rapid Recovery and Rise

Fred Vinson had no intention of just fading away. He hated to lose, and his personal code of honor required that a defeat be avenged. Beyond pride, though, were other reasons. He had unfinished business, such as the passage of a bonus bill for veterans. Most important of all, he desired a return to Washington because he had found his calling in public service. He summarized his feelings about serving in government in extended remarks he placed in the *Congressional Record* on his last day as a member of the Seventieth Congress, March 1, 1929: "Many people think that a public official serves merely for the salary. . . . That is far from true." The greatest reward, he said, "is the knowledge that his work is well done; that his efforts will benefit the people; that his labor will make better the land in which we live and perpetuate the institutions of which we are so proud." Vinson's remarks, which mainly covered what he considered his achievements during his time in Congress, in effect signaled the start of his campaign to reclaim his House seat in 1930. He made that clear in his concluding comments: "In retiring from office, it is not my purpose to relinquish interest in public affairs."[1]

Vinson left Washington in the spring of 1929 and returned home to eastern Kentucky to resume a full-time law practice, but his thoughts never strayed too far from again being the representative of the Ninth District. The likelihood of that happening rose as the roaring twenties gave way to the roiling thirties. The stock market crash in 1929 was the dark harbinger of the Great Depression, which would convulse the country for much of the coming decade. President Hoover, who had won the White House in a landslide in 1928, became for many the most reviled figure in the land, seeming cold and comatose to the catastrophic conditions of the country. The dramatic reversal of fortune for the president and the party in power, the Republicans, naturally increased the possibility of Democratic gains in the off-year elections of 1930.

Vinson, who would have run for Congress in 1930 regardless of favorable prevailing political conditions, approached the race in his typical plotting and careful way. He did not want his intentions to be known until he felt the time was right. Explaining his strategy to a supporter in late 1929, Vinson said he wanted to announce "as late as possible, mainly on the account of the fact that I am practicing law, and being an announced candidate, always cuts in on the do-re-mi, which is a necessity of life." Nevertheless, Vinson did not want to delay too long, because that might mean competition in the primary, "which is a lot of worry and costs lots of money."[2]

Concern over having the wherewithal to finance his comeback and earn a decent living led Vinson to move both his law practice and his family, which by 1930 included sons Fred junior, nearly five years old, and Jimmy, still a toddler, to Ashland, thirty miles north of his hometown of Louisa. Ashland, as the largest city in the district, provided higher visibility to his candidacy and more opportunities for his legal practice. In Ashland, Vinson easily formed a circle of friends drawn from the city's legal and business elite who would aid him politically and professionally. These acquaintances included prominent attorneys John Diederich, who had been a classmate at Centre College, and Simeon Willis, a future Kentucky governor; Paul Blazer, founder of Ashland Oil, a gas and oil exploration and production company that grew into a diversified Fortune 500 business; Ben Williamson, a businessman who had served in the U.S. Senate; and B.F. Forgey and James T. Norris, publishers of the *Ashland Daily Independent.*

Vinson's best-laid plans to avoid a primary fight in 1930 were dashed when two challengers emerged. Ironically, one opponent was former governor William J. Fields ("Honest Bill from Olive Hill"), an erstwhile political ally whose move from Ninth District congressman to governor had paved the way for Vinson's first run for Congress in 1924. The other challenge came from commonwealth attorney William C. Hamilton of Mt. Sterling. Vinson, always piqued by primary opposition, was especially agitated by having to battle for a nomination that he felt should have been his by default because he "went down for my party" in the GOP juggernaut of 1928. Privately, he disparaged his opponents as fair-weather opportunists who had declined to run for Congress two years earlier when "it looked like rain" but wanted into the action now that "it looks like the sun will shine."[3] Publicly, though, he stayed to the high road, saying in a statement opening his campaign that the "race should be based upon the official records of the candidates, and their qualifications for the service—performance rather than promises. Nothing will be said or done by me in this campaign that will weaken our party."[4]

For his part, Fields, who represented the strongest challenge to Vinson, was not reticent to play hardball. In his opening campaign address in Owingsville on June 7, 1930, he criticized Vinson as being overly ambitious and more concerned with achieving personal recognition and glory than serving the needs of the Ninth District. In this regard, Fields said, Vinson caused his own defeat in 1928 by seeking and accepting a campaign position with the national party instead of concentrating his time and efforts at home. "Vinson sought every available honor, chased every rainbow in the political sky to the neglect of the district until he let it go Republican," Fields said. Furthermore, he warned that if Vinson was returned to Congress, he would quickly leave that office to run for governor in 1931. "In other words Mr. Vinson is running a double header with full intentions of discarding the Congressional engine just as soon as he can reach Frankfort."[5]

When the primary balloting was tallied, it was clear that the organization Vinson had built up among Ninth District Democrats during his five years in Congress and had maintained since his defeat was as solid as ever. He won overwhelmingly with 17,903 votes, coming out on top in fifteen of the nineteen counties. Fields finished a distant second with 6,016 votes, and Hamilton had 4,417 votes. The November election, which pitted Vinson against the man who had defeated him two years earlier, Republican Elva R. Kendall, was proof positive that Vinson's political prowess had been restored. He swamped Kendall by a margin of nearly 14,000 votes—42,671 to 28,850—and won every county in the district but Carter and Lewis.

Among those rushing to congratulate Vinson on his resounding victory was Texas congressman John "Jack" N. Garner, the House minority leader with whom Vinson had formed a close friendship during his previous stint in the House. Garner had sensed—correctly as it turned out—that the Democrats would take control of the House once the political lineup of the Seventy-second Congress was settled. After the 1930 elections, Republicans still held a 218 to 216 advantage over Democrats, but as a result of deaths in the following months and the special elections that filled the vacancies, Democrats gained control of the House by a margin of 219 to 214. "As you know," Garner wrote Vinson, "the great ambition of my life has been to serve as Speaker, and I sincerely appreciate your kind tender of assistance in aiding me in the materialization of that ambition."[6] Responding, Vinson said, "It is almost unthinkable that anyone would oppose you, but it is always best to keep our weather eye open." Vinson felt that seven in Kentucky's Democratic delegation, which now numbered nine, could be counted on to support Garner, though he noted, "Gregory (William) and Gilbert (Ralph) will probably be alright, but they are rather uncertain quantities, when it comes to playing the game." With Democrats holding a majority in the House for the first time since 1919 and Garner as Speaker, Vinson's second tenure in Congress was destined to be markedly different from his first, when, as he told Garner, he "chafed over inaction during the five years I served."[7]

Inactivity would not be a problem for Vinson over the next six and a half years. It became apparent as soon as the Democratic caucus met in early December of 1931 to organize the House that Vinson had been identified by the Democratic leadership as an up-and-comer who was worthy of being entrusted with considerable responsibilities. As an indication of this, he was given a spot on the all-important Ways and Means Committee, an unusual action because his service in Congress had been relatively brief and nonconsecutive. The committee, which is the starting place for all legislation dealing with revenue and taxation, was certain to be in the thick of things throughout the thirties as Congress grappled with the most severe and sustained economic depression in the nation's history. His work during this period on Ways and Means and as chairman of a special subcommittee on taxation earned Vinson the reputation of being one of the country's leading experts in tax and fiscal matters.

Before Vinson started down the road that led to such esteem, he seriously contemplated taking a detour in his political career toward the governor's office in Frankfort. The new Congress would not convene until more than a year after the 1930 election—December 7, 1931—so Vinson had plenty of time to study his options.[8] He had been encouraged to enter the gubernatorial race in 1927 but had decided it would not be in the best interest of the state's Democratic party for him "to muddy up the waters."[9] Now, as another election cycle neared, he clearly was drawn to the idea of running for governor in 1931, as his opponent in the primary, William Fields, had prophesied. Less than a week after his election in 1930, Vinson wrote James A. Thompson, editor of the *Bracken Chronicle* in Augusta, that he was "feeling the matter out for the Governorship. In fact, I think it is in splendid shape for me."[10] To Richmond newspaper publisher Keen Johnson, himself a future governor, Vinson stated frankly, "I want to be Governor," but clearly he was proceeding cautiously. "I really want to know that the folks are behind me, and want me to run before I enter the lists," he told Johnson, adding, "I am 'watchfully waiting.'"[11]

Throughout the early weeks of 1931, Vinson continued sounding out friends and party officials about the wisdom of entering the race. In correspondence with Jouett Shouse, chairman of the national party's executive committee, he expressed concern that giving up his congressional seat might cost Democrats the chance to take control of the House. "Possessed with a personal ambition to be the Governor of our State, I believe that I could be nominated and elected," Vinson wrote. "Yet, I could never forgive myself, if, with a few days' dead-lock, it would cause the loss of the organization's fight. Hence, I am between two fires."[12] In his response, Shouse said, "I don't believe you should let this question (organization of the House) be compelling in your decision." More important to Shouse was "the propriety, at least the political wisdom" of being elected to Congress "and then becoming a candidate for another office before one has even taken his seat."[13] The exchange with Shouse seemed to cool Vinson's ardor for the race after all. Shortly thereafter he wrote to Maja Eudaley, secretary of the Democratic State Campaign Committee, that he was not "very hot to run. In fact, I am happy to be out of the campaign rather than in it."[14] To Thompson, the Augusta newspaper editor, Vinson said, "I would really like to be Governor, and I believe I could get the nomination in a primary or a Convention. But I was elected to Congress, and I am going to serve there."[15]

As he assumed his duties in the House in early December 1931, Vinson might well have thanked his lucky stars that he was in Washington, not Frankfort, where events and enemies gnawed "away the foundations of Laffoon's administration from the beginning." The new governor, Democrat Ruby Laffoon, a judge from Madisonville, faced a mountain of economic difficulties piled high by the spreading depression. He was bogged down almost immediately by a host of nightmarish and intractable problems, including a shortfall in state revenues of more than $11 million, rising unemployment, banks and municipalities nearing financial collapse, and a swelling number of Kentuckians in desperate need for the basics of food, clothing, and shelter. The political front was just as stormy for Laffoon, with many of the waves being churned by his own lieutenant governor, the ambitious A.B. "Happy" Chandler. From the very beginning of Laffoon's term, Chandler took every opportunity to challenge and undermine the governor and devoted "his energies and the facilities of his office to full-time politicking."[16] He had his sights set on becoming Kentucky's next governor, but having made an enemy of Laffoon and his forces, he knew that advancement would be blocked by the governor if the party convention system remained in place. So when Laffoon went out of the state in early 1935, Chandler, as acting governor, called the legislature into special session to consider adopting party primaries. Although his gambit encountered some snags, the change was made, and Chandler, who won his party's gubernatorial nomination and then the election in 1935, was on his way to becoming one of the state's most powerful and colorful politicians of all time.

To help battle the ravages of the depression, Laffoon and countless other state and local officials like him looked to Washington, but the prevailing economic orthodoxy of the time, which was embraced by the Hoover administration, was that there was little the national government could or should do about the economy except to keep its own financial house in order. The keys to economic recovery, the president reasoned, were the prudent management of federal finances and a balanced budget. Nevertheless, as the depression worsened, Hoover was willing to try initiatives such as the Reconstruction Finance Corporation, which Congress, including Vinson, supported. The RFC was designed to stimulate domestic production and consumption by making low-interest loans to banks, railroads, insurance companies, and agricultural organizations. When such remedies proved inadequate to make much of a dent in the nation's crisis, the president veered to the left and signed in July 1932 a massive $2.1 billion relief bill that included $1.5 billion to finance public works construction of income-producing projects and $300 million in loans to states for direct relief.

At the beginning of the Seventy-second Congress in December 1931, Vinson was in an even more parsimonious mood than Hoover, but by the summer of 1932 his passion for fiscal restraint likewise had ebbed. In House debate over the relief bill, Vinson said, "There are those who do not agree that hungry and starving Americans should be cared for by the Federal Government. I would not counsel such legislation except *in extremis*." He noted that the "Glass-Steagall banking bill, and many other bills, have been brought upon this floor and passed," but "everything that has been done to this good hour has failed to start the wheels rolling in the right direction."[17]

Vinson, though, was still fixated on balancing the budget and reducing government spending when a constituent wrote in the spring to complain that the national government "is spending a constantly increasing sum each year" and "will have spent an amount exceeding comparable figures for 1927 by over ONE BILLION TWO HUNDRED AND THIRTY DOLLARS."[18] Vinson replied, "I am doing my dead-level best to cut the cost of Government in every reasonable manner possible." Noting that he led the fight in Ways and Means to reduce spending, he said, "I do not think there is a question but what the Budget could well be reduced one billion dollars, but that could only be done after a complete study of the situation by Congress. We have not had the co-operation of the Executive Department looking toward the cut. In fact, every one has insisted that their's must not be cut."[19]

Taking his argument to the full House, Vinson asserted that Hoover's proposed fiscal 1933 budget could be even more frugal. "No more wholesome thing could go to the country than that Congress was cutting appropriations, the executive departments saving money, all of which would mean a lessened burden upon the taxpayers of our nation," Vinson said. He claimed that 10 percent, or $242 million, could be cut from Hoover's proposed budget of $4.1 billion, whereas the administration claimed that at most only $125 million in savings could be achieved. "The country demands, and rightfully so, that the expenditures of government must be decreased," Vinson said. "It is a source of genuine regret to me that when the executive branch . . . has a real opportunity to practice what they have long preached, they are not willing to assume their share of the responsibility."[20]

One economy measure Vinson advocated, to no avail, was consolidating the administration of the military into a unified department headed by a secretary of defense with Cabinet rank; there would also be assistant secretaries for war, the navy, and aviation. He estimated that the consolidation would save $50 million to $100 million a year. In addition, Vinson said, there would be a "material increase in the efficiency of the national defense service if there was a single driver at the wheel." Discussing his proposal on the House floor, Vinson said his experience on the Military Affairs Committee "fully acquaints me with the failure of the Army and Navy to coordinate in their functioning for national defense." The love of power, jealousies, and animosities caused conflicts between the army and the navy whether the country was at war or not, Vinson said. "During the war the Army and Navy were in competition for the purchase of the same steel. They wrangled over priority of shipment. For many years they have been haggling over the jurisdiction of the defense of a coast line, arguing whether the Air Corps of the Army or the Navy had the duty of coastal defense."[21]

Vinson's fiscal fluctuations during 1932 were most apparent in the area of taxation: he supported on the one hand a sales tax of 2.25 percent and staunchly defended tobacco against increased taxes on the other. Vinson joined with twenty-three of his colleagues on the Ways and Means Committee in the spring to pass what was called a manufacturer's excise tax, which meant that consumers would pay the sales tax on the cost of the finished product, not on the retail price. Food and inexpensive clothing were to be exempt. It was estimated that the measure, whose lone opponent in the committee was Democrat Robert L. Doughton of North Carolina, would generate nearly half of the $1.24 billion needed in new revenue to balance the 1933 budget. The tax proposal created a storm once it reached the full House, and a bipartisan bloc, led by Republican Fiorello H. LaGuardia and Doughton, defeated it, reviving instead the wartime surtaxes on wealth. Vinson did an about-face on the sales tax, voting with the majority to strike it from the revenue bill.

There was no retreat on his part, though, when the issue was lower taxes on tobacco, which was grown on small plots by hundreds of farmers in Vinson's Ninth District and, of course, was Kentucky's premier cash crop. He used his chairmanship of two Ways and Means subcommittees in 1932 to defend tobacco against additional taxation. He first made his case for tobacco as head of a five-member panel that crafted an alternative budget bill to the Hoover administration's proposal, which called for a one-cent tax increase on a pack of cigarettes, from six cents to seven cents. Vinson was able to persuade the subcommittee, the full Ways and Means committee, and the House to eliminate the higher cigarette tax. Explaining the action to a radio audience over Washington, D.C., station WJSV, Vinson said, "We are convinced beyond doubt that the point of saturation in tobacco taxes has been reached, if not passed." Calling tobacco "the largest and most dependable tax source for Uncle Sam," Vinson noted that tobacco taxes would account for one-fifth, or $434 million, of the revenue collected by the federal government in fiscal 1933, far exceeding individual and corporate income taxes combined. "The federal government has a direct interest in the consumption of cigarettes," Vinson said, adding that the treasury collects three dollars for every fifty packs sold.

Increasing the cigarette tax, Vinson said, "would bring into action the law of diminishing return, which in everyday parlance simply means killing the goose that lays the golden egg." Higher taxes mean decreased sales, he explained, noting that yearly per capita consumption in the thirteen states that added their own tax to the federal levy was 431 cigarettes compared with 975 cigarettes per capita for the country as a whole. Decreased consumption "means a decreased price for the farmer's product," Vinson said. "Only when there is a demand for his product can a fair price be secured." Lastly, smokers pay enough in taxes, Vinson said, adding, "A man using one pack per day already pays a tax of $21.60 a year to his government. With the additional one cent per pack his tax would be $25.50 per year." This tax, he said, "is more than the income tax required of a married man with a wife and three children, under existing law, who has a net income of $7,000."[22]

Writing to thank Vinson for his efforts, D.P. Newell, cashier at the State National Bank in Maysville, said, "We folks here greatly appreciate the fight you have made in Washington and particularly your assistance in blocking the additional tax on tobacco."[23]

Vinson got another opportunity to make his case for tobacco in 1932 when he chaired a subcommittee appointed to study double taxation, or the imposition of taxes on the same thing by federal, state, and local governments. In a July 6 national radio address on the subject, he said the "present tax burden is oppressive," adding that "city, county, state, and nation will tax anything that will yield returns. It is a permitted right in law, but an unjust exercise in application." He said the committee hoped, by studying the duplication, overlapping, and lack of coordination in the tax system, to find ways "to lessen the burden of taxation. In no sense are we seeking new taxes."

Conveniently, Vinson used tobacco to illustrate the problem of double taxation, noting there was a federal tax of 6 cents on a pack of twenty cigarettes and that thirteen states had "invaded this tax field." Arkansas, for example, levied a 5-cent tax, raising the cost of a pack of cigarettes in that state to 15 cents compared with 10 cents a pack in states where there was no additional tax. The combined federal-state tax yield of 11 cents on a pack of cigarettes "is 2,100 percent more than the average price the farmer received for its tobacco content," Vinson said. He added that the reverse is also true: that is, that the federal government tapped sources previously the domain of state and local governments. "In the recent revenue bill, for the first time, the federal government invaded the gasoline field, which had heretofore been subject to state taxation only," Vinson said, noting the imposition of a one-cent-a-gallon federal tax. "This invasion was made because of the attractiveness and certainty of yield—which is far from justification of the act."[24]

A childhood friend from Louisa, then living in Los Angeles, wrote Vinson that she was "thrilled because at last I am going to hear your speech on the tax question of which every-one seems to be so interested nowdays." She added, "I've seen your name in our papers every now & then & listened in a few wks. ago to the ball-game [the annual baseball game between House Democrats and Republicans] in which you were playing. They said Vinson at the plate & mentioned that you weighed 190 lbs."[25] Vinson wrote in reply that it was "good to know that old friends were listening in, even though the miles separated us. I have been working mighty hard this session. It has been the most strenuous session that we have had for many years. However, I feel that I have accomplished some things that will be of real benefit to my District and State."[26]

In releasing the subcommittee's study at the end of 1932, Vinson had no illusions that its findings would lead to sweeping reforms. Instead he held out modest expectations that the report would "aid in the scientific study of our tax problems and throw some light on what the public receives for their tax dollars" and should serve as a "basis for the intelligent discussion of the subject of double taxation."[27] Although the report called on federal, state, and local governments to eliminate duplication of taxes, it pinpointed reducing the cost of government at all levels as the best way to achieve tax reform. The report said a more equitable distribution of the tax burden and its ultimate reduction could come through "a judicious curtailment in expenditures."[28] The subcommittee found 326 instances of duplicate taxation between the federal government and state governments, an inflated figure because the gas tax, imposed by 48 states, 1 territory, and the District of Columbia, was counted as 50 duplications. Total tax collections for 1931 amounted to $9.5 billion, with federal taxes accounting for $2.4 billion, state taxes nearly $2 billion, county taxes $958 million, city taxes nearly $3 billion, and other local taxes $1.2 billion. This put the per capita tax bill for Americans in 1931 at $77.53.[29]

Vinson also demonstrated support for tobacco through his work on a voluntary allotment plan contained in legislation proposed in the waning days of Hoover's presidency. The scheme would have provided a price-support system for farmers of various commodities, tobacco included, who voluntarily limited their production. Under a bill passed by the House, farmers would have been paid from a fund created by excise taxes levied upon the manufacturers of their products, for example, cigarette companies for tobacco, meat packers for hogs, and textile mills for cotton. Vinson's main contribution to this legislation was to get the parity price for tobacco changed. Originally, it was to be equal to the average price over the 1909–1914 period, or 10.5 cents a pound. Under his amendment to the bill, the period used was changed to 1909–1918, which raised the average price to 14.5 cents.

Raising objections to the legislation in a letter to Vinson, one Kentuckian wrote, "I have discussed the proposed plans for agricultural relief with a great many intelligent people, and the almost unanimous opinion is that the Domestic Allotment Plan, or any similar plan is absolutely unsound." The writer opposed the plan because he believed it would result in higher prices for consumers because manufacturers would simply pass along their increased costs and because the plan "would be very difficult to administer thoroughly or justly."[30] In his reply, Vinson countered that the proposal would have a rippling effect throughout the economy. "If you can get an increased price to the farmer, they will have increased purchasing power, increased purchasing power means increased production of the manufactured article. That means wages for men with which to purchase commodities. You can buy the farmers products and other manufactured products and you have an endless chain." Acknowledging that some might think the proposal "very radical," Vinson added that "we are in an unusual condition and unless something is done to increase purchasing power, there is no hope for us."[31]

The House passed the allotment plan in the lame-duck session of the Seventy-second Congress, but the Senate failed to act upon the measure. Farm relief would have to wait for Roosevelt and his New Deal.

Coal, another vital Kentucky commodity that had fallen on hard times, also commanded Vinson's attention in 1932. In arguing that the Hawley-Smoot Tariff Act of 1930 be amended to stimulate foreign trade, Vinson blamed higher duties imposed by the legislation for causing calamity in the state's coalfields, and he chided Republican Charles Finley of Kentucky's Eleventh Congressional District for supporting Hawley-Smoot. "I am astounded that he could defend the . . . tariff bill or his party for acts . . . that have so detrimentally affected his district. He represents a great coal district. Its money crop is coal. This great industry in Kentucky is paralyzed, lying prostrate . . . with thousands of the constituents of the gentleman . . . at this moment hungry for work and food." He noted that "American commerce has been shut out from many markets of the world" because other countries raised their own tariffs in retaliation for Hawley-Smoot. Therefore, Vinson said, it was "of the highest importance to secure a lowering of foreign tariff barriers, repeal of the retaliatory tariff measures in order that our commerce, the products of the farm, mine, and factory, might again move in the channels of world trade."[32]

Vinson's efforts in behalf of the beleaguered extended to veterans as well. His inherent zest for fiscal restraint evaporated when the issue concerned cash bonuses for World War I veterans, an issue he began campaigning for during his earlier time in Congress and one he continued championing until he achieved success in 1936. In 1932, with 2 million veterans out of work, Vinson pushed for immediate full payment of the previously authorized adjusted service certificates, which were paid-up life insurance policies collectible in 1945. Such an action would have required the issue of $2.5 billion in treasury notes, something the Hoover administration adamantly opposed, as did a host of expert witnesses testifying before the House Ways and Means Committee. "If you are not going to couple this measure with a scientific control of the currency . . . then I would say that it is a dangerous thing to embark on," warned Dr. Williford I. King of New York University. He added, "I can see immediately somebody else will want $5,000,000,000 for roads and somebody else will want $10,000,000,000 for unemployment and there will be no end to the demands to put out money."[33] Professor Edwin W. Kemmerer of Princeton University agreed, saying, "The minute you break from gold . . . the force of your resistance is greatly weakened because if you issue $2,500,000,000 and then go off the gold basis, why not issue two billion more for the farmers, for this class, and the other class?"[34] The governor of the Federal Reserve Board, Eugene Meyer, said, "The debasing of the currency will, of course, create distrust and disorganization of business, and evils and difficulties so great in comparison with any that we are now suffering from that I hesitate to contemplate them." He foresaw Gresham's law—good currency being driven out by inferior currency—as one effect. "That was the reason for the great flow of gold to the United States from all over the world in the early nineteen twenties and the middle nineteen twenties," Meyer said. "They had inferior currency, and gold left them, and it went to the only important country having a stable, sound currency."[35]

Vinson was in the forefront of a heated House debate on the cash payment issue during mid-June of 1932. He said opponents of the legislation "paint a picture of havoc and near chaos" should the measure be enacted. "I would remind them that we have already arrived at the brink of ruin. We have reached this point without any urge from this legislation." Many of the measures that Congress passed to aid the economy— Reconstruction Finance Corporation and Glass-Steagall, among others—had helped, Vinson said, but "they are superficial palliative treatment of the disease without getting to the roots of the disease. This measure, in my judgement, goes at the basic conditions underlying our weakened economic structure."

To critics concerned about the gold standard, Vinson said, "They would enshroud the gold dollar with the cloak of divinity and declare to be heretics all those who would not worship at its shrine. They would have the country believe that the currency of this country is backed by gold and that money not so protected is 'fiat' money." But, Vinson noted, "We do have money without gold reserve." He then proceeded to support his statement: "On March 31, 1932, our total outstanding currency was $5,459,085,385. Our total gold reserve held by the Treasury and the Federal reserve bank was $3,594,694,087. In other words, the currency outstanding in excess of the total gold reserve was $1,864,391,298." He then noted that national-bank notes, totaling $700 million, had no gold reserve and that federal reserve notes required only a minimum of 40 percent in gold reserve. "My friends," Vinson said, "the fact that the gold reserve of this country will support expansion of the currency admits no argument. The mere statement of the amount of gold used as the reserve of the Federal reserve notes shows beyond contravention that an expansion of currency can be had."

Continuing, Vinson said, "There is never any argument about how to get money or where to get it when the direct interests of the big interests is involved. When human rights become involved, then immediately the vested interests strike out, hitting in every direction all those who stand in their way." He said the $26 billion in war expenses, the $3 billion to war contractors, $2 billion to the railroads after the war, and the billions of dollars to European nations in the form of war debt reductions "certainly inclines me to the idea that this Nation could pay the adjusted-service certificates."

In closing his fifteen-minute speech, Vinson, who throughout had relied upon cold, hard facts and figures to carry his argument, made a stirring appeal to the emotions. "I can not, in my mind and heart, forget the boys of yesterday who were the proud defenders of our flag," he said. "How many billions of dollars has this country taken from them in their physical and mental inability to pursue their hopes and their ambitions?" Soldiers, Vinson said, "did not serve for monetary reward. Patriotic fire stirred their breasts; love of country imbued them with a world-admired zeal." Veterans were told that "America would ever be grateful" for their sacrifices, but now "in a matter which they are much interested, their names would be defamed, their motives attacked." To applause, Vinson ended by saying, "Before you attack them in this forum, boys, remember who they are—lest you forget; lest you forget."[36]

The House approved the bonus bill by a vote of 209 to 176, but the Senate overwhelmingly rejected it 62 to 18. Even if the measure had cleared both bodies, it almost certainly would have been vetoed by President Hoover.

Veterans from every state had traveled to Washington in the summer of 1932 to lobby for the bonus bill, and although many departed once the outcome was decided, some ten thousand stayed on to press their cause. Their continued presence and agitation led Hoover to order the eviction of the so-called Bonus Army, which troops under an overzealous Gen. Douglas MacArthur accomplished with a barrage of tanks, guns, and tear gas. This rout of a helpless, ragtag band of veterans added to the public's perception that Hoover and his administration cared little about the needy and was a major factor in his defeat when he ran for reelection in the fall.

As Vinson contemplated his own reelection prospects that summer, he had to be buoyed by a telegram he received on July 13 from his brother-in-law Robert Dixon, then working in Frankfort as secretary to the Workmen's Compensation Board, informing him that "Clay, Watson and Stevens [all of whom had filed to oppose Vinson in the primary] have withdrawn. These withdrawals have been acknowledged and their names stricken from book in secretary of states office."[37] Vinson's relief over being spared a primary fight, which would have saved him money and allowed him to spend more time with his family and his law practice, was short-lived. A few weeks later came the devastating news that Kentucky's congressional redistricting law, enacted after the 1930 census resulted in the loss of two seats in the House of Representatives, had been declared unconstitutional by a panel of three federal judges; they ruled that the new districts were not contiguous and did not equally distribute the state's population. The effect of the decision, which came only days before the August 6 primary, was to force congressional candidates to run on an at-large basis to be nominated and elected.

Instead of having no opposition, Vinson now found himself vying for one of the nine nominations in the statewide Democratic primary with twenty-six other candidates. With precious little time to mount the meticulous type of campaign he preferred, Vinson nevertheless did the best he could. He blanketed the state with a form letter that highlighted his experience and growing influence in Congress and appealed for support in the name of fairness for his region of Kentucky. Noting that his district encompassed twenty counties and nearly three hundred thousand people, Vinson said unless he was nominated, "this vast territory and great people will not be represented on the ticket."[38] Vinson's efforts were helped by favorable newspaper editorials. One in the *Cynthiana Democrat,* under the headline "Remember Vinson," urged Harrison County voters to "search out the name of Congressman Fred M. Vinson, which they will find eighteenth down the list of twenty-seven congressional candidates, and stamp opposite his name."[39] The *Carlisle Mercury* published a similar opinion with the headline, "Vote First for Vinson for Congress." The paper said that "the Democrats of Nicholas owe the cause of able representation in Congress a debt that they should repay by voting for Fred Vinson."[40] "Vinson should be returned to Congress without fail," said a piece in the *Bracken Chronicle,* complete with Vinson's picture and a headline that read, "Has Earned the Support of All Loyal Democrats."[41]

Other Vinson supporters also did what they could. A few days before the primary, a Vinson supporter in Bath County informed him, "The soldier boys are 100 per cent O.K. and have done a good deal of work in the short time they had since it became known that you would have to engage in a state wide primary." Another confidant, writing to apprise Vinson of the situation in western Kentucky, said, "I am going to do all I can and wish you success. However, do not expect too much as there seems to be considerable displeasure on the part of the people and they may not vote."[42] One western Kentucky resident, a Hopkinsville banker, did intend to vote, but before he made any commitments, he had some questions for Vinson. The questions mainly concerned economy and efficiency in government. For example, he asked Vinson, "What is your position on the question of consolidation of Bureaus and abolishment of others in order to reduce the number of Government employees?" To this, Vinson replied, "The Congress would have abolished many agencies and consolidated others, if they had had any help from President Hoover. I favor businesslike administration." The banker also wrote, "If my memory serves me right, you voted against the recent Bonus Bill, for which many of us thank you."[43] His memory, of course, was faulty, but Vinson, normally so quick to correct any error in fact, let this one slip by without comment, undoubtedly worried about losing any potential voter in the risky statewide race.

The results of the campaign that Vinson and his allies put together in a matter of days convincingly demonstrated that his popularity and appeal stretched the breadth of the Bluegrass. He finished first in the field of twenty-seven with a total of more than 100,000 votes. In a letter of congratulations, a Murray State geography professor wrote, "I had students and friends working all over western Kentucky for you and Jack May [who finished second to Vinson with more than 97,000 votes]. I talked [about] you two so much that your names became a by-word in many homes of this region." He closed by saying, "Your election in November is assured. This is a Democratic year; Roosevelt will be our next president."[44]

Vinson took to the hustings to make sure the professor was right in his prophecy. In reporting on his frenetic campaign activity to House Speaker Garner as election day neared, Vinson noted, "I have spoken in ten of the eleven (old) Congressional Districts, and have covered more miles and made more speeches in Kentucky than anyone in this campaign." In four weeks leading up to the election, Vinson wrote, "I have not been home but three nights." He told Garner, "Everything looks good in Kentucky," adding, "I may be wrong but I believe it is going to be record breaking."[45]

It was. Democrats captured all of the nine congressional seats, and Vinson led the pack with 575,191 votes. Roosevelt won in 95 of the state's 120 counties, polling nearly 60 percent of the vote, and Alben W. Barkley was reelected to the U.S. Senate, the first time a Kentucky senator had won reelection in forty-two years. Vinson and the eight other Democrats would be at-large representatives of the state when the Seventy-third Congress went into session on March 9, 1933.[46] But when the next congressional elections were held, two years later, they would be according to the 1930 redistricting plan, which the U.S. Supreme Court eventually declared valid. This meant that Vinson would run in 1934 and 1936, his last races, as Eighth District representative.

He was still representing the old Ninth, though, when he returned to Washington for the last lame-duck session of Congress, which met from December 5, 1932, to March 4, 1933. With the curtain about to ring down on the repudiated Hoover administration and poised to rise for the greatly anticipated Roosevelt presidency, Vinson should have been able to revel in the moment. Out with old and in with the new, however, proved far more vexing than he could have imagined. In the lame-duck session, he had to cast a vote that put him at odds with a long-held position, while in the aborning Seventy-third Congress, he opposed the new president's economic recovery bill that slashed government spending. Vinson was ready with ample explanation and justification for his actions, but that did not make the fallout from these decisions any easier to handle.

Little had been expected to happen in Washington while the nation waited for Hoover to depart and Roosevelt to ascend. Certainly nothing of any consequence happened on the economic front. Congress did, however, take up the hot-button issue of repealing prohibition, which had been called for in the Democratic Party's 1932 convention.

Having to vote on this matter undoubtedly was a bitter pill for Vinson, whose stand on repeal had corkscrewed suddenly from his long-held, unequivocal opposition to support of congressional action in February 1933 that sent to the states the Twenty-first Amendment, repealing the Eighteenth. As late as his 1930 campaign for Congress, Vinson was still taking the pledge. He reaffirmed his position on September 9, 1930, to the president of the Association against Prohibition Amendment, who had asked him whether he favored repeal. He replied: "It is a pleasure for me to answer the question for you. My answer is 'No.'"[47] When others wrote to question Vinson's fidelity to the cause, he was quick to state his allegiance. For example, on October 10, 1930, Vinson, in a response to Rev. W.C. Pierce of Catlettsburg, said, "I have never given anyone any right to believe that I have changed my attitude upon prohibition from that which I had long [held] before I ever entered political life." He added that "without equivocation" he was dry and "would oppose any effort to weaken the enforcement statutes affecting prohibition, and would oppose the repeal of the Eighteenth Amendment."[48]

Less than two years later, shortly after repeal won nearly unanimous approval at the Democratic National Convention, Vinson again responded to a letter from Reverend Pierce about prohibition. This time he had a different answer, and he acknowledged "that my statement to you will not be pleasing." He delivered the news obliquely, using uncharacteristically strained and formal phrasing in his letter, which indicated his discomfort in being forced to disclose that he had switched sides. Vinson never directly declared support for repeal; rather, he recited the fact that he had taken an oath as a congressional candidate "before the action of the Convention" to support the party's principles and policies. "The Democratic platform adopted at Chicago is the statement of the principles and policies of that Party," Vinson said, adding, "I am standing upon that platform in accordance with the oath that I have taken." Furthermore, he pointed out that if elected as an at-large representative in 1932, he would have a statewide constituency to consider. "As such, it is my sworn obligation as well as an implied Party obligation to express the sentiment of the people whom I represent." As one indication of that sentiment, Vinson noted that the Kentucky delegation at Chicago voted unanimously for the repeal plank in the platform. Lastly, Vinson justified his position by saying that the "enforcement of prohibition has completely broken down. The Nation is in the most critical condition of its history. The people are demanding changed conditions."[49]

Vinson was not one to change positions on issues lightly, especially on one that had been such a touchstone. He valued consistency in himself and others, but he also could put party loyalty ahead of personal considerations, especially in the critical year of 1932 when all signs pointed to a Democratic sweep. To Vinson, having the party in control of national government far outweighed any concern he might have felt for the fallout that was sure to result from repudiating a long-held position. His commitment to being a team player is obvious in a letter he wrote to a political ally on the eve of the national convention. Although he was discussing the need to make the selection of a permanent convention chair as harmonious as possible, the sentiments expressed might just as easily be used to explain his turnabout on prohibition. "We have the Republicans on the run the worst that I ever saw, and we will elect a president, hands down, if we do not mess things up at Chicago." He added, "As a Democrat, desirous of winning, I do not want any more mistakes made than we can possibly help."[50]

Vinson's dream of Democratic domination, of course, was realized. When the Seventy-third Congress opened, Franklin D. Roosevelt was in the White House, and Democrats, in control of the legislative branch for the first time since 1916, held substantial margins over Republicans in both chambers—60 to 35 in the Senate and 311 to 116 in the House. Vinson would be at center stage in the formative years of the New Deal, helping to shape such landmark legislation as Social Security and taking on the difficult assignment of wringing out more tax dollars to fund the administration's adventuresome and expanding efforts to revive the economy. He was in lockstep with Roosevelt on just about everything that came before Congress from the spring of 1933 until his departure more than five years later for the federal bench. His devotion to the New Deal was so deep that he even introduced the House version of the president's court-packing plan, a scheme so transparent and brazen in its attempt to corral the Supreme Court that it was roundly criticized by even some of Roosevelt's most loyal guard in Congress. About the only time Vinson parted company with the president was over the issue of funding for veterans. Unhappily for Vinson, the first parting of the ways on this matter came only one week after Roosevelt's inauguration.

CHAPTER 4

The Loyal Lieutenant

Opposing Franklin D. Roosevelt in the early, heady days of his administration, a time when most Americans saw him as the savior come to lift the country out of the despair of the Great Depression, bordered on sacrilege. "People are looking to you almost as they look to God," one person wrote to the White House a few days after the president's inauguration on March 4, 1933.[1] The weather on that Saturday—cold and gloomy—matched the country's dire economic condition. Millions had lost their jobs, their homes, their savings, and their futures. In the new president, though, "tens of millions of frightened Americans found a much-needed tonic in the self-assurance and strength that FDR projected."[2]

Roosevelt had promised the country a New Deal and he wasted little time in trying to achieve it, calling Congress into special session five days after taking office to act on his sweeping legislative agenda. The first hundred days of the Roosevelt administration set the standard by which the activities and accomplishments of future presidents in their first days in office would be judged. None before or since can match Roosevelt's prodigious record. His first one hundred days, according to a summary of that special session in the *American Political Science Review,* were "unparalleled for the speed and discipline with which Congress was brought to face and finish its task, for the political adroitness and firmness of the presidential leadership, and for the extraordinary importance and far-reaching effects of the legislation enacted."[3]

By the time Congress adjourned on June 16, 1933, exactly one hundred days after convening in special session, it had written into law fourteen major pieces of legislation designed to deal with the banking crisis, unemployment, hunger, homelessness, farm relief, business and industrial recovery, conservation, securities fraud, energy needs, and the budget deficit. America was transformed in those exhilarating days from March to June, not only as a result of the specific measures enacted, but just as significantly because confidence and energy had been restored to the nation. "It's more than a New Deal," Harold Ickes, Roosevelt's secretary of the interior, said. "It's a new world. People feel free again. They can breathe naturally. It's like quitting a morgue for the open woods."[4]

Fred Vinson was in the front lines battling for the president's New Deal revolution with one big exception—Roosevelt's Economy Act, which was his plan to reduce federal spending by $500 million. Vinson, normally a champion of such frugality, opposed this particular measure because it would slash $400 million from payments to veterans. Vinson was not alone in his opposition. The Democratic caucus in the House decided to withhold its support, and when the bill reached the House floor, ninety Democrats besides Vinson voted no, including such liberals as Wright Patman of Texas and John McCormack of Massachusetts. The Economy Act still passed by a comfortable 266–138 margin. When he went home the evening after the House vote, Vinson said to his wife, Roberta, "I committed political suicide today."[5]

Vinson was wrong about his fate, though. Far from being relegated to a political wasteland, over the course of the next five and a half years he found his stock as a legislator and politician steadily rising in Washington and in Kentucky. Time and again, he demonstrated his value to Roosevelt, the New Deal, his state, and his district. While taking on difficult legislative assignments that were national in scope, mainly finding the money to finance the New Deal, Vinson never lost sight of taking care of critical back-home issues, aiding tobacco farmers and the coal industry in particular. If he had chosen to remain in elective office instead of accepting a position in the federal judiciary in 1937, eastern Kentuckians almost certainly would have continued reelecting him to his seat, or his career might have veered into a successful run for the U.S. Senate or for governor. Had he remained in the House, he no doubt would have ascended to a leadership position, logically as majority leader under his close friend Sam Rayburn, who first became Speaker in 1940 and who considered Vinson practically indispensable to the functioning of Congress.

In early 1933, however, Vinson understandably was feeling very dispensable after his vote on the Economy Act. Defending his opposition in the name of veterans was a hard sell because many, including some veterans themselves, believed pensions for war service were unwarranted. But even if they could be justified, the belief was that veterans should still be willing to accept reductions in benefits if everyone else in the country was being asked to sacrifice for the sake of economic recovery. It was Vinson's unhappy lot to be cast as a turncoat and a tool of the veterans' lobby. The charges cut him to the quick, and he flared back at those who dared question his decision, even friends and political allies.

Vinson was put on the defensive as soon as the news of his vote reached Kentucky. The *Louisville Courier-Journal,* the state's most prominent and widely circulated daily newspaper, led the charge. Because Vinson and *Courier* publisher Robert Worth Bingham were from opposing factions in the state Democratic party, criticism from that quarter was not unexpected. Still, Vinson was stunned by the vociferousness of the attack. In an editorial headlined "Assassin's Bullets," the paper accused Vinson and the three other Kentucky congressmen who opposed Roosevelt's budget-cutting proposal—Virgil Chapman, A.J. May, and Finley Hamilton—of "desertion of their duty to their President and to their country." In addition, the newspaper said the four had "chosen to represent not the body of their constituents, but the gratuity-clinging veterans and the Federal employees who rebel against the economies to which all others are subjected."[6]

He was accustomed to taking shots from predictable sources like the *Courier-Journal,* but Vinson obviously was stung when darts flew from friendlier quarters, as his exchange with Ashland businessman and supporter Walter Mayo illustrated. In a "My Dear Fred" letter, Mayo wrote, "When we picked up the paper Sunday morning we were shocked at your vote on the Economy Bill. Our first place to go was to Bible Class at Methodist Church where it was the sole discussion before and after class. Not a voice was raised in your defense."[7]

In a huff, Vinson responded, "Your letter wounded me," adding that Mayo had "jumped at conclusions, indicted me, found me guilty and executed me without an opportunity for hearing, just because the Courier-Journal, who has wanted to operate on me for a long time, reached an editorial conclusion—mind you, the conclusion of one man—that I was not standing in with the President."[8] Actually, it was Vinson who had jumped to conclusions, as Mayo gently pointed out in a later letter. Vinson had assumed, wrongly as it turned out, that Mayo had been influenced by the stinging opinion in the Louisville paper.

Answering Vinson, Mayo pointed out that he had not seen the *Courier-Journal* editorial when he first wrote; he was merely responding to the news of Vinson's vote as reported in the *Ashland Independent.* "If you feel wounded you have taken the letter just opposite to what we intended," Mayo wrote. "It is easy to be a fair weather friend and send only roses. Tried to be a friend in time when you needed them but guess our efforts turned into a cactus."[9]

A friend in Cynthiana informed Vinson that his "vote on the President's economy bill Saturday has stirred up a lot of Hades around here."[10] Similarly, V.V. Adkins, another friend and supporter in Ashland, wrote to tell Vinson that the "comments on the streets" were running against him. Adding his own assessment of the situation, Adkins said that "the world war boys through concentration and organization have absolutely taken charge of congress, and I believe that this bill was the only way to break an absolute dirty draft upon the treasury of the United States."[11]

Desha Breckinridge, a scion of one of Kentucky's most distinguished families and a man Vinson greatly admired and respected, politely eased into his displeasure over Vinson's position. "I feel sure there is no need for me to tell you that I treasure implicit confidence in your intellectual integrity and courage," wrote Breckinridge, longtime editor and publisher of the *Lexington Herald,* noted horseman, and a leader of the party faction to which Vinson belonged. Still, he said he regretted that Vinson had let himself become captive to the special interests of veterans: "You are . . . a representative of all the people, not a faction of the people." He said he had been opposed to pensions and bounties for veterans "since as a college lad, when visiting my father in Washington, I saw the subserviency of congress to the greed of the Grand Army of the Republic." He would make exceptions, of course, for "those whose bodies were mutilated or health impaired as a direct result of service." Breckinridge, noting that as a veteran he was entitled to a pension and free hospital care, said, "I can see no possible justification for the nation caring for me because I served in the Spanish War, when I had no ill effect from that service."[12]

The tone of other correspondence that Vinson received was far more harsh and carried threats of political retribution. For instance, J.C. Courtenay of Anchorage wrote that Vinson's vote was "a disgraceful sacrifice . . . to political expediency." He added, "You no doubt think you were looking after the interests of World War veterans. I am one of them who saw service overseas, and I am very sorry indeed that I voted for you last November. Furthermore, I shall remember this unpatriotic conduct at the next election and see that all with whom I come in contact remember it too."[13] An Owensboro correspondent wrote, "My reason for writing is that I want to fix your name in my memory so that I will know what to do if I ever see it on any ballot handed to me."[14] In a testy, one-sentence response, Vinson wrote, "Just to advise you that I have a good memory also."[15] John C. Hatcher, of Ashland, also warned Vinson that he would turn from a supporter to an opponent if Vinson ever again veered from backing Roosevelt. "I want to tell you candidly and truly that if this happens again I certainly will use my moral influence to eliminate you from the Democrat party, even if I have to vote a Republican ticket. The people demand that you get on the job and give us a new deal."[16]

Vinson and Joe T. Lovett, editor of the *Ledger & Times* in Murray, had a particularly nasty exchange over the issue. "Sorry you saw fit to knife your President and your country on the Economy Bill," Lovett wrote, adding, "You have made a great political mistake and your vote on this measure makes it impossible for me ever to support you again on any ticket or platform."[17] Vinson shot back: "I charge your statement that I 'knifed my President' on the so called economy bill as an untruth. Because an editorial [*Courier-Journal*] reached an erroneous conclusion as to my intentions and purpose, you go off half-cocked and blindly follow their thought."[18]

Lovett raised the stakes in his next letter. "Embroiled in the morass of your gross error you seem convinced that you must make a complete ass of yourself," he wrote. "Neither the Courier-Journal nor any other newspaper voices or sponsors my political convictions." Noting his service in France during the war, Lovett said, "I utterly detest demagogues of your ilk who will gut the treasury to feather your own political nests by granting pensions to tin-soldiers who served a few months in camp." He continued: "There are a few veterans, Mr. Vinson, who cannot be bought. You had a right to vote as you damn please in Congress; we have a right to vote as we damn please at the polls. You have signed your political death warrant, now rant and rave until you make your former supporters vomit with disgust."[19] Vinson, obviously not wanting to prolong the exchange, wrote a brief letter in response, saying in part, "I want to be careful not to say anything to which you may take personal exception, as you seem to be some 'ranter and raver' yourself."[20]

In defending his vote to less vociferous critics, Vinson argued that past pledges to veterans bound him to oppose the measure, that the proposal was pension reform disguised as emergency budget-cutting, and that the *Courier-Journal* misconstrued his position in its editorial simply because the paper was out to get to him. In one letter Vinson wrote, "I have made pledges repeatedly that I would be friendly to the interests of veterans of all wars. I have lived up to that pledge to the letter."[21] In another he wrote, "The job I have to do is to do the best I can with such experience and limited sense as I possess, but they will have to hunt a long way before they find some jay-bird that can say I broke faith with him."[22] Saying that the real intent of the Economy Act was to reform the pension system, Vinson wrote to a friend that although Civil War veterans and their widows would not be affected by the legislation, "the power was given to rewrite all other veterans legislation of every kind and description. Instead of a 15% cut, in many instances you would have had 100% cut. The Spanish War Veterans would have been required to prove their cases service connected, even though at the time the pension was granted such was not the case."[23] In blaming the *Courier-Journal* for causing the criticism that coursed his way, Vinson wrote to Breckinridge, "It is clearly demonstrated to me again that which I have frequently observed—the helplessness of one from the maligning tongue of slander."[24]

Amid the tumult also came letters of comfort and support. A friend from Louisa wrote, "I desire to tell you that you have not only not lost any prestige down in your old home town but stand 100% as one of the four Kentucky Congressmen who kept their word, and, boy we are 100% for you any time, any where and for anything."[25] Another supporter wrote, "I want to compliment you on your loyalty to your constituents. Personally I believe you have gained many votes by the stand you have taken on the economy measure. I am a Republican, but have always voted for you when you was running, also my wife and close friends, both personal and business, and I control quite a number of votes here."[26] An attorney in Mt. Sterling wrote Vinson to let him know "that all of your friends have not deserted you. I know that it took much more real honest-to-goodness COURAGE to vote your honest convictions on this measure, than it possibly could have taken to have followed the majority."[27]

The economy bill passed both houses of Congress in just two days after it was introduced, but the strain and stain of the debate lingered for Vinson. He could not resist taking parting shots at Bingham and the *Courier-Journal* and at a fellow Kentuckian in the House, John Young Brown, who had also attacked Vinson's vote. In an extension of remarks on the issue in the *Congressional Record,* Vinson said his "vote upon this measure has been misunderstood, even to the point that disloyalty to the President of the United States was charged in the Courier-Journal and Times. In short words, such a charge is a malicious, willful, damnable lie."[28] He noted that there was opposition to the bill in the Senate, from both Democrats and Republicans, but that no "character assassination of them has appeared upon the pages of his newspapers. The fact that his name appeared before them being nominated for the Ambassadorship to England probably closed his mouth in attacks upon them." Vinson charged Brown with flip-flopping his position, having first voted in caucus to bind Democratic members to supporting an amended version of the bill that would have restricted cuts in veterans' benefits to 25 percent and then changing his mind to oppose the proposal. "Every member of the Kentucky delegation voted to bind the bill with said amendment," Vinson said. "Brown alone changed his vote."[29]

A few days later, the Vinson-Brown feud erupted on the House floor. Brown drew first blood when he accused Vinson of inserting his extended remarks in the *Congressional Record* for "essentially no purpose other than to promote his own future" in Kentucky. "This gentlemen has spent $225 of the taxpayers' money to explain a vote of his, so that in the future he can get votes by virtue of this explanation of this vote," Brown said. He added that if Vinson sent a copy of his speech to every voter in his district it would cost taxpayers $3,240.78, and the cost would be $29,166.99 if copies went to every voter in the state. Brown, defending Bingham against Vinson's charge that "his papers are unfair to him personally, and have always been," noted that "on the very day he was making that attack Judge Bingham, upon the front page of his paper, was carrying an article, 'Vinson Seeking Amendment to Aid Burley in Farm Measure.' What more propitious place could he have found to put this speech favorable to this gentlemen."

Naturally, Vinson was ready with a rejoinder, responding partly in patronizing fashion. He said he wanted "to apologize to you for the lack of understanding of the new Member from Kentucky" when he claimed sending copies of the speech to Kentucky would cost taxpayers more than $29,000. "You all know that if any speeches are sent out by me I will have to pay the entire cost of printing," Vinson said, adding, "He displays the same kind of misunderstanding that he has shown throughout his whole political experience." He then turned to Brown's comment on the House floor that anyone opposing the Economy Act was disloyal to the president: "Loyalty is part of my religion, and I resented the charge of disloyalty to my President, because no man in this House will stand by him longer or suffer more for him than will I." He added, "Wait until the storm clouds hover low, wait until support of the President may not be so popular, and then see the young gentleman from Kentucky take cover, as he always does."[30]

By the time Vinson faced voters again in 1934, the acrimony over his vote on the Economy Act had not completely faded, and he confronted an even bigger challenge in his bid for reelection. Kentucky lawmakers were again fiddling with the composition of congressional districts, and Vinson's Eighth District had been targeted for change. A Democratic state legislator friendly to Seventh District congressman A.J. "Jack" May proposed taking four Democratic counties from Vinson and giving them to May, making his district more safely Democratic. It was a move that Vinson felt would guarantee his defeat. "I understand they are trying to put me out of Congress," Vinson wrote to a friendly state senator in early 1934 as he began his campaign hundreds of miles away in Washington to head off the redistricting attempt. "I would appreciate anything that you can do," Vinson said to the state senator, "and believe that if you could go to bat on this matter, you can protect the interests of the Democratic Party in Kentucky, and, incidentally, my own personal interest."[31] As the legislative tug of war proceeded, Vinson maintained a steady stream of correspondence with his supporters in the state capital and was prepared to travel to Frankfort if it became necessary. His presence was not required, as it turned out. He had enough support in the state legislature and even from the governor to beat back redistricting. On the morning of March 16, 1934, Vinson received a telegram from a friend in Frankfort informing him, "Successful in defeating all efforts of redistricting."[32] Another supporter wrote that day, "You are in luck. Several were gunning for you but you had some real friends looking after your interests," specifically mentioning state representative C.L. Cropper of Burlington. "This Cropper boy was at the top in the House, none better. He did some very effective work for you and was at all times watching."[33]

The good news from the redistricting fight was tempered for Vinson by the fact that he would again confront a primary challenge from William Fields, the erstwhile friend turned foe who had opposed him in the 1930 Democratic primary. Fields managed to poll 32 percent of the vote in 1934, a better showing than in 1930, but Vinson was too formidable, winning with more than 67 percent of the vote and taking every county in the twenty-county district except two. In the fall, Vinson was sidelined much of the time because of an illness, which required a two-week hospital stay and a minor operation. In a form letter to supporters about his situation, Vinson urged them to work extra hard in his behalf, saying, "I am compelled to depend upon you, in this campaign, more than ever" because "of my being unable to campaign in my usual vigorous fashion." Although his reelection appeared certain, Vinson warned "that feeling of confidence must not ripen into over-confidence."[34] Despite being hobbled, Vinson rolled to an impressive win, beating his Republican opponent in every county but two while amassing nearly 60 percent of the total vote.

That Vinson never allowed himself to be lulled into overconfidence is illustrated by his actions in the year following his overwhelming 1934 victory and a year before he would be up for reelection in 1936, which turned out to be his final campaign. In the 1935 Democratic primary for governor, he actively supported Thomas Rhea, chairman of the state highway commission, against then lieutenant governor A.B. "Happy" Chandler. "It is just simply a question of self preservation with me," Vinson wrote to a friend, explaining his involvement with Rhea's campaign.[35] "I know that the fellows who are wholly behind the Chandler candidacy, namely the Louisville newspaper crowd, would make it hard for me along any line that I may decide to go if they can." Vinson's lingering bitterness toward the *Courier-Journal* for its scathing criticism of his vote on the Economy Act is apparent in another letter. Writing to a political ally in Mt. Sterling, he said, "It may be that I oughtn't to have such a good memory but it will be at some future date before I would support the Courier Journal crowd as I can't keep from remembering an editorial that they shot at me back in March 1933."[36] When his man lost, Vinson, ever the loyal party man, did support Chandler, but mainly because he believed that a Republican victory in an off-year election would damage Roosevelt's reelection chances in 1936. For example, in his standard stump speech during the 1935 campaign, which was more of a testimonial to the president than an endorsement of Chandler, Vinson said, "The November election in Kentucky means much to the national campaign. The stakes in a governor's race in Kentucky are large. However, the Presidential stakes are much more valuable." The election of a GOP governor, he said, "simply means the placing of powerful weapons and ammunition . . . in the hands of the enemies of the Democratic national administration." The arsenal stayed in Democratic hands in 1935 as Chandler won handily over the Republican challenger, King Swope.[37]

The outcome of Vinson's finale in elective politics in 1936 was never in doubt, although, much to his annoyance, he still could not escape having opposition in the primary. "It certainly is the devil to have to have primary trouble every two years!" Vinson wrote to a supporter. "I should be thankful, I take it, that it does not come every year."[38] His hapless intraparty rival, however, was reduced to winning three precincts in the entire district and received only 16 percent of the vote compared with Vinson's whopping 84 percent. In the general election, campaigning as an ardent Roosevelt supporter and New Dealer, Vinson beat his Republican opponent by nearly 60 percent to 40 percent, almost identical to the president's margin of victory in Kentucky over the GOP presidential candidate, Alf Landon.

Aligning with Roosevelt, at least until the recession of 1937, was a sensible strategy for politicians, but Vinson proved that opposing the popular president was not an automatic death sentence. He readily acknowledged in campaign speeches that he and Roosevelt disagreed on the issue of veterans' legislation, a rare policy dispute between the two. Vinson had been pushing for immediate cash payments of the adjusted service certificates to World War I veterans for many years, and Roosevelt, just like presidents Harding, Coolidge, and Hoover before him, saw bonuses for war veterans as an extravagant expenditure the government could not afford, especially at a time when the economy was still wobbly. The president, like his three predecessors, tried to blunt bonuses with his veto power. It worked for him in 1935 when the Senate failed to override his veto of a bill sponsored by Texas congressman Wright Patman that would have provided for immediate cash payments to veterans. As soon as Congress convened the next year, Vinson introduced his bill that again called for veterans to receive cash bonuses, which amounted to an expenditure of about $2.5 billion. Another veto by Roosevelt was promised and delivered, but this time both houses of Congress overrode the president, and Vinson finally won his most protracted legislative battle. Conditions for passage were more favorable in 1936 than in the previous year. The two major veterans' groups, the American Legion and the Veterans of Foreign Wars, which had backed competing proposals the previous year, joined to support Vinson's bill, as did the Disabled American Veterans. In addition, 1936 was an election year, making it more difficult for incumbent legislators to oppose the influential and united veterans' lobby.

Ray Murphy, national commander of the American Legion, wrote Vinson in early 1936 to thank him "for the magnificent work you did which made possible the passage of the Adjusted Service Certificate payment bill." He added, "Your complete knowledge of the subject, your evident desire to forego any personal pride of authorship, your final framing of the bill . . . which was the basis for final passage of the Act, your diplomacy and tact were all of such extraordinary quality as to cause me to marvel and to be eternally grateful."[39] Frank N. Belgrano Jr., former head of the Legion, said in a letter to Vinson, "No one knows better than I the time and effort you put into the fight last year, and that because of the stand you took the payment of these certificates was made possible in the first 21 days of this session of Congress."[40]

Vinson's electoral hold on his district also stemmed from the tried and true method of paying close attention to the needs and concerns of the folks back home. During this period of hard times, Vinson did what he could to improve conditions in Kentucky; he was especially active in supporting two of the state's most important commodities—coal and tobacco. He managed floor debate in the House on the Bituminous Coal Act, which had sought through regulation to correct some of the dire conditions in the coalfields, including appallingly low wages, overproduction, and cutthroat competition. The act created local boards that would set minimum prices for coal and provided for collective bargaining so that miners could negotiate for better wages and working conditions. After the Supreme Court ruled the legislation unconstitutional in 1936, Vinson and others started drafting new legislation to address the Court's contention that the Coal Act infringed upon the power of the states and was an unconstitutional delegation of power to people outside of the government. A revised coal bill, then known as the Guffey-Vinson Coal Stabilization Bill, passed the House but fell victim to a filibuster in the Senate.

Vinson's efforts did not go unrecognized, however. John L. Lewis, president of the United Mine Workers and a man sparing in words of praise, nonetheless was extremely complimentary of what Vinson had tried to accomplish. "Your masterful handling of the measure on the floor . . . has evoked the admiration of every one familiar with the fight," Lewis wrote. He added, "Your broad personal sympathies and comprehensive understanding of the problems of the workers in the mining industry has caused our people to regard you as one of their loyal champions."[41]

Vinson, not deterred by defeat, came back in early 1937 with the redrafted Guffey-Vinson Coal Bill, which restored much of the original Coal Act except for the labor provisions that had been invalidated by the Supreme Court. The measure eliminated the local district boards that the Court said were an unconstitutional delegation of powers, creating instead a new Bituminous Coal Commission appointed by the president with powers to fix minimum prices for coal. The bill also established a consumers' counsel, which reported directly to Congress. The Guffey-Vinson bill won congressional approval in less than five months' time and was signed by Roosevelt in late April 1937. Lewis said the legislation meant "rational stabilization" of the industry instead of the "ruthless and devastating competitive practices which have debauched the industry for decades, sweated labor and removed the industry as a source of tax revenue for the government."[42] Vinson later called this legislation one of his prime achievements in Congress.

Likewise, Vinson was proud of his efforts in behalf of the state's struggling burley tobacco farmers, who had seen their income drop from $71 million in 1929 to $31 million three years later.[43] Tobacco, like the six other crops targeted for rescue under the Agricultural Adjustment Act, suffered from overproduction, which caused the lower prices. The Triple A, enacted in the hectic first hundred days of the Roosevelt administration, sought to raise farm prices by getting farmers to agree to cut back their production. In return, the government paid participating farmers a subsidy that would be funded through taxes imposed on the processors of the seven commodities. Vinson worked out the tables for determining tobacco processing taxes, and he returned to Kentucky several times for meetings to help plan how the program was to be implemented in the state. He was also deluged with correspondence from growers with questions about AAA. The desperate conditions of growers in the state are made clear in a letter from a farmer in Augusta, Kentucky, trying to scratch out a living for his family of five on disability payments for war injuries and four acres of tobacco. "I am compeled to put a roof on my home which is in a very bad shape. $50. I owe $50 for food already consumed by my family. Taxes $18. Food for my family for a year is about $240. Coal about $25. Interest on $700 with F.L.B. [Federal Land Bank] $35. I never spend one cent unless it goes derect for the benefit of my family. I havent supported an Automobile for five years. My family and I walk where ever we go even if it is five or six miles."[44]

In his response, Vinson informed the farmer of a recent change that broadened the scope of AAA, adding, "I trust that this new option will be of benefit to you. I have been working on the tobacco situation for a long time, and feel that I have been able to do some real good in this connection."[45] Later, Vinson claimed that his efforts under Triple A resulted in subsidy payments of $21 million to burley tobacco growers in the state in the two years before the legislation was declared unconstitutional by the Supreme Court in 1936.[46] After AAA was invalidated, Congress quickly enacted substitute legislation known as the Soil Conservation and Domestic Allotment Act, which also paid farmers to decrease production, although the money had to come from sources other than the outlawed processing taxes. Vinson, as a member of a special committee from the tobacco growing states, sponsored an amendment that created a pool of more than $15 million from customs fees that was used to pay benefits to tobacco farmers.

Reducing taxes on tobacco continued to be on Vinson's legislative agenda during the mid-1930s. Actually, Vinson believed "there ought to be no tax on tobacco products."[47] Realizing that that was an impossible dream, he tried his best to at least get the taxes reduced. In 1934, as chairman of a Ways and Means subcommittee on tobacco taxation, he steered through his panel a recommendation for an across-the-board reduction of 40 percent in all tobacco taxes. The full committee adopted the proposal, but it failed to pass Congress. Vinson's efforts the following year to get the 40 percent tax cut enacted met the same fate. Nonetheless, he again impressed those who saw him in action. One industry veteran, who had been a buyer, warehouseman, and grower, commented, "I thought I knew considerable about the tobacco situation but Vinson indicated in the way he handled the hearing of the tobacco tax that he has absolute mastery of the tobacco question."[48]

Vinson believed his tax reduction proposal was a win-win situation for all concerned—the grower, the manufacturer, and the consumer. Smokers would get their cigarettes at a reduced cost, spurring demand for the manufacturers, who in turn would buy more burley from farmers. Obviously, the government would lose tax revenue, but Vinson felt the loss would be more than offset by the political gains to be won. In a letter to James A. Farley, one of the president's closest political advisers, Vinson estimated that the tax cut would mean a loss to the federal government in fiscal 1935 of between $50 million and $75 million, which, he said, "would not be of vital consequence, in view of the fact that it is not contemplated that the Budget will be brought to balance in that year." The vital consequence of the proposal, however, as Vinson made clear to Farley, was political. He noted that there were 432,000 tobacco farms, 3 million people directly dependent on tobacco for their livelihoods, and millions of consumers. The political payoff would be from smokers who would "know that under President Roosevelt's leadership, he is getting to him an essential pack of cigarettes for some two and one-half to five cents per pack less than that which he would have had to pay, except for President Roosevelt's attitude toward him," Vinson wrote.[49]

Whereas all segments of the burley belt could obviously get behind lowering taxes, another initiative that Vinson strongly supported—the creation of a federal system for grading and inspection of tobacco sold at auction—was not unanimously endorsed in Kentucky. In its editorials on the subject, the *Lexington Herald,* a paper normally in agreement with about any position taken by Vinson, opposed the measure, also known as the Flannagan Bill, on the grounds that it was a waste of tax-payers' money on a system that farmers neither wanted nor needed. In one opinion piece, the paper said, "It is the belief of the farmers that the bill really has for its purpose the eventual destruction of the open auction system of marketing."[50] Another editorial a few days later warned: "The real danger is the lurking prospect of a government-enforced co-operative. This would mean eventual government control on a far larger scale than the AAA has ever proposed."[51] In a letter to Thomas R. Underwood, the paper's general manager and a good friend, Vinson, noting that it was "a very unusual situation not to be battling on the same side with you," addressed the editorial's point that a governmental grading system was unnecessary because tobacco companies have trained, experienced, and well-paid buyers, who, in effect, grade the tobacco when they make their bids: "These trained, experienced and well-paid buyers, it seems to me would decide every doubt against the farmer insofar as the price they paid for his tobacco is concerned. They are employed by the Buyers and, as loyal employees, they would certainly protect the interests of the purchasers—the farmer has nothing to say about it."[52] Vinson prevailed on the issue of federal grading and received in acknowledgment of his efforts four pens that the president had used in signing the bill.

With the ravages of unemployment rife in the land and people increasingly looking to the federal government as the great beacon of hope, Vinson naturally was besieged by supplicants. For a variety of reasons, he often could do little more than write a letter of recommendation or provide advice on the application process. There were, for example, too many people competing for too few jobs. To a woman from Carlisle who wrote seeking "clerical work in some department in Washington," Vinson responded, "It is a difficult matter to secure a position of this character at long distance, and I hesitate to suggest your coming to Washington, because even then, there is no assurance that an appointment can be secured. There are hundreds of applicants for every available job."[53] Answering a request from a friend to find a job in the Library of Congress for his daughter, Vinson noted that there were more than twenty-nine thousand applicants for jobs in the library and that even Kentucky senator Barkley, who was chairman of the Library Committee in the Senate, had not been able to get anyone a job there. "I certainly would be happy to help your daughter secure a position," Vinson wrote, "but it has been impossible for me to place anyone in the Library of Congress."[54] Vinson's ability to help job seekers was also limited by Civil Service, which filled positions through competitive examinations. An Ashland man, upon learning that the Alcoholic Tax Unit of the Internal Revenue Service was adding one hundred workers to its enforcement staff, wrote Vinson asking if he would "endorse me for one of the jobs as you know I can get the solid endorsement of the Democratic organization of Boyd county and any other county in our district if necessary."[55] Vinson's reply noted "that the only prospective employment offered by that division will be to storekeeper-gaugers, and that, as you know, is under Civil Service."[56]

Vinson was also hampered by the dictum from Harry Hopkins, Roosevelt's chief administrator who was responsible for pouring billions of dollars into public works programs employing millions of workers, that there must be a separation between relief and politics. Responding to a letter from an Ashland resident, Vinson wrote, "The local relief work is totally in the hands of the local committee or those persons assigned by them to do it. Members of Congress and Senators haven't any control over it and our recommendations are not desired. I can say to you frankly, that if I had had anything to do with it, there would have been lots of things done differently."[57] He complained in particular about his lack of influence with the Civil Works Administration (CWA), a short-lived enterprise that spent about a billion dollars and employed more than 4 million people in early 1934 to build or improve roads, schools, airports, and playgrounds as well as to undertake other public works projects. To accomplish the Herculean task of mobilizing such a massive workforce in a short time, the organization of CWA was by necessity decentralized, meaning that decisions on whom to hire and what work was to be done were made at the local level. Vinson felt that, at least in parts of his district, Republicans had seized control of local CWA committees and were using their positions of power for political purposes. "In my home county of Boyd," he wrote to a friend, "the CWA has two Republicans in charge of the employment, one of whom is a very bitter, partisan political leader. I believe that Mr. Hopkins, the Federal Administrator, is getting his eyes open. He has been fully informed of the situation in Kentucky, but to date, there has been no change in his policy with reference to politics."[58]

A constituent in Catlettsburg wrote Vinson that Hopkins's nonpartisan approach to relief had only turned "the emoluments and the benefits over into the hands of the enemy, under the ruling of 'No politics in this deal,'" and had disheartened middle-class Democrats who "have been the backbone of the democrat party." From his vantage point as the owner of a grocery store that dispensed federal supplies, the correspondent said he had "witnessed many wrongs" committed by the local relief office. He told of one farmer who appeared to be prospering but never failed to be on the list of those qualifying for government food supplies. "Old men who are his neighbors, almost destitute, totter up to my desk to see if their names are on the list and go away disappointed. Is it an accident, that this favored man is a republican politician among the lower class." Another unworthy recipient described in the letter was a "ranting Republican ward healer" who, although in perfect health, "got his supplies regularly and his vouchers every week and he would bring his mistress with him to the store to spend the voucher." By contrast, the storekeeper said, "My nearest neighbor is an old man in the eighties, an Ohio River Pilot, a life time democrat, out of a job forever. He worked and paid for a home but he can't eat it. He does not belong to the high class, neither does he belong to the lower class, he is of the middle class and can get nothing, but on rare occasions, a one pound package of LARD, or in other words an insult, from the relief office."[59] To the man's letter of indignation, Vinson responded, "I agree with you that the Democrats are not in control in either the relief work or the unemployment end of it. Ever since the State failed to match federal money, it has been in the hands of the Republicans. They did not let the Senators or Congressmen have anything to do with the recommendations of the men in charge of it, either State, county or cities."[60]

Vinson experienced the same frustrations with the Works Progress Administration, an even more ambitious, expensive, and long-term public works undertaking than its predecessor agencies, CWA and FERA (Federal Emergency Relief Administration). An Ashland woman wrote to ask his help in getting employment with one of the WPA-sponsored sewing centers in the state, which hired women to make garments for their own families and for other needy families. In responding, Vinson, who by this time had left Congress and was a federal judge, said, "I must frankly say that if I were in the House I could do very little . . . because of the fact that at all times before I went on the Bench we were constantly kept advised that there was no politics in WPA and that as Members of Congress it wasn't our job to hire or fire the non-relief persons or to appoint or remove the relief persons in WPA. I can say truthfully that I never placed a single, solitary person on the relief rolls of WPA while I was a member of the House."[61] Though upsetting to him in one regard, Vinson's avowed lack of influence-peddling with the WPA at least spared him from being branded, as was Senator Barkley, as having used the WPA for political purposes.[62]

One relief activity during this period that proved to be more fertile ground for Vinson was the Civilian Conservation Corps (CCC), a program that put young men to work restoring and improving public lands and forests through such measures as soil conservation, reforestation, construction of national parks and dams, and wildlife protection. Vinson's district had about one-half of the more than forty CCC campus located in Kentucky, and he fought hard to keep them open as long as possible because of the economic boosts they gave to surrounding communities. For instance, he telephoned the White House upon learning of the planned closing of one camp to plead that it should remain open. "I never did have enough camps to start with and there have been one or two already discontinued," Vinson said, adding, "I am very anxious for this one to be kept going for a while."[63]

For all its good works, the CCC was but a temporary fix on the landscape, passing out of existence in 1942 after a highly productive run of nearly ten years. Vinson joined with others in legislative efforts to find more lasting solutions to the manifold problems in the environment, specifically flooding and water pollution. For Vinson, flood control became a priority when much of the state was deluged in 1927; it resurfaced on his agenda in 1934 when a portion of his district was hit by floods and again in the disastrous winter of 1937, when flooding of the Ohio River resulted in hundreds of deaths and property damage of some $200 million in Kentucky. In the aftermath of the 1937 floods, Vinson was elected chairman of a flood relief subcommittee composed of House members from flood-prone areas. His group explored various means of financing a comprehensive, long-range program of flood control by such means as a national sales tax or broadening the base of income taxes. Congress ultimately, however, took a more modest, piecemeal approach that year, passing legislation to construct emergency flood walls at various points along the Ohio, including Louisville, Paducah, Covington, and Russell.

In a measure that foreshadowed heightened national concern over clean air and water by thirty years, Vinson and Barkley sponsored legislation in 1937 for controlling water pollution. Their bill, which finally passed Congress in 1938 after Vinson had departed for the federal judiciary, was a modest $1 million proposal creating a water pollution control division in the U.S. Public Health Service, which would study the problem of contamination in navigable waterways and tributaries and make grants to states for studies, surveys, and other work in connection with preventing and controlling water pollution. Surprisingly, given the meager amount of money involved and the strong, bipartisan support in Congress for this initiative, Roosevelt killed the measure by a pocket veto. He objected to a single sentence in the bill that had recommendations for grants-in-aid going directly to Congress without presidential review--interpreting this as legislative assumption of responsibilities of the executive branch. The *Cincinnati Times-Star,* in a stinging editorial rebuke of the veto, wrote, "By incomprehensive action on the Barkley-Vinson bill, the President has slowed the gathering momentum of a movement to clean up the filthy rivers from which our drinking water comes. By no means has he stopped it."[64]

The disagreements over veterans' legislation and the water pollution bill were notable exceptions to Vinson's overall legislative record as a Roosevelt stalwart. The revenue demands of the president's new programs required an accelerated hunt for more tax dollars, either through new levies or plugging loopholes or both. From his positions on the Ways and Means Committee, a taxation subcommittee, and a joint House-Senate panel on tax evasion and avoidance, Vinson carried out his marching orders with skill and determination, earning in the process a lasting and deserved reputation as the preeminent tax authority in the House. Ironically, of course, Vinson had compounded Roosevelt's need for more revenue through his successful push for cash bonus payments to veterans, which added more than $2 billion to governmental expenditures. The Supreme Court contributed to the administration's budgetary shortfalls as well when it struck down the Agricultural Adjustment Act, depriving the government of about $500 million in revenue.

Vinson also was in the president's camp for two of his most controversial moves—to pack the Supreme Court and to reorganize the executive branch. The Court proposal, Roosevelt's scheme to increase the number of justices after so many of his New Deal initiatives had been struck down by a conservative majority on the Court, resulted in Roosevelt's worst defeat in Congress. Vinson introduced the measure, which the White House had unsuccessfully tried to masquerade as court reform legislation, on July 6, 1937. Under the proposal, for every justice who did not retire at age seventy, the president got to make an appointment to the Court, which at the time meant that Roosevelt could have appointed six more justices. After long and heated debate, the Senate killed the bill in late July by recommitting it to committee, and it was never debated in the House. Vinson maintained his interest in the contrivance nonetheless, sending the president a copy of a recently enacted Georgia law that created emeritus status for the chief justice and associate justices of the state supreme court who retire at age seventy. Such justices became members of an advisory appellate council and were entitled to two-thirds pay for life. In thanking Vinson for the information, Roosevelt wrote, "I was much interested in the copy of the Georgia Statute relative to the Judiciary of that State, and am glad you brought it to my attention."[65] The president suffered another humiliating loss with his plan to reorganize the executive branch to make it more efficient. Coming as it did in the wake of the Supreme Court fight and the rise of fascism in Europe and Japan, the proposal set off cries in Congress and throughout the country that the president was trying to install himself as a dictator. Efforts by Vinson and other Democratic leaders in the House to pass a reorganization bill failed in April 1938 when it was rejected by a narrow margin.

The failure of Congress to give the president what he wanted was an oddity, certainly during his first term, when ideas from the White House were transformed into law in a blur. Many of these signature New Deal measures bore Vinson's imprints, including the Social Security Act of 1935, the most enduring and important legislative achievement during this frenetic period.

Roosevelt made the issue of governmental assistance for the unemployed, the elderly, and the uninsured a top priority in the summer of 1934 with the creation of the Commission on Economic Security. In about six months' time, the commission, headed by Labor Secretary Frances Perkins, had drafted a sweeping proposal first introduced into Congress as the Economic Security Bill. Although he had a tough primary election to win that summer, Vinson did little campaigning, devoting his time instead to "working out the complicated tax features of the new social security legislation."[66] He also returned to Washington several times during the summer recess to meet with the members of the commission and others involved in weaving a broad safety net for the most needy.

Caring for the aged had long been of concern to Vinson, according to his son, Fred M. Vinson Jr., who recounted a story of his parents seeing an old man "all gnarled and ragged walking along the side of the road" while driving between Louisa and Ashland. Vinson, then just beginning his congressional career, remarked to his wife, Roberta, "that some day he was going to introduce legislation that would take care of old people who could no longer work."[67] Vinson did not get the opportunity to actually sponsor Social Security legislation, but as a leading member of the House Ways and Means Committee, he played a key role in shaping the final form of the proposal that passed Congress and the president signed on August 14, 1935. He was the dominant influence on Ways and Means during the committee's work on this legislation, according to Thomas H. Eliot, who, as counsel for the Committee on Economic Security, drafted the Economic Security Bill, later changed by Ways and Means to the Social Security Act. In an *Atlantic Monthly* article commemorating the twenty-fifth anniversary of Social Security, Eliot noted that the progress of the proposal through the Ways and Means Committee depended "on the behavior of one member as he first entered the room. That one member was Fred Vinson. If Vinson, on entering, walked directly to his seat, said an amiable 'Good morning,' and began perusing the bill, we were pretty sure of having a productive day. But if he came in either scowling or whispering jovial stories to a couple of his colleagues, the morning could be counted as lost."[68]

Vinson was in tune with some of modern-day political thought when, predicting in early 1935 a vast surplus in the Social Security fund of $50 billion by 1980, he pondered using reserves to invest in such securities as state, municipal, and county bonds. "But if they wanted to," Vinson continued, "they could find plenty of other places to invest it. They could make loans to industry, or to home owners, or they could expand the functions of our present Reconstruction Finance Corporation."[69]

Arthur J. Altmeyer, an assistant secretary of labor and chairman of a subgroup of the Committee on Economic Security known as the Technical Board, said Vinson and Jere Cooper of Tennessee were the most influential members in shaping the Social Security proposal as it made its way through the Ways and Means Committee. "Congressman Doughton, the chairman [of Ways and Means] introduced the bill at the request of the administration, but I don't think [he] necessarily understood what the bill was about," Altmeyer said. "But these men [Vinson and Cooper] worked at it very conscientiously and understood every bit of the bill as it was hammered out in the committee. So they were very important then and later." Altmeyer, later appointed a member of the Social Security Board and widely credited with getting this complex and unprecedented program up and running, said he got crossways with

Vinson and Cooper over the matter of patronage. "I just didn't realize how strongly members of Congress felt they should be consulted in making appointments," he said. "I failed to discuss key appointments . . . with the result that I found I had deeply offended these two men." Concerning Vinson, he said, "I had to refuse to appoint a man as personnel director who had no qualifications for the position. We offered him a position as office manager in Louisville, but he declined that; so Mr. Vinson was never satisfied that I had given him appropriate consideration to his views. And he felt as one of the influential supporters of the legislation, his view should have been taken more seriously."[70]

Vinson's work was also praised by Edwin E. Witte, executive director of the Committee on Economic Security, who was often called "the father of social security." In a letter responding to Vinson's request for information on social insurance plans in other countries, Witte wrote, "Permit me again to express the deep appreciation of our Committee for your valiant efforts in behalf of this measure."[71] Speaking on the twentieth anniversary of the Social Security Act, Witte included Vinson on his short list of politicians responsible for getting the proposal enacted into law. "Academic people are prone to give all the credit for social reforms to their original proponents," Witte said, "but, clearly, more should go to the men in public life, who risk their political future in championing and enacting these measures and to administrators who make the programs work."[72]

Vinson undoubtedly performed his greatest service to Roosevelt and the New Deal as a congressional spearhead in revenue and tax legislation. In his quest to expand the government's treasury, the president tried with limited success to shift the tax burden to the wealthiest individuals and corporations. In part, the president embarked on this course in response to the so-called thunder on the left, radical schemes such as Huey Long's Share Our Wealth movement to redistribute wealth and power. One administration proposal resulting from this approach was a graduated surtax on corporate income that had not been distributed as dividends, a levy the president thought would achieve tax reform while adding about $620 million in new revenue.[73] Roosevelt believed that companies purposely retained their profits instead of paying dividends as a way of shielding stockholders from income taxes. In addition, he felt that surpluses gave these companies an unfair business advantage, making it easier for them to attract capital for expansion and thereby increase their market share. A corporation that paid out all of its profits in cash dividends was not liable to the tax. The task of putting specifics to the president's plan fell to Samuel B. Hill of Washington, chairman of the Ways and Means subcommittee on taxation, and Vinson, his right-hand man. To Vinson, called by the *New York Times* "one of the most influential leaders in drafting the pending measure," the legislation would bring equity to the system of taxation. "All business profits should bear their just share of Federal taxes whether held in the enterprise or distributed to the beneficial owners," he said. Existing law, Vinson continued, "has been ineffective in preventing the retention of earnings in corporations controlled by wealthy individuals," and although Congress had attempted reform from time to time, "the evil has been a growing one."[74]

The evil seen by opponents of the proposal, mostly Republicans, although some Democrats were in opposition as well, was the administration's proclivity for taxation rather than reduced spending. They charged the White House with "spending hundreds of millions of dollars unnecessarily, wastefully, extravagantly and politically."[75] It also was argued that the measure would be destructive to business and that Congress had no right to use its power of taxation to tell businesses how they should operate. Furthermore, opponents called the proposal "a huge Chinese puzzle" that no one really understood. Vinson countered this point in House debate, saying that the bill was comprehensible to anyone who took the time to try to understand it. But he evoked smiles from Republicans when it took him more than an hour to explain the details of the proposal. Roosevelt eventually got his undistributed profits tax, although he had to settle for a watered-down version. Even then, the Revenue Act of 1936 "was probably the most dramatic closing of a tax loophole ever to be undertaken in an election year."[76]

Roosevelt wanted even more, as he made clear in his reelection campaign and in a message to Congress after his resounding victory in 1936. Congress created a special Joint Committee on Tax Evasion and Avoidance in response to his call for a stepped-up assault on loopholes that the wealthy, or "economic royalists" in the president's term, used to avoid or lessen their tax bills. Vinson, who had become chairman of the Ways and Means subcommittee on taxation after Sam Hill left Congress in 1936, was named to the panel. Hearings throughout the summer of 1937 uncovered a multiplicity of abuses and schemes used by the upper class to avoid taxes, one of which was the personal holding company, also known as incorporated pocketbooks. Through this device, some of the richest people in the country could reduce their individual surtax rates by incorporating various sources of personal income, gaining deductions in the process that would not otherwise be available to them. Though perfectly legal, the practice was ridiculed under the glare of congressional and press scrutiny as a blatant example of how the privileged could manipulate the system to their advantage. It was front-page news when the joint committee named names, sixty-seven in all, including such recognizable figures as Andrew W. Mellon, a former secretary of the Treasury; Alfred P. Sloan, chairman of General Motors; William S. Paley, head of CBS; and Jacob Ruppert, owner of the New York Yankees. Congress acted quickly on proposals emanating from committee hearings, and by the end of the summer the president was able to sign the Revenue Act of 1937. Although the legislation did not give Roosevelt the "evasion-proof" tax system he had wanted, it did close a number of loopholes and made it more difficult to escape tax burdens through personal holding companies.

In the next stage of the president's continuing tax reform crusade, Vinson assumed an even more prominent role as chairman of a Ways and Means subcommittee charged with examining the whole field of taxation and recommending changes for the overhaul of the nation's tax structure. However, the climate in Congress for making substantive changes in tax law during the 1937–1938 period, especially if it meant higher corporate taxes, was now less favorable. By this time a recession was under way, and the business lobby had a more a sympathetic hearing in Congress with its argument that Roosevelt's taxes, particularly the hated undistributed profits tax, had been responsible for causing the economic slump by discouraging investment. When the subcommittee began its work in early November of 1937, Vinson said the matter of taxing retained earnings was the top priority for study. "We are looking into the idea of relieving the sufferings and hardships of the tax," he said.[77] The panel's open-ended probe also extended into such realms as capital gains, estate and gift taxes, and excise taxes.

The subcommittee's deliberations, which took three months, propelled Vinson into the national spotlight. As proposals were offered, debated, discarded, or adopted, he was the source news reporters most often relied upon to explain what had transpired in the highly technical and complicated process of fashioning tax reform legislation. Vinson's comments and analyses became a staple of front-page stories in the *New York Times,* and he was widely quoted in other daily newspapers, weekly news magazines, and business periodicals. The editor of the *Saturday Evening Post* asked Vinson, as "the recognized authority of the Congress on the income tax," for his comments on a reader's observation that the tax system was grossly unfair to those whose earnings were crowded into just a few years. The reader cited the example of a business owner who, after spending a lifetime building up the concern, sells out at a profit, but the income tax he must pay is for the year in which the business sold. The reader also questioned the tax treatment of an author who might have no income during a six-year period of planning and writing a book but who would be taxed only when income started rolling in from royalty payments and sale of motion picture rights. "Clearly," the person wrote, "were justice done, the treasury should apportion this income over the whole number of years occupied in producing and in marketing the book."[78] In his response, Vinson noted that the example of the business owner selling out was wrong because Congress changed the law in 1934 so that the percentage of tax owed on capital gains decreased the longer a property was held. To the second example, Vinson said devising a scheme to tax work done in planning and writing a book would be "administratively impossible."[79] He said there was no basis in law to levy a tax upon study or the work done in planning and writing a book, adding that the government could not tax mental processes or physical labor, only the income derived from such activities.

Vinson had to give a lesson on capital gains to another editor, but in this case it was in response to an editorial that made it appear that he was pushing for a change in capital gains at the behest of the country's "forty-three" millionaires. The writer said the proposal from Vinson's subcommittee would permit someone in high-income brackets "to cut his capital-gains tax on a $100 quick profit from $76 to $30."[80] Responding, Vinson pointed out that the writer erred in using the $76 as the amount of tax owed when actually it would be the figure upon which a tax is based on a capital asset held for two years. Of more concern to him, though, was the writer's assertion that he was looking out for the interests of millionaires and "not worried at all about the millions of ordinary taxpayers." He said, "I have a record which I want to leave to my children of representing the folks rather than those who are sometimes termed 'the privileged' and I know that your great paper doesn't want to do injustice to one whose record at no time and in no sense has been that of a reactionary."[81] Vinson's attempts to educate the media and in the turn the public about the complexities of the business taxation proposals contained in the Revenue Act of 1938 also involved making addresses on nationwide radio broadcast, a technique so skillfully employed by the president. However, it is one thing to engage listeners in an intimate "fireside chat" and quite another to attempt to connect with a mass audience when the discourse is filled with a litany of corporate net income figures and the bewildering array of the different percentages that apply.

Another result of Vinson's sudden national prominence was the flood of letters he received from people all over the country asking for consideration of their positions on the sundry tax issues. A great deal of the correspondence concerned a proposed additional tax of 20 percent on retained earnings of family-owned or closely held corporations. Thruston B. Morton, later a U.S. senator from Kentucky, writing in behalf of his family's venerable flour milling business, Ballard & Ballard Company in Louisville, argued that such a measure would put his firm at a competitive disadvantage and force it to merge with a larger corporation.[82] Being allowed to accumulate surplus capital during the good times provided the means for the company to survive the bad times, Morton said, noting that when thousands of factories were idle during the depression, "this company guaranteed and paid its men for five full days work each week regardless of orders and regardless of whether the mills ran or not." He added that retained earnings also enabled the company to continue "its charitable munificence in times when most needed" and to survive "the disastrous Ohio river flood." Had the proposed tax been in effect during those years, Morton said, "none of this could have happened." He added that Ballard was in need of rebuilding its reserves so that it could modernize and expand.[83] A Cincinnati bank president, identifying himself as "an old Louisa boy," wrote to urge the repeal of the undistributed profits tax. If continued, he said, "it would practically disembowel all these Companies in the course of time, big and little, and take away their very life-blood; thousands of them need now to retain what they have earned this year."[84]

The owner of a furniture store in Kansas City, Missouri, wrote that if the proposed profits tax were enacted, he would "dissolve the corporation. I will not stand for this unjust tax when I have given all of my best years and efforts to building this business." Noting that during the depression his operation had lost an average of twelve thousand dollars a year, he said, "Now that our business is better, I am leaving in the business every dollar I make. This is necessary to build up the depleted capital."[85]

A hardware dealer in Detroit wrote that his business managed to keep most of its employees throughout the depression and had never closed down for a day, but only because it "used up all our working capital and borrowed from friends and relatives some thirty thousand dollars." He added that although earnings had improved, "due to expansion in business and with no working capital left, we have been forced to pay not only our local and federal taxes in installments, but have had to sell our receivables at usurious rates in order to operate." His business, he said, needs "numerous items in equipment, purchase of which would furnish employment all along the line and allow us to compete profitably with our larger competitors." He said he was willing to do his "share in carrying the cost of government, but you surely must realize that any business must have working capital in order to exist."[86]

The chairman of Crane Company in Chicago said his firm would not have survived the depression had it not been for a liberal surplus: "We were using the surplus to keep the organization together and the men off the dole. . . . It is apparent that a surplus acts as a balance wheel to carry a company over bad times and benefits the wage earners by saving their jobs and the stockholders by preserving their property."[87]

A friend who was the owner and publisher of daily newspapers in Huntington, West Virginia, neighboring city to Vinson's Ashland, wrote, "If the recommendations of your committee . . . are enacted we face very dark prospects for the future. You will force thousands of small businesses, which have been efficiently operated and which paid billions of taxes into the governmental coffers, to go broke or dispose of their holdings. At the same time you allow big business, giant corporations with hundreds of thousands of stockholders to go on without penalty."[88] In his response, Vinson said he was convinced "that no great burden would come from the imposition of this tax" because it would be assessed only on that portion of net income that is left after certain deductions were applied. He also questioned whether large numbers of companies would be affected. "There will be comparatively few," Vinson said. "In my judgment there will be between 350 and 600 corporations coming under the term of the provisions."[89] His objective, Vinson said, was to ensure that the government received the optimal amount of tax revenue from corporate earnings, adding that the tax proposal would correct a disparity between widely held corporations, which pay the normal corporate tax and then shareholders pay a tax on their dividends, and closely held firms, which were subject to the corporate tax only when earnings were not distributed as dividends.

No doubt Vinson was cheered when he received a letter from a man in Pittsburgh on this issue that began, "Accept please my enthusiastic congratulations upon your committee's proposals in re Close Corporations." This correspondent, calling the security holder in a closely held firm "the forgotten man," said the rights that shareholders have in large and publicly traded corporations are denied to the stockholder in closely held companies. Such a stockholder, the writer said, "finds himself . . . in a tough spot at best" because the owner-manager "by devious and varied means—and I speak with experience—was usually able to hold its earnings down and hold them free from distribution and the Government did not always receive its fair share of taxes from this source."[90]

Vinson also heard from those concerned about other tax proposals under consideration. An executive of a company that made dominoes and checkers asked for relief from what he called the "unfair and unjust" 10 percent excise tax his firm paid on its products. He added, "Recently Japan has entered this field, and it is needless to tell you that we are not able to meet this competition unless we are relieved of this 10% excise tax."[91] The president of Rutgers University, Robert C. Clothier, wrote of his concern that high gift taxes had hurt the endowments of colleges and universities to such an extent that "unless some means can be found to change the trend, the future of our institutions of higher learning is most precarious."[92] A woman in Boston also wrote to Vinson about the gift tax, complaining that she bore an unfair tax burden because she supported her children and their families with income from a trust fund. "Does it seem fair to levy an additional tax because I choose to divide my income with my children instead of spending it all upon myself?" she asked. "Every cent declared in my gift tax return has already been heavily taxed in my income tax return for the same year."[93] In a "Dear Fred" letter, an attorney in Ashland objected to Vinson's idea

Vinson, Sam Rayburn, and Harry Truman at a barbecue, May 1938. (Courtesy of Special Collections, University of Kentucky Library.)

for a withholding income tax on wages, a cornerstone of today's system but untried as yet in 1937. "It would seem to me that employers have enough on their hands now with their own taxes, governmental regulations, continual labor agitation and all these social security taxes, too," the attorney wrote. "To add to the employer the burden of doing the private and personal bookkeeping for each one of his employees looks to me to be the last straw."[94] Vinson replied that he was "trying to bring in taxpayers who were not paying income taxes and make certain of collection and, at the same time, relieve the smaller taxpayers from filing income tax returns."[95] His proposal applied only to taxable salaries up to five thousand dollars.

The report of Vinson's subcommittee, which was nearly one hundred pages long and contained sixty-three recommendations, became the framework for the Revenue Act of 1938 and marked Vinson's final major endeavor as a member of the House. Even before his panel completed its work, Vinson had been nominated and confirmed as a judge on the federal appeals court for the District of Columbia. He delayed taking his new position, however, until he could shepherd the proposed tax reform through Congress. It proved to be a rocky road. Although the subcommittee's proposals were adopted virtually intact by the full Ways and Means Committee, key portions of the bill were eviscerated in the full House and Senate. The legislation ultimately enacted clearly demonstrated that Congress had paid heed to the business community's argument that reducing taxes was the way back to economic health. The undistributed profit tax was substantially lowered and targeted for elimination in 1939; the special tax on closely held corporations was dropped; and the tax on capital gains was lowered. The president denounced the bill, but he let it become law without his signature, realizing that a veto most likely would have been overridden.

The House dispatched final debate on the Revenue Act of 1938 in about an hour and turned the remainder of the session into a tribute to Fred M. Vinson. To applause, representatives of both parties spoke at length about Vinson's service in the House and their regret at his leaving. Republicans offering warm words included Allen Treadway of Massachusetts and Frank Crowther of New York, both members of the Ways and Means Committee; and Thomas Jenkins of Ohio. Treadway, who had led the fight against the 1938 revenue bill, nonetheless expressed admiration for its chief architect, Vinson. Calling him a "constructive legislator," Treadway said Vinson provided the type of able and productive service that had endeared him not only to the "membership of our great committee, which he has ornamented so highly, but with the entire membership of this body."[96] Crowther said it was "during the long, dreary, laborious, and tiresome hours of committee work" that he grew to love and respect Vinson. "That is where I learned why he was here, and why after his masterful service in this House he has been elevated to a high judicial position" (6692). Jenkins, noting that he and Vinson were neighbors and longtime friends, said his only regret was that the president did not "place him on the Supreme Court bench, where he belongs. I hope the time may come . . . when he might reach the top in the judiciary as he has reached the top in the legislative branch" (6693).

Among the Democrats paying tribute to Vinson were John McCormack of Massachusetts, a Vinson colleague on Ways and Means and a future Speaker of the House; Robert Doughton, chair of Ways and Means from North Carolina; majority leader Sam Rayburn of Texas, also a future Speaker; and Speaker William Bankhead of Alabama. Vinson, said McCormack, "spoke and voted in an independent and courageous way—not responsive to a false public opinion, but casting his vote and expressing his views along the lines which he considered to be for the best interests of his people—for the best interests of our country" (6695). Doughton said Vinson had been "a tower of strength in the arduous duties which have fallen upon our committee during the past few years," and he had "ceaselessly labored to ascertain the facts and to bring about the enactment of tax legislation giving equality of treatment to all" (6697). Rayburn, whose campaign for majority leader had been managed by Vinson, spoke of the value of their professional and personal relationships, saying, "Few things in my life have come into it that have meant as much to me as this fine man and the fine friendship he has given me" (6698). Bankhead said that while it was sad that Vinson's "very brilliant and very distinguished legislative service" was ending, "all of us are comforted by the fact, and deeply comforted by the fact, that he will continue his public service in another tribunal" (6698).

CHAPTER 5

Vinson's Transition from Legislator to Jurist

When Fred Vinson was sworn in as associate justice of the U.S. Circuit Court of Appeals for the District of Columbia,[1] on May 12, 1938, at the age of forty-eight, it was a big transition for the Kentucky politician who had served twelve years in Congress and achieved great heights in legislative leadership. Vinson's devotion to his legislative responsibilities was so strong that more than five months elapsed between his confirmation for the circuit court and his swearing in. The delay was the result of Vinson's desire to steer the tax bill to passage in the House of Representatives. In his farewell address to the House, he urged adoption of the conference report on the tax bill, which was agreed to the same day.

Roosevelt wanted Vinson to stay in Congress until the tax bill was passed, but there was a legal question whether he could do so after being confirmed as a circuit court judge. The president discussed this matter with Attorney General Homer Cummings. Subsequently, Golden W. Bell, assistant solicitor general, drafted a lengthy legal opinion on the subject, which recommended that the president delay issuing the commission to Vinson "until the time he expects to render himself ineligible as a member of Congress by taking his oath of office as a judge."[2]

Vinson's elevation to the circuit court was seen by virtually all observers as a reward from Roosevelt for his strong support for the president's legislative proposals, including some of the more unpopular measures such as the Undistributed Profits Tax of 1936 and the court-packing bill. Roosevelt, however, was primarily interested in his own agenda, and Vinson's appointment served the president's goals extremely well.

Following his reelection in 1936, Roosevelt devised strategies to deal with what he considered to be a constitutional crisis resulting from the Supreme Court's invalidation of a number of New Deal policies. The most visible strategy was his court-packing scheme for the Supreme Court. A less visible approach focused on the composition of lower federal courts, that is, district courts and the circuit courts of appeals. The president was determined to appoint lower court judges, preferably Democrats, who could be counted on to support New Deal measures.[3] No one fit these requirements any better than Fred Vinson, a loyal, liberal Democrat with a proven track record of supporting the president's proposals. Vinson never lost his zeal for Roosevelt and his policies, a view not held by all his colleagues. In 1940 Harold Stephens, a fellow associate justice on the circuit court, expressed amazement that "Fred can maintain his enthusiasm for F.D.R."[4]

Vinson's age was also a point favoring his appointment. Given his obsession with getting rid of Supreme Court justices over age seventy, Roosevelt felt compelled to select younger judicial appointees at all levels. At forty-eight, Vinson was three years younger than the average Roosevelt circuit court appointee.[5]

Other factors, no doubt, were also influential in FDR's decision to appoint Vinson to the federal bench. He had been considered for a court vacancy in 1934 and again in 1937,[6] but at that time he was still a valuable asset to Roosevelt in the House. By 1938 the main components of the New Deal tax reforms were in place. A business backlash, the recession of 1937–1938, and increasing congressional hostility to tax reform spelled the end of Roosevelt's efforts to redistribute wealth through the tax structure. Furthermore, with the clouds of war casting shadows on the United States, FDR's attention began to shift more to international concerns. Vinson now could be more useful to Roosevelt in the judicial branch than in Congress.

In background and experience, Vinson was very different from the men who served on the circuit court for the District of Columbia; none of them had held an elective office. Most of them came with some previous judicial experience, and half of them came from the ranks of the law professorate. These characteristics reflected Roosevelt's overall pattern of staffing the circuit court. Approximately 61 percent of FDR's appointees in his second term had prior judicial experience, thus providing the president with some basis for judging their support for his policy agenda. Sixteen percent of Roosevelt's circuit court appointees in his second term had been law professors, who, according to court scholar

Vinson, top center, and his colleagues on the U.S. Court of Appeals for the District of Columbia in 1940. In front are Harold M. Stephens, D. Lawrence Groner, chief judge, and Justin Miller. Flanking Vinson are Henry W. Edgerton, left, and Wiley Rutledge, right.

Sheldon Goldman, "could articulate a judicial philosophy that would favor the New Deal and provide intellectual leadership on their courts supporting economic liberalism." Only 12 percent of FDR's appointees had been members of Congress.[7]

The chief justice of the circuit court was Lawrence Groner, a highly respected jurist from Virginia who had been a district court judge for ten years before his elevation to the circuit court in 1931. Although he was a Republican, in 1938 Roosevelt had named him chief justice. His appointment came only after Attorney General Homer Cummings assured FDR that Groner could "be ranked as a Liberal Republican."[8]

Groner's nomination to the chief justiceship came as part of a "package deal" in which Roosevelt was personally involved. The president had written to Attorney General Cummings that a vacancy in the chief justiceship of the Circuit Court of Appeals for the District of Columbia "clears the way for a disposition of the matter along the lines we originally discussed."[9] The package entailed promoting Groner to chief justice, appointing Henry White Edgerton, a liberal law professor from Cornell, to the associate justice vacancy left by Groner, and appointing Vinson to the vacancy created by the resignation of Associate Justice Charles Robb.

Associate Justice Harold Stephens from Nebraska was next in seniority to Groner. Roosevelt appointed him to the circuit court in 1935 after a career that included serving as a prosecuting attorney, a state judge, and a U.S. assistant attorney general. Stephens and Edgerton attended Harvard Law school together and had maintained a close relationship ever since. Although Edgerton had worked briefly as a special assistant to the attorney general, his main occupation was professor of law at such prestigious schools as George Washington University, the University of Chicago, and Cornell University.

The other two judges with an academic background were Justin Miller and Wiley Rutledge. Miller, of North Carolina, was appointed in 1937, just a few months before Vinson. He had been a member of the U.S. Board of Tax Appeals prior to his nomination. Before that he had served as dean of the Law School at Duke University and at the University of Southern California. Rutledge was nominated to the circuit court in 1939 after Congress passed an act in 1938 authorizing an additional justice for the court. His appointment brought the total number of judges to six. Like Edgerton and Miller, Rutledge brought to the court considerable experience as a law professor. He had taught at Washington University in St. Louis and at the State University of Iowa, where he was also dean of the Law School. Rutledge's appointment completed FDR's reconstruction of the circuit court for the District of Columbia.

Although Vinson did have legitimate credentials to serve as a judge, including his previous experience as a practicing attorney and his position as prosecuting attorney, the political nature of Vinson's appointment made him suspect in the eyes of some, including perhaps his colleagues on the circuit court bench. Several months before Vinson was appointed, Associate Justices Groner and Stephens, discussing a vacancy on the court, had expressed concern about the kind of person they might get as a colleague. "While the Attorney General indicated . . . that he would do everything within his power to get a first class lawyer appointed to the court," Stephens wrote to Groner, "he did not feel wholly sure that he would be able to accomplish his own desires." Stephens reported that Joseph B. Kennan, assistant to the attorney general, doubted that "it would be possible to get a non-politician appointed [because] jobs on this court were looked upon as plums and that some mediocre men had been put off in respect to other circuits with the statement to their supporters that vacancies would be coming along on the United States Court of Appeals." Stephens called the prospects "depressing."[10]

There is no record of Stephens's reaction to Vinson's appointment, but the fact that Vinson had led the fight for the court-packing scheme might have been a strike against him. Stephens was "unqualifiedly against the President's program." He called it "a very grave mistake both from the standpoint of the merit of the plan and from the standpoint of its political effect."[11] Ironically, Stephens's close friend on the circuit court, Henry White Edgerton, strongly endorsed the Roosevelt plan, because "the present system has been, on the whole, harmful to the majority." Edgerton supported a constitutional amendment forbidding any court to hold any act of Congress unconstitutional and an amendment requiring judges to retire at seventy.[12]

Although Vinson's circuit court brethren may have had misgivings about his political connections, they were not reticent to make use of those connections when it served their interests to do so. Two years after Vinson left his judicial position and was head of the Office of War Mobilization and Reconversion, Stephens sought his influence for a forthcoming appointment to the circuit court. Stephens reported to Groner that Fred "has talked with the President along the lines [we discussed] ... I am sure he has done the best he can do for us.[13]

If Vinson had any apprehensions about making the transition from the legislative to the judicial branch, he did not openly acknowledge that he did. After a few months on the job, Vinson was asked whether he liked judicial work better than legislative work. He replied, "They are so much alike that there is not much difference. ... Making laws is more or less a judicial procedure."[14]

There are indications that Vinson never completely severed his legislative ties. Two members of the Washington Bureau for *Newsweek* wrote in 1946 that Vinson never got used to the "cloistered atmosphere of the federal bench." They claim that to relieve boredom he developed a "pay-as-you-go" revenue plan based on a withholding tax and that he was "frequently consulted by the Congressmen who pushed through the withholding tax bill."[15]

Certainly the judicial life had advantages over legislative life for Vinson, not the least being financial security. The necessity of campaigning every two years for his seat in Congress had put a serious strain on the family finances. A judicial career, with its guarantee of a lifetime appointment, offered economic stability, even if the compensation was relatively modest. His annual salary increased from $10,000 to $12,500 with his court appointment.[16]

However, Vinson had to pay a price for that financial security. He had to leave behind the excitement of partisan politics and colleagues on both sides of the aisle who had held him in high esteem. No one was more eloquent about Vinson's abilities than House Speaker Sam Rayburn. "No man out of the 435 Members here could leave this House in my humble judgment, and the House suffer a greater loss," Rayburn said. "I have never served with a man of finer character, of greater patriotism or of more outstanding ability than is possessed by the gentlemen from Kentucky."[17]

One aspect of political life that Vinson had to forgo was that of helping friends and constituents receive the benefits of government. Even after donning his judicial robes, he received hundreds of requests from constituents who did not understand that he could no longer help them. Usually they sought help with getting a job or an appointment, and Vinson's stock answer was that he was no longer in a position to help. "I've withdrawn from the fray," he told one petitioner.[18] He even had to tell his mother-in-law that he could not do anything about her plea to reduce the sentence of her son and Roberta's brother, Bob, who had been jailed for a criminal offense. Vinson explained to her that the sentencing judge's hands were tied. "I don't think that there is anything that could be done even if the Judge did have the power to reduce the sentence after Bob went away."[19] The tone of Vinson's letter to his mother-in-law suggested a slight irritation at being asked to intervene.

In a letter to another former constituent, who sought his help shortly after he took his seat on the bench, Vinson reflected on his new job. "The opportunity for real service presents itself here," he said. "It is along different lines than that to which I have been accustomed, but I like it."[20] Although Vinson enjoyed a cordial and friendly relationship with his fellow circuit court judges, he never had the kind of bonds with them that he did with congressional colleagues like Sam Rayburn. As a group these judges appeared to have amicable relationships, although some were closer than others. Stephens and Groner, who served together for several years before the others came, were especially close. Edgerton and Stephens had a long-standing friendship prior to the latter's arrival on the bench. A former law clerk, Willard Pedrick, who served Vinson on the circuit court, said that Vinson was especially close to Chief Justice Groner and to Wiley Rutledge.[21] Indeed, Vinson's tribute to Rutledge after his death reflects his affection: "The fellowship which I shared with him on the bench and in the conference rooms on two courts was made precious by his unfailing courtesy and good humor. To know of Justice Rutledge was to admire and respect him. To know him was to love him."[22]

As a body the Circuit Court of Appeals for the District of Columbia was growing in importance during Vinson's years there. Despite the fact that many considered it to be the second highest court in the nation, members of the court were sensitive to views to the contrary. In 1937 Stephens told Groner that he took exception to a comment by the attorney general that the court ranked "below two or three of the circuits in importance." Stephens recalled that when the appointment had been offered to him, Attorney General Cummings had told him "distinctly that he regarded it as the most important Federal court next to the Supreme Court."[23] Roosevelt himself wrote to a potential nominee to the court in 1937 that the "D.C. Circuit" has taken on wholly new importance in the last few years—is now easily the second most important Federal court in the country."[24] One sign of the circuit court's importance is that it was seen as a source of potential Supreme Court nominees. In 1943 Rutledge was elevated to the Supreme Court, and Vinson joined him there in 1946 as chief justice. All of the other judges—Groner, Stephens, Miller, and Edgerton—at one time or another were touted as possible Supreme Court appointments.

Certainly the Circuit Court of Appeals for the District of Columbia was, as it is today, in a singular position in the federal judicial structure. In addition to exercising the same jurisdiction as the other circuit courts, it has unique powers deriving from its location at the seat of government. Thus the court heard cases of national importance, and it was this aspect of the court's jurisdiction that explained Roosevelt's personal involvement in selecting the judges sympathetic to the New Deal for that court. The court also heard appeals stemming from the municipal courts for the District of Columbia.

The members of the District of Columbia circuit court worried about how they measured up to other circuit courts. Their level of productivity was a matter of great concern. In this regard the District of Columbia court did not compare favorably to other courts. This problem grew progressively worse during Vinson's tenure on the court, and in November of 1942, Chief Justice Groner advised his colleagues that in the number of cases terminated in the period between July 1 and September 30, 1942, their court "was behind every Circuit except the First and the Fourth, and in each of those Circuits there are but three judges; and in cases pending we have a greater number than any other circuit."[25] A year and a half earlier, Groner had admonished his fellow judges to resolve the backlog problem. One suggested approach to the problem was to hand down more decisions either without opinions or with per curiam opinions. The latter are opinions that speak for the court without being attributed to any one judge. Vinson's response to this suggestion offers a good insight into how the circuit court handled its review of cases.

Vinson defined the situation as a "practical problem," which lay in the nature of their conferences, where they initially discussed cases. After conference the judges reached a tentative conclusion about a case, and the judge writing the opinion determined whether it should be per curiam. Vinson thought the court should determine this only after a thorough consideration of the case, "with the deliberate conclusions of the Judges expressed in conference both as to the conclusion reached and the nature of the opinion." All this should occur, Vinson said, before an opinion is assigned to a judge.

In a memorandum to his colleagues, Vinson explained, "It is apparent that when any of us are thoroughly saturated with a case we are prone to magnify the importance of the case and we properly desire to give expression upon many issues which have been decided many, many times. We restate the principles involved, and in such expressions, may at times be more confusing than helpful to the Bench and Bar." Vinson's practical nature is seen in his desire to make both conference deliberations and opinion writing more efficient. His political instincts also were apparent in his advice to colleagues that "unless we do speed up our work we will soon have bogged down [to a state] of which Mr. John Public, the Bar and we complain."[26]

There is no indication that the court resolved the problem of productivity by the time Vinson departed in May of 1943. The court was still handing down the same number of per curiam opinions in 1943 as it had in 1938, an average of about seventeen per year, slightly less than 4 percent.

Perhaps it was the tensions produced by concerns such as their lower productivity that prompted Stephens to complain to Rutledge that their court was a "lugubrious place."[27] Rutledge agreed, adding, "There isn't enough cheer here. . . . We take ourselves maybe a little too seriously and I wonder whether sometimes we aren't all too damned conscientious." Rutledge thought it might be a "good thing for all six of us to get out about once a month and get dead drunk—I mean privately of course. Maybe halfway drunk would be better." If that form of release should be too "nonjudicial," Rutledge recommended "just sitting around now and then chinning or kidding each other or playing tiddlywinks."[28]

There were lighter moments in the corridors of the circuit court, as shown in a concurring opinion that Rutledge wrote to go along with Vinson's majority opinion in a saga of two dogs.[29] It seems that Popo was the perpetrator of a fatal assault upon Little Bits, a pet Pomerian. The owner of Little Bits had apprised Popo's owner of the dog's malevolent tendencies but to no avail. Following the fatal attack, Little Bits's owner sought to recover from the loss of the dog. From a judgment in favor of the plaintiff, Popo's owner appealed. He argued that Little Bits was not licensed as required by statute and therefore could not be regarded as personal property. Vinson carefully reviewed the statutory provisions, along with his common sense, and concluded that Congress did not intend for an unlicensed dog to lose its status as personal property. He affirmed the judgment in favor of the owner of Little Bits.

To inject a little humor into their proceedings, Rutledge entered a concurring opinion that consisted mainly of a poem written by Justice Miller, the unofficial court poet. He cited the poem as "additional authority."

> This saga of Popo, malevolent pooch,
> And Erck's Pomeranian pet;
> Your etymological-legal approach
> To canons of dog etiquette,
> Persuade me that canines are property still
> Whether licensed, unlicensed or tagged;
> Not *ferae naturae,* or fair game to kill
> So long as there's a tail to be wagged. (344)

Exchanges between the circuit court judges were not always light-hearted banter, as is apparent in an exchange of letters in a case about the interpretation of a will.[30] Miller wrote a dissent highly critical of Vinson's majority opinion in a case decided in July 1938, just a few months after Vinson joined the court. Although Vinson seemed overly defensive about the criticism, it was Chief Justice Groner who first remarked on the intemperate nature of the dissent in a letter he wrote to Vinson. Groner called the language in which Miller had framed the dissent "unfortunate." He said Miller had "attempted to belittle the main opinion in a way in which I think it ought never to be indulged by members of the same court." Groner acknowledged that Miller had the right "to express his contrary views as fully as he cares to," but he said it was "unwise to attempt by ridiculing the main opinion to destroy the confidence of the litigant and the public in the expressed view of the court." Such disagreement is appropriate in the conference but not in public.[31]

Vinson's response to Groner was in total accord with the chief's. He said "the language carried me back to heated arguments in the court room; heated debates on the House floor, or even ill-considered language used in the political campaign. . . . If my college days were not so far behind me, I would be inclined to think that it was a hazing." Perhaps, Vinson said, "it might be the effect of the weather."[32]

In a few days' time, Vinson received a gracious letter from Miller. He said, "You are the last person on the court whom I would desire to offend and I hasten, therefore to assure you that no reflections of any kind were intended upon you, and that I had no other intention than merely to comment as frankly and critically as I could upon your write up."[33] Later, Miller wrote Vinson to say that he had revised his dissent in the case. The final version of the dissent is toned down considerably from the earlier circulated draft, which had been a point-by-point, sharp attack on Vinson's logic.

On another occasion Vinson took exception to Justice Stephens's attempt to correct sentence structure in one of his opinions. Stephens had suggested that Vinson eliminate a double negative in a sentence in order to make a rhetorically stronger sentence. Stephens wrote a lengthy letter of explanation and apology. "In respect to the double negative: Please believe me . . . that I did not intend to criticize your sentence structure. I meant only to suggest the clearing up of what I thought was one of those inadvertent ambiguities in which I find myself so often indulging."[34]

Disagreements over language and sentence structure aside, the members of the circuit court displayed fairly strong unity in their judicial opinions, owing perhaps to Roosevelt's carefully crafted selection process. In the five years that Vinson sat on the court, he participated in 439 cases, an average of 88 cases per year. In all of these cases, there were only 25 dissenting opinions, slightly less than 6 percent of the cases heard. Vinson himself dissented only five times, about average for his court. His files contain drafts of several dissenting opinions that he later withdrew.

As chief justice, Groner was responsible for constituting the three-judge panels who would sit during a specific week to hear cases. Each judge sat two different weeks of each month, with the combination of judges changing each time. In approximately 68 percent of the cases in which he participated, Vinson sat with Groner. He sat with Miller in 50 percent of the cases and with Edgerton in 40 percent of the cases. For whatever reason, the chief justice did not pair Vinson with either Stephens or Rutledge nearly as often as with the other three judges.

Pedrick, his former law clerk who later became a law professor at Northwestern University, described Vinson's process for reviewing a case. The judge would study the record diligently before listening to arguments of a case. After a tentative decision was reached in conference, Vinson paid close attention to the circulated opinions, where "the real decision process took place." Occasionally he would ask a law clerk for a memorandum on certain aspects of a case.[35]

During his tenure on the court, Vinson wrote 107 majority opinions, 5 dissenting opinions, and only 3 concurring opinions. He also wrote 2 separate opinions in which he concurred in part and dissented in part. Petitions for certiorari to the Supreme Court were filed in 25 cases in which Vinson wrote the majority opinion. In all but 4, the petitions were denied. Of these, the Supreme Court reversed Vinson in 3 and affirmed in only 1.

Vinson's work habits on the bench did not change substantially from his days in Congress. He would arrive at work around ten and remain there until seven or eight in the evening. Much to the chagrin of his law clerks, he expected them to remain until he left. Pedrick said "it was often these after-six sessions where work on a particular case gave way to general conversations" in which they came to really know "the Judge." Their conversations ranged from Kentucky politics, to baseball, to the problems of the New Deal, to their families, to Kentucky stories. Pedrick, recalling these sessions fondly, said they were enjoyed by the judge and his law clerks.

The cases in which Vinson participated covered a wide range of issues, from the monumental to the mundane. Cases pertaining to the national government involved requests for judicial directives to public officials to carry out their official duties, known as mandamus; injunctions against federal officials; appeals of rulings by administrative agencies in the areas of patents and trademarks, taxation, war risk insurance, condemnation of lands, bankruptcy, and the Selective Service; and reviews of orders by the Railroad Retirement Board, the Federal Communications Commission, and the Wage and Hour Division of the Department of Labor. Much of this litigation was the direct result of the expanded role and responsibilities of the federal government, a consequence of FDR's social and economic reforms aimed at overcoming the effects of the depression and restoring confidence in the economy.

Appeals of decisions made by government officials implementing federal programs were the main source of cases brought before the Circuit Court of Appeals for the District of Columbia. Of the 107 cases in which Vinson wrote the majority opinion, 36 were the result of administrative action. These included decisions about patents, war risk insurance, workmen's compensation, FCC licenses for radio stations, actions by various secretaries of Cabinet-level departments, and rulings by the Railroad Retirement Board and the National Mediation Board. Nearly 85 percent of these opinions favored the government's decisions. In only 6 instances did the opinion go against the government.

The rulings in federal cases had important implications beyond the immediate litigants in the case. The cases pertaining specifically to the District of Columbia were narrower in their scope and impact. They involved more common concerns about wills and trusts, real estate transactions, negligence, insurance, domestic and family relationships, contracts, and banking. Approximately one-third of the cases Vinson heard were in the area of private law, where the state had no direct interest.

Rarely were the members of the court called upon to determine whether particular statutes or governmental actions were constitutional, the kind of issues that Vinson regularly had to confront later on the Supreme Court. The more routine nature of many of his opinions on the circuit court, involving the application of laws rather than their validity, make it difficult to distinguish a clear and underlying judicial philosophy at this stage of his judicial career. Nonetheless, some tendencies were already apparent and later became major themes in his Supreme Court years.

One characteristic was Vinson's propensity to defer to the power of the legislature. In cases involving statutes of Congress, Vinson was very meticulous about reviewing the history and wording of the legislation to determine the lawmakers' intent. Another trait was his strong reliance on precedent. It is not unusual for judges to rely on precedents as a basis for a decision, but Vinson was especially inclined to be guided by previous rulings. In cases where there was no judicial precedent or clear statutory authority, Vinson "reached his decisions by the rational analogical processes of common law rather than by introduction of personal view." Judge Stephens said of Vinson, "He is a believer in government according to law and regards it the duty of judges to apply the law and not to make it."[36]

Pedrick attributed Vinson's approach to judging to two key experiences of his life: his legal education at Centre College and his long tenure in Congress. "On questions dealing with subject matter that he had studied at Centre and which his practice had confirmed, such as the law of evidence . . . he tended to view the law as a relatively closed system." In these types of cases, Vinson "viewed the judging process as largely a search for previously established rules."[37]

Vinson's legislative experience resulted in a different approach on questions relating to the exercise of federal power. In such cases, Vinson "viewed the law as a dynamic institution and the courts as a partner in the affirmative process of government." Vinson did not bow unquestioningly to congressional and administrative actions; rather, "when he thought a problem calling for the exercise of governmental power existed he was certain that government had the power to act, if it went about the task in an acceptable way" (58–59). Taken as a whole, these characteristics indicate that Vinson was inclined toward a philosophy of judicial restraint, according to which judges give greater leeway to policymakers in the elected branches of government. Given his strong defense of FDR's court-packing plan, aimed at justices who consistently invalidated New Deal legislation, it was unlikely that Vinson would have assumed a more activist stance as a judge.

In his deference to legislative intent and reliance on precedent, Vinson was very much like his fellow judges. His opinion writing, however, was distinctly different. Vinson took a more practical approach to opinion writing than did his intellectual brethren on the circuit court. His opinions, "plain and unadorned,"[38] were usually briefer than those of his colleagues. His formula was to state the facts, identify the pertinent legal authority, and explain the conclusion demanded by the logical analysis. Vinson's reputation for logical analysis had been established in the House. Speaker William Bankhead said he had "the best organized and analytical mind I ever came in contact with."[39] Another former House colleague, congratulating Vinson on one of his opinions, said he was "pleased to find that attention to detail and comprehensiveness of view which always characterized you up here."[40]

Vinson relied very heavily on his law clerks in the drafting of his written opinions. Usually the clerks prepared an initial draft of the opinion after discussing the case with the judge. Then Vinson reviewed the draft and pressed the clerks on legal points. In these deliberations Vinson's "Kentucky-isms" often came out. Arguments or propositions Vinson thought were valid were "sound as old wheat in a mill." When law clerks advanced arguments that Vinson thought were suspect, he would say, "We had better get out the lead pencil on that one." Pedrick said the "lead pencil" reflected Vinson's tough-mindedness and skepticism. Vinson was not impressed with statements clothed in fancy rhetoric. The statement had to be written, he said, "so that folks can understand it." Pedrick summarized Vinson's views on written opinions this way: "[His] emphasis on simplicity and communications was the product of a long experience in public life and at the same time a testament to his faith in an informed democracy as the proper mode of government. He had great faith in the 'folks.'"[41] Perhaps this was part of Roosevelt's scheme—to nominate Vinson, a man with political instincts and a practical bent, to a court that was filled predominantly with men who had extensive judicial experience or careers in academia.

The key to Vinson's rulings about administrative decisions lay largely in how he construed the statute being implemented. He must have felt some ownership for many of these, for a significant number of the congressional statutes at issue were passed while he was in Congress and with his support. These included the Railway Employee Retirement Act of 1934, the National Labor Relations Act of 1935, and the Fair Labor Standards Act of 1938. Vinson's familiarity with the statutes and their legislative history is vividly demonstrated in several of his opinions.

Vinson was generally inclined to defer to the expertise of administrators charged with implementing a statute unless he could be convinced that administrative discretion was exercised in a manner contrary to legislative intent. A good example of his approach to reviewing administrative discretion is found in his opinion in *Railroad Retirement Board* v. *Bates*.[42] The case involved a railroad employee who worked for two railroads jointly. When one ceased operations, she was granted a pension, which was later assumed by the government under the Railroad Act of 1937. While receiving this pension, she continued to work for the other railroad company. When she ceased her employment with the second company, she applied for an annuity, which provided a much larger monthly payment than her pension. The Railroad Retirement Board interpreted the 1937 Railroad Act to mean that a pensioner could not receive an annuity because she was already receiving a pension. The employee petitioned the district court, which directed the Railroad Retirement Board to determine the employee's eligibility for an annuity, irrespective of the fact that she was currently a pensioner, and if she was found eligible, the board was to grant an annuity in lieu of pension benefits.

Vinson began his opinion by stating that "proper weight" should be given to the board's interpretation because it "is familiar with problems in its field and has had experience and understands that Act which creates it." However, because this was a relatively new area for the board, Vinson felt more attention should be given to legislative intent. "[The] question is a question of law, one of statutory interpretation," and that, he said, "is a field in which courts are regarded as having some expertness" (643). Vinson proceeded to dissect in minute detail the relevant provisions of the Railroad Retirement Acts of 1935 and 1937. He concluded that the unique position of the employee had never occurred to Congress, leaving the court with the additional burden of trying to decipher congressional intent "from the history, the outlines, and the purpose of the act, as well as the specific language."[43] Applying logical analysis, Vinson concluded that Congress could not have intended a retiree to receive *both* a pension and an annuity, nor could it rationally have intended that one who draws a pension be automatically excluded from receiving an annuity in lieu of a pension. Following this logic, Vinson determined that the district court had properly directed the Railroad Retirement Board to determine the retiree's eligibility for an annuity. Rutledge praised Vinson's opinion for doing "a good job of supplying what Congress left out."[44] Intended as a compliment, Rutledge's remarks suggest that Vinson was really engaging in policymaking, rather than following legislative intent.

Once Vinson was convinced that the intent of Congress in passing a statute had not been violated, he would generally allow administrators broad discretion in their rulings. He did this in the case of *National Association of Wool Manufacturers* v. *Fleming,*[45] when the woolen industry questioned how the administrator of the Wage and Hour Division of the Department of Labor defined what products constituted the woolen industry for the purposes of determining prescribed wages. The definition was crucial because of wage differentials for workers producing cotton and woolen products and the impact of established minimum wages on competitiveness between industries. The law in question was the Fair Labor Standards Act (FLSA), of which Vinson had been an avid supporter while in Congress. Although it did not pass until June 25, 1938, after his departure for the circuit court, Vinson understood how crucial the FLSA was to the legacy of the New Deal. He wrote majority opinions in three cases that involved the powers of the Wage and Hour administrator under the FLSA, upholding the administrator's power in every one.[46]

Vinson's opinion in *National Association of Wool Manufacturers* contains a highly detailed analysis of the minutiae of the law and its application to the competitive advantages and disadvantages of the woolen and textile industries. Vinson determined that the ruling of the Wage and Hour administrator regarding the definition of a woolen product, which hinged on such technical details as what percent of wool a product must contain to be classified as woolen, was consistent with the legislative goal of eliminating competitive advantages that result from low wages, but that elimination, Vinson wrote, "is to be done only as rapidly as practicable. That is primarily a matter for administrative decision and we are not an administrative tribunal. The scope and extent of judicial scrutiny over administrative action depends upon the statute, the adequacy of the process below, and a sound relationship between the two branches of government."[47] Satisfied that all requirements of the law had been met, Vinson allowed the ruling of the Wage and Hour administrator to stand.

In one opinion in which Vinson construed a congressional statute regarding administrative discretion, he was reversed by the Supreme Court. The dispute was between two labor organizations over representation for collective bargaining for employees of a railroad carrier, New York Central Railroad. The Brotherhood of Railway Trainmen sought to be the representative of all the yardmen employed by the company. The Switchmen's Union of North America sought to represent a smaller group of employees.[48] The National Mediation Board designated *all* yardmen for the carrier as participants in the election and, based on the results, certified the Brotherhood as the sole representative. The Switchmen brought suit in district court challenging the board's determination about who could participate in the election and seeking cancellation of the certification. They claimed that the board should have recognized that certain portions of the New York Central Railroad represented separate crafts and classes and were entitled to a separate vote on representation. The board maintained that its only power extended to determining whether New York Central was a single carrier and that, having done so, it had no additional authority to separate yardmen by different crafts and classes.

Vinson determined that the board had fulfilled legislative intent in declaring that New York Central was a single carrier for the purpose of collective bargaining and that the board did not have the authority to treat the switchmen as a separate class. "It is for Congress to determine policy," he said. "Our province is to keep the Board within the confines of that policy" (796). Rutledge dissented in this case, mainly on the question of whether the statute required the board to designate that all yardmen employed by the carrier constituted a single unit.

Nine months after the opinion was handed down and seven months after Vinson's departure from the circuit court, the Supreme Court reversed the decision. Rutledge, now a Supreme Court justice, did not take part in the case. Justice William O. Douglas wrote the majority opinion, which did not discuss the merits of the controversy but focused exclusively on whether the district court, and subsequently the circuit court, had any grounds to intervene at all once the board had made its ruling. The majority determined that the board's decision was final because Congress had not specifically authorized judicial review. In effect the majority ruling reached the same result as Vinson but on different grounds. Justice Stanley Reed wrote a dissenting opinion joined by Justices Owen Roberts and Robert Jackson. The dissenters argued that Congress did not intend to deprive employees of a judicial remedy in protecting their rights in selecting representatives in collective bargaining.[49]

One of the more interesting opinions that Vinson wrote regarding administrative action involved a petition for a writ of mandamus directing Secretary of the Treasury Morgenthau to pay twenty-five thousand dollars to the estate of the petitioner.[50] This was the sum specified in the congressional appropriations bill in 1937. Morgenthau refused to pay the money on the grounds that Roosevelt had vetoed the measure and returned it to Congress within the ten-day limit allowed by the Constitution. The plaintiff claimed that the bill had not in fact been returned properly within the specified time. Although the record showed that Roosevelt's veto message had been delivered in writing to the Senate on the tenth and last day allowed by the Constitution for presidential action, the plaintiff claimed that the message was not properly presented to the Senate with a formal announcement of the president's objections. The administration claimed it had followed a thirty-year practice for sending veto messages to the Senate and that the Senate itself had failed to properly record the receipt of the veto message and present it to the members.

The *Prevost* case presented something of dilemma for Vinson because it pitted Congress and the president against each other, and Vinson felt a kinship with both. In the end he concluded that the evidence supported the president. Vinson argued that to require a presidential messenger to do more than deliver the written veto message with stated objections created an artificial formality and erected a barrier to the exercise of a constitutional power. Some of Vinson's former colleagues in Congress squawked to him about his ruling. To placate them, Vinson sent a copy of his opinion to Lewis Deschler, parliamentarian of the House of Representatives. In reply Deschler admitted that Vinson's reasoning in the opinion was "sound and clear" and "amply cleared up any fogginess that remained."[51] Deschler could not help but comment that House procedures, being much more efficient than those of the Senate, would never have allowed such a gap in procedures to occur.

Tax cases, not included in the previous discussion of administrative rulings, constituted about 18 percent of Vinson's majority opinions. Given his extensive involvement with tax legislation in the House of Representatives, Vinson relished dealing with tax matters. The cases represented a mixture of tax issues and consisted mainly of appeals from the rulings by the Board of Tax Appeals, for in tax cases Vinson was not as inclined to support the government's position as he was in other areas of law. Here he could draw on his own expertise on tax legislation and not feel obliged to defer to administrative experience. In all of his opinions in tax cases, Vinson wrote for a unanimous majority, another indicator of the influence of Vinson's expertise in tax matters. That other members of the court respected Vinson's acumen in tax matters is shown in comments his colleagues sent to him about his opinions. For example, in one tax case,[52] Vinson reversed the government on the question of timeliness of appeal because he determined that the petitioner, who had gone to extraordinary lengths to meet a filing date, should not have his appeal barred, because the failure was not his fault. Chief Justice Groner said, "Well written—If this is not the law it ought to be the law and I challenge any court to say the contrary and ordinarily what ought to be is. Certainly in a case like this."[53] Justice Edgerton also praised the opinion as "a beautiful job,"[54] and Justice Stephens described it as "good law, good sense."[55]

In another tax case, which upheld a decision of the U.S. Board of Tax Appeals,[56] Justice Rutledge described Vinson's opinion as "an excellent and interesting opinion. You leave the appellant pretty much . . . in the position of the minister who announced alum-lipped, that 'there will be no services today.'"[57] Justice Miller, who had previously served on the U.S. Board of Tax Appeals, called the same decision "clear, concise and convincing."[58]

Vinson ruled against the government's position in ten of the nineteen tax cases in which he wrote the majority opinion. Three of these ten opinions involved appeals of rulings by the Board of Tax Appeals for the District of Columbia. Seven involved appeals from the U.S. Board of Tax Appeals.

Five of the seven tax opinions that went against the federal government consisted of several insurance cases that were consolidated because they all involved the same beneficiary. The main opinion for these insurance cases was *John Hancock Mut. Life Ins. Co.* v. *Helvering, Com'r of Revenue.*[59] The issue revolved around the question of who was liable for unpaid taxes on the interest earned on deposits from an insurance estate; the deposits had been left with the insurance company at the direction of the beneficiary, who was now deceased. The Board of Tax Appeals had upheld the ruling of the commissioner of internal revenue that the insurance companies, with whom the beneficiary had similar policies, were liable for the tax.

To resolve the question, Vinson meticulously analyzed the provisions of the relevant statute, the Revenue Act of 1926, and concluded that Congress clearly intended the beneficiary alone to be liable for the tax in the case of an insurance estate. Not content to let the decision rest on the most recent statute alone, Vinson proceeded to conduct a comparative analysis of provisions of two previous revenue statutes, which left him with no doubt that the legislature intended the beneficiary to be liable for the insurance estate tax. For good measure, he included an excerpt from a report by the Ways and Means Committee on the subject. His opinion in the insurance estate tax cases clearly illustrates Vinson's empirical bent, a trait honed as a legislator. Just as he approached the development of legislation with an eye toward the facts, Vinson had great faith that sufficient study of all relevant facts inevitably leads to the correct answer to a question.[60]

Although known for his faithful reliance on precedents, Vinson did not accept them with a blind eye, and in the insurance tax cases he was skeptical of the one precedent cited by government lawyers. That case, he said, "is not on all fours," and he offered a detailed explanation of why it did not square with the issue at hand.[61]

Among the cases involving an appeal from a ruling by an administrative agency was the only one of Vinson's majority opinions that dealt with racial discrimination.[62] The case was about a dispute over union representation between the National Federation of Railroad Workers, a black association that represented the coach cleaners employed by the Texas Pacific Railway Company, and the Brotherhood of Railway Carmen of America, affiliated with the American Federation of Labor. The National Mediation Board investigated the dispute and called for an election. Based on the results, the board certified the Brotherhood as the proper representative for the coach cleaners. The Federation sought an injunction from the district court to void the election.

Several issues were raised by the Federation to prevent the board's certification from taking effect. One of the issues was the effect of Brotherhood representation on its employees. In particular, the Federation objected to rules established by the Brotherhood that required black members to participate in separate lodges and stipulated that officers bargaining with the carriers would not be black. The Federation claimed that these rules would deprive them of their Fourteenth Amendment rights under the equal protection clause, which states that "no state shall deny any person within its jurisdiction the equal protection of the laws."

Vinson disagreed with the Federation's claim. The Fourteenth Amendment, he noted, prohibits discrimination by state governments, and in this case no state action was involved. The only possible constitutional rights that might be pertinent were those guaranteed by the Fifth Amendment, but, as Vinson noted, it relates only to actions by the federal government and not private parties. Therefore, the Brotherhood, being a private association, could limit the rights of minority employees without offending the guarantees of the Constitution. Vinson explained: "It may be that certification of the Brotherhood will mean that white, rather than colored men will represent the coach cleaners in negotiations with the carrier. If so, that condition will obtain because a majority of the coach cleaners voted for it, and not by reason of any governmental action. Moreover, it can continue only so long as they desire it. It cannot be that the Constitution denies colored workmen the right to select a white representative or vice versa."[63]

The Federation case was on the cusp of cases about discriminatory practices that soon flooded the federal courts. Vinson's determination that private discrimination was not subject to the restrictions of the Fourteenth Amendment was consistent with Supreme Court precedents going back to 1883, when the Court invalidated the public accommodations section of the Civil Rights Act of 1875. That statute, passed by Congress to implement the Fourteenth Amendment, sought to prohibit discrimination in privately owned public accommodations.[64] Several years later, when Vinson was chief justice of the United States, the Supreme Court found ways to apply the Fourteenth Amendment to private forms of discrimination. A good example is Vinson's 1948 majority opinion in *Shelley v. Kraemer*,[65] in which he found a way to effectively end racial covenants, which allowed private discrimination in the sale of housing. Vinson also supported the Supreme Court's ruling in 1953 that outlawed the unofficial primary held in Texas by the Jaybird Democratic Association, an all-white organization.[66]

Vinson's tendency to side with the government is readily apparent in criminal cases. He wrote twelve majority opinions in criminal cases, and of these only three favored the defendant. Because these cases dealt with constitutional issues more than with other areas of the law, Vinson's opinions in this area offer some of the clearest insights about his judicial philosophy. A good example, and one of his more noted opinions, was *Viereck* v. *United States.*[67] George Sylvester Viereck was convicted by a jury for violating the Propaganda Agency Act of 1938, which required persons acting as agents for foreign governments to register with the secretary of state. It provided criminal sanctions for willfully omitting a material fact on the original registration forms and on subsequent biannual statements. In answer to a question on the registration form asking for a "comprehensive statement and nature of business," Viereck simply wrote "author and journalist." He omitted information about extensive propaganda activities in which he was engaged.

The trial began in 1942, shortly after the United States entered World War II, and in pretrial publicity Viereck was vilified as a "Master Nazi Agent" by such notable publications as the *Washington Post.*[68] At his trial the government proved that Viereck had been engaged in German propaganda activities, but Viereck argued that he undertook such activities in his own behalf and that, according to his interpretation of the statute, he was not required to provide the nature of these activities to the secretary of state. Vinson disagreed with that argument. He wrote, "When the concern is with disclosure of propaganda, a measure would be a half-way one if it did not require one to reveal propaganda he puts out on his own as well as the propaganda he puts out as an agent."[69] Vinson's dislike of the petitioner's numerous activities as a propaganda agent is palpable as he recounts in vivid detail the varied ways in which Viereck promoted the pro-German cause.

A second issue raised by Viereck was whether the act had authorized the secretary to ask the petitioner for all of his activities, including those undertaken in his own behalf. Vinson, who normally sought to follow legislative intent to the letter, in this case was willing to "read a little more liberally the Act's authorization to the Secretary to do that which will make the statute work and a full disclosure of all political activities of an agent as agent or as his own is a *sine qua non* for feasibility" (951). In Vinson's view the secretary of state had acted completely within the scope of legislative authority when he promulgated rules requiring a full disclosure of all political activities of a registrant, and Viereck "knew that he was skirting the line of demarcation in leaving unrevealed many of the things he did" (958).

A third set of issues raised by Viereck concerned misconduct on the part of the prosecutor and certain procedural errors by the trial judge. Vinson acknowledged that the conduct of the prosecuting attorney "was not exemplary, particularly in view of his office." This he blamed in part on the defense counsel, and he claimed that both attorneys had made remarks that were uncalled for. Vinson also agreed that the prosecuting attorney had made "inflammatory" remarks in his closing statements but that these did not result in "prejudicial error" (962). As to certain theatrics in which the prosecutor had engaged, Vinson said, "This appears to us to be unnecessary stage business on the part of the prosecutor, [but] . . . the ends of justice would not be served by reversing on instances of improper action like this, considering the many aspects of this case" (963). The crux of Vinson's opinion is summed up in these closing comments: "The alleged looseness of the Act, the regulations, and the forms, is not sufficient to allow a willful evader to succeed in a technical claim that he has not been legally brought to task. The evidence presented against the defendant is strong and he has no quarrel with its deficiency" (964). In other words, Vinson was convinced that the defendant was guilty in this case and that none of the procedural shortcomings could have changed that fact.

Viereck petitioned the Supreme Court for a review of the circuit court's ruling, and in March of 1943, shortly before Vinson left the court, the Court reversed the decision.[70] In the majority opinion, Chief Justice Stone pointedly rejected the reasoning of Vinson's opinion. As to the interpretation of the statute itself, Stone wrote: "The unambiguous words of a statute which imposes criminal penalties are not to be altered by judicial construction so as to punish one not otherwise within its reach, however deserving the punishment" (244). Taking aim at Vinson's obvious dislike of Viereck's activities, Stone said, "Men are not subject to criminal punishment because their conduct offends our patriotic emotions or thwarts a general purpose sought to be effected by specific commands they have not disobeyed. . . . For the courts are without authority to repress evil save as the law has proscribed it and then only according to law" (245). The majority of the Court also thought that the prosecutor's inflammatory remarks to the jury had in fact deprived the petitioner of a fair trial.

An unlikely pair of Supreme Court justices dissented from the majority opinion—Hugo L. Black and William O. Douglas. Black wrote the dissenting opinion, which argued that "the general intent of the Act was to prevent secrecy of any kind of political propaganda by foreign agents" and that the act could legitimately be interpreted to grant the secretary of state the latitude to ask for all propaganda activities in which a foreign agent had engaged. Black's opinion rested squarely on his strong commitment to the rights guaranteed by the First Amendment. "Resting on the fundamental constitutional principle that our people, adequately informed, may be trusted to distinguish between the true and the false, the bill is intended to label information of foreign origin so that hearers and readers may not be deceived by the belief that the information comes from a disinterested source. Such legislation implements rather than detracts from the prized freedoms by the First Amendment. No strained interpretation should frustrate its essential purpose" (251).

The irony of the judicial lineup in this case is rich. Vinson's opinion was reversed by an opinion written by the chief justice he would eventually succeed. A pair of justices who frequently disagreed with Vinson, especially over issues of individual rights, voted to uphold him in this case, albeit for entirely different reasons. In his zeal to promote First Amendment freedoms, Black happened to end up on Vinson's side, but during their time on the Supreme Court, they were often at odds over the extent of First Amendment rights. The Supreme Court's opinion in the Viereck case did not end the matter. Only four months later, in July 1943, Viereck was retried and reconvicted. Again the circuit court of appeals affirmed the conviction,[71] although Vinson was no longer there. The Supreme Court denied certiorari.

Vinson did on occasion take the defendant's side, even when he thought the defendant was guilty. In *Nueslein* v. *District of Columbia,*[72] Vinson offered an impassioned defense of the Fourth Amendment's protection against unreasonable search and seizure. The defendant in the case had been convicted in the Police Court of the District of Columbia of driving while under the influence of liquor. The saga began when a taxicab struck a parked vehicle. The two police officers summoned to investigate found a cab close to the damaged car. In the cab they found the registration card and a character license of the owner, but the driver had left the scene. The officers went to the owner's home, and when their knock was not answered, they entered. They called to the occupant, who answered from upstairs. The officers went upstairs and spoke with the defendant through a bathroom door. He said he would be right down. After fifteen minutes, he presented himself and stated that he was the owner of the vehicle. The officers, accepting this statement to be true and also believing him to be intoxicated, arrested him.

The conviction hinged mainly on the officers' testimony that the defendant said he was driving the taxicab at the time of the accident. Citing other evidence that corroborated the charge of intoxication, Vinson thought that the defendant was most likely guilty. However, he concluded that the officers' behavior of entering the suspect's home without his permission and without a search warrant or an arrest warrant was a blatant disregard for the defendant's Fourth Amendment rights. This left the question of whether the officers' testimony could be admitted as evidence.

In 1940 the issue of admissibility of evidence obtained by an unlawful search was far from settled. Vinson noted that under common law practice evidence would have been admissible no matter how obtained, and most state courts were following the common law rule. Until 1914 the federal courts followed the same principle. But the landmark case of *Weeks* v. *United States* changed that.[73] Under the rule established by *Weeks,* illegally obtained evidence became inadmissible. Although there were exceptions to this rule, Vinson determined that this case was not one of them. He said, "When two interests conflict, one must prevail. To us the interest of privacy safeguarded by the Amendment is more important than the interest of punishing all those guilty of misdemeanors."[74] Adding emphasis to this position is Vinson's conclusion that it is "more important to effectuate the vital constitutional policy of security in the home from general investigations directed toward the hope that some evidence will turn up [than to pursue a] policy that all misdemeanants be brought to task" (696). This emphasis on the individual's rights is somewhat surprising, given Vinson's own prosecutorial background as well as his position on rights of the accused while he was on the Supreme Court.

A case concerning the power of a federal district court to punish for criminal contempt charges presented Vinson with an opportunity to expand on that most profound legal question, What is the law?[75] The issue was raised because of a change in the Supreme Court's construction of an 1831 statute governing obstruction-of-justice offenses and punishment for such acts. In 1939 the defendant, Emmett Warring, pleaded guilty to a charge that he had used money to influence a prospective juror and to charges that he had investigated the possibility of influencing another prospective juror. These acts occurred several days prior to the trial and some distance from the courthouse. The defendant challenged his sentence for these acts, claiming that the district court's contempt power did not extend to any cases except the misbehavior of any person in their own court or *so near thereto* as to obstruct the administration of justice.

A 1905 Supreme Court construction of this provision of the statute established that it included all attempts to influence jurors, wherever they were, and this ruling had been reinforced with subsequent decisions. In April 1941, the Supreme Court overturned its previous rulings and said that the words "so near thereto" must be given a geographical and not a causal construction. The question before the circuit court was whether the 1941 interpretation of the statute took away the district court's power to punish Warring for his acts in 1939. Vinson said it did not.

Vinson's opinion provides a lengthy analysis of the implications of both courts and legislatures changing "the law." "This discussion on the effect of altering the law can be pretty well tied together," he said, "when it is realized that the law is not a pure science, that law loses its vital meaning if it is not correlated to the organic society in which it lives, that law needs some stability of administration, that law is more for the parties than for the courts, that people will rely upon and adjust their behavior in accordance with all the law be it legislative, judicial or both."[76] He concluded that a change in the meaning of a statute applied only to actions from that time forward and not to previous actions, acting under the authority of a court ruling in effect prior to that time. He said, "We reject the idea that if a court was considered to have the power in 1939 to do a certain thing under existing statutory construction, and in 1941 that construction is changed so that it no longer has the power to do that thing, it should be concluded that it never had the power in 1939" (647).

To Vinson it boiled down to a matter of maintaining order, which requires that people conform to the rule of law, and they can only conform to the law as it is laid down. He wrote in conclusion: "It has often been said that the living should not be governed by the dead for that would be to close our eyes to the changing conditions which time imposes. It seems even sounder to say that the living should not be governed by their posterity, for that, in turn would be downright chaotic."[77] The Supreme Court seemingly validated Vinson's opinion a few months later when it refused a petition of certiorari to review the case.

As a Supreme Court justice, Vinson heard numerous cases involving civil liberties. While on the circuit court he heard relatively few. The Cold War, in full force during Vinson's tenure on the Supreme Court, had not yet started to heat up. Besides his opinion in the *Viereck* case, the only civil liberties case in which Vinson wrote a majority opinion was *United States* v. *Offutt*.[78] In 1942 Dorsey Offutt, a lawyer, and his client, Robert Sopourn, were indicted on charges of conspiring to violate the Selective Service and Training Act. They challenged the sufficiency of the indictment.

Before Sopourn had been ordered to report for induction, he had consulted with Offutt, and subsequently both men had spoken with members of the local board and presented them with a letter and two affidavits. Offutt had spoken with the appeals agent for the local board on the date his client was to have been inducted and subsequently advised his client not to report. Both men were charged with conspiracy to avoid the draft. They claimed that for a conspiracy to exist there had to be an *overt act* and that failure to report was not an overt act. Vinson, however, determined that failure to report met the test of an overt act. In part he was influenced by the gravity of the times. The United States had just entered World War II and was "preparing for what has become our nation's crisis" (340).

Nonetheless, Vinson was clearly troubled by the possibility that instead of agreeing to take the law into their own hands, the defendants were merely attempting to bring all facts and consideration to the attention of the local board, which he said was "a natural function of a lawyer and a registrant." Vinson recognized that the right to be represented before a government body was essential to protecting individual rights, and he tried to weigh this right against the government's need to recruit soldiers. He said: "In the interests of a free people, preserving the dignity of the individual as much as possible while organizing our nation's forces to battle in that behalf, we make it our concern to flash a signal of warning. Perchance this is not adjudication as usual, but if we can add one title to the preservation of man's worth behind the lines, we accept the concomitant responsibility."[79] Vinson revealed a surprising sympathy for a draft dodger. Perhaps the case reminded him of his own reticence at the onset of World War I to leave behind a life of relative luxury to become engaged in military action. Even when he did "sign up," he was never on the battlefront but was safely "behind the lines," at military bases in Kentucky and Arkansas. It was not a happy experience for Vinson, and in later years he recalled the disruptive effects of the military, which included "the heartache and misery of separation from home and family."[80] The *Offutt* decision was a tough call for Vinson, but others saw it as the correct decision. Rutledge sent him a brief note describing it as "a very well written opinion—and—curbstone. I would agree."[81]

Whenever the circuit court was reviewing appeals from trial courts, Vinson almost always voted to uphold the lower court's ruling. In *Parmelee* v. *United States,* a case that involved imported materials determined to be obscene, Vinson wrote a blistering dissent, highly critical of the court majority, which had reversed the lower court's determination of what is obscene.[82] The materials in question were copies of imported books, entitled *Nudism in Modern Life,* which contained a few small nude photos. A U.S. customs officer deemed these materials to be a violation of federal customs laws and confiscated the books. The trial court determined that the books were obscene and should be destroyed.

The majority opinion wrestled with the meaning of the term *obscene* and concluded that it "is not susceptible to exact definition" (731). The majority put heavy emphasis on the literary, scientific, and educational merit of the materials. Vinson thought that the Tariff Act's ban on obscene materials called for a broader definition of the term than the standard established in precedents where obscenity was associated with criminal statutes. In an opinion that is highly unusual for him because of its strident tone, he pointedly attacked on the reasoning of the court majority.

Vinson thought the court majority had overstepped its bounds as appellate court judges in holding that the book was not obscene within the meaning of the statute. This was not an issue of the First Amendment right of free speech but a question of whether the district court correctly followed the mandate of Congress. Vinson considered the issue of whether the materials were obscene to be a factual question, and the verdict of the lower courts on matters of fact is "final and conclusive," he said. For Vinson the issue turned on whether reasonable men could differ, and if so, "the question is one for the fact trier." In this logical vein, Vinson reasoned that "whether a book is obscene presents a question of fact, if reasonable men could differ on that question" (740). In deference to the trial court, Vinson argued that the appellate court could not disturb the trial court's determination "unless it is prepared to say that no reasonable men could have found as did the [court]." Normally such a determination is done by a jury, but in this case the trial court judge was the arbiter, and as such, Vinson said, precedent dictated that the court "may not apply to the facts its own method of analysis or process of reasoning as a judge, but should try to reflect in its findings the common experience, observation and judgment of the jury of average intelligence" (741).

On this point Vinson is vehemently in opposition to the majority opinion, because it tends to rely more on the judgment of social scientists, who "do not always reflect, or even intend to reflect, the sentiment of the community." Furthermore, he argued, "this publication . . . is to be judged in light of the present day standard, not that of the world of tomorrow."[83]

The *Parmelee* dissent provides clear evidence that Vinson adhered to a philosophy of judicial restraint in limiting the role of the court in matters he thought were best left to others. He chose to focus on the powers of the trial court under the statute rather than to examine the larger issue of what is obscene. In this and other regards, the *Parmelee* opinion also reveals once again Vinson's pragmatic nature. He is clearly deciding the case based on the climate of the times rather than announcing an abstract standard for the future. Vinson rarely wrote dissenting opinions. As a person known for being a team player, it went against his grain. The tone of the *Parmelee* dissent revealed how much the majority opinion violated his basic judicial philosophy.

Vinson has been taken to task by some critics for using an overly narrow standard to determine the meaning of the term *obscene,* but at least two of his fellow judges thought that Vinson had made a persuasive argument. Rutledge wrote, "You made a good case for this point of view."[84] Edgerton was even more complimentary. He described the opinion as "excellent, good-tempered and devastating." Edgerton said that although he "did agree heartily with Justin [Justice Miller], I am now inclined to agree with you that the judgment should be affirmed—tho I do not 'approve' the judgment below."[85] Both judges, and Edgerton in particular, imply that although they might have made a different determination than the trial court judge made, they thought Vinson was right in arguing that it was his call and not that of the appellate court. One senses, however, that Vinson agreed with the trial court judge's determination that the materials in question were in fact obscene. The materials offended his own sense of decency.

The *Parmelee* opinion also shows how important the average person was as a point of reference to Vinson as a politician and a former legislator. He takes offense that the appellate court would give more credence to experts than to the views of those in the community at large. It was this aspect of the opinion that appealed to one of his former colleagues in the House. Rep. Frank Crowther of New York, praising Vinson's opinion, wrote, "We have surely traveled a long road . . . and modesty in our women folks no longer seems to be an attribute. . . . I feel a measure of obscenity of various types has been hiding behind the mantle of art for a long time. I am for your dissenting opinion."[86]

In March 1942 Chief Justice Harlan Stone appointed Vinson to serve as chief judge of the Emergency Court of Appeals. This court was established by the Emergency Price Control Act, passed January 30, 1942, to hear complaints about price ceilings for commodities and rents set by the price administrator. Vinson served on this court with two other members—Judge Albert B. Maris of the Third Judicial Circuit, and Judge Calvert Magruder of the First Judicial Circuit. Vinson held this position simultaneously with his seat on the circuit court, and the members often met in circuit court offices. The court's powers were limited to setting aside a regulation or price schedule, dismissal of the complaint, or remanding the decision back to the price administrator. Relatively few complaints were filed with the Emergency Court of Appeals in its first ten months. In January of 1943, Vinson made a speech before the Bar Association of the District of Columbia, in which he remarked on the paucity of complaints, fifteen altogether. He attributed this to one of three possible factors or a combination of them: "(1) that Congress did an acceptable job in the enactment of the legislation; or (2) that the Price Administrator has done an acceptable job in the administration of the Act . . . ; or (3) that the American people affected by the legislation, visualizing its purpose, have buckled their belts and are taking it; that the business men of this country, large or small, are as patriotic as we would have them be, and though pinched in spots, they yield to their financial discomfiture for the good of the country."[87] After the first year, complaints came more readily. By January 1944 the number had increased to 113.[88]

There were other explanations for the limited number of appeals from the Office of Price Administration (OPA) decisions. The procedures for appealing OPA rulings were so restrictive that they may have discouraged complaints. For example, the administrator was directed to consult with industry representatives "as far as practicable," but no right to a hearing was guaranteed. Further, Congress adopted novel procedures that made it more difficult for parties to challenge the validity of the OPA regulations. In giving the Court of Emergency Appeals exclusive jurisdiction to review the validity of price orders, Congress sought to avoid delays that could be caused by litigation in separate district courts and thereby enhance the effectiveness of the national price regulation program.[89]

Vinson served on the Emergency Court of Appeals for fourteen months. During that time he wrote four majority opinions and issued one dissent. Petitions for certiorari were filed in two of his majority opinion cases, and both were denied by the Supreme Court. In the case in which he dissented, Vinson's opinion went against the ruling of the price administrator. In one of his longest opinions, he determined that a warehouse was a public utility and as such was entitled to an exemption under the Price Control Act. On certiorari the Supreme Court reversed the majority and sustained Vinson's dissent.[90]

Although it was not apparent at the time, Vinson's tenure on the Emergency Court of Appeals was a prelude to his appointment as director of the Office of Economic Stabilization, to which Roosevelt appointed him in May 1943. As chief judge of the Emergency Court of Appeals, Vinson had jurisdiction over price controls for commodities and rents; but as director of economic stabilization, his responsibilities were much broader. Both jobs placed him squarely in the administration's scheme for managing the economy during the war.

Pedrick, his former law clerk, surmised that Vinson, missing the "rough and tumble of politics," welcomed his first opportunity to serve the war effort. He thought it likely that Vinson would have left the court even if the world had remained at peace. According to Pedrick, Vinson "entered the executive branch of government with real enthusiasm and with only minor regrets over the seeming end of his judicial career."[91]

Nonetheless, his five-year tenure on the circuit court of appeals was an invaluable asset for Vinson. Without that experience it is not likely that he would have been considered for the chief justiceship in 1946. As a member of the circuit court, Vinson had established a reputation as a competent but cautious judge. Judge Stephens wrote that Vinson's work on the court of appeals was characterized by "integrity of mind, courage, common sense and balance, a natural sense of justice, and diligence."

His judicial philosophy had all of the traits of judicial restraint. His deference to legislative intent, to administrative expertise, and to the discretion of trial court judges resulted in a consistent progovernment stance. In upholding the decisions of administrative agencies, he helped to sustain the legacy of the New Deal in areas such as labor mediation, wage and hour policies, and economic policies. His strong penchant for following the dictates of precedent meant that he would not be a trailblazer in setting new precedents. His colleague Stephens said that Vinson recognized, like Justice Benjamin Cardozo, that "adherence to precedent . . . must be the rule rather than the exception if litigants are to have faith in the even-handed administration of justice of justice in the courts."[92] When it came to the law, Vinson placed a high value on societal order and believed that stability and continuity in the law were essential to that end.

His opinions were methodical in their presentation of detail and fact and their emphasis on logical analysis. Except for rare occasions, his writing did not exhibit much passion or humor. Although Vinson's direct, dry, methodical approach to opinion writing was not highly valued by judicial scholars, it had appeal for a president like Truman in 1946, when he was looking for a sturdy hand to guide the Supreme Court through the troubled waters in which it foundered.

CHAPTER 6

Available Vinson

On New Year's Day 1945, a Monday, Tennessee congressman Estes Kefauver wrote a short note to Fred M. Vinson, who at the time had been director of the Office of Economic Stabilization (OES) for a year and a half. "Today, I am in my office thinking of the past year and of the things and people we should be thankful for," he began. "My thoughts turn to you and of the hard work, vision and unselfish service you have rendered our country. I just wanted to express my confidence in you and to wish you good health in the new year."[1] Also in his office that day was James M. Proctor, a judge on the appeals court for the District of Columbia, and he too had been thinking of his friend and former colleague. "I frequently hear your able and patriotic service commended, often by those who do not know you personally," Proctor wrote to Vinson. "Yet, I dare say little of praise comes directly your way. So I hope this kind of New Year greeting may bring some pleasure and encouragement."[2] It did. In his reply Vinson noted that warm words for the OES "are few and far between" and that Proctor's kind gesture helped in "lightening the burden of the many problems confronting us and bringing to us a realization that our efforts are valued by those who understand."[3]

The burden Vinson bore as head of the OES, a position he held for nearly two years, was to preside over practically every facet of the home-front economy, making decisions to control rents, prices, production, and wages so that inflation would not add to the cost of fighting the war as it had in World War I. To achieve President Roosevelt's goal to keep the lid on prices and wages, Vinson more often than not fought multifront battles against the demands of farmers, businesses, and workers. The job had been so draining for Vinson's predecessor, James F. Byrnes, the first economic stabilizer, that he wanted out after just a few months and lobbied the president for something more grandiose; he wanted to make policy instead of setting the price for "potatoes and beans."[4] Roosevelt responded by creating the Office of War Mobilization and installing Byrnes as its first director. In this position, which acquired the informal title of "assistant president," Byrnes had responsibility for running all phases of the war effort except those that were strictly diplomatic or military. His relief at shedding OES was obvious. "It's a happy job— happy for me to turn it over to you," Byrnes said at Vinson's swearing-in ceremony in May 1943. For his part, Vinson, then fifty-three, said, "I'm smiling today for the last time."[5]

Although his smiling days might have been over, Vinson neverthe-less was eager to be serving in a job of such importance and one that propelled him into the midst of the frenzy swirling in wartime Washing-ton. Being a federal judge had provided him with security because it was a lifetime appointment, and Vinson found the work satisfying, but it was also a cloistered existence and far removed from the epicenter of political action in which he had thrived and excelled as a congressman. As the nation's chief inflation fighter, he could again get out his lead pencil, as he liked to put it when confronted with difficult problems, and work out a solution, just as he had done so many times in drafting com-plicated tax and revenue legislation. Explaining his decision to leave the judiciary, Vinson said, "I had a feeling that I was not making much of a sacrifice in the war and it was up to me to do something more than sit on the bench and listen to lawyers' arguments." Furthermore, Vinson said, he was "constantly reminded of my eldest boy in the air force ready to sacrifice his life if God willed it, while his father was living a life of ease." He said when Roosevelt offered him the job of economic stabi-lizer, "I was glad to do it. After all, we've only one life to live and when the country needs one's services, I believe that it is one's duty to serve."[6] His wife, Roberta, left no doubt that she too was pleased with the move. Noting that Byrnes also had given up lifetime tenure as a Supreme Court justice to become OES director, she said, "I remember thinking how magnificent it was of him to do so. Now that practically the same thing has happened to us, I realize that it is, indeed, a privilege rather than a sacrifice to be able to contribute toward winning the war."[7]

Vinson's stay in the executive branch lasted only three years, but in this brief period he became a household name, earning a reputation as a tough-minded, honest, and able administrator who could be relied upon to handle whatever troubleshooting task came his way. During this time he became known as "Available Vinson," because whenever Presidents Roosevelt and Truman needed someone to tackle a difficult assignment,

Vinson left the federal bench in 1943 to head the Office of Economic Stabilization. (Courtesy of Special Collections, University of Kentucky Library.)

whether it was managing the domestic economy during wartime or making plans for the postwar period, they reflexively turned to Vinson. He always answered the call, even if he had to take a pay cut of three thousand dollars, as he did when agreeing to give up the job as economic stabilizer to become federal loan administrator in 1945. The great repository of goodwill that Vinson had cultivated while in Congress was a valuable asset once he crossed over into administrative ranks. It assured him of easy congressional confirmation and made him an effective advocate for important administration programs. Vinson's success in the executive branch, as in Congress, also was due to his genuine warmth and gentility in dealing with people. He might disagree with someone but still leave that person "convinced that he has given their viewpoint the most careful consideration." Though not in any sense a backslapper, "he makes you feel that he has a deep and abiding interest in your happiness, the state of your wife's health, the progress your children are making in school, the welfare of your family's pet dog."[8]

The near-universal acclaim Vinson received for his work in the executive branch naturally led to talk of him as a potential presidential candidate. That never happened, but it was a logical assumption given the mark Vinson made in performing assignments of ever-increasing importance and complexity for both the Roosevelt and the Truman administrations. After nearly two years as economic stabilizer, Vinson took charge of government loan policies at the Federal Loan Agency, a job he held for less than a month; he then succeeded Byrnes again, this time as director of war mobilization; and finally he was named secretary of the Treasury.

Shortly before Vinson had assumed command at OES, the president, worried that creeping inflation would soon add billions to the cost of the war, issued his "hold the line" order to freeze wages and prices, with some exceptions, at their adjusted 1942 levels and to roll back the cost of some food items. To Vinson's literal way of thinking, his marching orders from Roosevelt were clear and specific: hold the line meant exactly that. In a nationwide broadcast over CBS on July 8, 1943, Vinson spelled out in dramatic fashion the vexing economic difficulties facing the country and pledged his resolve to hold the line. "Soaring wages, skyrocketing prices, frantic migration and turnover of labor, uncertainty in food production, black markets, shortages, slowdowns, strikes—those are the body sores of inflation," he said, adding that eliminating "this dread disease in its initial stage is our primary task." Failure to do so, Vinson said, "will gravely impair the nation's effective support of our heroic forces abroad; will delay the hour of military victory; and will sow the seeds of bankruptcy, panic, deflation and poverty in the peacetime which follows." Stabilization, in contrast, he continued, "will strengthen us in our job of supplying the armed forces; will hasten the hour of victory; and will lay the solid economic foundation for a prosperous and productive peace. On the home front, then, we are fighting the fires of inflation."[9]

Extinguishing those fires proved to be far more formidable than Vinson could have imagined when he moved into OES headquarters in the Federal Reserve Building in mid-1943. Dancing around the flames and poised to add fuel to the fire were organized labor, business interests, farmers, members of Congress, Cabinet secretaries, and even FDR himself. But Vinson, perhaps as well as anyone else in public life at the time, was suited for the task of reconciling conflicting interests and fashioning compromise. In Congress and on the court of appeals, he had earned the reputation as a hard bargainer, "but a bargainer all the same, a man with convictions but no hard and fast dogma, with a spirit of compromise and a willingness to move ahead slowly, so long as he does move ahead."[10] One of his many sayings, certainly one apropos to the heat he faced as economic stabilizer, was "Things go better when you don't get hot and bothered."

The appellation "judge," which followed Vinson from the judiciary to OES, was also appropriate to the job, because in a sense he remained a judge, "settling disputes between warring Washington agencies at the rate of about one a day and handing down dour decisions against every interest that sought to sneak or bully its way across the anti-inflation line."[11] In addition he tried to remain judicial-like by staying above the political fray, rendering judgments independently, objectively, and impartially. He took great offense at the suggestion that anything other than the evidence at hand could be a factor in his decisions, as one indiscreet lobbyist for southern cotton cloth manufacturers discovered. In a report to the group on his meetings in Washington with various officials, including Vinson, concerning a textile wage dispute case, William P. Jacobs claimed that a decision favorable to the industry might be forthcoming. He explained that because of "pressure we know has now reached him [Vinson] it is possible that for political reasons he may be forced to indefinitely hold the matter, or he may recommend a basis somewhat lower than the WLB [War Labor Board] would authorize."[12] The so-called confidential report was obtained by the Textile Workers Union, which in turn made it public through the press. Vinson was furious. In a scorching letter to Jacobs, he told the lobbyist he had blatantly distorted their meeting by stating in his report that "effective pressure from higher up" might sway the wage decision. "Nothing in my interview with you could have given a color of truth to these statements," Vinson wrote. "Naturally, I deeply resent any intimation from whatever source, that I am subject to political pressure in discharging my duties."[13]

Willard Pedrick, who had been a law clerk for Vinson on the circuit court and was on his staff at OES, recalled how carefully Vinson avoided conflicts of interest. He noted that when orange or mushroom growers might be given a small price increase, they would send a crate of oranges or mushrooms to OES. When Pedrick and others asked Vinson what to with the bounty, "he would say, get rid of it. He wouldn't touch it, not one piece," Pedrick said, adding that Vinson "wanted to be in a position to say that his office, and this was true, never accepted any showing of gratitude or anything else."[14]

In reaching decisions on especially tough and complex issues, Vinson relied upon the decision-making technique he used on the bench and throughout his career, which he called the saturation method. That meant soaking himself in information and then letting the facts suggest the answer.[15] For Marvin Jones, in charge of the War Food Administration, Vinson's slow, deliberate approach sometimes was frustrating. "Frequently when we would go to him with troublesome questions," Jones recalled, "he would listen and then say, 'I will think over this and let you know.'" Urging a quick decision, especially if the issue affected perishable food, Jones told Vinson he would rather have a wrong decision than to have it delayed. Vinson "would laugh and say, 'Better be careful, I might decide against you.'" Jones allowed, however, that Vinson was "an exceedingly busy man with a terribly difficult job" who rarely "made a wrong decision."[16]

Vinson's methodical ways also must have been chafing to his young and brash legal assistant at OES, fellow Kentuckian Edward F. Prichard Jr., whose father had been a classmate of Vinson's at Centre College and his teammate on the baseball team. Prichard, a Washington wunderkind who had graduated with honors from Princeton University and Harvard Law School, started at OES shortly after its creation as head attorney under Byrnes. He had risen rapidly in the Roosevelt administration through his intelligence, political acumen, and connections. Prichard was a law clerk and protégé of Supreme Court justice Felix Frankfurter and a presidential insider who was influential in shaping the New Deal; he also, interestingly, became Vinson's chief antagonist on the Supreme

Court. A memo Prichard wrote Vinson in spring 1944, in which he mixes business and politics, illustrates the range of his interests, his egocentricity, and his impetuous nature. Prichard, who had not yet turned thirty, listed four things he wanted Vinson to do. In his first point, he said it was "most urgent" that Vinson meet with Donald Nelson, who headed the War Production Board, and Chester Bowles, who was in charge of the Office of Price Administration, on the issue of low-cost clothing.[17] "I suggest you set it up for Monday without fail," Prichard said. Secondly, he told Vinson, "I think you should sit tight on strawberries. If you make him sweat it out, it will be interesting to see what Chet's [Bowles] reaction will be." In his third instruction, Prichard wrote, "I think you should call Justice Byrnes and tell him how important it is for somebody to defend the Montgomery-Ward seizure on the Hill, particularly in the Senate." He thought the issue, which involved the government's unpopular takeover of the mail-order firm in a labor dispute, "will come back to harm us in the campaign again and again." Finally, Prichard suggested "you talk to Justice Byrnes and Judge Rosenman [Roosevelt adviser] about Lyndon Johnson. It would be a most excellent move."[17] According to Prichard's biographer, he was "seeking an expanded role for an up-and-coming Texas congressman."[18] Despite the incongruity of their personalities, Vinson took Prichard with him as a top aide when he moved to higher and higher positions in the executive branch.

The staff at OES, which numbered fewer than fifty, also included two other Kentuckians—Paul L. Kelley and Paul A. Porter—who were valuable assistants to Vinson. Kelley, from Ashland, was Vinson's right-hand man not only at OES but also earlier while he was in Congress and on the court of appeals and later when he was chief justice. Porter, who as a young Kentucky newspaper editor and lawyer was drawn to Washington by the New Deal, was general counsel and deputy director of OES. He went on to become chairman of the Federal Communications Commission and head of the Office of Price Administration.[19]

Some of the biggest challenges Vinson and his staff at OES faced came from organized labor, which was especially effective in pressing its demands for increased wages in the face of higher living costs. Unions, despite their no-strike pledge at the beginning of the war, used strikes and threats of strikes to win concessions, weakening the "Little Steel" formula that was designed to fix all pay increases to 15 percent above a 1941 base for the duration of the war.

In dealing with the upheavals in 1943 staged by unions representing coal miners and railway workers, Vinson discovered that Roosevelt's

Vinson with longtime aide Paul Kelley, a native of Ashland. (Courtesy of Special Collections, University of Kentucky Library.)

interpretation of his own hold-the-line dictum contained shades of gray, which undercut his effectiveness and credibility as the strict stabilizer he intended to be. For his part, the president bought labor peace at the risk of adding to inflation; he needed the mines open and the rails running because of their obvious importance to waging war. He also wanted to keep labor in his camp in the likely event he would make a fourth run for the White House in 1944.

John L. Lewis, the monomaniacal leader of the United Mine Workers, led the assault against the Little Steel formula through tactics such as short-term, selective strikes. Roosevelt responded by seizing the mines, but Lewis held the upper hand, as was apparent when the final settlement was reached at the end of 1943. An attempt was made to camouflage the miners' wage gains by using a different method of calculating the length of the work day, paying them for the travel time from the mine entrance to the workplace and back again, for example. But it was clear that Lewis, by doggedly and defiantly bucking the administration, had gotten most of what he wanted for the miners, whose annual wages went from $1,715 in 1942 to $2,535 two years later, an increase of nearly 50 percent. Although his methods proved successful, they also earned Lewis the overwhelming antipathy of the American public and Congress. Lawmakers, responding to the anti-Lewis feelings in the country, enacted the War Labor Disputes Act, also known as Smith-Connally, which added to the president's power to seize strike-bound plants during wartime.

Another setback for the administration on the wage front occurred when the railroad unions, those representing operating employees such as conductors, firemen, engineers, and switchmen and those for the nonoperating employees such as maintenance workers, sought pay raises. In late spring of 1943, a special labor railway panel recommended to Vinson that the more than 1 million nonoperating railway workers be given an increase of eight cents an hour. To Vinson, the answer was a simple no; he ruled that it was not warranted in part because these employees had already received a raise under Little Steel. That should have ended the matter as far as Vinson was concerned, but in next few months his black and white decision faded against the combined forces of congressional involvement, public opinion, union intransigence, and presidential intervention.

After Vinson's decision, the railroads and the unions reached a settlement on the eight-cent-an-hour increase and sought legislative endorsement of their agreement. Vinson returned to the familiar terrain of Capitol Hill to argue that his original judgment on the pay hike should be upheld. If he expected his long congressional service to afford him any special treatment, he was mistaken, at least in the Senate. Ironically, given the close relationship that they would later forge, Vinson came in for a scolding from Sen. Harry Truman, sponsor of a measure to grant the union pay request. He called Vinson's original decision "entirely silly" and a later settlement proposal "perfectly absurd." The Senate passed the bill overwhelmingly, with even Vinson's old Kentucky colleague, Majority Leader Alben Barkley, voting in support. Enactment of the legislation, Vinson said, would mean "Congress itself will have broken the Little Steel formula" and "will have told the country that a privileged group is outside the stabilization program and is not to join the battle against inflation."[20] The legislation stalled in Congress because the House failed to take it up before leaving for the Christmas recess, most likely as a result of action by Vinson's close friend, Speaker Sam Rayburn. He refused to delay adjournment so that a vote could be taken on the bill. By the time Congress returned in January 1944, peace on the railroads had been achieved, but not before the railway unions called for a strike, the government prepared to seize the railroads, and the president negotiated a settlement. Using the expedients of overtime pay, travel expenses, and vacation pay, the agreements preserved the Little Steel formula in name only. In the end, the nonoperating employees were given pay raises on a sliding scale of nine to eleven cents an hour, and operating workers got a raise of nine cents an hour.

Despite these well-publicized breaches in the administration's anti-inflation efforts, Vinson said in a report marking the first anniversary of the economic stabilization program that the line had been held fairly well against inflation. "The workers who have gone out on strike have been too much in the limelight," he said. "They have obscured the millions who have worked harder and longer than ever before, and worked without let-up, even when they felt they had legitimate grievances." Although there had some advance in prices, it "was not as great as it could have been in view of the inflationary pressures, or in comparison with the price rise which occurred during the last war." During World War I, prices shot up by nearly 30 percent, he said, but they had been held down to 12 percent since the beginning of World War II. Inflationary pressures remained as serious as ever, however, because there was still about $36 billion "more in our pockets than there are goods and services available for us to buy," Vinson said. "The battle against rising prices is by no means conclusively won," he said, adding, however, that it was "inconceivable that the American people would let down now after the progress that they have made in the fight to hold prices down."[21]

Vinson's power over the everyday lives of Americans at home was most pronounced in the decisions he made affecting prices for clothing, food, and gasoline. A particularly vexing problem for him on the price front involved the scarcity of low-cost clothing, which he called in a report to Roosevelt "the biggest stumbling block to the entire stabilization program." He added, "The textile and clothing industries can howl louder and make more money than any group with which I have dealt in my present post."[22] At the heart of the problem was the "highest-price line" order of the Office of Price Administration in early 1943, which froze clothing prices at their one-year-earlier levels. Manufacturers, faced with increased labor and material costs, virtually stopped making cheaper lines of clothing, because they determined that to do so would be unprofitable; instead they produced higher-priced items and lowered the quality of popular-priced merchandise. This resulted in the near-disappearance of low-end clothing from retail stores and increased pressures on the cost of living.

Vinson responded to the crisis in late 1944 by ordering stepped-up action by the War Production Board and the Office of Price Administration. His exhortations got results, according to *Business Week,* which reported, "Activity in OPA and WPB textile divisions indicates that . . . Vinson really meant business last week when he called for tightened price and production controls on textiles and clothing."[23] The Works Progress Administration (WPA), the agency responsible for overall wartime production, directed that 75 percent of the total yardage available for civilian use be used in the manufacture of low- and medium-priced children's clothing and such essentials as men's shirts and shorts and women's slips and housedresses. Manufacturers of higher-priced clothing would be forced to scramble for the little yardage remaining in the free market. In addition, the OPA, the agency responsible for pricing policy, ordered clothing prices rolled back about 6 percent, or to their level in mid-1943. To make sure that retailers passed along the savings to customers from the rollback in manufacturers' prices, the OPA required that each individual garment be "preticketed" by the manufacturer with the retailers' ceiling price. In addition, volunteers were used to visit stores to check on compliance.

When it came to controlling food prices, Vinson was able to wield the weapon of subsidies. Through a program of massive government funding by the Reconstruction Finance Corporation, he was able to ensure that food producers and manufacturers could make a profit while still adhering to price ceilings. In 1943, for example, he ordered the War Food Administration to purchase from canners and processors their output for the year of peas, snap beans, sweet corn, and tomatoes at prices that reflected their higher wage costs and then sell the products back to them at lower costs so that they could sell to consumers at prices set by the OPA. Without subsidies, Roosevelt believed that inflation would balloon with workers constantly demanding more money to pay for the ever-increasing living costs. The program faced strong opposition, however, from some farm-belt legislators who believed that subsidies were slow and complex and that higher prices were the simplest solution. Congressman Jesse P. Wolcott, a Republican from Michigan, who authored a bill to end all subsidies, also claimed that the program was intended to socialize agriculture. Similarly, a lobbyist for cattle producers equated subsidies with bribes and said they grew out of a desire on the part of the federal government to regiment the nation completely. Responding to the criticism, Vinson said that to prohibit price supports would "torpedo our stabilization policy as effectively as any U-boat ever torpedoed a Liberty ship."[24] In early 1944, Roosevelt vetoed legislation that would have eliminated subsidies, saying that enactment of the bill "would increase food costs at least seven percent, increase the whole cost of living materially, and destroy the price and wage stabilization program."[25] The veto was sustained.

With the president's blessing, Vinson freely used his power to grant subsidies. For instance, annual subsidies of $100 million went to grain mills to keep the price of flour and bread from rising; another $100-million-a-year subsidy program was approved to reduce the prices of apples, onions, oranges, potatoes, peanut butter, lard, and edible vegetable oils; and subsidies were given dairy producers as a means of offsetting their increased costs while keeping retail prices stable. In other actions involving food, Vinson set ceiling and floor prices for the cattle industry, and he restored the grading of beef, veal, lamb, and mutton after Congress had taken such authority away from the OPA.

One of Vinson's most important decisions at OES was to deny the oil industry its request for a price increase of thirty-five cents a barrel, which would have raised the cost of gasoline and heating fuel. He held firm to his judgment despite pressure from powerful quarters, including his old House confederate Speaker Rayburn from oil-rich Texas. Secretary of the Interior Harold Ickes, who also functioned as petroleum administrator for war, had proposed the increase in crude oil prices as an incentive for increased production. The proposal was opposed by Bowles of OPA, and it fell to Vinson to make the final decision. Porter, general counsel and deputy director of OES, took several weeks to analyze the issue for Vinson and concluded in his two-hundred-page report that the increase was not necessary and would not achieve its purposes. After reading the study, Vinson said, "I'd better take it home with me and study this more and think about it."[26] He boiled the study down to a twenty-nine-page decision, which reached the same conclusion that Porter had: the increase could not be justified.

But before announcing his decision to deny the increase, Vinson called Rayburn, who had said he would make a legislative push for the increase if OES turned it down. Upon hearing what Vinson had decided, Rayburn said, "Fred, I'm gonna have to fight you for the first time in my life on the floor of Congress."[27] During subsequent House debate on the measure, Rayburn descended from the Speaker's box to the well of the House to make a speech in support of increasing oil prices. The Speaker's advocacy notwithstanding, legislative efforts failed. Bowles said that he and Vinson were able to "convince Congress that OPA's subsidy plan to the oil industry, which cost the government only $50 million, was to be preferred to Ickes' prices increases, which would cost $525 million."[28]

Given the range of his edicts, it is understandable that in the public's eye Vinson was seen as nearly omnipotent and the one to contact to get something done. But he was unwilling to intervene, even for friends from Kentucky, if the matter fell outside his jurisdiction. When the Kentucky Department of Welfare was denied its request to purchase new milk pasteurization equipment for its mental health facility in Frankfort, a department official, who had been a Vinson ally for years, wrote him asking for help. After having his office investigate why the planned purchase had been refused by the War Food Administration (WFA), Vinson reported to the state official that there was "a terrific shortage" in this type of equipment and that the WFA "is endeavoring to make distribution of the available equipment . . . where they are most needed." He suggested the department try to locate used equipment, adding, "I do not feel, that in view of their [WFA's] adopted policy, that there would be much that we could do to have an exemption made in this instance."[29] Vinson responded similarly to a friend from Ashland who felt he deserved an increase in gasoline rations because of necessary trips to his doctor's office in nearby Huntington, West Virginia. "I regret to inform you that this is a matter over which I have no control whatsoever," Vinson wrote. Noting that the distribution of gas for civilian use was in the hands of the OPA, he then outlined the appeal procedure his friend needed to follow if he chose to do so.[30]

Although his twelve-hour workdays at OES left little time for anything else besides an occasional hand or two of bridge with old friends such as Rayburn and Barkley, Vinson did leave the hurly-burly of Washington behind for nearly a month to serve as vice chairman of the American delegation at the U.N. Monetary and Financial Conference held in July 1944 at Bretton Woods, New Hampshire. Representatives from more than forty countries attended the conference, the first one of its kind since 1815, to work on ways to establish financial and economic cooperation and stability in the postwar world. Using the plans and ideas of U.S. Treasury undersecretary Harry Dexter White and the preeminent British economist John Maynard Keynes as their foundations, the delegates created the International Monetary Fund (IMF) and the International Bank for Reconstruction and Development, better known as the World Bank. The IMF was intended to function as an orderly international monetary system whose clear and precise rules on the money flow between member states would facilitate world trade, and the World Bank's role was to be a source of loans to assist in the reconstruction of war-torn countries and in the growth of developing nations. A key component in the international monetary scheme was the establishment of a fixed relationship among currencies, which White wanted based on the U.S. dollar and its ties to gold. Vinson was given the responsibility of devising the system of quotas, which determined how much each country would contribute to the international funds. According to Keynes, this question was "the thorniest of the conference, and his [Vinson's] handling of it, which was forceful, but at the same time tactful, helped to bring matters to a peaceful issue."[31] The main obstacle to final agreement at Bretton Woods had to do with quotas. A higher quota meant more prestige and was a sign of a country's relative economic importance. America and Great Britain, not surprisingly, ranked one and two. Just as an agreement was about to be reached, China and France hesitated to sign because both wanted higher rankings.

Vinson, who was an expert at soothing bruised egos, stepped in and appealed to the recalcitrant delegations not "to make the task of friends more difficult."[32] He told the Chinese that the United States revered "the historic friendship that has existed throughout the years between China and our country." To the French, Vinson invoked the name of Lafayette, saying "we learned it at our mother's knees that France came to us years ago when we were in need." Vinson's performance was called a classic

Vinson taking a break at the Bretton Woods conference in July 1944. (Courtesy of Special Collections, University of Kentucky Library.)

case of diplomatic apple-polishing, but his ploy worked. The objections were withdrawn and the way was cleared for the creation of a single new monetary system.[33] After mollifying the Chinese and the French, the next hurdle for Vinson and other leaders of the U.S. delegation, including White and Treasury Secretary Henry Morgenthau Jr., was to sell ratification of the Bretton Woods agreement to Congress.

As the world's leading economic power, the United States had pledged to contribute the biggest shares of the initial IMF and World Bank capitalization. According to a quota system that Vinson helped devise, the United States would fund $2.8 billion of the $8.8 billion proposed for the monetary fund, which intended to use the money to make short-term loans to help developing nations pay their debts. To the World Bank, whose money would be used for long-term loans to support commercial and infrastructure projects, the United States would provide $3.2 billion of the $9.1 billion total. Vinson, in an appearance before the House Banking and Currency Committee in the spring of 1945, said had something like the Bretton Woods institutions been created following World War I, World War II might not have occurred. "When we tried to walk the single path and failed to accept our responsibilities, it became every nation for itself—a race for trade." The best proof of the merit of the agreement, according to Vinson, was that it did not become an issue in the 1944 presidential campaign. Thus, he added, "It must square off pretty well with the interests of the people."[34] Despite predictions from political prophets that Bretton Woods faced tough sledding in Congress, both the Senate and the House overwhelmingly approved the agreement. Final congressional approval came in July 1945, exactly one year after delegates had convened in New Hampshire.

By the time of ratification, Vinson had become secretary of the Treasury, his fourth and final major position in the executive branch. He was appointed by the new president, Harry S. Truman, who had assumed the office when President Roosevelt died in April 1945. Vinson's elevation to the Cabinet post came only a few months after Roosevelt had, in rapid succession, made him federal loan administrator and then director of the Office of War Mobilization and Reconversion.

Upon ending his nearly two-year reign at OES in early March 1945, Vinson reported to Roosevelt that the economic stabilization program "has not worked perfectly, but it has worked," noting that living costs had risen only 2 percent since the president's "hold-the-line" order of April 1943. However, he said the pressures to keep wages and prices under control would increase rather than decrease in the coming months.

Vinson, fourth from right, at swearing in of Harry Truman as president on April 12, 1945, in the Cabinet Room at the White House. Next to Vinson is his good friend House Speaker Sam Rayburn. (Copyright *Washington Post,* reprinted by permission of the D.C. Public Library.)

"General belief that the war was about to end has, to some extent, jeopardized the saving psychology which has so firmly underpinned our entire system of control." Controls were also being endangered by creeping price increases, which made it harder to hold the wage line, according to Vinson. He thought the culprit was the so-called product standard policy of the Office of Price Administration, which allowed a particular product in an industry to go up in price even though the earnings of that industry were more than ample. Vinson wanted a return to past practices when price increases were denied to any industry that made more money than it had earned during a peacetime base period: "Since almost every industry is earning far more than this, such a rule would permit few if any price increases."

In closing his report to Roosevelt, Vinson said, "I believe we can fairly say that in no other country, during this or any other war, have inflationary tendencies been more firmly checked in the face of greater difficulties, both political and economical." Credit for this accomplishment, he believed, largely belonged to "those in OPA, the War Food

Administration and the War Labor Board and other agencies . . . and to you and Justice Byrnes who have given the program such earnest and understanding support."[35] Although Vinson was too modest to credit his own efforts, others certainly did so. A resident of Mt. Sterling, Kentucky, wrote that although he was anti–New Deal and had been "anti-Vinson, politically," he was now a big fan. "I must confess a swing to the Vinson column and in which I am joined . . . by thousands of Kentuckians who have, heretofore, been equally as anti as myself. . . . You have, sho', done a splendid job and we are extremely proud of you."[36] Even more pleasing for Vinson than having a former foe turned into a friend was the thanks he received from soldiers. "After having returned to the U.S. to find that the dreaded inflation, which was so feared in 1942 & 1943, has not materialized, I should like very much to offer my sincere thanks to you," wrote an air force sergeant. He added, "The fact that a lid was kept on wages & prices, thus protecting the buying power of those of fixed incomes as my wife and mother, is due, I judge, almost wholly to your efforts."[37] A navy lieutenant who was in Europe awaiting orders to the Pacific wrote Vinson to let him know "how appreciative so many of us overseas are of the fine job you have done. . . . Most of us hope to be civilians again before too much longer, and as you certainly understand, the hope that inflation will go no further than now is perhaps our most sincere wish, as many of us will return to the old job at the pre-war wage scale."[38]

Vinson's adroit performance as economic stabilizer in balancing the interests of warring groups made him the logical choice to help steer Roosevelt through the storm he created when he picked his former vice president, Henry A. Wallace, to replace the legendary Jesse H. Jones as secretary of commerce. In addition to heading the Commerce Department, Jones, a wealthy Texas businessman, also held the position of federal loan administrator, which gave him authority over the government's vast lending activities and war plant operations. The prospect that Wallace, considered by many to be a left-wing loose cannon, would now control what was in effect the world's largest banking institution set off alarms on Capitol Hill and in the business community. When Congress responded to the fear about Wallace by passing legislation separating the Federal Loan Agency from Commerce, Roosevelt called upon Vinson to head the newly independent entity. The decision immediately calmed the troubled waters. Vinson won unanimous and unusually speedy approval from a normally polarized U.S. Senate. When he heard of the appointment, Paul Porter, by now chairman of the Federal Communications Commission, said he turned "cartwheels in the office and yelled with great glee," adding that it was "the best thing that has happened since the election."[39]

The reaction in the press, though not as exuberant as Porter's, nevertheless was positive irrespective of a publication's political bent. The liberal *New Republic* said the appointment "was received with more general approval than any other choice he [Roosevelt] has made in a very long while."[40] The conservative *Business Week,* which ran a glowing three-page spread that chronicled Vinson's life and career, said his record in Congress and at the OES had "demonstrated that he has a stubborn independence" and that Vinson "will never be anybody's symbol for ideological warfare."[41] The *Louisville Courier-Journal,* which treated Vinson more favorably as an administrator than as congressman, used the occasion of his latest appointment to ridicule the common refrain of protest "against this or that figure in the New Deal that he 'never met a pay roll.'" The newspaper said the payroll yardstick had been made to appear "in the last 12 years as the *sine qua non* of the public servant," especially if an official's responsibilities in any way intersected with business. Calling the catchphrase threadbare, the editorial said it was "self-evident that public administration is something entirely apart from the administration of private business; that it requires imagination instead of the rigidity of the pay roll–meeting routine, a sense of human value rather than of cost-accounts, an awareness of the involvement of destiny before dividends." Vinson, the paper said, having fortified himself against the shibboleth by his accomplishments, "may have performed the added service of putting an end to it for all time."[42]

Going from economic stabilizer, where it was his job to keep wages, prices, and profits down, to supervising and coordinating the network of government finance agencies grouped under the Reconstruction Finance Corporation was akin to being transformed from Scrooge to Santa Claus. Vinson obviously relished the prospect of being able to give rather than restrict. "The job of director of the loan agencies is no cinch, but I have a feeling I'll be able to say 'yes' once in a while," he said.[43] In his first press conference as federal loan administrator, Vinson indicated that he wanted to use the government's multi-billion-dollar lending might to rocket postwar America into an economy of full employment, high prices for agricultural products, high wages for workers, and big profits for industry. In less than a month, however, Vinson had to leave behind his ambitious plans as loan administrator to take on a different assignment. Again, it was a disgruntled James Byrnes who precipitated the latest

change in Roosevelt's administration; in early April 1945, he quit his
position as director of the renamed Office of War Mobilization and Reconversion after twice being disappointed by FDR. The first slight, being passed over for vice president in 1944, was compounded when the
president chose someone else to be secretary of state when Cordell Hull
resigned because of failing health.

In the last major appointment before his death on April 12, 1945,
Roosevelt again picked Vinson to replace Byrnes. Without delay, the
Senate unanimously confirmed his appointment to the second most powerful job in Washington, one known unofficially as "assistant president,"
and Vinson moved to the east wing of the White House. Although he
held the position for only three months, his tenure came during the critical period from V-E (Victory over Europe) Day to just before V-J (Victory over Japan) Day when decisions had to be made on what wartime
controls could be lifted, how best to reallocate production and man-
power resources for a one-front war, and how to begin the process of
converting the country from wartime to peacetime. Despite taking aggressive and decisive actions on these pressing matters as well as others,
"Vinson ended his stay without substantial attacks from any quarter,"
according to a history of the agency by a staff member. "He left OWMR
with his reputation for wisdom, balance, and forthrightness unsullied."[44]

Shortly after Germany surrendered in early May 1945, Vinson ended
two so-called "nuisance" restrictions by lifting the midnight curfew on
entertainment places and the ban on horse and dog racing, but he made
it clear that civilian life for the duration of the war against Japan would
continue to be lean and difficult. "All our effort toward war, and toward
production will be needed up to the last minute," Vinson said, noting
that virtually all of the economic controls then in place, including rationing, high taxes, and wage and price ceilings, had to remain until the
war in the Pacific was won.[45] Vinson's decision on racing, incidentally,
cleared the way for the seventy-first consecutive running of the Kentucky Derby, good news for his fellow Kentuckians even though the
event had to be moved to June 9 from its normal time on the first Saturday in May. Vinson also dealt with a meat shortage in the country, the
worst since rationing had begun, by ordering more government subsidies to boost production and controls to prevent black-market activity.
The wife of a former House colleague had another crisis she wanted
Vinson to tackle, suggesting facetiously that he divert some of the rubber used for tires to corset manufacturers "before I spread all over these
wide open spaces. This synthetic stuff just won't fence me in."[46] Amused

by the letter, Vinson responded in kind with the assurance "that I am struggling with the rubber situation. I hardly know which plea is more forceful and persuasive in regard to the girdle situation—yours or Roberta's. I have first-hand information on the situation that exists, but assure you that your evidence will not be overlooked."[47]

The influence and power Vinson wielded as "assistant president" had limitations; that was evident in the summer of 1945 when he lobbied hard, but unsuccessfully, in the House in behalf of Truman's efforts to make the Fair Employment Practices Committee, which was created in 1941 to help minorities get and keep jobs, a permanent governmental agency. A rebuff from Joe Bates, who held his old seat in Congress, created a sore that never healed. Vinson tried to persuade him to provide the one vote needed to report the controversial FEPC proposal out of the Rules Committee so that it could be debated by the full House. Bates refused, and "Vinson has had nothing to do with him ever since."[48]

Amid signs pointing to the imminent defeat of Japan, Vinson in early July issued a report to President Truman and Congress entitled "The Road to Tokyo and Beyond," which was his blueprint for the postwar American economy. The document also set the stage for the big debate that ensued in postwar America over how large a role government should play in the economy. In Vinson's vision, the United States would enjoy such prosperity in peacetime that Americans would be in the "pleasant predicament of having to learn to live 50 per cent better than they have ever lived before."[49] That level of economic bliss could only be achieved, Vinson believed, through the combined and coordinated efforts of government and private business and industry. On the one hand, his report advocated lower corporate taxes to encourage business and industrial development and to keep venture capital moving into new enterprises or expansion of older ones. On the other hand, Vinson recognized that government had major roles to play in the economy as a stimulator and regulator. His litany of governmental involvement included public works projects to bridge unemployment gaps during business slowdowns, payments to farmers to stimulate production of scarce commodities, financial assistance and information services to small businesses, arbitration and other orderly procedures to protect workers' rights to organize and bargain, more comprehensive unemployment insurance and old-age pensions and more attention to public health measures, and a vigorous antimonopoly policy to ensure fair competition.

Vinson's prescription for a healthy postwar economy was a tonic for some and cod-liver oil for others. *Collier's* magazine called Vinson's report "an excellent instrument with which to orientate your own thinking about how to keep a prosperous peacetime economy," adding that it "may turn out to be a reliable road map to the most widely prosperous and happiest era that Americans have yet enjoyed."[50] The most important elements of Vinson's program, said the *Chicago Sun,* were "the direct governmental measures he proposes as a balance wheel to keep the economy operating at high levels." The paper said the broadening of Social Security, a long-term public works program, and a fiscal policy to compensate for the fluctuations of private investment and expenditures were measures that "cannot be avoided by a democracy which has the courage to look ahead."[51] The *Courier-Journal* also praised Vinson for the idea that government's proper function is to make sure that a balance in the economy is maintained: "Government is the instrumentality for doing things which need to be done for the welfare of all the people, and this means . . . positive action for protecting standards of living and rejecting the idea that these must be left to chance or the automatic operation of so-called nature forces."[52]

Other editorials, however, decried the thought of more governmental involvement in the economy. "The idea of prospering by shoveling out tax money has bitten deep when a man like Fred M. Vinson accepts it," said the *Arkansas Democrat.* Vinson's program, it said, "reaches for the New Deal Santa Claus suit" and was a "recipe for more taxes, and an invitation to pressure groups to demand new kinds of government spending."[53] In a similar vein, the *Macon Telegraph* in Georgia said, "It is alarming to the last degree to hear a man in high position blandly committing this government, so far as he can, to a policy of paternalism, in face of the catastrophic experience we went through during the depression which preceded the artificial prosperity of the present World War."[54] The *Standard-Examiner* in Ogden, Utah, which was especially critical of Vinson's proposal for a public works program, concluded, "Uncle Sam has looked after his nephews so generously in their periods of trouble, the nephews have assumed the happy-go-lucky attitude of refusing to worry until an emergency arises and then to appeal to Uncle."[55]

The ink hardly had time to dry on the postwar report before the president, who was quickly reshaping the Cabinet he had inherited from Roosevelt, named Vinson secretary of the Treasury on July 6, 1945, after forcing out Henry Morgenthau Jr., who had held the post for nearly twelve years. Vinson's appointment, like the previous ones, won unanimous approval in the Senate. Under the law at the time and because there was no vice president, he was now second in line to succeed the president behind Secretary of State Byrnes, who had only a few days before finally gained the position denied to him by FDR. With his well-founded expertise in tax matters and his genius for numbers, Vinson was a natural for the Treasury job. In his wartime positions, Vinson had also demonstrated his skills as an administrator, but his chief asset was his ability to deal with Congress. Truman could expect that his economic plans would get a far better reception from legislators when presented by Vinson, a shrewd politician who enjoyed wide and friendly relationships on Capitol Hill, than if they were proposed by Morgenthau, whose chief difficulty had been his inability to get along with lawmakers. When he went to the Hill, Morgenthau was accompanied by a coterie of experts to whom he would turn when asked questions. Vinson, however, "strolled into hearings unencumbered by aides or by voluminous documents and testified out of the wealth of tax knowledge filed in his own mind."[56]

As if to underscore his congressional ties, Vinson's swearing-in ceremony was held in the large Ways and Means Committee room where he had spent so much of his time when he was a member of the House. Senators and representatives of both parties praised Vinson, as did his predecessor, Morgenthau, who said, "If I had had to pick among all the people for my successor, I would have picked Fred Vinson." Republican Rep. Bertrand W. Gearhart of California, alluding to speculation that Vinson might be either a presidential or vice-presidential candidate in 1948, said, "I have been beating the drum for Fred Vinson ever since I have been in Congress. Maybe I'll be beating a drum for him for an even higher office."[57] Senate Majority Leader Barkley of Kentucky added a bit of levity to the proceedings when, after noting that Vinson was moving into his fourth position in six months' time, he quipped, "I hope he will stay here long enough to identify the rack where he hangs his hat."[58] The setting and the tributes obviously meant a lot to Vinson, who recounted the day's events in a detailed letter to his old friend and colleague Robert Doughton, chairman of the Ways and Means Committee, who was unable to attend. "The audience filled the room—all seats were filled, and the back and sides were packed, as a matter of fact I think they could have very properly hung out the 'Standing Room Only' sign. The boys were most generous in their remarks—it was truly a field day." After the oath of office was administered by Chief Justice D. Lawrence Groner, with whom Vinson had served on the appeals court, "news-reels and news pictures were taken. Then I shook hands with the folks, and thence, back to your office for awhile." After lunch on the hill with

Official portrait of Vinson as secretary of the Treasury. (Courtesy of Special Collections, University of Kentucky Library.)

House Speaker Rayburn "and the boys," Vinson said he then "came back down to 'run the show' for John Snyder who was taking over as my successor. These ceremonies took place in the Rose Garden on the White House grounds. When this was over, I came on over to the Treasury and started in."[59]

The domain Vinson now oversaw as the nation's fifty-third secretary of the Treasury was one of the largest in government, employing nearly ninety-seven thousand people in far-flung operations that included making coins and currency, protecting the president and other important officials, collecting tax money, enforcing drug laws, and supervising national banks. Though he was chiefly concerned with postwar tax and fiscal policies during his eleven months as secretary, Vinson counseled Truman on a variety of other matters as well. "I valued his judgment and advice very highly, and until he was appointed to the Supreme Court he was in on nearly every conference on every subject," the president said.[60]

Less than a month after Vinson took office, the war with Japan was over and he was confronted with the difficult task of trying to put flesh onto the broad outline of the recommendations contained in his "Road to Tokyo and Beyond" manifesto. His biggest fear was massive unemployment among the 12 million men and women in the armed forces, all but about 1.5 million of whom would be returning to civilian life, and among the 10 million workers who worked in strictly war-related production jobs. To forestall what some were forecasting as another depression, Vinson made full employment the cornerstone of his postwar economic program. This could be achieved, he believed, through a balanced approach that would unleash the engines of free enterprise through

Vinson talking via a walkie-talkie on October 8, 1945, at a football game between the Washington Redskins and Detroit Lions. With him is his son Jimmy. (Courtesy of Special Collectons, University of Kentucky Library.)

tax relief for businesses and provide compensatory spending by government to take up any slack. The remarkable transition of Vinson, who as a Congressman was a champion of higher corporate taxes, into what in contemporary parlance would be a supply-sider, is best explained by his lifelong devotion to the welfare of veterans. He was chilled by the prospect that the men and women who won the war would suddenly be discarded in peacetime. Vinson often stated that he hoped his work "will make some contribution toward the kind of country we desire for the boys when they return after the 'shooting' is over."[61]

In a Congress dominated by moderate to conservative Democrats, it was, not surprisingly, much easier for Vinson to win support for the component of his full-employment plan that called for tax cuts than for the companion piece seeking government underwriting of jobs when private endeavors fell short. In fall 1945 Vinson became the first secretary of the Treasury since Republican Andrew Mellon to go before Congress with a program of tax reductions. His proposals called for cuts of some $5 billion for 1946, including the repeal of the excess profits tax on corporations, which had been enacted in 1940 as a way to prevent war profiteering. Even though the tax had raised large amounts of revenue, Vinson considered the tax "too erratic a tax engine to turn loose for even one full year of the postwar period."[62] Others disagreed, most notably Marriner Eccles, chairman of the Federal Reserve Board, who opposed repeal on the grounds that it would further damage a federal budget already heavily unbalanced, it would benefit large corporations that needed it the least, and it would be inflationary by igniting a wage-price spiral. In one of the few policy disagreements the two ever had, Ed Prichard, who had gone with Vinson to Treasury as his assistant, also opposed repeal. "I strongly urged and felt that the excess profits tax should be repealed in driblets, should be staged out, because of the necessity for continued fiscal strength or as an anti-inflationary measure," Prichard recalled. Calling Vinson's advocacy of the measure "one of his few economic mistakes," Prichard said that although repeal probably aided the rapid reconversion, it may also have been "one of the contributing factors to the very large postwar inflation that we had."[63]

Congress, with an eye toward the 1946 elections, wanted to be even more generous than Vinson in giving tax relief to corporations and individuals, which put him in the position of trying to hold cuts to his recommended $5 billion level. At a hearing before the Senate Finance Committee, that task was made more difficult because he had stepped on and broken his eyeglasses the morning of his appearance, forcing him to try to read his prepared remarks with borrowed glasses. As the comical scene unfolded, Vinson first borrowed a pair of glasses from one aide, but those made him squint; another borrowed pair made him see double. The ever-helpful Alben Barkley pulled off his own glasses, handing them to Vinson with the comment, "These may be too young for you, but you can use 'em." He saw triple, went back to a previous loaner, and "with time out for arguing with Republicans, plowed through his 11 pages of facts and zeros with hardly a bobble."[64] In the end, though, Congress cut nearly $1 billion more in taxes than Vinson and the administration wanted.

The second part of Vinson's full-employment program, which called for the government to spend what was necessary to assure a job for virtually everyone in the workplace, also emerged from Congress in a form different from what he had intended. Although the Employment Act of 1946, which Truman signed on February 20, 1946, created the Council of Economic Advisers to analyze economic developments, established a joint congressional committee on the economy, and required the president to submit an annual economic report to Congress, the legislation "contained no guarantees, no firm policies or policy mechanisms, no embodiment whatever of the liberal Keynesian ideal."[65] A disappointed Majority Leader Barkley wryly commented that the legislation "promised anyone needing a job the right to go out and look for one" (366). One commentary observed that even though the administration's proposal was emasculated by Congress, "it made a start and it is doubtful whether anyone in the administration other than Vinson could have accomplished even that."[66]

During his reign as Treasury secretary, Vinson also used his political skills in the arena of foreign economic policy, most notably in mobilizing public and congressional support for a $3.75 billion loan to Great Britain and nurturing the Bretton Woods agreements into fruition. The abrupt end of Lend-Lease on the heels of V-J Day caused great alarm in England, which hurriedly assembled a team of emissaries, including Lord Halifax, the ambassador to the United States, and Lord Keynes, economic adviser to the chancellor of the exchequer, to plead for financial assistance to help the nation deal with a staggering load of foreign debt and other pressing economic needs in the postwar period. Negotiations opened in the fall of 1945 at the Federal Reserve Building in Washington with Vinson and William L. Clayton, assistant secretary of state for economic affairs, leading the U.S. delegation. Truman, Vinson, Clayton, and other top officials in the administration were more than sympathetic, but most Americans and many in Congress had already turned inward, preferring that the country's economic might be used at home rather than abroad now that the war was over, even if it meant ignoring the plight of such a longtime and staunch ally as Britain. Keynes had envisioned an outright gift or grant of $6 billion, but Vinson and Clayton, a self-made man who was as practical and pragmatic as Vinson, knew that for any deal to win approval on Capitol Hill and in the heartland, the size had to be smaller, it had to be in the form of an interest-bearing loan, and there had to be some reciprocity from the British. In terms of amount, Vinson came in low at $3.5 billion, Clayton high at $4 billion, and Truman split the difference, deciding that the final loan figure would be $3.75 billion. The loan, hammered out after three months of hard bargaining, also called for an interest rate of 2 percent, repayment over a fifty-year period, and a reduction in tariff and exchange restrictions and other trade concessions by Great Britain.

After sealing the deal with the British, Vinson and Clayton went on the offensive to win over public opinion and Congress, delivering numerous speeches, supplying facts and figures to influential columnists and broadcast commentators, and testifying on Capitol Hill. In his talks and testimony, Vinson emphasized the free trade aspects of the agreement, arguing that the loan could usher in a new era of international cooperation, with peace and prosperity for all. Speaking to a meeting of the American Academy of Political and Social Science in Philadelphia, Vinson said that the significance of the agreement with Great Britain "goes far beyond its economic effects, important though they are. This is a world in which all countries must work together if we are to live in peace and prosperity. The alternative—God save us—is to perish together. Mankind certainly has the wit and the will to choose not death but life."[67] Vinson did not discount the amount of money involved, which he said "is a lot of do-re-mi in anybody's book," but he added that "war, including its aftermath is costly business. This loan represents about two weeks of our expenditures for war toward its close. In my judgment, this is not an expenditure but an investment. It is sound business for America."[68] When asked during a call-in program on the NBC radio network whether the United States could afford to make the loan, Vinson replied that the credit was an investment, not an expenditure. "We will get it back with interest," he said. "And in view of what's at stake—a healthy Britain and a healthy world trade—I don't think we can afford not to make the loan."[69] Vinson continued to focus on the trade aspects of the agreement during the several days he spent before the Senate and

House banking and currency committees, warning during one appearance that failure to approve the loan would "compel the British to weld the sterling area and British commonwealth into a militant trade group" with the United States forming one of its own to compete. "Two rival blocs would mean economic warfare," he said. "Probably we would win, but it would a Pyrrhic victory."[70]

While the House was still deliberating the British loan after its passage in the Senate by a 46-34 margin, Vinson suggested to Truman that a statement of support from World War II hero Gen. Dwight Eisenhower might be helpful to the cause. The president, however, did not think it necessary "to use him for every occasion that comes up," and besides, he said, "Rayburn assures me that they are going to get it through." Truman said that he was "just as strong for the British loan as any man could be, and I have pulled every possible string I can to get it approved, but I still believe it would be best not to ask Eisenhower to make a statement."[71] The House finally approved the loan on July 13, 1946, by a vote of 219 to 155, and two days later Truman signed the legislation into law at a White House ceremony.

Vinson's other major involvement in international economic affairs came during early March of 1946 when he presided over the organizational meeting in Savannah, Georgia, of the two Bretton Woods institutions, the International Monetary Fund and the World Bank. As chairman of the board of governors of both groups, Vinson had the power to shape the major questions to be decided at the conference, and he used it, much to the annoyance of Lord Keynes, who headed Britain's delegation. The two men, who developed an intense dislike for each other during the loan negotiations, clashed in particular over where the offices of the fund and the bank should be located and over the management structure of the two organizations. With the British loan still pending in Congress, Vinson, of course, held the upper hand over his English counterpart. Nevertheless, Keynes fought for his positions as best he could. He thought New York City made the most sense as a headquarters location because the United Nations was there and because of the city's position as a center of international finance. Vinson, however, had decided it was to be Washington, D.C. This rankled Keynes, who in a memorandum after the conference complained that Vinson had used his authority to make his choice of Washington "an absolute instruction to the American Delegation from which they were not to be free to depart in any circumstances." As a result, he said, it was impossible for U.S. delegates "to listen to our arguments."[72] The American position was that Washington

Vinson at the Savannah Conference in March 1946. Seated to his right is John Maynard Keynes, who headed the British delegation. (Courtesy of Special Collections, University of Kentucky Library.)

was the logical selection because having embassies there made it easier for IMF and bank members to communicate with their countries and because information on the economies of countries throughout the world would be readily available. Another compelling reason for Vinson, though one not articulated at the conference, concerned the growing tensions with the Soviet Union. He thought it wise to keep a close eye on the organizations, realizing that decisions made "at the headquarters of the Fund and Bank might have important political consequences affecting the national security of the United States."[73]

On the issue of management, Vinson and Keynes agreed that the fund should be headed by a managing director and the bank by a president, but they were at loggerheads over the U.S. proposal that each institution have a governing board consisting of twelve full-time directors and twelve full-time alternates. To Keynes, who argued for part-time directors, the plan meant gross overstaffing that would hinder the efficient operation of the organizations. The American position, with just a minor change, prevailed, and Keynes suffered another disappointment. It would not be the last one.

Keynes had assumed that Harry Dexter White, his coarchitect of the

Bretton Woods institutions, would become the first managing director of the IMF. He found out at Savannah that it was not to be. The explanation from Vinson was that Truman had decided that an American should be head of the World Bank to assure the confidence of the financial community in New York and that it would not be appropriate for Americans to be in charge of both organizations, making White ineligible for the position. The truth of the matter was that White had become a potential time bomb for the administration. What to do with White became a top priority for the White House in the late winter of 1946 after he had been accused in an FBI report of passing government information to Soviet agents. The timing of the report made the decision even more complicated because it came after Truman had nominated and the Senate had confirmed White to serve on the governing board of the IMF as an executive director. The president, Vinson, Secretary of State James Byrnes, Attorney General Tom Clark, and FBI director J. Edgar Hoover discussed several possibilities, including firing White and making no public statement, asking him to resign, and allowing him to take the IMF job but keeping him under surveillance. The last option was decided upon, and White was allowed to join the fund when it began operations later in 1946, playing "a highly influential role during the IMF's first year."[74] He resigned the next year because of failing health and died of heart failure in 1948, three days after forcefully testifying before the House Committee on Un-American Activities that he had never been "a Communist, nor even close to becoming one" and that the principles he believed in and lived by "make it impossible for me ever to do a disloyal act or anything against the interests of our country."[75]

Shortly after the Savannah conference and the White affair, Vinson got a much-needed breathing spell when he returned to Kentucky in the spring of 1946 for pleasure and politics. The relaxation came at the Kentucky Derby, where he and his wife Roberta played host to the president's daughter, Margaret. Not only did Truman entrust the care of his daughter to Vinson, he gave his Treasury secretary five dollars to bet on the Derby. In a playful confession of his inability to "pick 'em," Vinson wrote to Truman, "Your Trustee came, saw and was conquered." He still possessed the tickets that represented "your misplaced confidence in order to produce them in court to meet any action, criminal or civil, that you might bring against me," Vinson added. In closing, he said, "And now having made this worthless investment for you, and thereby losing your confidence and friendship, may I call you what I truly think you are, 'A damn sucker'!"[76] The political event of his spring sojourn in

Kentucky was a speech to four hundred of the party's faithful at a Jackson Day dinner in Louisville to raise money for the Democratic National Committee. Vinson's appearance came amid reports that he was being lobbied hard by party officials in the state to run for the U.S. Senate in 1946. As he introduced Vinson, Louisville mayor E. Leland Taylor said Kentuckians were hoping that Vinson would cap his eminent career by filling "the shoes Henry Clay wore as U.S. Senator."[77] Vinson made no reference to his intentions, discussing instead the pending loan to Great Britain and the administration's domestic and international economic policies.

The next and final step in the public life of "Available Vinson," however, would not be to fill the shoes of Henry Clay, but rather those of Harlan Fiske Stone, the chief justice of the United States, who died unexpectedly in April 1946.

CHAPTER 7

The Chief Justice
and His Court

On June 24, 1946, as thousands watched, Fred M. Vinson was sworn in as the nation's thirteenth chief justice. President Truman, who said he had "labored long and faithfully" in his duty of selecting a chief justice, declared that the only regret he had was "losing Vinson from the cabinet." The president voiced confidence that respect for the Supreme Court would be "enhanced" by Vinson's appointment. Despite the fact that Vinson was the thirteenth chief justice, Truman said his appointment was "lucky for the U.S. and lucky for Mr. Vinson."[1] The next seven years, however, did not live up to the hope and optimism of the colorful swearing-in ceremony.

Although it came as a surprise to many, there was much to justify Vinson's appointment in 1946. Two overlapping considerations were preeminent. One was the diminished respect for the Supreme Court resulting from the highly visible personal infighting, especially that between Justices Hugo L. Black and Robert H. Jackson. The other was Vinson's reputation as a mediator and respected politician who had proved his mettle in Congress and a succession of key positions in the Roosevelt and Truman administrations. Truman thought that Vinson, known for his amiability and collegiality, could play the role of peacemaker and bring some order to the splintered Court.

That Vinson was not as successful in achieving this goal as Truman hoped is the result of many factors and can best be understood by examining the controversy leading up to Vinson's appointment, the personal and philosophical rivalries on the Court, Vinson's own personality and his relationship with the other justices, and his continued close ties to Truman that by today's standards may have bordered on the unethical.

To many observers, Vinson's appointment smacked of cronyism, and some thought that he did not display enough independence from his friend and political benefactor.

When Chief Justice Harlan Fiske Stone died on April 22, 1946, most people in and outside of Washington expected Justice Jackson to succeed him. This widely shared expectation dated to FDR's elevation of Stone in 1941 to be the twelfth chief justice. Before making that appointment, Roosevelt consulted retiring chief justice Charles Evans Hughes about his successor. Specifically, the two discussed Stone and Jackson, who was attorney general at the time. Although Hughes endorsed Stone, who had served on the Court for sixteen years, he also recommended that Jackson be appointed to succeed Stone.[2]

Stone's death set in motion a series of political activities that could only occur in a place like Washington, D.C., in the postwar environment of intense ideological disputes about the future social and economic direction of the country. The Court could not escape being embroiled in these disputes, and the composition of the Court was vitally important to people of every political stripe. Truman moved cautiously to select a new chief justice. One week after Stone's death, he invited retired chief justice Hughes to the White House to discuss appointments. Exactly what took place in that meeting became a matter of dispute, which can be partially untangled through the public record.

One of the first public signs of the struggle over the appointment appeared in the *Washington Post* on May 2, 1946, in a column by Marquis Childs. Referring to Truman's meeting with Hughes, he wrote, "The weight of the advice" that Hughes gave Truman "was that the Chief Justice should be selected from outside the ranks of the court."[3] Merlo J. Pusey, who was writing an authorized biography of Hughes at that time, claims that the former chief justice wondered where Childs got his information, which he said was not an accurate account of his meeting with Truman. The Childs column was followed by several media reports about a bitter fight between Justices Black and Jackson, which had serious ramifications for the appointment of the new chief justice. The most extensive account appeared on May 16 in a story by *Washington Star* columnist Doris Fleeson. She recounted in detail the origins of the Black-Jackson "blood feud," which stemmed from the *Jewell Ridge* case in 1945.[4] Black had refused to disqualify himself from a case involving the Jewell Ridge Coal Company and the United Mine Workers. Black's former law partner, Crompton Harris, was counsel for the United Mine Workers, and a five-to-four majority, which included Black, sided with the mine workers. The coal company petitioned for a rehearing and asked specifically that Black be removed from the case. Jackson was so incensed with Black's failure to disqualify himself that he attached an unprecedented statement deploring Black's actions to the Court's denial of a rehearing in the controversial case. The angry Black considered Jackson's attack to be a "gratuitous insult" to his personal and judicial integrity. Fleeson reported that the information about this "clash of wills" had been provided to Truman. "The harassed President, a southerner himself," Fleeson said, "was quick to perceive the affront which Mr. Black feels he suffered." She reported that Truman had confided to a senator that "Black says he will resign if I make Jackson Chief Justice and tell the reasons why. Jackson says the same about Black."[5] Fleeson's article was slanted in favor of Black, and Jackson was convinced that some member of the Court had breached the confidence of the conference table.[6]

A week after the Fleeson article appeared, Fred Rodell, a Yale law professor who wrote widely on legal subjects for law journals as well as for the popular press, reported in the *Progressive* that when the progressives got wind of the possibility of Jackson's being elevated to the chief justiceship, they "poured protests into the White House—by phone, by emissary, by personal appearance—to block Jackson." Rodell said, "They succeeded, and they probably succeeded permanently."[7] Another blow against Jackson was struck by retired Supreme Court justice Owen J. Roberts, whom Truman invited to the White House on May 2 to discuss the appointment. Truman claims that Roberts also advised him that Vinson was the best choice.[8] Several years later, Roberts refused to comment on the advice that he gave to Truman, but Jackson told his biographer, Eugene Gerhart, in 1951, "I have no doubt that Roberts advised that the appointee come from off the bench." The following year, Jackson told Gerhart that "it was probably Roberts" who recommended Vinson to President Truman.[9]

It was Black whom Jackson held responsible for his not being chosen. On June 8, two days after Truman announced Vinson's nomination, Jackson, who was in Nuremberg as the lead U.S. counsel prosecuting the Nazis for war crimes, sent the president a fiery telegram blasting Black. After perfunctory congratulations to Truman for "having named as Chief Justice an honest, forthright and trustworthy man," under whom he said he would be happy to serve, Jackson spewed forth his venom over the events that had transpired. He said that he had read reports that Black had threatened to resign if Truman promoted Jackson to chief

Vinson is sworn in as the nation's thirteenth Chief Justice on June 24, 1946, by Chief Justice D. Lawrence Groner of the U.S. District Court of Appeals for the District of Columbia. (AP/Wide World Photos.)

justice and that "thereupon you agreed to do so. These events were at once given wide publicity either by the White House or Mr. Justice Black." Jackson said: "I would be loathe to believe that you would concede to any man a veto over court appointments. Every justice, every aspirant, every judge on lower courts, and every litigant before the court, is now given the impression that a judge may be denied promotion if he incurs the displeasure of Mr. Justice Black on grounds however trivial."

Jackson was grieved that Truman had not bothered to contact him in Nuremberg, "on a mission undertaken at your request," to inquire about the "truth of the insinuations." Jackson then wrote approximately six pages describing his version of the events surrounding the *Jewell Ridge* case, which resembled in some ways tales of two high school boys bullying each other over perceived threats to their reputations. Finally, he told the president that the "protection of my own name lies in disclosing the facts heretofore suppressed. I must meet the situation forthrightly and over my own signature." He concluded with a request. "Unless you can suggest some better method of making my position clear to the public and to the bar of the country or unless you think it preferable that I release this cable myself from here, I am compelled to ask you to release it."[10]

Truman's reply to Jackson was swift and forceful. "You have been grossly misinformed," he said, and he assured Jackson that he had "not discussed the question of the appointment of a new Chief Justice with any member of the Court. I received no information from anyone that even insinuated that you were unfit for promotion. There may have been some newspaper comment regarding differences existing within the Court, but I took no notice of them nor did they enter into my decision in any way. I did not see the article in the *Star* you refer to nor had I ever heard of it before. Justice Black has given me no information either orally or in writing on this subject." In no uncertain terms, Truman said, "The reputation and the position of the Court are of paramount interest to me and no purpose can be served by making this controversy public." He ended the telegram cordially, telling Jackson that he was "doing a splendid job and performing an outstanding service," and he appreciated "the difficulties with which you are faced."[11]

Despite Truman's urging him not to make public the details of his feud with Black, Jackson did so anyway. On June 11 he sent another telegram to the president. In it he said, "I regret that I could not accept your conclusion that this matter should not be made public. I think no good can come from further suppression of the facts that are favorable to me since part of the facts have been peddled." Jackson informed Truman that he had forwarded to the chairman of the House and Senate Judiciary Committees "a statement confined strictly to answering the one case which had already been given out as the inside cause of the feud. I have tried to handle it so as to cause no embarrassment to you or to Vinson. It is far better that this matter be cleaned up now than left to break in some form after Vinson takes over, or to embarrass him by smoldering in the secrecy of the conference room."[12] On the same date that Truman received Jackson's cable, the story broke in the *New York Times*.

So why did Truman pick Vinson? He stuck by his claim that Hughes advised him to nominate Vinson. Pusey, Hughes's biographer, and Gerhart, Jackson's biographer, both question the reliability of that version of Truman's meeting with Hughes. In a series of letters exchanged between Gerhart and Joseph Short, secretary to the president, and between Pusey and Short in 1951 and 1952, the three protagonists laid out their claims.

Truman's last statement on the matter was sent to Pusey on April 29, 1952, by Short. He asserted again Truman's recollection "that Chief Justice Hughes' final recommendation was Mr. Vinson. The President recalls that he and Mr. Hughes discussed every member of the Supreme Court, a number of Federal Circuit Court Judges, and several members of the State Supreme Courts. Mr. Hughes, the President recalls, spoke highly of Justice Jackson but ended the conversation with the recommendation of Mr. Vinson as the late Chief Justice Stone's successor." Signifying that the president would not engage in any more debate about the issue, Short's letter stated, "If this conflicts with the understanding of other people like yourself, it still stands as the President's version of a two-man conversation on which apparently no notes were made by either one." Truman indicated his approval on a copy of the letter with a handwritten comment, "This is as correct as can be, H.S.T."[13]

It is virtually impossible to verify what did transpire in the conversation between Truman and Hughes. Gerhart offered one possible scenario that lets both men stick to their version, in a letter he wrote to Truman in November 1951. Gerhart suggested that Hughes "may have considered Mr. Justice Jackson as 'the better man' so far as his legal and judicial qualifications are concerned . . . [but] that he regarded Chief Justice Vinson as 'the better man' from the point of view of his ability to harmonize the conflict on the Court."[14] Gerhart leaves no doubt in the Jackson biography that he believes Hughes's version of the meeting with Truman and accepts the view of Rodell that the publicity about Black's threatened resignation was inspired by Black's friends who did not want Jackson to be elevated over him. The stories, Rodell said, were leaked to the press to impress upon Truman the serious nature of the Black-Jackson feud. Although he denied it vehemently, there is some evidence to suggest that it was Justice William O. Douglas who leaked stories about the *Jewell Ridge* case to the media.[15]

Tom C. Clark, who served as attorney general under Truman and was later appointed by him to the Supreme Court, supported Truman's recollection of the events. Clark said that in discussing the nomination with Truman, "we had to figure out just who would be the best peacemaker." The president asked Clark to talk with Chief Justice Hughes. Clark called the former chief justice and asked if he could come and see him. Hughes replied that he would come to see Clark. "We decided we'd go to the White House and he told the President that in his view Vinson would be an ideal person for it."[16]

Independently of the Hughes advice, Truman's decision to select someone off the bench seems perfectly justifiable. Whether Vinson was the best person for the job may be questioned, but in light of Jackson's ill-tempered cable to the chairmen of the judiciary committees in Congress, which he made available to the press, there is ample reason to guess that choosing Jackson would have only intensified the internecine warfare that had been laid bare. To close observers of the Court, the whole episode further diminished the Court's already tarnished reputation. When the story of the Black-Jackson feud broke in the press on June 11, Vinson's former colleague on the circuit court, Chief Justice Groner, wrote to another colleague, Justice Stephens. "What a nasty mess," he said. "Its destructive influence on public opinion will be widespread and the man in the street will consider it a joke to be told that trust and confidence in the courts and of the administration of justice is at the basis of free government."[17] Stephens agreed wholeheartedly with this assessment and blamed the whole thing on Roosevelt. He said, "It all stems from the character of 'the Great White Father's' appointments to the courts."[18]

Without doubt, the infighting on the Supreme Court among Roosevelt's appointees convinced Truman that Stone's successor must be someone off the Court and that it should be someone who had the ability to bring harmony to the court. Clark Clifford, one of Truman's most intimate advisers, said, "Once the President had heard about the problems in the Court, I rather doubt he seriously considered anyone else."[19] Vinson had a reputation as a person who could get along with almost anyone. Richard Kirkendall, who wrote Vinson's profile for Leon Friedman and Fred L. Israel's anthology on the lives of Supreme Court justices, identified Vinson's personality as the most influential factor in Truman's decision to appoint him chief justice. The qualities Truman admired were Vinson's "sociability and friendliness, his calm patient and relaxed manner, his sense of humor, his respect for the views of others, his popularity with the representatives of many factions, and his ability to conciliate conflicting views and clashing personalities, and to work out compromises."[20] Kirkendall did not mention loyalty, but that too was of utmost importance to Truman. In his memoirs, Truman wrote that Vinson had "a sense of personal and political loyalty seldom found among the top men in Washington."[21]

In his study of presidential appointments to the Supreme Court, Henry Abraham noted the similarities among all four of Truman's appointees to the Court: "They had all held public office; they were his political, professional, and personal friends; he understood them; he liked them; they liked him; he liked their politics."[22] Vinson matched these criteria perfectly. He and Truman had developed a close personal friendship between 1945 and 1946 and interacted on both a personal and professional basis. Vinson had become a trusted adviser during Truman's first year in office and was a frequent visitor to the White House for social occasions, including late-night poker games. As former members of Congress, both men felt strongly that Congress and not the Court should shape national policy and write laws.

Matthew Connelly, who was serving as appointments secretary to President Truman in 1946, said that Truman valued Vinson's legislative experience: "As a legislator he had achieved a great reputation. Mr. Truman, naturally having been in Congress for many years, liked those things about Vinson."[23] In 1945 Truman described Vinson in his personal diary as a "straight shooter, knows Congress and how they think, a man to trust."[24] Truman was the last president to appoint a member of Congress to the Supreme Court. Relatively few of the Court appointees since Truman's time have had previous legislative experience. Thomas Corcoran, adviser to President Roosevelt and lifelong companion to Supreme Court justice Oliver Wendell Holmes, wrote to Vinson shortly after his nomination about the importance of his legislative experience. Corcoran said that Holmes had once told him that Edward Douglass White was the greatest chief justice, "greater than either Taft or Hughes, because White had been a legislator and had been compelled to know the men and to feel the tug of the deep currents of his times . . . and to understand to his marrow the reasons and the processes which bring law into being."[25]

Although the turmoil on the Court and Vinson's personal traits and close personal relationship with Truman were the most obvious reasons for Vinson's nomination to the Court, a pragmatic political consideration may have also played a role. Elevating Vinson to chief justice gave Truman the opportunity to name his lifelong friend and fellow Missourian John Synder as secretary of the Treasury. Truman announced both appointments on the same day. Snyder, a Missouri banker from St. Louis, had held many positions in the Truman administration. At the time of his appointment, he was the director of the Office of War Mobilization and Reconversion, a post Vinson had once held. It is an ironic twist that Vinson's elevation to the Court opened the door for Snyder to succeed him. Vinson, along with Robert E. Hannegan, postmaster general, chairman of the National Democratic Party, and Truman's chief political lieutenant, had fought vigorously to deny Snyder the treasury position. Snyder had become anathema to party liberals and organized labor, and he and Vinson had never had a high regard for each other. Snyder had wanted to be appointed to the presidency of the International Bank and Reconstruction, and both Vinson and Secretary of State James F. Byrnes had successfully thwarted that move. Vinson's nomination had been held up while the battle over Snyder raged. Once Vinson got the president to appoint his candidate, Eugene Meyer, publisher of the *Washington Post,* to the International Bank for Reconstruction and Development, Vinson felt he gained as much as he could from the president and gave up his opposition to Snyder for the treasury post.[26]

There were only a few glitches when Vinson's nomination was sent to the Senate. One member of the seventeen-member Judiciary Committee, E.H. Moore of Oklahoma, a Republican, voted against his confirmation. The floor vote on his nomination was delayed a week because of protests filed by two citizens.[27] These were determined to be inconsequential, and he was confirmed unanimously by the Senate on June 20, 1946. Senator Moore was not present.

The eyes of the media were riveted on the Court's opening session on October 8, 1946, when all nine justices would be sitting for the first time since April 1945, when Jackson had accepted assignment as chief prosecutor at the Nuremberg war crimes trials. The *New York Times* described the atmosphere as "the tensest surrounding the opening of a term in all of the 157 years of the tribunal's life."[28] Of immediate interest was the first public meeting between Justices Black and Jackson since the latter's public attack on the former four months earlier. As the justices took their places on the high bench, there was no evidence of public animosity. Seated far apart because of differences in seniority, the two justices did not look at each other.[29] Two days later, as the justices convened for their initial conference of the term, Associate Justice Harold H. Burton recorded in his diary the first exchange between the feuding justices. Burton said Jackson was seated beside him when Black entered the conference room: "Justice Black shook hands with him immediately and Justice Jackson said, 'Good Morning, Hugo.'" During the conference Burton reported that Jackson and Black "joined in a brief discussion—all in the best of quiet manners." Following the conference, all of the justices ate lunch together.[30]

Although the personal animosities between Black and Jackson were kept in check as Vinson stepped to the helm, the Court's voyage under his guidance was not smooth sailing. The deep philosophical and personal rivalries from the Stone court kept the waters churning. A few

Vinson and his messenger, Robert H. Marshall, on the opening day of the Supreme Court on October 7, 1946. (Courtesy of Special Collections, University of Kentucky Library.)

months before his death, Chief Justice Stone used a simile to describe the bickering among the justices. He said he felt "a good deal like the man who sticks his head through a sheet at a country fair and lets the boys throw baseballs at him."[31] Justice Felix Frankfurter described the Court's problems in more philosophical terms. He wrote his assessment of the Stone Court's shortcomings to his colleague Justice Frank Murphy on June 10, 1946, the day Vinson's appointment was announced.

If I were translated into a classroom and had to tell my students what I thought about the period just closed, I would say the following. . . .

1. Never before in the history of the Court were so many of its members influenced in decisions by considerations extraneous to the legal issues that supposedly controlled decisions.

2. Never before have members of the Court so often acted contrary to their convictions on the governing legal issues in decisions.

3. Never before has so large a proportion of the opinions fallen short of requisite professional standards.[32]

This is the environment into which Vinson stepped in October 1946. The president and the nation, having grown weary of the Court's divisiveness, held high hopes that Vinson would be able to bring harmony and order to the nation's highest tribunal. It was not to be. As court scholar Melvin Urofsky observed, "Given another lineup at a different time, Vinson might well have been considered a good chief, but he proved unable to control or guide his colleagues."[33]

Urofsky described the Stone and Vinson courts as "transitional courts, located between the conservative, property-oriented courts of the Taft and early Hughes era and the individualistic activism of the Warren years" (1). In the first four decades of the twentieth century, the Court was preoccupied with protecting the property rights of business owners from government regulations. These policies were largely the product of the Progressive movement, which sought to counteract the social dislocations caused by rapid industrialization. To that end, the Progressives succeeded in passing a wide range of laws, under the police powers of the state, to protect employees in the workplace and to regulate relations between management and labor. These included workmen's compensation laws for injured workers, safety and health standards for working conditions, maximum working hours, and minimum wages.

These regulatory laws were challenged by business owners as violations of their freedom of contract and their right to control their property. They found a sympathetic ear among a majority of the Supreme Court justices, who interpreted the Fifth and Fourteenth Amendment prohibitions against depriving a person of "life, liberty or property without due process of law" to mean that business should operate largely unfettered by interference by the states or the federal government. In

The Court Will Be In Order—Or Will It

Justice Jackson   Chief Justice Vinson   Mr. Justice Black

A political cartoon that illustrates the divided Supreme Court that Vinson inherited in 1946.

doing so, the Court relied on the doctrines of economic due process and liberty of contract.[34]

The economic hardships caused by the depression in 1929 prompted further economic regulations, and the federal government took a much more active part following Roosevelt's election in 1932. Heavily Democratic Congresses passed broad, sweeping regulations with breathtaking speed. Fifteen measures were passed in 1933 alone, including the National Industrial Recovery Act (NIRA), which directed industry groups to draw up codes of fair competition that governed production, prices, and labor relations, and the Agricultural Adjustment Act (AAA), which subsidized farmers in order to control crop production. In 1935 Congress followed with the National Labor Relations Act, establishing the right of workers to organize and bargain collectively; the Bituminous Coal Act, which applied wage and price controls and collective bargaining rights to the coal industry; and the Social Security Act, which created old-age pensions and unemployment insurance. In rapid succession the Supreme Court invalidated the NIRA, the AAA, and the coal act. As a member of Congress, Vinson felt the sting of the Court's rulings, for he had been intimately involved with many of these acts. He had helped to write the tobacco processing taxes under the AAA and was instrumental in the passage of the Guffey-Vinson coal bill that Congress passed after the Court invalidated the Bituminous Coal Act. The hostility of the Court's majority to these measures precipitated the constitutional crisis of 1937 and prompted FDR to propose his famous court-packing plan.[35]

As a counterbalance to the Court's laissez-faire majority, Roosevelt proposed adding one court seat for each justice over the age of seventy, which most of the property rights justices were. Although Congress and the public in general disapproved of Roosevelt's court-tampering efforts, the plan succeeded in nudging the Court to take a different stance. The historic case of *West Coast Hotel Company* v. *Parrish,*[36] which upheld a Washington state minimum wage law for women, signaled the Court's turning point. Decided by a slim five-to-four majority, *West Coast Hotel* marked the beginning of the end of the Court's hostility to economic regulation. Two weeks later the Supreme Court upheld the constitutionality of the National Labor Relations Act by the same five-to-four majority.[37] This abrupt switch in the Court's direction in 1937 signified that a constitutional revolution was under way. The new direction of the Court was sealed when Justice Willis Van Devanter resigned at the end of the Court term in June, presenting Roosevelt with his first opportunity to appoint a Supreme Court justice.

Between 1937 and 1945, FDR appointed eight men to the Court and elevated a ninth to be Chief Justice. The Court that Vinson joined in 1946 comprised seven Roosevelt appointees and one Truman appointee, Harold Burton, a Republican, who was appointed in 1945.[38] All of

Roosevelt's appointees had been staunch New Dealers and approved the Court's about-face on economic regulation in 1937, but beyond that they did not share a common judicial philosophy. Once the constitutionality of the New Deal had been firmly established, the philosophical unanimity of the Roosevelt Court disappeared. As new issues, particularly those relating to civil liberties and civil rights, began to dominate the Court's agenda, two opposing blocs emerged on the Court. One bloc coalesced around Hugo Black and consisted of Justices William O. Douglas, Wiley B. Rutledge, and Frank Murphy. The other group coalesced around Felix Frankfurter and consisted of Justices Jackson, Stanley Reed, and Burton. The nation waited to see with which bloc Vinson would align.

The doctrinal fault lines separating these two groups revolved around two fundamental questions regarding the exercise of judicial powers. The broader question concerned the proper role of the court in relation to the other branches of government, especially when determining whether the decisions of those branches were constitutional. One view, the judicial restraint position, holds that the court, whose members are appointed, should show deference to the elected branches. According to this view, when weighing constitutional questions, the court should strive to uphold legislative or executive decisions unless there is some clear constitutional prohibition against such action or an equally compelling reason why the action should be invalidated. Frankfurter was the Court's leading advocate of judicial restraint. He firmly believed that the elected representatives of the people should be given adequate opportunity for experimentation. If the people's representatives made a bad or unwise decision, the proper remedy in a democratic society was the ballot box. When issues came before the Court involving governmental infringement of an individual freedom, such as speech, Frankfurter's approach required the judge to balance the rights of the individual against the government's interest in maintaining order and security.

This view is rooted in the "clear and present danger" test established in 1919 by Oliver Wendell Holmes.[39] The test serves as a guide for judges in weighing the individual's freedom of speech against government's concern with order. Speech that poses a serious and imminent threat to public order and safety can be prohibited. It is through this balancing of interests that the judge is able to defer to other institutions. Ironically, although this perspective enhances the role of the judge, it is more consistent with a limited role for the court, one imposed by the judge himself. For Frankfurter, judicial discretion was the route to self-restraint.

Given Vinson's long career in elected office, he was naturally inclined toward this view. He was particularly sensitive to the issues of national security that were of preeminent concern during the Cold War era, and his views on the subject are most clearly articulated in one of his most famous opinions, *Dennis* v. *United States.*[40] In addition, Vinson surely understood and shared Truman's expectations that his judicial appointees would "find the law," not "make the law."[41] A former law clerk said that Vinson's "whole conception of the democratic process counseled caution when, as a judge, he was invited to set aside the equilibrium of social interests represented by a legislative pronouncement."[42]

Black, who has been described as a "result-oriented" justice, was less concerned about the virtue of judicial deference to the other branches if that stood in the way of the desired result, as it often did. Black also advocated judicial restraint, but he approached that concept differently. His position is best illustrated by his stand on the absolute and literal meaning of the First Amendment. According to Black, the language of the First Amendment, that "Congress shall pass no law respecting" freedom of speech meant just that, no laws restricting speech or expression. To Black there was "no place in the First Amendment for the clear and present danger test."[43] He would not tolerate any exceptions to free speech, even in the face of threats to public order or national security. The idea that a judge should, as Frankfurter advocated, have the discretion to "balance" the interests of the individual against the interests of government was simply wrong. A consequence of limiting judicial discretion to a fixed meaning of the Constitution, which is how Black conceived of judicial restraint, meant that laws passed by legislative bodies might be invalidated. "I believe," he once wrote, "it is the duty of the Court to show 'deference' to the Constitution only."[44]

Even in the intense heat of the Cold War, Black uniformly voted against the government and for the individual. This put him on the opposite side from Vinson, whose instincts and experience made him sympathetic to government's need to address public fears about order, safety, and national security. Most of Vinson's service in the executive branch had been done under emergency conditions, and "he tended to think of the problem of freedom largely in terms of the affirmative use of political power to create and preserve such conditions as are favorable to freedom."[45] Vinson never voted against the government where national security matters were at issue.

The other source of philosophical differences between the Frankfurter and Black camps stemmed from sharp disagreements over the interpretation of the due process clause of the Fourteenth Amendment and what restrictions it imposed on the states. Black took the position that the due process clause of the Fourteenth Amendment incorporated all of the first eight amendments of the Bill of Rights, thus imposing the same restrictions on states as it did on the national government. Consequently, the states, like the federal government, were prohibited from infringing on individual freedoms such as speech, press, religion, and free association, and they were also required to guarantee the same procedural rights as the federal government, such as the protection against self-incrimination and unreasonable searches and seizures.

In contrast to Black's absolutist view of total incorporation, Frankfurter espoused "selective incorporation," which again required a "balancing view." Rather than accepting a fixed meaning for any individual right, Frankfurter chose to weigh the individual right against "the necessity for allowing play at the joints of the crude machinery of government."[46] He also argued that "due process of law" was an extremely vague concept, which required judicial discretion and a flexible interpretation. Again, Vinson was inclined to Frankfurter's point of view. His natural bent toward pragmatism and his experience in seeking compromise to achieve desired goals made him wary of any absolutist stance or interpretation. One of his law clerks said his judicial approach had a predominantly "pragmatic cast" and that "as a judge he ordinarily reacted suspiciously to the grand generalization."[47]

These sharp philosophical differences among the members of the Vinson Court were often exacerbated by intense personal rivalries and conflicts. On occasion these personal animosities were even reflected in the wording of opinions. Theories of leadership on the Supreme Court developed by such scholars as David J. Danelski and Robert J. Steamer help to explain why Vinson proved no more capable than Stone at unifying the Court.[48] Leadership on the Supreme Court requires the performance of two kinds of functions: task leadership and social leadership. Social leadership concerns how the chief justice conducts himself with his colleagues and his efforts to make the Court a more harmonious body. Vinson's ability to provide social leadership was aided by his personal affability, and he worked hard to foster good relations with his colleagues. He went out of his way to accommodate the personal needs of the justices. This was especially noticeable in his consideration of illnesses that affected various Court members. On two occasions Douglas was away from the Court for health reasons. Vinson diligently kept him informed about the Court's business and was very solicitous in en-

Vinson in his judicial robes at the Supreme Court. (Harris & Ewing, courtesy of Special Collections, University of Kentucky Library.)

couraging him to recover his health before returning to the bench. He showed the same consideration for Justice Murphy's prolonged health problems. He willingly rescheduled any Court business when another justice had a personal conflict. Vinson's files are replete with notes of appreciation from his colleagues for his kindness to them. One thing that stands out about Vinson's relationship with his colleagues is that there is no record of his ever having said anything to another member of the Court or to one of his law clerks that demeaned any of his colleagues. The same cannot be said for some of his brethren. Success in social leadership, though, does not equate with task leadership.

Task leadership has managerial and intellectual components. Managerial leadership relates to keeping the docket up to date and using political skills in guiding the conference, in assigning opinions, and in choosing when to write opinions for the Court. Intellectual leadership is displayed at the conference debates and in writing the opinions.[49] A critical measure of the chief justice's leadership is how he manages the conference, where the justices meet to discuss cases. As the presiding officer, the chief justice speaks first and votes last. He can exercise task leadership through his presentation of cases, by facilitating compromise, and by ending debate when necessary. In the process of decision making, disagreements can become high-spirited, leading to antagonisms and tensions. Dealing with these negative consequences of conference debate requires skills in social leadership. This task is necessary to keep the Court socially cohesive. Rarely will a chief justice excel at both types of leadership. Others on the Court may fulfill one of these functions. If both functions are performed well, the consequences for the Court as an institution are highly positive. Conflict is reduced, and social cohesion and satisfaction with the conference increase. Also, production, in terms of the number of decisions per time spent, increases.

Three characteristics determine a chief justice's actual influence over the Court: esteem, ability, and personality.[50] Of these three characteristics, Vinson's strongest asset was his congenial personality, but it was not enough to overcome his weakness in the other two areas, esteem and ability. From the beginning some of his colleagues harbored doubts about Vinson's judicial credentials. On October 15, 1946, following a visit with President Truman at the White House by all the justices, Frankfurter asked Reed, also from Kentucky, his candid opinion of Vinson. Reed, who was not known as one of the Court's intellectual leaders, replied, "He is just like me, except that he is less well-educated and has not had as many opportunities." Although Reed had held some expectations that he might be selected as chief justice, he told Frankfurter that had he been president he would not have appointed either Vinson or himself. "I know a good deal about the history of Chief Justices of this Court and the great ones have been men like Marshall, Taney and Hughes, men of recognized pre-eminence before they [came to the court]."[51]

Another justice who expressed reservations was Douglas. He liked the chief justice personally. He described him as a person with "a gentle voice and gentle manners." But he did not consider Vinson to be a great jurist. Douglas said that like Truman's other appointees, he was "mediocre." He theorized that Truman harbored some feelings of inferiority, noting that the president once said to him, "You know Bill, you are the one person I see who does not try to make me feel inferior." From this exchange and others with the president, Douglas speculated that "the reason he named people like Fred Vinson to the Court was in order to be surrounded by men whose stature did not exceed his own."[52]

The justice who harbored the greatest doubts about Vinson's abilities and who became his chief antagonist was Frankfurter. He expressed reservations about Vinson following the first conference at which argued cases were taken up. Frankfurter recorded in his diary on October 19 that the way Vinson dealt with the cases "gives further evidence that he is likely to deal with complicated matters on a surface basis." He described the chief justice as "confident and easy-going and sure and shallow."[53] In fairness, Frankfurter said that "one must give him ample time to show his qualities, but he seems to me to have the confident air of a man who does not see the complexities of problems and blithely hits the obvious points." Yet, said Frankfurter, "he does it all in good temper and dispatch." A few weeks later, Frankfurter again observed that "Vinson conducts the Conference with ease and good humor, disposing of each case rather briefly by choosing, as it were, to float merely on the surface of the problems raised by the cases" (283).

Edward F. Prichard, a Kentuckian who at one time had been a Vinson protégé when he worked for him in the executive branch and who had served as a Frankfurter law clerk prior to Vinson's appointment, described the "personal rancor" that developed between the two men. "Frankfurter," he said, "did not have high regard for Vinson's judicial capabilities and . . . was not very adept at concealing his views on things of that sort." The antagonisms between the two men stemmed from differences in background and personality. Prichard described Vinson as "a practical day-to-day kind of person, he didn't spin out and articulate philosophical positions—just the opposite of Frankfurter." Although Vinson was an affable man by nature, "he could take offense if he were affronted and Frankfurter was a good affronter."[54]

Early on, Frankfurter tried to lure Vinson into his camp, which was his standard approach to newly appointed justices. Flattery and instruction were the key elements of his strategy. Soon after his appointment,

Vinson replied to a congratulatory letter from Frankfurter. "I want to tell you," he wrote, "how happy your letter made me, and how much I welcomed your generous prophecy in regard to my conduct of the office of Chief Justice."[55]

During his first year on the Court, Vinson sought out Frankfurter's advice. On one occasion a baffled Vinson asked Frankfurter about a pending case. "What is happening around here? I haven't heard anything for several days." Frankfurter, sensing an opportunity to instruct the Chief Justice, discussed with him how they might "smoke out" the majority. Vinson replied, "I am ready to move in whenever I have to, but I want to take my time about it and not do it too soon. If I have any special ability, it is that of getting on with folk and I want to do it here without making people feel that I am unduly moving in and that this is why I rather thought it would be unwise for me to move in on [this] case." Frankfurter surmised that Vinson was reticent in "taking the initiative on questions before the Court and asserting such intrinsic authority as the position of the Chief Justice gives."[56] To show signs of weakness such as this was an open invitation to Frankfurter, who had a reputation for trying to dominate those whom he considered to be intellectually inferior.

In his psychological biography of Frankfurter, H.N. Hirsch explains Frankfurter's behavior toward Vinson and other members of the Court as the result of his neurotic personality. He had a strong need to manipulate people and an even stronger desire to win. When he failed to win, he became bitter and vindictive.[57] Such was the situation with Vinson. Beginning in early 1950, his attitude toward Vinson turned vengeful, and he began to criticize him at every opportunity. This change in his behavior coincided with two major changes in the Court's personnel. Over the summer of 1949, two of Roosevelt's appointees—Frank Murphy and Wiley Rutledge—died suddenly. Truman appointed Attorney General Tom C. Clark to fill the Murphy vacancy and Sherman Minton, whom the president had known since their days in the Senate together, to fill the Rutledge vacancy. Clark is on record as saying that he thinks Vinson lobbied Truman for his own appointment.[58] Clark and Minton were very much in the Vinson mold, and their appointments produced what many court scholars labeled the Truman Court. With the four Truman appointees, all of whom supported a passive judiciary and a progovernment stance on most civil liberties issues, Vinson had an almost automatic majority. He could usually count on Reed, Frankfurter, or Jackson to join their bloc. Perhaps it was the realization that his own stature had been diminished with the appointments of Clark and Minton that caused Frankfurter problems.

Newton Minow, who served as a clerk for Vinson in 1951–1952, maintained that the real intellectual leaders on the Court while he was there were not Frankfurter and Black but Vinson and Black. Minow argues that scholars "tended to underestimate Vinson as a power in the Court because they didn't regard him as a scholar." In calling Vinson one of the Court's intellectual powers, he was defining *intellectual* in terms of "strongly held, strongly articulated views." Minow's thoughts on the matter were shaped by the prominence of the steel-seizure case during his clerkship, but in that context his observations ring true. When a big case like steel seizure came along, "Vinson had a view and Black had a view and others would fluctuate around them. Frankfurter and Jackson were more colorful in their legal language and they could write more artful opinions with better quotes. But in the real tough cases there was Vinson and Black on opposite sides."[59]

Howard Trienens, who served as a Vinson clerk along with Minow, recalled that Frankfurter became very unhappy whenever he learned that Vinson did not always vote the way Frankfurter wanted him to. Accord-

Vinson at a dinner given in his honor by his law clerks on June 5, 1951. Front row, from left, David Feller, Willard Pedrick, Vinson, Karl Price, Francis Allen, and Lawrence Ebb; second row, Ike Groner, Art Seder, Newton Minow, Murray Schwartz, Wilbur Lester and Howard Trienens. (Courtesy of Special Collections, University of Kentucky Library.)

ing to Trienens, there was a period when Frankfurter would not sign a Vinson opinion no matter what it said. Although he eventually got over it, Trienens said their relationship remained strained in a "professional sense."[60] Frankfurter, even though he agreed with every word, would write a separate concurrence, a practice that greatly irritated Vinson.

Another thing that irritated Vinson was Frankfurter's habit of standing up in conference while addressing the other justices. His demeanor was that of a college professor; sometimes he would go and pull a book down from the shelves. On one particular day, recalled Tom Clark, Frankfurter was standing and talking about a case "and he said something that irritated the Chief."[61] Vinson thought the remarks reflected on his integrity, and "the Chief pushed his chair back . . . and was sort of making toward Felix." Douglas recalled that the chief justice said, "No son of a bitch can ever say that to Fred Vinson."[62] Minton and Clark intervened and held Vinson until he could cool off. Later that day he apologized to Frankfurter.

Although Clark said that this was the only incident in which Vinson lost his temper, there were many other situations in which the chief justice and Frankfurter locked horns. One issue that was perennially a matter of concern to all the members of the Court was petitions for certiorari, the procedures by which a litigant could ask the Court to review a case from a lower court. Four justices must vote to grant review before a case can be brought to the Court. During Vinson's tenure as chief justice, there was an increasing number of petitions for certiorari. Frankfurter felt that the Court granted too many petitions. Vinson was sympathetic to this view but no doubt resented the officious way in which Frankfurter instructed the Court on the mater of a "serious evil" in the Court's work. In a memo sent to all members of the Court, Frankfurter wrote, "The evil is the filing week-after-week of utterly baseless petitions."[63] In a comment that reflected on Vinson's leadership, Frankfurter said that the situation "offends every consideration relevant to the efficient and economic conduct of our business." He then identified several cases that should not have been accepted for review and laid out his own formula for stemming the number of petitions for certiorari.

It is not known how Vinson replied to Frankfurter's complaint about the matter of granting too many petitions for certiorari, but he did respond at length to another Frankfurter memorandum sent to all members of the Court. This complaint was about extending the amount of time within which to file a petition for certiorari. Frankfurter's main concern was about the need to notify the opposing party in a case that an extension had been granted. The issue had been raised in a case on which Frankfurter was working. To his memo he attached a proposed new rule, drawn up by the clerk of the court.[64] In less than a week, Vinson sent a memo to all the justices saying, "It doesn't strike me that [the proposed new rule] does the job," and he proceeded for two pages to explain how his view of the problem differed from Frankfurter's view, to elaborate on the concerns he had about Frankfurter's proposal, and to suggest a solution of his own.[65] This prompted another lengthy memo by Frankfurter. Vinson's proposal, he said, "arouses sympathy in me," but upon reflection he was persuaded that "practical considerations preclude the desirability of such a change." Two days later Frankfurter followed with yet another memorandum, which he said was not circulated "for the pleasure of arguing but to aid if possible in dealing with questions to which my original memorandum had given rise."[66] Later that same day, Vinson responded with a five-page memo restating his own views and explaining why Frankfurter's proposal was not desirable. This exchange of memos, stemming from Frankfurter's need to tell Vinson how the Court ought to be run, was not an everyday occurrence, but it happened frequently enough to frustrate Vinson. It is striking that these justices wrangled before the members of the Court via memoranda when a simple face-to-face discussion might have resolved their differences. It is a classic situation of Frankfurter the professor instructing the chief justice and the latter taking exception to it.

Indicative of Frankfurter's constant needling of Vinson are the numerous occasions on which he wrote notes of apology to Vinson. In one handwritten note, he said, "Don't let me irritate you. I don't mean to. Sometimes I over tease."[67] On another occasion he wrote, "If I spoke unduly on what was an unemotional and technical matter, I'm sorry and apologize."[68] One other time he apologized for his "slipshod English" in saying to Vinson "'You don't know what will happen' when I meant 'nobody knows.'"[69]

Sometimes Frankfurter quibbled with Vinson over the conduct of the Saturday conferences in which the justices discussed pending cases. At the beginning of the October 1950 term, Frankfurter sent one of his familiar "Dear Brethren" memos to the Court members asking for their "indulgent consideration" of suggestions for improving the disposition of already argued cases. He contended that the Court did not take enough time before reaching a decision or before writing and circulating opinions. In typical fashion he stated that his suggestions did "not imply criticism of the present Court or of its doings,"[70] which it obviously did.

At the end of the term, he sent another memorandum to his colleagues reiterating his concerns. "It would greatly surprise me if all of us did not feel cases this Term had not been adequately informed." Specifically, he said, "there was no adequate opportunity to study a case" before the justices voted. "I do not recall," he said, "any instance—there may have been such—in which we postponed a vote on an argued case."[71] Frankfurter requested that the justices meet in conference at the beginning of the next term to discuss the problem. Vinson obliged by calling the conference that Frankfurter requested, but he also took issue with his facts. "My recollection is very definite that we have postponed many such cases. I will make a check in regard to this feature to see whose memory is correct on this point." Vinson said that his policy had always been to pass any argued case upon the request of a single justice. Vinson, the master of doing his homework, was so eager to prove Frankfurter wrong that he already had the data in hand before the ink had dried on his memorandum. Attached to it was a four-page list of all the cases from the 1946 term through the 1950 term in which votes were not cast at the first conference following argument.[72] The scheduled conference kept being postponed because individual justices were unable to attend. In the end, "the uniform lack of enthusiasm by his brethren finally made Frankfurter realize there was no point in insisting on a special conference."[73]

One of the most important powers of the chief justice is to assign the writing of opinions to individual justices. If the chief justice is in the majority, he may assign an opinion to himself or to another member of the majority. If he is in the minority, then he assigns the justice to write the dissent. The senior justice in the majority assigns the opinion for the majority opinion. The more often the chief justice is in the majority, the greater his control over opinion assignment. Vinson maintained a tight control over the assignment of opinions by bending himself to the majority. He was in the majority in over 86 percent of the cases. He averaged only nine dissents per term, far less than Stone's annual average of eighteen.[74]

How the chief justice assigns opinions has several ramifications for the Court. It can affect the value of the decision as a precedent, make the decision more acceptable to the public, help to hold the chief justice's majority together in a close vote, and influence dissenters to join the Court's opinion.[75] Law clerks Minow and Trienens offered some insight about the chief justice's approach to assigning opinions. They noted that he "went into that kind of calculation of analysis of how he could assign cases in a way to keep a majority if he was on the majority." By the time Trienens and Minow became clerks in 1951, Vinson was almost always in the majority, because the four Truman appointees usually voted together. This meant that his task was to assign opinions in a way to get the fifth justice, and he would discuss his strategies with his clerks. "For example he would say now if I assign Bill [Douglas] to this, then he'll write such and such an opinion and you might lose Jackson or Burton. So I think what I'll do is assign [it] to [Jackson] and Burton may be able to go along."[76]

Often a chief justice assigns important cases to himself. When he speaks for the Court, he lends the prestige of his office to the decision. Vinson had a reputation for assigning the "plum" cases to others. In fact, one of the more favorable assessments of Vinson's role as chief justice was that he was fair in assigning opinions. A frequent Vinson critic, Yale law professor John P. Frank, observed that Vinson did not play favorites when assigning opinions. There was "no hazing period of dull statutory and tax cases for the younger justices."[77] Vinson's law clerks agreed that "in the vast bulk of cases the Chief's sole motivation was the equitable sharing of the work load." In order to distribute opinion writing fairly, Vinson kept a large chart with nine columns, indicating which opinions had been assigned to each justice and when each opinion was handed down. Vinson had difficulty in maintaining an equitable distribution of cases because of the varying speed with which the respective justices completed opinions, and as a result the assignment of opinions on the Vinson Court favored those justices who wrote more expeditiously.[78] Delay in completing opinions increased in importance as the term drew to a close, because the Court could be forced to sit for extra weeks waiting for some justices to get caught up.

The problem of timeliness in completing opinions is illustrated by an incident that occurred at the end of Vinson's first term in the well-known *Securities & Exchange Commission* v. *Chenery Corporation* case.[79] The case had originally been assigned to Burton after oral arguments were heard in December 1946. By June, Burton had not produced a draft of the opinion, and with only a few weeks left in the term, Vinson reassigned the case to Murphy. Frankfurter, who wrote a dissenting opinion, commented in the first draft that he circulated to his colleagues about the lack of time available to him to write the dissent because of the delay in receiving the majority opinion. Rutledge counseled Frankfurter against making the issue of late opinions so public because it would disclose the "confidential routines of the Court." It would also have the effect, he said, or making it appear that Murphy, "who took over [the case] not by request but by the Chief's assignment" was the cause of the delay, and it would not "be quite fair to Harold."[80] For once, Frankfurter accepted the advice of a colleague. At the end of the Chenery opinion, handed down June 23, 1947, is a notation that Justices Frankfurter and Jackson dissent, "but there is not now opportunity for a response adequate to the issues raised by the Court's opinion." The two justices indicated that the detailed grounds for dissent would be filed in due course.[81] The actual dissent, written by Jackson and joined by Frankfurter, was filed October 6, 1947, and printed with the majority opinion.

Critics laid the blame for the Court's inability to get its work done on time squarely on the shoulders of the chief justice. Fred Rodell, like Frank a Yale law professor and no fan of Vinson's, wrote that "either he does not know or does not care how to make most of his colleagues get at their work and get it done. . . . He lets a backlog of opinions-to-be-written pile up for months, so that the Court's two or three most efficient work-horses get assigned far more than their share."[82] Rodell may have been trying to burnish the image of the Court's most efficient "work-horses," Black and Douglas, with whom he had an intimate relationship. Through their personal interactions with Rodell and in a steady stream of correspondence, the two justices shared with him their thoughts about the Court and its justices and about each other. Rodell's admiration for both justices was no secret.

The issue of getting opinions written in a timely fashion was a problem that plagued the circuit court when Vinson was a member. Chief Justice Groner, who presided over the D.C. circuit court, went to great lengths to prod his colleagues to be more productive. There is nothing in Vinson's extensive files on the Supreme Court, or those of the other justices, to suggest what specific measures if any he took to speed up opinion writing. However, a thorough analysis of the amount of time taken by Vinson Court justices to process opinion concluded that with the 1949 October term, when Vinson had the benefit of a solid majority, "he succeeded in his efforts to get opinions written more expeditiously." Cases were completed approximately one month faster during that time.[83]

One result of Vinson's efforts to share the responsibility for writing the plum opinions was that "sometimes a whole year might go by without his having reserved anything of real significance for himself." The drawback of this strategy for him was that "the number of Vinson's majority opinions of any profound consequences can be counted on one hand."[84] In fact, Vinson was frequently criticized in scholarly publications for his limited productivity in opinion writing. Rodell wrote that Vinson "sets his brethren the worst example of any chief justice in memory by making no effort to carry his fair share of the Court's real workload—that is, the writing of opinions."[85] In his seven years on the Court, Vinson averaged twelve majority opinions per year, which was actually very close to the Court's average of thirteen. In his first three terms, Vinson wrote thirty-eight majority opinions.[86] Only two justices wrote fewer opinions, Rutledge, who wrote thirty, and Burton, who wrote a paltry twenty-two. In contrast, Douglas wrote seventy-one and Black wrote sixty-nine. In his last four terms, when he was more often in the majority, Vinson wrote forty-one majority opinions; the range for the other justices was a low of thirty-seven for Burton and a high of fifty-seven for Black. Black and Douglas were less often in the majority during Vinson's last four terms.

Opinion writing was clearly not Vinson's favorite part of being a justice. Some have suggested that Vinson did all of his writing "with his hands in his pockets, outlining the general approach to his clerk[s] and then suggesting but few revisions in the draft."[87] Minow and Trienens confirm that his law clerks were given a great deal of responsibility in drafting opinions. "The fact that he wasn't going to sit down with a blank yellow pad and start from scratch was characteristic of an administrator," but Vinson would go over the opinions with his clerks, expressing his ideas before and after the drafting of the opinion. The final product clearly reflected Vinson's views.[88]

The most prolific opinion writers were the Court's most liberal members—Black and Douglas. Even though their views were significantly different from Vinson's, he often favored them in assigning cases because they were the most productive. This suggests that Vinson, unlike some chief justices, did not rely on ideology alone as the basis for assigning opinions. He was not, however, indifferent to the basis on which a case would be decided. Frankfurter recalled an incident in Vinson's first term when the chief justice was disturbed over an "outrageous" majority opinion in a labor case written by Reed, which "in effect took labor unions out of the Sherman law." When Frankfurter asked Vinson what he thought ought to be done about the opinion, he said, "By gad, something has to be written and I wondered whether you wouldn't want to write the dissent." Frankfurter agreed, and then Vinson asked him to write the majority opinion in another labor case. Vinson said it was a complicated case, and "since Stanley [Reed] had some doubts about it, I probably was more likely to persuade him in what I wrote than anybody else."[89]

There were some tensions in the relationship between the two Kentuckians Reed and Vinson. These surfaced early in Vinson's tenure as chief justice on the occasion of his first opinion, *United States* v. *Alcea Band of Tillamooks*.[90] Vinson was overly sensitive about the rather strong dissent written by Reed, and he asked Frankfurter "why Stanley would write a dissent in such strong terms." Frankfurter asked Reed about the reaction of the chief justice, and Reed replied: "He is very sensitive. You must remember he comes from the mountain region of Kentucky. It makes a difference whether you come from a community where you assume everyone is ready to help everyone else, or from the mountains where you are brought up to be suspicious and distrustful. And as I said some time ago, Fred Vinson has all those qualities."[91] Reed recalled that Vinson had once pressed him about why he opposed one of his opinions. Vinson asked, "Are you opposing me because I was appointed Chief Justice instead of you when you wanted to be Chief Justice?" Reed replied, "Of

President Truman participates in a four-way handshake with Vice President Alben Barkley, left, Vinson, and Stanley Reed on inauguration night, January 21, 1949, at a Kentucky society ball for Barkley. (AP/Wide World Photos.)

course I would have liked to have been appointed Chief Justice. All I looked at as to your choice over me was that I felt that my experience on the Court had been wider than yours."[92]

Vinson was very much concerned about the reputation of the court as an institution, and he tried in vain to bring more unity to the Court's decision making. Under his predecessor Stone, a large number of decisions were not unanimous, and many of those were decided by a slim majority of five to four. Things got progressively worse under Vinson. In his first term, 36 percent of the Court's opinions were unanimous; in his third term it was 26 percent. In his final term, there was a record low of only 19 percent agreement on cases,[93] bringing the Court the distinction of being "the most fragmented in history" up to that time.[94] Vinson felt that the reputation of the Court suffered as a result of the fragmented decisions, and because of this he wrote very few dissenting opinions. In seven years he voted in approximately 760 cases and dissented only 26 times. Of his 91 authored opinions on the Court, only 12 were dissents. Vinson hoped to use his powers of persuasion to reduce the number of dissents. He was not up to the task.

Not only was the Court plagued by closely decided opinions, but often those in the majority disagreed on the basis for the decision. An indication of Vinson's inability to reduce the divisiveness on the Court is the large number of concurring opinions filed by justices. Vinson's nemesis Frankfurter was notorious for writing separate opinions. Frankfurter resisted Vinson's efforts to reduce the number of multiple opinions. One of the first encounters Vinson had with Frankfurter over the matter was the case of Willie Francis, a black man who had been sentenced to death in Louisiana for murder.[95] The state's first attempt to electrocute Francis failed when the chair malfunctioned, and the state set a second date for his execution. Francis sought judicial relief, arguing that to put him through that experience again amounted to a denial of due process by subjecting him to double jeopardy and cruel and unusual punishment. Reed was assigned to write the majority opinion, which took the position that sending Francis to the electric chair a second time did not constitute cruel and unusual punishment. On the majority side, in addition to Reed, were Vinson, Frankfurter, Jackson, and Black. On the dissenting side were Murphy, Rutledge, Douglas, and Burton, who had been assigned to write the dissent. Several justices planned to write concurring opinions. After Vinson pleaded with his colleagues to eliminate multiple opinions, Jackson joined in Reed's majority opinion and Murphy and Rutledge withdrew their dissents and joined Burton. Frankfurter, however, insisted on filing his separate opinion, leaving the court without a majority opinion.[96]

Vinson and Frankfurter had divergent views about the value of multiple opinions. Vinson was mainly concerned with the resolution of a dispute, and he favored unanimous decisions "because they provided a better guide for judges and lawyers interpreting the law."[97] Frankfurter, in contrast, stressed the educational function of the Court, which he felt was well served by multiple opinions. One case in particular provoked a sharp exchange between the two justices. In *Kovacs* v. *Cooper*,[98] Vinson persuaded Reed to drop language in his majority opinion to which Frankfurter objected, and then he asked Frankfurter to drop his concurring opinion and join in the majority. He refused because he thought the case was "disposed of on the basis of what I deem a misleading formula. I see no intrinsic harm, and often much good, in multiple opinions." Frankfurter concluded that although there may be things that hurt the Court, the "writing of conscientious opinions courteously expressed, whether for the Court in concurrence, or in dissent, is not one of them. We are here largely for that purpose."[99]

In response, Vinson replied that of course there was a place for "conscientious opinions courteously expressed. . . . But that the Bench, the Bar, and the public generally have a right to be critical of the many opinions that sometimes appear in the disposition of cases. I know that the Bench and Bar have great difficulty, at times, in knowing what to do when we get through with some cases."[100] The next day, Frankfurter sent Vinson a long memo describing in detail the history of dissenting opinions under various chief justices as far back as Taney. He then aimed another dart at his chief justice. "If there is one thing that the history of this court proves, it is that very little attention should be paid to the ephemeral griping of an uninformed laity and too often of an unlearned or narrowly preoccupied bar."[101] Vinson's reply the next day was swift and caustic. He thanked Frankfurter for his "charming recitation" of the history of multiple opinions but said that Frankfurter "missed the boat" in terms of his attitude about multiple opinions. Obviously irritated by Frankfurter's dismissive attitude toward the bench and bar, Vinson vigorously asserted that "any judge worth his salt" should be influenced only by "a conscientious resolution" of the issues before him. "I do believe," he said, "that our function is to decide the issues which are presented in such a way that judges and the Bar may know how to conduct themselves in the future." Then, his anger clearly showing, Vinson concluded, "Thanks for the lecture, even though you misjudged my position and set up a straw man to attack. I would have preferred to have it face-to-face. It started in that manner—it will only be continued in that way."[102] Determined to have the last shot, Frankfurter wrote, "I'm sorry to miss a boat—particularly if it is a good one. I hope there's another one—even if I catch it tardily. Nobody is more ready . . . for face-to-face talks than I."[103] There is no record of the two justices having a face-to-face talk over this issue, but two things are clear. Frankfurter not only ignored Vinson's pleas to drop his separate concurrence in the *Kovacs* case; he also continued until Vinson's death to file numerous concurring and dissenting opinions.

Although the reputation of the Court may have been further damaged by the declining number of unanimous decisions and the large number of multiple opinions, the aspect of the Court's business that generated the greatest criticism among judicial scholars was its low productivity. Indeed, the number of cases decided by the Court declined significantly under Vinson. In his first term the Court accepted 142 cases for review. In the prewar years the Court had accepted more than 200 cases for review.[104] The most significant change in the caseload began in 1949 when Truman's last two appointees, Minton and Clark, joined the Court. In that year the number of cases dropped to 94. In the two subsequent years, it went even lower—88 in 1950 and 89 in the 1951 term. In Vinson's last year on the Court, when many cases of pressing national importance were presented to the Court, the number of cases increased to 104.[105]

The Court controls the number of cases it hears each year through its power to grant or deny petitions for certiorari, the procedure by which litigants can petition the Court for a review in cases where the Court is not mandated by statute to hear a case. By the time Vinson became chief justice, most of the cases reached the Court through the route of certiorari rather than a right to appeal. This was largely the result of a law passed in Congress in 1925, which limited the number of mandatory cases the Court must accept on appeal, thus allowing the Court greater discretion over the cases it would hear each term. Those justices who were apostles of judicial restraint were less inclined to grant review of cases. With the arrival of Minton and Clark, there was a solid block of seven justices, the four Truman appointees plus Frankfurter, Reed, and Jackson, who generally wanted a limited role for the Court and thus were more likely to deny certiorari petitions. As long as they stuck together, the number of cases heard would be limited. This perturbed liberal judicial scholars, such as Frank, who favored a more active Court.

By their estimates, the Court should have been accepting approximately 60 more cases per year for consideration,[106] and they often listed cases that they thought should have been heard. Vinson's success in limiting the Court's caseload can be counted as a measure of his success at task leadership, but those who wanted a more activist Court were not willing to give him that much credit.

Vinson firmly believed that the Court's caseload should be more limited. He thought the Supreme Court should not function as a "mere revisory body to correct errors of lower courts, but as a tribunal whose judgments should be reserved for cases of high national importance or clear conflict below."[107] Vinson had both personal and policy reasons for his view. His personal considerations stemmed from his belief that the pressure of the Court's work was responsible for Justice Rutledge's untimely death. In terms of policy, he would sometimes vote to deny certiorari on grounds of practical policy, "believing that conflicting opinions then in prospect would unsettle more law than they could settle." One of his law clerks put it best: "In general, the Chief's philosophy regarding applications for review was that he couldn't run the world from his chair—a philosophy that made him much less anxious than some other justices to grant review of cases involving such matters as the administration by the states of their criminal processes" (29).

Less charitable critics attributed the Court's decreased productivity to "laziness," but others offered different explanations. One was that there was a decline in the number of cases worthy of consideration.[108] Another was that the increasing number of dissenting opinions "set some limit to the number of cases which can be handled by the Court in its present temper; it is the most industrious members who are at the same time the most constant dissenters. In the 1950 term, when the Court had only 98 majority opinions, it also handed down 23 concurring opinions and a whopping 60 dissenting opinions.[109] A chief justice is frequently described as "the first among equals." He is equal to his colleagues in that each has only one vote in a given case. Yet he is also the person who is assigned the responsibility for providing leadership to the Court. When Truman chose Fred Vinson to be chief justice, he was counting on his leadership qualities, demonstrated successfully in a series of positions, to provide much-needed unity to a Court torn by personal bickering and sharp philosophical disagreements. Although the personal animosities did not disappear, they were hidden behind the "purple curtain" that shields the Court from public scrutiny. Vinson tried his best to reduce the excessive dissents and concurrences, but he was unable to get his colleagues to accept the responsibility for acting as an institution rather than a group of individuals. In his view, the Court was better served by unanimous decisions that would enhance the certainty of the law and the ability of judges and lawyers to understand and implement them.

Writing shortly after Vinson's death, one of his sharpest critics, John Frank, observed that Vinson's main shortcoming was not in his failure to stifle dissent, for "the will of one man, Chief Justice or not, is not enough to have any great effect as to dissents." To Frank, the more telling indication of Vinson's weakness as a leader was that "the bulk of his own outstanding opinions were for a less than unanimous Court, and in a surprisingly large number, he did not unequivocally speak for five Justices."[110] Frank, of course, did not write from an unbiased view. He had previously served as a law clerk to Black and had written a highly favorable biography of the justice. They remained close friends until Black's death.

Although there may be merit in the arguments of Frank and other critics, they were remiss in failing to recognize the impossible odds Vinson faced. As chief justice, his only real power was persuasion, and the people he had to persuade, especially Frankfurter, had already served on the court eight to ten years prior to his appointment and already had established national reputations. To men like Frankfurter, Vinson was a "Johnny-come-lately and an upstart."[111] Frankfurter's insistence on writing numerous dissenting and concurring opinions made it difficult if not impossible for Vinson to unify the Court. There is the possibility that no one could have succeeded any better than Vinson. Further, any assessment of Vinson must account for the social and political tensions of the time during which he served on the Court as well as his brief tenure. With more time, Vinson might have developed into a stronger leader of the Court. As Steamer noted, none of the chief justices deemed to be among the best ever served such a brief term.

Vinson's main difficulties stemmed from the fact that his colleagues recognized him as the "first among equals" in name only. Many of them, especially the Roosevelt appointees, did not consider him to be equal in intellect and ability. The real blame may lie with Truman. As one observer noted, "If the justices do not have the desirable sense of acting as an institution . . . it is not necessarily the fault of any one or more justices. . . . It is perhaps because to the appointing power it has been irrelevant that the incumbent justices may not respect the capacity of the new appointee."[112] Truman was interested in appointees who thought like he did, whose political instincts and abilities he trusted. These are the traits of a politician, and although a chief justice must possess political skills, these alone are not sufficient for effective leadership of the Court. In Truman's view, Vinson lived up to his expectations of what a chief justice should be. Some scholars of the Court, however, rated him a failure. Perhaps Vinson's chief shortcoming was his inability to move far enough out of Truman's orbit to act independently of the president, to define for himself what a chief justice should be.

CHAPTER 8

The Chief Justice, the President, and the Politics of Economic Stabilization

Fred Vinson, puffing on his pipe, leaned forward and spoke in confidential tones to Harry Truman. "What would the people of the United States of America think if they knew that the President and the Chief Justice were playing poker with five aces?" The two men were playing poker at Key West at the time, when they discovered that two decks of cards had inadvertently been mixed together. The American people might have been less concerned about the makeup of the card deck than the fact that the president and the chief justice maintained such intimate contact. Vinson's occasional visits to Key West with the president were not kept secret, but the full extent of his involvement with Truman during his seven years as chief justice was not widely known, much less publicized.[1]

The closeness of these two leaders raised questions about how Vinson voted on some important cases before the Court. Two in particular, *United Mine Workers* v. *United States* (1947) and *Youngstown Sheet and Tube* v. *Sawyer* (1952), demonstrated that Vinson may have been acting more as a friend of the president than as an impartial jurist. Both of these cases pertained to strikes that threatened the president's postwar economic stabilization program and the government's subsequent seizure of the industry assets in order to avert the strikes.[2] In fact, on virtually every issue of importance that came before the Supreme Court, Vinson did not fail to serve Truman's interests.

Truman and Vinson had a genuine affection for each other, and their friendship, which began in earnest shortly after Truman assumed the presidency, strengthened over time. Before appointing Vinson to be chief justice, Truman included Vinson in almost every conference because he "valued his judgment and advice highly."[3] Truman was particularly impressed with Vinson's ability as a peacemaker, and Clark Clifford, Truman's legal counsel, who also served as a confidant of the president, said, "Once the President heard about the problems in the Court, I rather doubt he seriously considered anyone else."[4] No one may have been more surprised about the choice than Vinson himself. In early May he told Tom Corcoran, a former Roosevelt adviser, that no one had spoken to him about going on the Court, and furthermore he was not "too interested."[5] However, on June 5, the day before Truman announced that Vinson was his choice for chief justice, he was at the White House for a lengthy visit with the president, prompting speculation that he was being considered for the Court appointment. Pressed by reporters as he left the White House, Vinson "chuckled" when asked if the Court appointment was the subject of the conference, but he would not deny that it had been discussed. Truman did not officially tell Vinson he wanted him to serve as chief justice until the following day at a White House reception. There was little time for him to decline; the president sent his nomination to the Senate in less than an hour.

After Vinson joined the Court, he and Truman continued to see each other socially, and Vinson also continued to advise Truman about various matters of politics and state. By the standards of today, such a relationship between a president and the chief justice would be highly suspect, but in fact there was ample precedent of Supreme Court justices serving the interests and needs of presidents. Bruce A. Murphy, who wrote about the secret political activities of Justices Louis D. Brandeis and Vinson's antagonist Felix Frankfurter, says, "The whole notion of a judiciary totally secluded from politics appears to be more myth than history."[6] He found that two-thirds of the Court's justices had engaged in some form of extrajudicial political behavior, either on an informal basis or in response to official government requests. These activities included "advising presidents, suggesting legislation to Congress, proposing executive and judicial appointments, participating in informal diplomatic missions, writing articles, delivering speeches, and sitting on governmental tribunals." Murphy documented numerous ways in which Frankfurter, who was publicly outspoken about the impropriety of such extrajudicial involvement, was actively involved in political activities while on the bench.

Part of the attraction between Truman and Vinson was the similarity in personality and background. They were both "border-state, middle-of-the roaders, and practical New Dealers."[7] They could also be quite earthy in their language, a trait that was in evidence at regular poker games. Sometime these were held at Blair House, the Trumans' temporary residence while the White House was under repair, but often the poker games took place on the *Williamsburg,* the presidential yacht. Justice Tom Clark, who was also a regular at these events, said he and Vinson would leave the Court after the Saturday conference and then fly down to Norfolk to catch the launch, which took them to the boat. They would stay until late Sunday evening. According to Rear Adm. Donald MacDonald, commander of the *Williamsburg,* there were two groups of people who played poker with Truman. One group played a game in which no one could lose more than a certain amount of money, but others played for unlimited stakes. Vinson, he said, was in the "expensive group."[8]

Clifford told of one particularly tense game of poker on the occasion of Vinson's birthday in January. The birthday party was an annual event arranged by Clifford at the request of the president and usually held at Clifford's home in Chevy Chase, Maryland. In a game of high-low, with most of the cards showing on the table, the pot had grown to about three thousand dollars. Vinson had a good hand and stood to win at least half of the pot if he got any card from a jack down. He turned to Truman, who was dealing, and said, "OK, Mr. President, hit me." The president flipped over a queen of spades. Vinson looked straight at the president and without blinking said, "You son of a bitch." There was a moment of stunned silence, because even in the informal setting of the poker table, everyone still called Truman Mr. President. Vinson stammered an apology, "Oh, Mr. President, Mr. President." Clifford recalled, "Never did President Truman, or the rest of us laugh harder than we did at that moment."[9]

Fred and Roberta Vinson occasionally socialized with Harry and Bess Truman. In some respects they were practically "family." Mrs. Truman and their daughter Margaret called the chief justice "Poppa Vin."[10] Truman even named a version of stud poker that he particularly liked "Papa Vinson,"[11] although within the family he referred to Vinson as "the Big Judge."[12] Reportedly, Roberta Vinson was one of the few women—if not the only woman—besides Mrs. Truman and Margaret who ever visited the president at Key West.[13] On occasion, the Vinsons hosted the Trumans at a dinner, either at a restaurant like the F Street Club or at their Wardman Park Hotel apartment.

Vinson's relationship with Truman went well beyond socializing.

He was one of Truman's closest confidants, and the president constantly sought his advice and counsel on many matters. They reportedly conversed late at night, "after the last caller has left the White House and after the President himself is presumably tucked away for the night."[14] Vinson was also a participant in some key meetings regarding partisan political decisions. In 1948 Vinson participated in discussions about whom Truman should select for his vice-presidential running mate. As an indication of how different things were then, Clifford said that at the time he "saw nothing improper in Vinson's presence; the meeting had no bearing on any matters pending before the High Court, and Vinson was a close friend whose views President Truman respected." Clifford also noted that there were precedents for such close relationships between presidents and members of the Supreme Court, including Herbert Hoover and Harlan Fiske Stone, and Franklin Roosevelt and Felix Frankfurter.[15] Clifford later changed his mind on the appropriateness of Supreme Court justices serving as presidential confidants. "There is simply too much at stake to permit the risks and temptations that can arise in such circumstances. Discussions with the President inevitably involve the Justice, at least subconsciously, in the President's political fate— and this could affect his opinions on a variety of issues before the Court" (216).

In 1948 Vinson became entangled in one of Truman's campaign initiatives—the incident that has become known as the Moscow Mission or the Vinson Mission. Vinson had reluctantly agreed to the president's request that he meet with Soviet premier Joseph Stalin, ostensibly to promote a peaceful understanding between the two nations. The original purpose of the proposed mission, however, was to boost public support for the president, who lagged far behind his Republican opponent for the presidency in public opinion polls. To accept the president's request to undertake the mission meant he would have to resign his position as chief justice, for Vinson was on record as strongly opposing extrajudicial assignments for Court justices. He reminded the president of that when Truman proposed the plan. He said, "Justices should confine themselves to their Court duties and stay out of all side activities."[16] Fortunately for the president, the chief justice, and the country, Secretary of State George C. Marshall reacted so strongly against the plan that Truman canceled the proposed trip, but he never forgot the sacrifice that Vinson was willing to make for him. In 1950, in a letter to Bess, Truman recalled Vinson's loyalty during the 1948 campaign. "He didn't want to go," Truman reminded her, "but he said,

'I'm your man to do what you want me to do for the welfare of the country.' How many Congressman, Senators, even cabinet secretaries would have said that?"[17]

Marshall was so upset about not being consulted about the Vinson mission that he threatened to resign. Questions about his intention to resign were heightened when he returned to the United States in November 1948 for the removal of a diseased kidney. This prompted speculation about who his successor might be. Vinson's name surfaced as a possible candidate. Marshall did resign in 1949, the day after Truman's inauguration, and was replaced by Dean Acheson. Within a year, Acheson was under heavy fire from Republicans in Congress for a number of reasons. One was his strong defense of Alger Hiss, a former midlevel State Department employee who had been accused of spying by Whittaker Chambers, a former editor at *Time* and an admitted Communist. Hiss could not be tried for espionage because the ten-year statute of limitations had run out. However, he was tried twice for perjury. His first trial ended in a hung jury, but on January 22, 1950, he was convicted on evidence produced by Chambers. Following his conviction, Acheson declared, "I will not turn my back on Hiss." The Hiss affair was coupled with charges from Wisconsin senator Joseph McCarthy that the State Department was heavily infiltrated by Communists. Adding oil to these troubled waters for Acheson was the fall of mainland China to the Communists, an event hung squarely on Acheson's shoulders.

Amid this turmoil, Truman was reported to be considering appointing Vinson as secretary of state and nominating Acheson as chief justice. Speculation about Vinson's appointment increased on March 19, 1950, when Vinson visited Truman, who was vacationing at Key West. The next day the president scotched the rumors with a public denial issued by his press secretary, who said the president believed Acheson was doing his work "admirably." The rumored swap between Vinson and Acheson was described as "completely erroneous" and the chief justice's visit was labeled "purely social."[18]

Despite the president's denials, speculation continued about Vinson's being named secretary of state. Fueling the fires this time were strong demands from Republicans in Congress. On December 12, 1950, Republican senators had scheduled a vote on whether to issue a formal demand to Truman that Acheson be relieved as secretary of state. The most prominent candidate to replace Acheson was Vinson. He was seen as a person "with whom Congress will cooperate to the limit permitted by normal partisanship and divisions over foreign policy in both parties."[19] The idea of Vinson's being named to head the State Department invoked some criticism by those who thought that members of the Court should not be transferred to the arena of politics. Nonetheless, it was agreed that "his appointment would be highly popular at the Capitol, and that the present ill-feeling would vanish at the sight of his name on the Presidential commission." In response to the press coverage, on December 13, Vinson assured his colleagues on the Court that he had "never been asked about becoming Secretary of State and that he did not want to do so." He did, however, tell his colleagues that he could not predict what might happen in "actual circumstances." Burton reminded him that Chief Justice Hughes resigned to run for the presidency. Vinson said he "thought resigning to become Secretary of State might be better understood and accepted than doing it to run for the presidency."[20]

The presidency was exactly what Truman had in mind for Vinson. Truman said in his memoirs that he had decided on his inauguration day in 1949 that he would not run for the presidency again. He felt burdened by the "grave problems that confronted the nation."[21] Margaret Truman said that her father began the search for his successor as early as 1949, when he approached Vinson with the possibility of his seeking the presidency. She reported that her father first raised the question with Vinson in a March 1949 visit to Key West and that he was noncommittal.

According to Truman, he first approached Vinson with the idea in the summer of 1950 but was turned down. Truman persisted. He approached Vinson again on October 11, 1951, at a meeting at Blair House, and again in November 1951, when Truman invited the Vinsons to join him and his family at Key West for Thanksgiving. In private conversations the president vigorously urged Vinson to run. Vinson told the president he wanted to speak to his wife about it. After discussing the matter with Roberta, and after further consideration, Vinson told Truman "he felt honestly and in his heart that he did not think he should use the Court as a steppingstone to the presidency." Truman reminded him that Chief Justice Charles Evans Hughes had done so, and in his own opinion there was nothing wrong with his becoming a candidate (490).

Truman made one last try, only this time he tried to persuade Mrs. Vinson that her husband should run. Vinson did not give Truman a definite answer before he left Key West. Charles Murphy, who was special counsel to the president at the time, grew impatient with Vinson's delay in answering the president and took it on himself to visit him at the Wardman Park to ask when he was going to answer and what he was going to do. Vinson asked, "Charlie, did the President send you to ask

Vinson and his wife Roberta at Key West, Florida. (Photo archives FDR Library.)

me this question?" Murphy said he had not. Vinson replied, "Well, I'm not going to tell you. I'll tell him."[22]

When Vinson did tell him, sometime in December or January, the answer was no. The reason he gave this time was his "physical condition."[23] Vinson was not the healthiest of men. He was overweight, a chain smoker, with dark circles under his eyes and a pasty complexion. Although at one time he had been a good athlete, he apparently did very little exercise. It is not clear that Vinson was aware of any serious health problems in late 1951, when he gave Truman his final answer. As it turned out, he had less than two years to live. Aside from health considerations, there may have been something more significant that caused him to turn down a request from his close friend—his concern about the potential damage to the Court's reputation. He had expressed reservations in 1950 about a chief justice moving into a political position such as secretary of state, and he believed that the public would be even less accepting for a chief justice to use the Court as a springboard to the presidency.

Although Vinson was unwilling to pursue the presidency, he was not reluctant to participate in party politics behind closed doors. On February 18, 1952, Truman invited six of his closest advisers, including

Vinson and Truman relax on the lawn of the Winter White House in Key West on March 23, 1950. (AP/Wide World Photos.)

Vinson and Clifford, to a highly secret dinner meeting to discuss the presidential campaign. The main topic was who should be the party nominee for president. According to notes kept by the president, Vinson turned the tables on Truman, saying he did not see how Truman could refuse another term. Others agreed, but other names, including Adlai Stevenson and others, were discussed. No agreement was reached.[24] Vinson attended another "off-the-record" meeting on February 25, 1952, with members of Truman's senior staff. They reached a nearly unanimous decision that the President should not run. Following that meeting, Vinson exclaimed, "That was the frankest meeting I ever heard in my life."[25] He was amazed that so many people close to Truman advised him against running.

The depth of Truman's and Vinson's affection for each other was cemented by a deep sense of duty and obligation to each other. Truman was profoundly grateful for Vinson's strong sense of loyalty. He wrote in his memoirs that Vinson had a "sense of personal and political loyalty seldom found among the top men in Washington [where] too often loyalties are breached for political advantage."[26] This loyalty was tremendously important to Truman when he was buffeted by the storms of the presidency. In 1950, when Truman was under heavy fire from the media and members of Congress over the loss of China and charges of Communist infiltration of the State Department and other government agencies, he wrote his wife a letter from Key West, where he had gone at her urging to regain his equilibrium. He despaired because "everybody shoots at me . . . and the general trend of the pieces is that I am a very small man in a very large place." In this letter he mentioned a visit from Vinson and added, "The Chief Justice is one man in high place who still believes in me, trusts me and supports me."[27]

One of his first opportunities to support the president came in a case in which the pot was already boiling when Truman nominated Vinson to be chief justice and which reached a full head of steam shortly after Vinson took the center chair on the Court. As the Supreme Court was making a transition under a new chief justice, the nation was also making a transition from a wartime to a domestic economy. Vinson had helped to facilitate that transition in his post at the Office of War Mobilization and Reconversion and after that as secretary of the Treasury, his last two positions before becoming chief justice. In this shifting, highly volatile economy, industrial labor disputes began to take center stage. Pent-up labor demands, most of which had patriotically been suppressed during the war, began to be unleashed. Perhaps the most prolonged and devastating dispute was between coal miners, led by the fiery John L. Lewis, and the soft coal mine operators. The ensuing battle brought the feisty Truman toe-to-toe with the pugnacious Lewis. It ultimately landed on the doorstep of the Supreme Court, with a brand-new chief justice, Harry Truman's close friend and adviser, Fred Vinson. The timing proved to be Truman's good luck and Lewis's misfortune.

Although increased wages were part of the demands made by the coal miners, their primary concerns were the establishment of a health and welfare fund, supported by royalties from the coal companies, and more rigorous mine safety enforcement. Talks between the miners and the operators, which had begun in early March 1946, failed to bring any agreement. Lewis threatened a strike on April 1 if the miners' demands were not met. In order to avert a strike, which he believed would have devastating effects on his reconversion and stabilization programs, Truman became personally involved in trying to resolve the differences between the operators and the miners. These efforts failed to bring agreement on the terms of a contract, and the miners struck on April 1, 1946.

As the strike dragged on, the nation reeled under its effects. Industries were shut down, energy consumption was drastically curtailed, and financial losses resulted. Truman continued to intervene in the dispute. He met with Lewis and spokesmen for the coal operators six times in the White House between March and May,[28] but he could not produce an acceptable solution. After a month, the strike was being called a "national disaster." Truman released a report from the War Mobilization and Reconversion office that manufacturing plants all over the nation were shutting down.[29] As the strike proceeded, Truman assumed an even more visible role in trying to resolve the dispute. On May 10 Truman denounced the strike as "nearing the status of a strike against the government" and predicted government seizure of the mines if necessary.[30] A day later, the miners and the operators agreed "in principle" to a plan endorsed by Truman that included a provision for the controversial welfare fund, and Lewis announced a two-week truce in the strike.

Agreement on the proposed plan broke down as quickly as it had materialized, and on May 17 both the operators and the miners rejected Truman's request that they submit their differences to arbitration. Fearing that the strike would resume at the end of the two-week truce, on May 21, Truman, acting under the authority of the War Labor Disputes Act, also known as the Smith-Connally Act, ordered his secretary of the interior, Julius A. Krug, to seize the nation's soft coal mines and operate them under government control. The War Labor Disputes Act authorized seizure and operation of facilities necessary for the war effort. Even though the war was over, the act remained in effect for six months following the end of hostilities, and the U.S. government had not officially declared an end to hostilities. Subsequent to seizure, Krug worked with the miners and the operators to achieve agreement on the terms and conditions of employment during the period of government control. Truman also kept his hand in the negotiations, including face-to-face meetings with Lewis, and on May 29 what became known as the Krug-Lewis agreement was reached.[31]

A period of relative calm prevailed over the summer while Krug, Lewis, and the operators negotiated the terms for a contract with the unions, which would return the mines to the owners. On September 13 the negotiations broke down, and on October 21 Lewis fired the next salvo in the battle. He charged that the government had breached the contract by failing to carry out some of its terms. Lewis demanded a conference with Krug and administration officials on November 1 to discuss reopening the contract with the government but was turned down. He then sent a telegram to Krug stating that failure to honor the meeting would void the Krug-Lewis agreement and obliquely threatened a strike of four hundred thousand soft coal miners on November 1, four days before the congressional elections. Although Truman remained silent on the developments, the controversy, coming just before the congressional elections, was seen as an embarrassment to the president. Truman later said that Lewis contributed to the Democrats' losing control of Congress that year.[32]

Lewis claimed that under the Krug-Lewis agreement, either party could give a ten-day notice of a desire to renegotiate the terms of the agreement and the other party was obligated to attend. Although the government disputed Lewis's interpretation of the agreement, it did eventually enter into negotiations before the November 1 strike deadline. Despite Truman's active involvement, the talks went nowhere. On November 15 Lewis announced that the union would terminate the agreement on November 20 and that a strike would ensue. The government's response was that the miners had no power to unilaterally terminate the agreement and that under the War Labor Disputes Act it would seek an injunction to prevent the miners from striking. Failure to comply with such an action would carry fines of five thousand dollars per day and a possible prison sentence of one year.

Truman lost patience with the defiant Lewis, and he ordered Attorney General Clark to "fight John L. Lewis on all fronts."[33] The next day, November 18, Clark, citing the "great loss and irreparable damage to the country" that would result from a work stoppage, sought a declaratory judgment from the federal district court, stipulating that the miners had no power to unilaterally terminate their agreement with the government. The government also requested a temporary restraining order against the union. U.S. District Court Judge for the District of Columbia T. Alan Goldsborough issued a temporary order restraining the union from carrying out the strike. Close associates of Truman confirmed to the media that Truman "had decided the time had come for a final showdown with the mine union chief who several times had forced the government into its [stand.]"[34]

Lewis and the miners defied the district court order and began a strike on November 21. Truman, who had given an order "to fight Lewis to a finish," instructed the Justice Department to press for a contempt citation against the union. In short order Judge Goldsborough ordered Lewis to appear in court for contempt hearings. He refused on the grounds that the court had no jurisdiction to issue the order because the Norris-LaGuardia Act of 1932 prohibited courts from issuing injunctions in labor disputes. Judge Goldsborough rejected the argument that the Norris-LaGuardia Act applied to the miners' dispute with the government and held both Lewis and the union in civil and criminal contempt. Lewis was fined ten thousand dollars and the union was fined $3.5 million. The judge also made the temporary restraining order against the strikers permanent.

On December 5 the United Mine Workers (UMW) filed an appeal of the contempt convictions and the $3.5 million fines with the District of Columbia circuit court, Vinson's old court. The following day, the government filed a petition of certiorari in both cases directly with the Supreme Court. Now, for the first time, Vinson entered the picture. On December 7 the lawyers for the coal miners met with Vinson on the government's petition for certiorari, and immediately after the meeting, Lewis unexpectedly called for an immediate end to the strike and ordered workers to continue working until April 1, 1947. The headlines of the *New York Times* boldly declared, "Lewis Ends Strike, Mines Open Tomorrow; Surrenders after Lawyers See Vinson."[35]

Drew Pearson, syndicated Washington columnist and a close friend of Vinson, reported in his weekly broadcast on December 8 that one of the factors that caused Lewis to back down occurred on Saturday, December 7, when "Chief Justice Vinson held a very significant meeting with President Truman in which he expressed his private opinion that the Supreme Court would uphold the lower court injunction against the United Mine Workers . . . and afterward word of the Chief Justice's view was quietly transmitted to the United Mine Workers."[36] In his broadcast the following week, Pearson corrected the impression "that Chief Justice Vinson took any sides in the coal strike case or conferred with anyone in such a way as to indicate he might decide against the miners." He said that the chief justice, "for whom I have the highest regard, took absolutely no sides, except to express himself very forcefully that the Supreme Court owed it to the nation to try this injunction case in a hurry."[37]

The following day, in his weekly column, "The Washington Merry-Go-Round," Pearson reported what happened in the Supreme Court's chambers on December 7, when the lawyers for the miners and the government met with Vinson for the purpose of determining whether the Supreme Court would take immediate jurisdiction in the dispute and to set a time for argument. The miners asked for a twenty-five-day delay to prepare their case. Attorney General Clark asked that the date for arguments be set on December 16. "Would you like to know what I think?" asked Vinson. "I had in mind setting argument for next Thursday [December 12]." His words, said Pearson, "fell like a bombshell" on the lawyers for the miners. This left them with only five days to prepare their case. Two hours later, John L. Lewis called off the strike.[38] Although there is no independent source to verify what Pearson reported, his closeness to both Truman and Vinson lends credibility to his version of what happened.

Vinson's declaration that the case would be argued on December 12 was just a bluff. Shortly after the strike had ended, Vinson asked to meet again with the attorneys for the mine workers and the government. The chief justice asked both sides their views as to when the case should be reargued. The mine workers argued for a date in February or March. Attorney General Clark wanted it set in January. On December 9, the Court announced that it would take the coal case on direct appeal, but it set oral arguments for January 14, 1947, a month later than the date Vinson had originally proposed.[39]

Frank Murphy's conference notes reveal that the Supreme Court began discussing whether to grant the petitions for certiorari on December 6, the day before Lewis announced the end of the strike. On that day, which was a day before Vinson met with Clark and the lawyers for the miners, the Court agreed to grant the petitions; however, after learning that the strike had been halted, the justices decided to reconsider. Only Vinson, Reed, and Burton still favored granting petitions. Black, Douglas, and Frankfurter voted to deny certiorari. Murphy, Jackson, and Rutledge thought further discussion was needed before making a decision. Yet, two days later, on December 9, seven justices voted to hear the case. Only Black and Douglas opposed.[40]

The following week, the UMW won an important concession from the Supreme Court when it agreed to broaden the appeal to allow the

Court to consider the question of whether the Norris-LaGuardia anti-injunction act applied to the situation with the miners under their agreement with the government. The *New York Times* predicted, "The legal battle before the Supreme Court may well be the 'battle of the century' in so far as some aspects of the Norris-LaGuardia Act and, perhaps, the Constitution are concerned."[41]

Oral arguments in the case were held on January 14, 1947, before a packed courtroom, and the questions by the justices were so exhaustive that the hearing lasted almost four hours. The most active questioners were Frankfurter, Jackson, Black, and Douglas. Vinson, who was still fairly green in his role as chief justice, asked very few questions. Vinson directed a question at Joseph A. Padaway, counsel for the UMW, about whether the union had challenged the government's seizure of the mines the previous May. Padaway said that it was not necessary to do so.[42]

The justices met in conference on January 20 to discuss the Lewis case. Douglas's copious notes on the conference revealed the sharp differences among the justices on the central issues before the Court.[43] The case boiled down to four questions: whether the Norris-LaGuardia Act was applicable to the government; whether the United Mine Workers could be held in contempt even if the Norris-LaGuardia Act prohibited the issuance of a restraining order; whether the trial judge had improperly commingled civil and criminal intent; and whether the fines imposed by the district court were excessive. Vinson was able to muster a decisive majority only on the question of whether the miners were obligated to obey the court order even if they thought it was illegal and thus should be subject to fines. On the crucial question of whether the Norris-LaGuardia Act pertained to the government, the Court was split five to four.

Vinson was never in doubt about any of the issues. He supported the government in every one of them. His colleagues recalled him railing against Lewis, saying he was "getting too big for his britches."[44] Vinson at one time had an amicable relationship with Lewis, owing especially to the "great fight" he made in behalf of the enactment of the Guffey-Vinson Coal Stabilization Act in 1936. Lewis called Vinson "one of the loyal champions" of the mining industry.[45]

What had set Vinson against the miners in the decade since he had received Lewis's laudatory remarks? Two things stand out. One was Lewis's bitter attack on Truman. In October, at the annual meeting of the UMW, Lewis had denounced Truman as "a man totally unfitted for his position. His principles are elastic, and he is careless with the truth.

. . . He is a malignant scheming sort of an individual who is dangerous not only to the United Mine Workers, but dangerous to the United States of America."[46] These were hard words to swallow for a person as close to Truman as Vinson was. A second factor was Vinson's strong suspicion of individuals or groups that posed threats to the nation's well-being. The pugnacious Lewis had earned his threatening reputation when he called a strike of the miners during World War II, and he sharpened that image with this devastating strike. To Vinson, the rule of law was at stake, and the only way to preserve it was to support the government. He worked to achieve support among his fellow justices for that purpose. He had his work cut out for him.

As things stood coming out of conference, there was no solid majority on any single point, an indication that the internal divisions within the Court had not subsided much in Vinson's brief tenure as chief justice. In the ensuing weeks, various justices worked to sway others to their point of view. On the day following the conference, Frankfurter, hoping to shore up Robert Jackson's tentative view in conference that the Norris-LaGuardia Act did apply to the government, wrote his colleague a lengthy discourse on the history of the Norris-LaGuardia Act. Persuaded by Frankfurter's argument, Jackson sided against the government on that issue. Black, who had been somewhat tentative in conference, finally supported Vinson. None of the other justices changed their positions on the issue of applicability of the Norris-LaGuardia Act, leaving a bare five-to-four majority in favor of the government's position.

The remaining negotiations among the justices were over the contempt charges and the appropriateness of the fines. First was the issue of whether the defendants were required to obey an injunction that they thought was invalid. Fowler V. Harper, Rutledge's biographer, maintained that the Court could have avoided the question but that Vinson was motivated by other considerations. Justices Black and Douglas thought it was unnecessary to decide on this question once the validity of the injunction had been established. Douglas expressed concern to Vinson about the danger of making the obligation to obey so broad that it might undermine the effectiveness of Norris-LaGuardia.[47] The chief justice, however, because of the importance and the highly controversial nature of the case, "wanted to bolster the decision with as many affirmative votes as possible." Had the Court not taken up the question of obligation to obey the court order, the Supreme Court's opinion would have hung on a narrow majority of five to four.[48] This, of course, was the most famous point established by the decision.

Frankfurter and Jackson had already indicated their agreement that the defendants were bound to obey the court's order whether it was valid or not. This gave Vinson a seven-to-two majority on the necessity of compliance and added a more positive note to the Court's ruling. This aspect of the case was given more emphasis in media reports the day after the opinion of the Court was delivered. Vinson must have gotten great satisfaction out of the headlines in the *New York Times:* "Lewis Conviction Upheld by Highest Court, 7-2."[49]

The most extensive negotiations among the justices were over issues about the fines and whether they were excessive. There was the question of whether Goldsborough erred in commingling the convictions and fines for civil contempt, which was for the refusal to comply with the initial order, with the convictions and fines for criminal contempt, which were levied for punishment. Assessing fines for civil contempt required different procedures and considerations than assessing fines for criminal contempt. Although Vinson himself thought that both fines were appropriate, he was willing to modify his position in order to get more majority support. The ill will toward Lewis was such that eventually seven justices were willing to uphold the contempt citation and the ten-thousand-dollar fine against him, which meant that Truman's nemesis would not be let off the hook. Now Vinson's challenge was to gain as much consensus as possible about the fines for the union. The initial draft of the opinion that Vinson circulated to the Court revealed how far he was willing to go to get agreement. It contained a statement that a majority of the Court "concluded that the fine against the union was unwarranted and proposed remanding the case to the district court."[50] The response to this draft revealed how difficult creating a majority opinion would be.

Frankfurter was adamantly opposed to the idea of remanding the Lewis case to the district court for a reassessment of the fines. Such an action would be "deplorable" and could have "seriously undesirable consequences," such as the perception that the result would be a victory for Lewis.[51] Douglas favored overturning the judgments not only for the union but also for Lewis and remanding the case to the district court with instructions to segregate the civil and criminal fines. He wrote Vinson that he was not convinced that any damage was shown. He argued, "The evidence of damage seems to be very speculative and in the realm of possibility, perhaps probability, but not certainty." Douglas added that he thought it would be "desirable to give the District Court some standards by which a remedial fine can be imposed."[52]

Other than Rutledge and Murphy, both of whom opposed any fines, the person who was most concerned about the fines was Stanley Reed. He wrote his colleagues a memo stating that the fines were "excessive in both the discretionary and constitutional sense." However, he said he could "acquiesce in fixing fines at $10,000 for Mr. Lewis and $500,000 for the Mine Workers," a sum that Reed still thought was excessive. He wanted to make a proviso that the district court judge be given the power to reduce the fines even further in light of further developments.[53] Frankfurter's reaction to a conditional fine was conveyed to Vinson in a handwritten note penned on a draft of Reed's proposal. "This is skillful eyewash and makes it all the more important that we conclude this business without any *ifs, ands* and *buts*." He added that he had "talked fiercely to Stanley and told him his proposal is ignominious and stultifying."[54]

Vinson strongly preferred that the fines imposed be unconditional, but Black and Douglas thought that all fines should be conditional. This left Reed as the key to obtaining a majority, and Vinson was prepared to negotiate a sum for the fine against the UMW that could secure Reed's agreement. Reed showed great sympathy for the miners because he thought they "acted in accordance with their concept of their legal rights."[55] Frankfurter tried to win Reed over to the idea of unconditional fines by proposing wording in his own concurrence that referred to the strong ties of solidarity among the mine workers and between members of the United Mine Workers and their president. "Fellowship in labor vital to the Nation and loyalty to a leader in promoting their legitimate interests are sturdy virtues. But all of the gains that the miners have made in the past are ultimately due to the fact that they enjoy the rights of free men under our system of government."[56] Frankfurter's objective was not only to win over Reed but also to appeal to Burton. It did not work. Burton said it sounded too much like "soft soap." Referring to wording that Vinson was working on, Burton said, "I believe it should not hand out bouquets and compliments to anyone—but confine itself to the thought there may have been good faith which failed to appreciate the seriousness of the step taken."[57] Frankfurter sent Burton's reply on to Reed with the comment, "See what the Christian Burton thinks of my emollient."[58]

Burton's diaries revealed the extensiveness of the efforts to negotiate an agreement that would satisfy the four justices, besides himself, who were the most supportive of fines—Vinson, Frankfurter, Jackson, and Reed. The meetings among these justices moved from a weekly basis in early February to an almost daily basis in late February.[59] Reed eventually agreed to an unconditional fine for the miners of $700,000, with a *conditional sum* of $280 million if they failed to abide by the orders of the district court. Vinson's victory, with Frankfurter's help, kept the decision from being remanded to the district court by a narrow five-to-four majority. The outcome of his efforts to craft a solid majority for the government in the UMW case was a mixed bag for Vinson. He won important concessions but failed to unify the Court to the extent he had hoped.

While the members of Supreme Court worked feverishly behind the scene to settle the issues, media speculation began to build as to when the Court would announce its opinion. It came in a surprise move on Thursday, March 6. Nearly fifteen years had passed since a decision had been handed down on any day but Monday.[60] There was no advance notice to anyone outside of the Court, not even the Court's public relations officer or the attorneys in the case.[61] One explanation for the surprise timing of the opinion is provided in a memo that Reed sent to Vinson. He said, "It might be wise for the Clerk to advise our public relations man that printing requirements were a factor, as on Monday other opinions come down, and there were requests for an unusual number of the opinions."[62] *Time* magazine suggested that the real reason for the unusual timing was that the opinions were written and "Vinson knew they were too hot to keep from a watchful press."[63] At noon, Vinson began to read his majority opinion. Within half an hour the attorneys for both parties arrived. It took two hours and twenty-six minutes for the opinions to be read, and even then all documents were not read in full.

Although the timing of the opinion day may have been unexpected, Vinson's majority opinion upholding the government's position on every issue should not have come as a surprise. For a person who had played a key role in the government's efforts at economic stabilization during and following the war, he could not help but be alarmed at the threat that labor demands for increased wages constituted for the country's efforts to keep inflation under control. Vinson devoted the bulk of his opinion to defending the district court's authority to issue the injunction. This required a declaration that the Norris-LaGuardia Act, which prohibited courts from issuing injunctions in labor disputes, did not apply to the government as employer. His argument rested on his reading of legislative intent. Here he had some firsthand knowledge, because he had voted for the Norris-LaGuardia Act when he was in Congress. First he noted that nothing in the language of the act indicated that it was intended to apply to government. He wrote, "We cannot construe the general term 'employer' to include the United States where there is no express reference to the United States and no evident affirmative grounds for believing that Congress intended to withhold an otherwise available remedy from the Government."[64] He referred to "an old and well-known rule that statutes which in general terms divest pre-existing rights or privileges will not be applied to the sovereign without express words to that effect" (272). Furthermore, Vinson argued that the Norris-LaGuardia Act withdrew the power of injunction from federal courts only in certain cases, those "involving or growing out of any labor dispute" that is a dispute involving "persons." Vinson noted that the act itself did not define "persons" and that "in common usage that term does not include the sovereign, and statutes employing it will ordinarily not be construed to do so. . . . The absence of any comparable provision extending the term to sovereign governments implies that Congress did not desire the term to extend to them" (275).

Next, Vinson sought to determine legislative intent by reviewing the floor debate on passage of the bill. He noted that Representative Blanton of Texas had proposed an amendment to the Norris-LaGuardia Act that would have specifically made an exception to the provision limiting injunctive power "where the United States Government is the petitioner." Although this amendment was rejected by the House, Vinson relied heavily on the views of Rep. Fiorello LaGuardia, the House sponsor of the bill. LaGuardia had opposed the amendment, but only because such "express exception was not necessary." After reading the definition of a "person participating in a labor dispute," LaGuardia said, "I do not see how in any possible way the United States can be brought in under the provisions of the bill" (277). Two days after the Court's opinion was announced, LaGuardia, coauthor of the act, told the labor committee of the Senate that the Court was correct in its interpretation of congressional intent.[65]

Vinson rejected the defendants' arguments that when the mines were seized under the War Labor Disputes Act, they did not become employees of the government because the mines were still under private management. The Krug-Lewis agreement, Vinson wrote, "was one solely between the Government and the union. The private mine operators were not parties to the contract nor were they made parties to any of its subsequent modifications." As further evidence he offered that private operators had vigorously opposed many of the provisions incorporated into the agreement.[66] Even though the government utilized the services of the private managers, the government retained ultimate control.

Vinson then turned his attention to the question of the district court's power to issue the temporary restraining order. In addition to the holding that the Norris-LaGuardia Act did not prevent the court from issuing injunctive relief, Vinson argued that alternative grounds supported such power. The district court had "unquestionable power to issue a restraining order for the purpose of preserving existing conditions pending a decision upon its own jurisdiction" (290). Vinson noted that the injunction was issued two and one-half days before the strike was to begin but that the defendants did not file a motion to vacate the order. Instead, he said, "they ignored it and allowed a nationwide coal strike to become an accomplished fact." To support his argument, Vinson relied on a 1906 opinion by Justice Oliver Wendell Holmes in *United States* v. *Shipp*.[67] In that case the Court ruled that a court order had to be obeyed even though its legality was in doubt. Citing the Shipp precedent, Vinson concluded that "the District Court had the power to preserve the existing conditions while it was determining its own authority to grant injunctive relief."[68]

The third question that Vinson addressed concerned the commingling of citations and fines for civil and criminal intent. Judge Goldsborough had tried the civil and criminal contempt charges together and levied fines without segregating the fines for each type of contempt. The defendants claimed that they did not know they had been charged with criminal contempt, but Vinson summarily dismissed this claim. Even though the defendants were not advised that they were subject to criminal contempt, he said they "were quite aware that a criminal contempt was charged" and had mentioned it in one of their motions to the Court (297). "Common sense would recognize that conduct can amount to both civil and criminal contempt. . . . Disposing of both aspects of the contempt in a single proceeding would seem at least a convenient practice" (299).

Vinson staunchly defended the district court's convictions for criminal contempt. On this point his pique at Lewis's defiant antics was evident. "One who defies the public authority and willfully refuses his obedience, does so at his peril. In imposing a fine for criminal contempt, the trial judge may properly take into consideration the extent of the willful and deliberate defiance of the court's order, the seriousness of the consequences of the contumacious behavior, the necessity of effectively terminating the defendant's defiance as required by the public interest, and the importance of deterring such acts in the future." Vinson described Lewis's policy of defiance as "the germ center of an economic paralysis which was rapidly extending itself from the bituminous coal mines to practically every other major industry of the United States. It was an attempt to repudiate and override the instrument of lawful government in the very situation in which governmental action was indispensable" (303).

Vinson concluded that the fine of ten thousand dollars against defendant Lewis for criminal contempt was warranted. A majority of the Court, however, felt that the fines against the miners were excessive. They reduced the fine to $700,000 but stipulated that the union would pay the additional $280 million unless the union complied fully with the court orders within five days. Acknowledging the seriousness of the fines, Vinson said, "The majority feels that the course taken by the union carried with it such a serious threat to orderly constitutional government, and to the economic and social welfare of the nation, that a fine of substantial size is required to emphasize the gravity of the offense." In wording aimed at smoothing over differences among the justices in the majority, Vinson added, "Loyalty in responding to the orders of their leader may, in some minds, minimize the gravity of the miners' conduct; but we cannot ignore the effect of their action upon the rights of other citizens or the effect of their action upon our system of government." In words that reflected his own long-held view about loyalty, Vinson said, "In our complex society, there is a great variety of limited loyalties, but the overriding loyalty of all is to our country and to the institutions under which a particular interest may be pursued" (306).

Frankfurter's concurring opinion strongly defended the majority argument that the district court had the power to issue an injunction and to punish Lewis and the miners for failure to obey it. To hold otherwise, he said, would be to "deny the place of judiciary in our scheme of government. . . . There can be no free society without law administered through an independent judiciary. If one man can be allowed to determine for himself what is law, every man can. Legal process is an essential part of the democratic process" (312).

Frankfurter devoted most of his opinion to his disagreement with the Court majority about the applicability of the Norris-LaGuardia Act. He criticized Vinson's "artificial canon of construction" and argued that this case was clearly a labor dispute as defined by the act. Further, he said, the provisions of the act that denied the courts injunctive powers in labor disputes under the act were not based on the "character of parties." He said Congress intended to withdraw from courts the power to intervene in labor disputes, regardless of whether the parties were private or public (313).

Black and Douglas wrote a concurring opinion in which they said that they agreed with the Court's opinion that neither the Norris-LaGuardia Act nor the War Labor Disputes Act barred the government from obtaining an injunction. They agreed that the Norris-LaGuardia Act pertained to labor disputes between private employers and their employees, that the court had the power to issue an injunction pending adjudication of the controversy, and that the court had the power to coerce obedience to those orders and to impose conditional sanctions necessary to compel obedience. "Courts could not administer justice if persons were left free pending adjudication to engage in conduct which would either immediately interrupt the judicial proceedings or so change the *status quo* . . . that no effective judgment could be rendered" (330–31). What the two justices could not agree to was the unconditional fines levied as criminal punishment. In contempt proceedings, courts must rely on the "least possible power adequate to the end proposed," they said, and the fines levied against Lewis and the miners were far more than that. They thought that conditional civil sanctions would have produced the obedience desired. To Black and Douglas, the $700,000 fine set by the majority was excessive. They argued that the fine on Lewis and the union should be conditional, "subject to their full and unconditional obedience to the injunction" (335).

Murphy's blistering dissent followed. He argued forcefully against every position in the Court's opinion. He acknowledged that the government was confronted with the "necessity of preserving the economic health of the nation and it was imperative that some effective action be taken to break the stalemate." However, Murphy argued, "those factors do not permit the conversion of the judicial process into a weapon for misapplying statutes according to the grave exigencies of the moment. That can have grave consequences even more serious and lasting than a temporary dislocation of the nation's economy resulting from a strike of the miners" (336). The court did not have the power to issue the injunction, and the miners were not obligated to obey it. "We lack any power to ignore the plain mandates of Congress and to impose vindictive fines upon defendants. They are entitled to be judged by this Court according to the sober principles of law" (342).

Rutledge's vigorous dissent is nearly as long as the Court's opinion. He began with an admonition to his colleagues about the public furor over Lewis and the coal strike. He said, "This case became a *cause cele-*

bre the moment it began. No good purpose can be served by ignoring that fact. But it cannot affect our judgment save only to steel us to the essential and accustomed behavior of judges" (342). Rutledge reminded the justices that their job was to decide the case according to their conscience and what the law commands, and he was of the firm conviction that the law in question prohibited the district court from issuing an injunction. Congress, he said, clearly intended to limit the jurisdiction of the courts in labor disputes, which was its prerogative under the Constitution. There is no precedent, he said, that holds "that a refusal to obey orders or judgments contravening Congress' mandate is criminal or affords cause for punishment" (351). Thus, like Murphy, he thought neither Lewis nor the miners could he held in contempt.

The reactions to the UMW decision were predictable. Legal scholars widely condemned the majority view. The strongest criticisms of Vinson's opinion were aimed at his dismissal of the language of the Norris-LaGuardia Act and the intent of Congress that the legislation applied to "any labor dispute." It was variously called "one of the poorer—if not the poorest—opinions written by Vinson,"[69] "legal gymnastics,"[70] and a "blundering treatment of the Norris-LaGuardia Act."[71] The sharpest criticism was an article in the *University of Chicago Law Review.* The author took the Court to task for what he labeled "judicial policy making." He said, "The Supreme Court may have believed, as thoughtful men with the interests of the nation at heart, that the country would be bound for hell in a hay-rick if Lewis and his union were not stopped in their tracks. But that is none of their business. Their business is to apply the law as written and to let Congress do the worrying about matters of economic convenience."[72]

Although Vinson had a long history of deferring to the legislative will, he was on the horns of a dilemma in this case. A careful reading of legislative intent might have spelled victory for Lewis and the miners and an embarrassing loss for the Truman administration. Vinson was not prepared to do that. In the opinion of one scholar, James J. Bolner, who wrote a doctoral dissertation on the chief justice's opinion, Vinson "was intent upon supporting the executive in its fight with Lewis."[73] He was, in fact, less than discreet with his colleagues about his concerns. In trying to persuade Murphy to support the government's position, Vinson is reported to have said, "Frank, the blue chips are down. . . . We've got to help the administration out of this mess."[74] The chief justice's attempts to persuade Murphy did not succeed. Instead, a law clerk reported, Murphy was "infuriated" by Vinson's plea to rescue the government.

Even without his sense of loyalty to the president, it is doubtful that Vinson would have ruled any differently. His opinion is completely consistent with his long-standing view that government has the power to promote public order and provide for the nation's defense. The idea that government should be helpless in the face of threats to the nation's well-being was anathema to him. As director of economic stabilization during the war, he had been prepared to seize the railroads and the mines. One of the most highly publicized cases was the government's seizure in 1944 of Montgomery Ward, the nation's second-largest mail-order house handling civilian goods. The government acted in the heat of a labor dispute that threatened to shut down Montgomery Ward, which it thought would impede the effective prosecution of the war. Wilbur Lester, a former Vinson law clerk on the court of appeals, was working with Vinson at the time. Lester said that Vinson never had any doubts that the "President in times of emergency had to assume leadership and to take such action as was necessary to preserve the country and the government."[75] A federal circuit court of appeals upheld the government, and before the Supreme Court could rule on Montgomery Ward's appeal, the federal government withdrew control. So there was no legal validation of the government's action.

Vinson's experiences as director of war mobilization and treasury secretary, which followed his term as head of economic stabilization, gave him firsthand knowledge about how precarious the nation's economy was after the war. The soft coal miners were not the only workers whose demands threatened economic stabilization. While Truman was confronted with the miners' strike, he was dealing with almost exactly the same situation with the railroad industry. Other labor disputes were on the horizon.

The Court's opinion received more favorable treatment from the popular press, reflecting public opinion, which was more concerned about the threats to the nation's economy and the potential ramifications of a decision that supported Lewis and the miners. The *Washington Post* declared, "The Court has struck a blow for law and order." It called the decision "a clear and forceful application of law to an area of lawlessness [and showed] that the United States is not a helpless victim in the face of such an assault. It can act to protect the public interest."[76]

The *New York Times* said, "Our highest court has grappled boldly with one of the greatest problems of our times," and called the ruling "a moral injunction toward a greater sense of public obligation." Fearing that this would not be the end of labor strife, the *Times* called upon

Congress to pass "better legislation" authorizing the president to take over any vital industry when its operations are halted by an employee-employer dispute.[77] The *Times* editorial reflected the same concerns as those expressed by members of Congress, and the most significant aftermath of the Court's opinion may have been its stimulus to new legislation that imposed stricter regulations on the right to strike.

Members of Congress uniformly praised the Court's ruling, and several of them called for tougher antilabor laws. Antilabor sentiments had already emerged in Congress as early as 1945 when the first postwar strikes began. Among the main targets was the National Labor Relations Act or Wagner Act, passed in 1935, which protected workers' right to collective bargaining. Several antilabor measures aimed at curtailing the power of labor to carry out disruptive strikes were introduced and failed. In May 1946 Truman himself proposed the Temporary Disputes Settlement Act, which included some rather strict measures to deter "labor disputes interrupting or threatening to interrupt the operation of industry essential to the maintenance of the national economic structure and to the effective transition from war to peace."[78] In 1946 Truman vetoed an even stricter law proposed by South Dakota representative Francis Case that included provisions for a sixty-day cooling-off period before any strike could occur.

After the Republicans gained control of both houses of Congress in 1946, a victory fueled in part by diametric forces—the public's disgust with labor and labor's frustration with Truman—even more antiunion bills were introduced. The most significant of these measures to succeed was the Taft-Hartley Act, passed in 1947, which amended the Wagner Act. The national emergency strike provisions were among the most important aspects of Taft-Hartley. These empowered the president to obtain an eighty-day temporary injunction if he thought that a threatened strike would present a national emergency. The Federal Mediation and Conciliation Service would then assist the two sides to reach a settlement. Subsequent procedures spelled out in the law effectively established an "eighty-day cooling off period" in labor disputes. Taft-Hartley was passed over Truman's veto. A prime consideration behind his veto was the need to woo labor support, which had been badly frayed by Truman's actions against the coal and railroad strikes. He made his veto of Taft-Hartley a major issue in 1948, and Truman was convinced that labor support was responsible for his reelection.[79] On the morning after the election, Truman exclaimed, "Labor did it."[80]

Truman's failure to use the national emergency provisions of the

Taft-Hartley Act in another labor crisis in 1952—a threatened strike by the steelworkers during the Korean War—became the basis for one of his major defeats at the hands of the Supreme Court. The story of the steel strike and subsequent rulings by the Supreme Court has striking parallels to the coal miners' strike in 1946. Both strikes involved government seizure of affected industries, and both issues landed on the doorstep of the Supreme Court while Vinson was chief justice. As in 1946, Truman was concerned about his program for economic stabilization, and just as in 1946, the looming elections were a consideration. Only this time it was a presidential election, and though he was not expected to run again, he was concerned about his party's chances of holding the White House. In 1946 the nation was operating under wartime economic policies, such as the War Labor Disputes Act. In 1952 the United States was in actual combat in an undeclared war in Korea.

Truman recognized the necessity of intervention when the first indications of conflict between the United Steelworkers of America and the steel companies surfaced in December 1951. Steelworkers were pressing their demands for a hefty wage increase, which the steel companies would have been willing to grant if they could raise prices. However, with the existence of price controls, the steel companies had to petition the government for a price adjustment. In the meantime, the Steelworkers contract was due to expire on December 31, 1951, and with no progress in contract negotiations, Truman referred the dispute to the Wage Stabilization Board (WSB). He stressed the importance of preventing an interruption in the production of steel. At the same time, Truman urged the steel unions and operators to continue working and to cooperate with the WSB. "The national interest demands it," he said.[81]

On March 20, 1952, the WSB, which was comprised of representatives from government, unions, and industry, issued a report that was very favorable to the unions. The industry representatives on the board issued a minority report, criticizing the WSB ruling as being decidedly prolabor. The Truman administration's immediate reaction to the report of the WSB was that it was too generous to the workers; Truman feared that it would undermine the stabilization program. Within a few days, however, the WSB changed its mind.

In the next two weeks, various officials in the Truman administration worked directly with the unions and the steel owners to settle their disagreement. On April 3 a tentative agreement was reached, but it hinged on government approval of a price hike. Truman was reluctant to yield to the industry's demand for a price increase because he believed that it would threaten his entire stabilization plan. Yet the absence of an agreement increased the likelihood of a strike. That too was intolerable. His various war advisers had painted dire scenarios of what a stoppage in the production of steel might mean.

Truman began to explore options available to him in the event that bargaining failed and a strike was imminent. He no longer had the option provided to him in the War Labor Disputes Act, under which he had seized the coal mines to keep them operating in 1946. In the interim Congress had passed the Taft-Hartley Act and, with it, provisions for an eighty-day cooling-off period when strikes threatened industries vital to the national interest. Truman and his advisers did not give much consideration to using the Taft-Hartley Act. First, there was the obvious political drawback—labor's staunch opposition to it. Truman and his advisers agreed that an injunction issued under Taft-Hartley would impose a hardship on workers by forcing them to work for wages they thought were inadequate. They felt that the burden to settle should be placed on the companies, because they were the ones that refused to settle. In addition, the Taft-Hartley Act would not achieve the objective of maintaining steel production, except for the eighty-day period of the temporary injunction.[82] Other options considered were seizing the steel mills under section 18 of the Selective Service Act or under the Defense Production Act or requesting seizure legislation from Congress. These were rejected as being either too complex, too time-consuming, or of questionable applicability.

After a lengthy and spirited debate about the advantages and disadvantages of each alternative, Truman and his advisers concluded that relying on the president's "inherent powers" under Article 2 of the Constitution was the most desirable approach. Article 2 contains three powers from which a president might infer a power to act. It vests executive power in the president, designates him to be commander in chief of the army and navy of the United States, and requires that he faithfully execute all laws. Relying on seizure under inherent powers allowed the president to pursue his goals of "continued steel production and reasonable price control" while at the same time permitting him to intensify his efforts to effect a settlement (80).

Advice from Vinson may have played a role in Truman's decision to seize the steel mills under his inherent powers. Robert J. Donovan claims in his book *Tumultuous Years: The Presidency of Harry S. Truman, 1949–1953* that "Vinson, in a most questionable act for a chief justice who might later have to weigh a case in court, privately advised the president to go ahead with the seizure, basing the recommendation on legal grounds." Secretary of the Treasury John Snyder argued strongly against seizure, but according to Donovan, "Truman was not persuaded and replied that the chief justice himself had assured him that the way was clear for the president legally to seize the steel industry and that such an act would be constitutional."[83] Although Donovan's book clearly implicates Snyder as the source of this claim, the author refused to verify that when questioned by reporters. Robert Ferrell's book *Harry S. Truman: A Life,* published four years later, reports that following Snyder's death, Donovan acknowledged Snyder as the source. Margaret Truman, in a book about her mother published in 1986, also claims that her father conferred with Vinson prior to seizing the steel mills and was assured that the move was legal and that the Supreme Court would uphold him.[84]

There is no direct evidence to corroborate these second-hand claims and some reason to doubt their accuracy. Ferrell noted, for example, that Truman, who studied law for two years in Kansas City, "knew that he could not properly receive information on the steel case from the chief justice." Another basis for questioning the accuracy of Snyder's claim is his dislike of Vinson, a feeling that was mutual. Even though they were both close and trusted advisers of Truman, no love was lost between them. Vinson had worked diligently to keep Snyder from positions in the Truman administration, and much to Vinson's regret, Snyder had taken his place as secretary of the Treasury when Vinson became chief justice. On more than one occasion, Snyder expressed negative views about Vinson. Snyder saw him as a person who was very ambitious, "always trying to step forward politically."[85] He credited him with being a good negotiator but a weak administrator as secretary of the Treasury. Furthermore, Truman, in his detailed account of the steel case, never mentions Snyder as a person who was consulted about plant seizures.

Yet two people who were close to Vinson during the time of the Court's deliberation of the steel case, law clerks Newton Minow and Howard Trienens, suspect that Vinson may have told Truman that seizure would be legal. They said the only time they ever saw Vinson, normally a mild-mannered person, get upset was over the Court's opinion in the steel case.[86] If Vinson did assure Truman that seizure of the steel mills would be upheld by the Supreme Court, it would not be the first instance of such a breach. There is extensive historical precedent for such advice, as noted in Bruce Murphy's work on extrajudicial behavior. Commenting on Vinson's reported advice to Truman, Murphy said, "You can argue that it's inappropriate or unwise, but you cannot argue that its unethical because there's no ethical standard governing that sort of behavior."[87]

Another factor that is said to have motivated Truman to seize the steel mills under his inherent powers was an opinion that Attorney General Tom Clark had sent to the Senate Committee on Labor and Public Welfare in 1947, regarding the possible repeal of the Taft-Hartley Act. Clark's opinion stated that "the inherent power of the President to deal with emergencies that affect the health, safety and welfare of the entire Nation is exceedingly great."[88] He offered as support for his opinion the precedent established in the *United Mine Workers* case in 1946. With Clark now on the Supreme Court, along with the chief justice and Truman's two other appointees, Harold Burton and Sherman Minton, Truman had good reason to believe that his seizure of the steel mills would be upheld if the issue ever reached the Court. The president may have overlooked one important fact about the opinion that Clark sent to Congress in 1947. It rested on the Court's interpretation of the War Labor Disputes Act, which was not a consideration in the steel case.

Armed with this conviction, on April 8, 1952, Truman announced in a nationwide radio and television address that he had ordered his secretary of commerce, Charles Sawyer, to seize the nation's steel mills, and he also announced that he was asking representatives of the union and the steel companies to resume collective bargaining to try to reach a settlement. Then, unable to resist a jab at the steel companies, he blamed them for the current state of affairs. "The companies have said . . . that unless they can have what they want, the steel industry will shut down. That is the plain unvarnished fact."[89] He criticized the steel companies for insisting on their price demands in the face of record profits. Commenting on the negative editorials in the nation's newspapers, Truman said: "Tell them to read the Constitution. . . . The President has the power to keep the country from going to hell."[90]

In less than thirty minutes following the president's speech, lawyers for the steel companies submitted a motion with the federal district court for the District of Columbia for a temporary restraining order against the president's seizure. On April 24 Judge David A. Pine, a Roosevelt appointee, presided over a hearing on whether to grant a preliminary injunction against the administration. Such a hearing would typically focus on the possible injury to each party and to the public that would result from issuing or not issuing injunctive relief, but because of a tactical error made by the government's lawyers, the proceedings before Judge Pine explored the merits of the case, that is, whether the president had the power to seize the steel mills. The government's lawyer boldly asserted at one point that the president had unlimited power in an emergency.

The audacity of the government's positions was too much for the "strict constructionist" Pine. He determined that "there is no express grant of power in the Constitution authorizing the President to direct this seizure. There is no grant of power from which it reasonably can be implied." Pine made specific reference to the Taft-Hartley Act as the remedy "provided by Congress to meet such an emergency."[91] On the question of damages, Pine rejected all of the government's arguments and concluded that the steel companies would suffer irreparable harm. Accordingly, he issued the preliminary injunction, and the steelworkers called for an immediate strike.

Faced with the reality of a stoppage in steel production and still determined not to use the Taft-Hartley Act, the Truman administration immediately filed for a stay of Pine's injunction with the court of appeals for the District of Columbia. There the government's claim got a more favorable review from a bench that included two of Vinson's former colleagues, Chief Justice Harold M. Stephens and Associate Justice Henry Edgerton. On April 30 the court of appeals, in a five-to-four majority opinion announced by Judge Edgerton, stayed Judge Pine's injunction for two days. In sharp disagreement with the district court judge, they declared that "there is at least a serious question as to the correctness" of Judge Pine's ruling that the president's seizure of the steel industry was illegal.[92] The judges stipulated that if petitions for writs of certiorari were filed in the Supreme Court within two days, the stay would continue until the Supreme Court acted on the petitions. Or if the request for certiorari were denied, the stay would remain in effect until further order of the court of appeals. Again the Truman administration lost no time in filing a petition for certiorari with the Supreme Court. Simultaneously, the president requested that the steelworkers terminate their strike, and they complied.

One day after receiving the petitions for certiorari, the Supreme Court, by a vote of seven to two, voted to grant certiorari. Only Frankfurter and Burton voted against accepting the case. The Court unanimously voted to stay the preliminary injunction until the final disposition of the case and set oral arguments for May 12. Burton recorded in his diary that the chief justice received word during the discussion that the president had said that unless the strike was settled by Monday, he would order wage increases, but Vinson did not report this information until after the decision to grant certiorari had been made.[93]

About a week before the oral arguments, Burton had lunch with Vinson, Black, Reed, Clark, and Minton, his regular lunch group. Burton left that meeting with the feeling that he was "largely alone in holding the President was without power to seize the steel plants in the face of Taft-Hartley."[94] His perceptions were wrong. On the day of oral arguments, it was abundantly clear that most of the other justices had serious doubts about the president's actions.

The significance of the case was apparent on May 12, 1952, when more than three hundred people packed the courtroom to hear the oral arguments in the case of *Youngstown Sheet and Tube v. Sawyer.* The Court relaxed its rule against standing during the session, which allowed an additional two hundred people to view the proceedings. Hundreds more stood outside the chamber. When John W. Davis presented the case for the steel companies, he was asked relatively few questions; but when Solicitor General Philip Perlman presented the government's case, he was subjected to a barrage of questions. Black, Douglas, Frankfurter, Jackson, and Burton were relentless in pressing Perlman. It was clear from their questions that they had reservations about an inherent presidential power to seize the plants and whether there was any statute that conferred such a power. Perlman was repeatedly asked to explain the president's failure to use the Taft-Hartley injunction to prevent the strike. Perlman kept returning to the idea that a steel strike at this critical time would create an emergency of such proportions that the president had to act, which he was empowered to do under the Constitution.

Vinson asked relatively few questions, none of which directly addressed the constitutional issues. At one point he asked, "What do I understand your position with regard to action by the Congress, vetoing or expressly disapproving of the action of the President?" Perlman responded that this was not an issue "because the President said he would abide by whatever Congress did . . . he made that crystal clear."[95] This allowed Perlman to demonstrate that Truman respected the authority of Congress to act. He noted that Congress had failed to take any action and therefore had in effect "acquiesced" to the seizure. At another point in the proceedings, Perlman asserted that if the steel companies were harmed by the seizure, they had an adequate remedy under the law—a suit for damages against the government in the court of claims. The resources of the government "are back of any damages they may suffer," he said. "How can you say that?" Vinson asked. "How are we to determine damage?"[96] Perlman was under relentless pressure from the justices, and at one point he had to request time to finish his answer to a question posed by Douglas before the justice pestered him with another question. Perlman's performance caused some consternation with Vinson, who complained that he "bounced around with this arguments and never finished a subject." Later, the chief justice felt compassion for Perlman and said, "I want you to do what you want to do."[97]

This allowed Perlman to turn to the question of seizure precedents established by previous presidents. He specifically mentioned Roosevelt's seizure of the North American Aviation plant in 1940 in order to use the airplanes for the war effort, which occurred while Justice Jackson was attorney general. The justice responded that the 1940 seizure was different because North American was under direct government contract, which made it a strike against the government. Minton was so disturbed about Jackson's seeming about-face that he confronted him with it later. Jackson replied, "But I was Attorney General then, and I'm a justice now."[98] During the oral arguments, Minton asked only friendly questions of Perlman. Clark's questions also reflected some sympathy for the government's position. He questioned the court's ability to pass on the merits of an emergency, "especially when there were many facts that could not be revealed for reasons of national security."[99]

The oral arguments were carried over to May 13, when the two parties made their closing arguments. Perlman was allowed extra time in order to answer the questions posed to him. If there was any doubt as to where the Court was headed, that was quickly erased on May 16, when the justices met in conference to discuss the case. Before they met that day, Vinson sent a memorandum to all members of the Court urging them "to take extra precaution to prevent any leak in respect of our deliberations."[100] Vinson began the conference with a strong defense of the president's actions. "History shows there is power," he said, and seizure does not have to be authorized by Congress. He argued that situations such as Korea or those involving NATO required the United States to furnish arms, materials, and men. These commitments, Vinson said, "placed serious responsibility on the President." He was not acting in defiance of Congress; instead, in his report to Congress, "he said if he was not right, let Congress choose the methods. . . . Congress has done nothing."[101]

Black followed Vinson and declared that "most of what the Chief Justice said is irrelevant." To him the question was whether the president had the power to seize without a statute, and Black concluded that he did not. He declared that to be a lawmaking power and said, "That power under the Constitution is in the Congress." Although Black thought the Court "must" address the constitutional issue, Reed was reluctant to do so. He said they "should keep the President in control of the plants to see what Congress may do." Although he preferred not to decide the constitutional issue, he felt that the president did have the power as commander in chief.

Frankfurter, ever insensitive to the need for unanimity on the Court, began with the comment, "Everyone should write in this case." He agreed with Black on the issues of separation of powers, and although he too would have liked for the Court to avoid the constitutional questions, he concluded that it could not. Jackson did not want the Court to pass on the question of whether there was an emergency. He accepted that there was an emergency and said the question was what the president could do in an emergency. Jackson claimed that the president "is in an untenable position. [He] can throw the Constitution overboard, but we can't."

Burton spoke mainly about the Taft-Hartley Act. The president, he said, had no power to seize apart from statute. He said that the legislative history of Taft-Hartley indicated that Congress would provide for seizure after the remedy in the act had been exhausted. Clark followed Burton, and he was the one justice whose position at the oral arguments was ambiguous. Now, Clark spoke against the president's actions. He began with the statement that the Court's decision "should be limited to this case," and in this case the president had no power. Clark said he could have avoided the situation "by two methods not involving seizure." In war situations, Clark clearly thought the president would have the power to seize plants, but, he said, "this is not war in Korea." Not surprisingly, Clark made no reference to his memo to Congress in 1947, supporting the existence of the president's inherent powers. Vinson must have been deeply disappointed at Clark's about-face. Sometime prior to the conference, he had told Vinson, "If you have four, I'll be the fifth."[102] After the conference, Clark said Vinson never spoke to him about his change of heart. "He was not that type. He wouldn't try to twist your arm."[103]

The last to speak at the conference was Sherman Minton, and he was adamant in his defense of the president's seizure to prevent the strike. Douglas noted that Minton was "very excited and pounded the table." He said, "There is no vacant spot in power when the security of the nation is at stake . . . the power is the power of defense and it rests in the President." Unlike Clark, he had no doubt that the country was at war and that "Truman seized the plants because the defense of the country required it." The conference lasted nearly four hours. In the end, six justices voted to affirm Pine's injunction. Justice Jackson was almost gleeful following the conference when he called his law clerks, including William O. Rehnquist, who later became chief justice, into his chambers. He said, "Well, boys, the President got licked."[104] One could almost interpret Jackson's words as a long-awaited payback for not being named chief justice.

Black, being the senior justice in the majority, assigned the case to himself. He tried to fashion an opinion that would accommodate all of the justices in the majority, but that proved impossible. In reality, their positions were not that compatible, save for the belief that the president lacked the power in this situation to seize the steel mills to prevent a strike. As a result, every justice in the majority wrote a separate opinion. This meant that the ruling lacked the force of a majority opinion. Vinson wrote the opinion for the minority. Neither Minton nor Reed, who joined him, was inclined to write separate opinions, but both contributed suggestions that were incorporated into Vinson's opinion. Reed's main contribution was to get Vinson to emphasize the temporary nature of the seizure near the beginning and end of his dissent.[105]

The nation had to wait only two weeks to learn the outcome of the case. On June 2 the opinions were announced. Black, who wrote the Court's opinion, went first and took only fifteen minutes to read his seven-page opinion. He said the president's authority to issue the seizure order could only come from one of two sources: a statute or the Constitution. Black said such authority was not found in any statute. He noted that when Congress contemplated the Taft-Hartley Act, it rejected an amendment that would have authorized government seizures in emergency situations. Nor, said Black, could the power be derived from the aggregate of his presidential powers under Article 2 in the Constitution. The president's action constituted lawmaking, and the Constitution vested "all legislative power" power with Congress. He argued that the president's role in lawmaking was limited to recommending and vetoing legislation and executing laws once they were passed. Black did not even leave open the possibility that under some catastrophic event, such as total war, the president could take property to settle labor disputes without statutory authority. Black declared that the president's seizure order could not stand and affirmed the judgment of the district court.

Douglas wrote only a five-page opinion. He was the only other justice who agreed with Black's absolute position denying inherent powers. His main thrust, however, was that the government's action amounted to taking private property, and when the government seized private property, it was bound by the Fifth Amendment to provide just compensation to its owners. According to Douglas, the president was without authority to raise revenues, and Douglas said Congress was the only branch that "has the power to pay compensation for a seizure [and therefore] is the only one able to authorize a seizure or make lawful one that the President has effected."[106] Thus, Douglas saw the president's action as violating the principle of checks and balances by getting into the realm of congressional power. The four remaining justices in the majority were not as unequivocal as Black and Douglas on the question of presidential powers to seize property when it served the national interest.

Although Frankfurter thought that courts should ordinarily avoid constitutional issues where possible, he said the issue could not be avoided in this case. Unlike Black's absolutist position, which rejected outright the notion of inherent powers, Frankfurter chose not to define the president's powers comprehensively, recognizing that the judiciary would be required to intervene at times to determine where the lines of authority should be drawn. He discussed the history of congressional statutes that had authorized executive seizure of the units of production and noted in each instance that Congress had carefully circumscribed the use of such power. His opinion contained fourteen pages of tables analyzing every statute that authorized presidential seizure. Frankfurter noted in particular that the authors of the Taft-Hartley Act had unequivocally denied granting the president the power of seizure as a remedy in labor disputes to insure production. Nor could any other statute passed subsequent to Taft-Hartley be construed as giving the president this power.

Jackson's opinion was also based on the separation-of-powers doctrine, but his approach was to establish categories of circumstances under which presidents might act, ranging from those that would be the least vulnerable to challenge to those that would be the most vulnerable. Under this scheme, Jackson argued that the president's authority to act would be at a maximum when he acted pursuant to an express or implied authorization from Congress. His power would be at its "lowest ebb" when the president took actions "incompatible with the expressed or implied will of Congress."[107] Jackson thought Truman's actions in this case fell into this latter category. The only justification for acting contrary to legislative intent would be if there were some residual powers in the presidency that were beyond the reach of Congress. Jackson concluded that the president's powers as commander in chief did not extend to seizing industries he thought necessary to supply the army. Rather, this was a congressional power derived from Congress's power to raise and support armies and navies. Jackson seemed to think that the president had enough power. The nation would not suffer, he said, "if the Court refuses to further aggrandize the Presidential office, already so potent and so relatively immune from judicial review, at the expense of Congress" (879).

Burton also addressed the separation-of-powers issue and devoted a significant portion of his five-page opinion to the language and legislative history of the Taft-Hartley Act. "The most significant feature of that Act," he said, "is its omission of authority to seize an affected plant" (657). Truman circumvented the procedures outlined in this act and chose a remedy that Congress had reserved to itself. Burton then rejected the notion that a president had inherent constitutional power to seize private property in this case, but he left open the question of whether such power might exist in "catastrophic situations" such as imminent invasion or threatened attack. The "controlling fact" for Burton was that Congress had acted within its constitutionally delegated powers when it passed Taft-Hartley, and Truman's order had "invaded the jurisdiction of Congress" (660).

Clark, in view of his pronouncements on the issue as attorney general, was the most reluctant to reject outright the inherent powers concept. He noted that "the limits of presidential power are obscure . . . [and] the Constitution does grant to the President extensive authority in times of grave and imperative national emergency" (661–62). If, however, Congress has laid down specific procedures for meeting a type of crisis confronting the president, he was bound to follow them, but "in the absence of such action by Congress, the President's independent power to act depends upon the gravity of the situation confronting the nation." In the steel situation, Clark noted that Congress had provided three procedures—the Defense Production Act, the Taft-Hartley Act, and the Selective Service Act. Truman invoked only the Defense Production Act and had exhausted the available remedies there. He did not invoke the other two. Clark concluded that in view of these various procedures prescribed by Congress, the seizure could not be sustained.

Vinson's dissent was a vigorous defense of the president's actions and criticism of those who opposed him. "Those who suggest that this is a case of extraordinary powers should be mindful that these are extraordinary times," he said. He devoted several pages of his dissent to discussing the measures taken by the United States since the end of World War II to assume its responsibility to promote peace and security in the world. Congress authorized these commitments with legislation and with funding, and it was the president's duty to execute these legislative programs. "Their successful execution," Vinson said, "depends upon continued production of steel and stabilized prices for steel" (672).

To accept the view that only Congress could authorize the seizure of the steel mills for public use, Vinson said, would leave the president "powerless at the very moment when the need for action may be most pressing, and when no one, other than he, is immediately capable of action" (680–81). In a seventeen-page analysis, Vinson reviewed previous presidential actions without specific authorization from Congress. Included in this discussion were references to opinions supporting presidential seizure by Jackson and Clark when they were attorney general. When reading his opinion from the bench, Vinson stopped and said extemporaneously, in what was considered to be friendly sarcasm, "Changing one's minds is evidence of strength."[108] At that point, Black turned and caught Jackson's eye and grinned at him; Jackson reciprocated.

Vinson made a pointed reference to Roosevelt's seizure of the North American Aviation company, which produced military aircraft, some six months before Pearl Harbor, and he cited at length Jackson's opinion in which he claimed that the president had a "moral duty to keep this Nation's defense effort a 'going concern.'"[109] Again, Vinson noted how Jackson stated his position then as vigorously and forcefully "as he ordinarily does now." Those in the courtroom caught the inflection in Vinson's voice on this last point, and there was a spontaneous outburst of laughter in which Jackson himself joined.[110]

Vinson continued. The president has not assumed he has unlimited power in this case, he said, and he pointed to the message Truman sent to Congress "stating his purpose to abide by any action of Congress, whether approving or disapproving of his seizure action."[111] Truman was not trying to defy the legislative will. The president was not mandated to follow the emergency procedures of the Taft-Hartley Act. Instead, he chose to follow the procedures of the Defense Production Act, which called for mediation under the Wage Stabilization Board. When these efforts failed, he was not then required to use the Taft-Hartley Act. Vinson said these were parallel, not consecutive, remedies. Vinson included a swipe at the justices in the majority for their "lack of reference to authoritative precedent, the repeated reliance upon prior dissenting opinions, the complete disregard of uncontroverted facts showing the gravity of the emergency, and the temporary nature of the taking." These serve to "demonstrate how far afield one must go to affirm the order of the District Court" (708).

Vinson rejected what he called the "messenger-boy concept" of the presidency implied in the majority opinion, a term that caught the attention of the news media the following day. In a comment directed at Judge Pine, he said, "The District Judge stated this is not time for 'timorous' judicial action. But neither is this a time for timorous executive action." The president had to act to prevent the "disastrous effect" that would result from interruption of steel production and thereby preserve the defense programs that Congress had enacted (709). Only the three dissenters were willing to grant the president that kind of unlimited power.

Reactions to the Court's opinion were varied and predictable. The person most affected was Truman, who was both surprised and disappointed about the decision. His anger was still palpable four years later when he wrote his memoirs. "I would never, of course, conceal the fact that the Supreme Court was a deep disappointment to me. I think Chief Justice Vinson's dissenting opinion hit the nail right on the head, and I am sure that someday his view will come to be recognized as the correct one."[112] Truman found it incomprehensible that the Court could ignore that gravity of the situation confronting the nation. Despite his disappointment, within two hours of receiving word of the decision, Truman ordered Commerce Secretary Sawyer to comply with the decision and return the plants to the steel industry. The strike continued until June 24, fifty-three days after it started, when Truman agreed to an increase in the price of steel so that an agreement could be reached.

Generally, the nation's media were favorable to the opinion. The *New York Times* editorial argued that the case was much more about the balance of power between the legislative and executive branches than about the immediate controversy between the union and the steel companies. The *Times* proclaimed that "the Supreme Court majority struck a blow for that balance."[113] Legal scholars of the day generally approved the Court's reaffirmation of the separation-of-powers doctrine, but there were criticisms as well.[114]

A major criticism of the Court's opinion in the steel case was about its applicability, particularly in view of the multiple opinions written by those in the majority. John Frank wrote in the *Chicago Law Review* that "all that was absolutely clear was that this particular seizure was invalid."[115] He noted that Jackson prefaced his own opinion from the bench with the remark that "Justice Black's opinion is the least common denominator on which five of us can agree." Only two justices took the absolute position that the president could never seize property without legislative authority, regardless of circumstances. The other four left open the possibility that executive seizure might be sustained under conditions of war, or even under Cold War conditions. A *Harvard Law Review* article agreed that precedent would have limited application. It said the opinion contained "extremely broad language and manifests a mood as well as a decision on particular facts; but there is no indication that it is intended to curtail the President's power in foreign affairs, and the use of formal power by the President in domestic matters is rare."

These criticisms aside, scholarly judgment in general was that the main thrust of the opinion was "a strong reaffirmation of the constitutional checks and balances, and the heartiest setback for executive power in more than a decade."[116] Frank described it as "a marked step toward restoring the balance of power between the Congress and the President, a balance which was tipping ever more toward the latter." He applauded the majority for "wisely putting general principle ahead of the immediate situation," even if it did leave the country without a sound basis for preventing production disruption in emergencies.[117] According to the *Harvard Law Review*, the "lasting importance of the decision would seem to rest with the political effect, the practical limitation on the activities of the President, rather than any legal effect."[118]

Contemporary scholars agree with the assessment of the long-term implications of the decision. In her landmark work on the steel case, Maeva Marcus said the case had "lasting constitutional significance" in that it helped to redress the balance of power among the three branches of government. It was equally significant in other ways, for it "served as a prelude to a more activist period for the Supreme Court." The Court could easily have resolved the issue on nonconstitutional grounds, but it chose not to do so. Its newfound assertiveness in the *Youngstown* case signaled the Court's willingness to tackle constitutional issues head-on. No one knew at the time, but a new era for the Court under a new chief justice was not that far away.[119]

As for Vinson, his dissenting opinion drew both praise and criticism. Frank, normally critical of Vinson, called it his "strongest single opinion."[120] He said it was "an opinion of necessity . . . but it offers a real, large-scale expression of the emergency powers of the President." He thought Vinson claimed far more power for the president than was necessary for the case, which was contrary to his tendency to decide cases on narrower grounds. In this regard it was like Vinson's *United Mine Workers* opinion. In both of these, Frank said, the fact that Vinson departed so far from his own accepted practices "is some indication of the emotional intensity with which he must have regarded them" (218).

Some Vinson critics think his emotional intensity was driven by his close relationship to Truman or a debt of loyalty for his appointment. The closeness of that relationship and the frequency of their personal interactions are not in doubt. However, some who were closest to Vinson at that time disagree that his relationship with Truman was the motivating reason behind his vociferous defense of presidential power. Trienens, who was his law clerk during the steel case, said that Vinson's feelings on the legal merits of the case were strongly held not because of Truman but from his own wartime experience as director of economic stabilization where "he had been the seizor." He thought it was in the national interest to seize firms when labor and management were doing something that was injurious to the economy. Trienens said Vinson "felt so strongly about that that it wouldn't have mattered who was President or if he ever knew him, it would come out the same way."[121]

Although the *United Mine Workers* case and the steel seizure case presented very different legal issues, they nonetheless provide an excellent prism for viewing Vinson's approach to issues involving the power of government, and especially the powers of the president, in emergency situations. As someone who normally followed as closely as possible the will of the legislature, in these cases Vinson seemed to find ways around their stated positions. The reason for this lay in his sympathy for the role of the executive as the person best able to respond quickly and decisively to crises. It also reflected his sympathy for Truman.

As far as Vinson's role as chief justice was concerned, these two cases resulted in very different outcomes. In 1946 Vinson managed to gain the Court's support in behalf of the government, but by 1952 the tide was running out for both Vinson and Truman. Vinson found himself writing for the minority, against a six-person majority in which every justice wrote a separate opinion explaining why the president lacked the authority to seize the steel mills. The steel case, coming on the cusp of what was to be Vinson's last year as chief justice, stands as stark testimony to Vinson's inability to unify the Court, much less to persuade a majority of his colleagues to accept his point of view.

The decision in the steel case had much larger significance for the Court as well as the nation. Marcus contends that the case not only helped to redress the balance of power among the three branches of government, but it also signaled the beginning of a more activist period for the Supreme Court. The Court abandoned its mindset against resolving cases on constitutional grounds if they could be decided on other grounds. The Court's newfound willingness to tackle constitutional issues head-on in the steel case was directly linked to the assertiveness the Court would soon display in resolving disputes involving school desegregation, reapportionment, and the Pentagon Papers.[122] Vinson's opinion in *Youngstown* showed that he was increasingly out of sync with a majority of his colleagues. His death in the year after the decision in the steel case not only marked the end of the Vinson Court but also ushered in a new era of judicial activism.

CHAPTER 9

Individual Rights in the Cold War Climate

When Fred Vinson became chief justice in 1946, the Red Scare era in American politics had already begun to boil. Responding to the spreading fear in the land that Communists were hell-bent on world domination, Congress the previous year had made the previously temporary House Un-American Activities Committee (HUAC) into a standing committee. Armed with the power of subpoena and the enthusiastic cooperation of FBI director J. Edgar Hoover, HUAC became a major power base for investigating and exposing subversive activities. Congressional Republicans blasted the Truman administration as being "soft on communism" and made this one of the major issues in the 1946 off-year elections. When the Republicans succeeded in winning both houses of Congress, Truman fought back. In response to charges that he harbored subversives in government jobs, he established a Commission on Employee Loyalty to assist in the creation of standards and procedures for investigating federal employees. The ultimate goal was removing disloyal and subversive workers. Then in 1947 Truman issued Executive Order 9835, which established the country's first loyalty program for federal employees.

A second strategy by the administration to fight the claim that Truman was soft on Communism was the vigorous prosecution of the leaders of the Communist Party of the United States. Truman's attorney general, Tom Clark, initiated aggressive prosecution of party members in 1948 following a combative session with the Republican-controlled House Un-American Activities Committee, in which he was grilled about his failure to use the Smith Act against subversive forces. Within a year the Justice Department had secured the indictments and convictions of the eleven top leaders of the Communist Party for violations of the 1940 Smith Act, which made it illegal to conspire to overthrow the government or to advocate the overthrow of the government.

Although the threat of Communism appeared very real to vast numbers of Americans, including some justices, others thought such fears were overblown. There was little doubt, however, where Vinson stood. As he dealt with these issues, he adhered strongly to one of his most cherished beliefs—that order must be secured for freedom to exist. When he had to balance society's need for order and stability against an individual's freedom of speech, Vinson usually came down on the side of order. As he said in a speech before the American Bar Association in September 1947, one year after becoming chief justice, "the only alternative to the supremacy of law is anarchistic chaos or the reign of a personal dictator."[1] Generally, Vinson's views were shared on the Court by Stanley Reed, Robert Jackson, Sherman Minton, and Tom Clark; Harold Burton occasionally sided with these five, but not always. Felix Frankfurter was in the middle. He was an avowed defender of free speech, but he was just as firm in his adherence to judicial restraint, causing him frequently to uphold legislative actions that restricted speech. The Court's staunchest libertarians, Hugo Black and William Douglas, believed that positions like Vinson's were an overreaction to a movement that posed little harm and were used to justify unconstitutional restrictions on individual freedom. Each camp was so fixed in its position that neither could accept the possibility of merit in the opposite view.

Scholarly research in the 1990s brought the question of Communist activities in the United States under new scrutiny and provided credible evidence that in fact party leaders in the Soviet Union did control the activities of the Communist Party of the United States (CPUSA). In 1992 the opening of the Soviet archives dealing with Communist activity in America yielded a wealth of data. Harvey Klehr, John Earl Haynes, and Fridrikh Igorevich Firsov, who examined these files in depth, concluded that "concerns about the subversive threat of the CPUSA and worries that Communists employed in sensitive government jobs constituted a security risk" were well founded.[2] A second work by Klehr, Haynes and Kyrill M. Anderson has also provided strong evidence that the American Communist Party was controlled, financed, and run by Communist Party leadership in the Soviet Union.[3] Various other scholars have drawn upon the data from the Soviet archives to document the significant number of individuals in government service who were engaged in espionage for the Soviet Union.[4] This evidence suggests that the worst fears of people like Vinson were not based on pure paranoia.

Vinson had more than an inkling about Soviet espionage in the U.S. government. In February 1946, when Vinson was serving as secretary of the Treasury, Truman forwarded to him a memorandum from FBI director J. Edgar Hoover containing "serious charges" that Harry Dexter White, then assistant secretary of the Treasury, was passing "materials which came into his possession as a result of his official capacity" to two Treasury Department employees who were part of a network of suspected Soviet agents who had been under intensive investigation by the FBI since November 1945.[5] Materials now available through the opening of this country's Venona files and from decrypted telegraphic cables between Soviet spies in the United States and their superiors in Moscow offer solid evidence that White was assisting a Soviet spy network in the United States.[6]

Even though the recently discovered data now make the views of the anticommunists in the decades of the 1940s and 1950s seem less irrational, they do not justify the assumption that every member of the Communist Party was part of the scheme to undermine the government. Many idealistic people joined the Communist Party for a variety of reasons, and the government's effort to rout out the true subversives was so broad and stringent that it swept many innocent victims into its net. The Court's libertarians were more inclined to think of the Communist Party in terms of these people, people who merely advocated certain beliefs but were not engaged in espionage, and thus they had little sympathy with their colleagues who were driven by theories of a Communist conspiracy. The underlying assumptions of the two camps on the Court were intertwined with the existing doctrinal and personal differences among the justices, and addressing these issues proved a daunting task for the Court.

American Communications Association v. *Douds* represented one of Vinson's strongest opinions in defense of government measures to thwart Communist influence.[7] *Douds* involved a suit by the American Communications Association, a union affiliated with the Congress of Industrial Organizations, over section 9 (h) of the 1947 Taft-Hartley Act, which denied protection under the National Labor Relations Act of 1937 to any union whose officers failed to swear that they were not Communists. Union leaders were required to take an oath that they were not members of the Communist Party nor affiliated with such party, nor did they believe in or support "any organization that believes in or teaches the overthrow of the United States government by any illegal or unconstitutional methods."

Vinson, joined by Burton and Reed, focused on the purpose of Congress in passing the National Labor Relations Act in 1937 and the subsequent noncommunist affidavit provision in 1947. These, he said, were aimed at eliminating impediments to interstate commerce. One such obstruction was the so-called political strike. Congress had amassed "substantial amounts of evidence" that Communist leaders had used and would continue to use strikes "in support of policies of a foreign government" and that Communists had infiltrated union organizations to use them as a means by which "commerce and industry might be disrupted when the dictates of political policy required."[8]

The union claimed that the statute violated fundamental rights guaranteed by the First Amendment, including the right of union officers to hold political views of their choice and to freely associate with political groups they desire and the right of unions to choose officers without interference from government. The National Labor Relations Board argued that there was no First Amendment problem, because it was only denying a "privilege"—the use of its service—to noncomplying unions. Vinson, however, recognized that neither position was entirely accurate. The Court could not treat section 9 (h) as if it was merely withdrawing a privilege "gratuitously granted by Congress," nor could the Court consider the provision as a licensing statute prohibiting those persons who do not sign the affidavit from holding union office. The question that emerged was much more difficult. Did Congress violate the First Amendment when it denied leadership positions to union members because of their particular beliefs and political affiliations? Vinson found that Congress did have such power. He likened the restrictions on labor unions to restrictions imposed on other enterprises, such as bank directors in the underwriting business and other rational schemes imposing restriction on specific occupations.

The heart of Vinson's opinion rested on his interpretation of the "clear and present danger test" as articulated by Justices Oliver Wendell Holmes and Louis D. Brandeis. Although the Holmes-Brandeis doctrine was originally intended to deal with speech or actions that posed a threat to national security, Vinson argued that the question presented in *Douds* was different. Instead, the government's interest in this situation was "in protecting the free flow of commerce from what Congress considers to be substantial evils of conduct that are not the products of speech at all." It is not the consequences of speech that Congress feared, but rather "the harmful conduct which Congress has determined is carried on by persons who may be identified by their political affiliations and beliefs" (396).

Vinson went to great lengths to clarify that the Court could not uphold restrictions on speech unless the evil it might produce is "substantial" and "relatively serious," but he rejected the idea that previous courts had intended to "lay down an absolutist test" to determine what constituted danger to the nation. Instead, Vinson said the Court must determine which of the conflicting interests demanded the greater protection "under the circumstances" (399). In weighing the circumstances, Vinson said the Court must give due deference to the "legislative determination of the need for restriction upon particular forms of conduct." Further, Vinson determined that Congress had not restrained "the activities of the Communist Party as a political organization," nor had it stifled beliefs. He noted that section 9 (h) affected "only a relative handful of persons, leaving the great majority of persons of the identified affiliations and beliefs completely free from restraint." Those who were affected, he said, were still "free to maintain their affiliations and beliefs" and were subject only to possible loss of positions that Congress had concluded were being abused "to the injury of the public by members of the described group" (404).

Another issue raised by the plaintiffs was that section 9 (h) was so broad that it could apply not only to members of the Communist Party and affiliated organizations but also to any person who believed in the overthrow of government by force. Vinson acknowledged that the breadth of the provisions, if read literally, could include "all persons who might under any conceivable circumstances, subscribe to that belief," but following his ingrained inclination toward judicial restraint, Vinson determined that there was no reason to construe the statute that broadly. He thought the Court had the duty to interpret a statute in a way that avoided the danger of unconstitutionality, as long as such construction of the statute was consistent with the legislative purpose. Vinson thought the legislative intent behind section 9 (h) was served by construing it "to apply to persons and organizations who believe in violent overthrow of the Government as it presently exists under the Constitution as an objective, not merely a philosophy" (407).

Vinson's avoidance of the First Amendment issue on this last point led Frankfurter and Jackson, who concurred with most of the Court's opinion, to dissent in part. Frankfurter was in total agreement that the Court had a duty to allow Congress some latitude in how it should regulate in order to protect the industrial peace of the country. However, he thought that Congress "had cast its net too indiscriminately" when it required someone to take an oath that they did not favor illegal or unconstitutional methods of changing the government" (420–21).

Jackson's lengthy concurrence actually went further than Vinson's opinion in limiting the Court's power to review the provisions of Congress except to determine if there was a "rational basis" for the proscribed remedies. He provided a lengthy analysis of the differences between the Communist Party and other parties in the United States to explain why Congress was justified in singling it out for differential treatment. Like Frankfurter, however, Jackson thought the belief provision of Section 9 (h) was unconstitutional. He did not think Congress had the power to "proscribe any opinion or belief which has not manifested itself in any overt act" (442).

Black took the "absolutist" position that section 9 (h) was an unconstitutional infringement of the First Amendment. "Individual freedom and governmental thought-probing cannot live together," he said. Congress could not use the commerce power to proscribe "beliefs and political affiliations." He noted that the First Amendment was added after the Constitution was adopted in order to prohibit Congress from using previously granted powers, such as the power to regulate commerce, to restrict freedom of belief or expression. "Freedom to think," he said, "is inevitably abridged when beliefs are penalized by imposition of civil liberties" (446).

Several points are noteworthy about the various opinions in *Douds.* One is that the case demonstrated how far Vinson was willing to go to support the government when it restricted individual freedom for the public's interest in security. On every issue raised in *Douds,* Vinson gave the benefit of the doubt to the government. The point for which he was most criticized was the way in which he applied the clear and present danger test, particularly with regard to the standards to be applied in deciding whether a clear and present danger existed. John P. Frank said Vinson set the standards so low "that almost any act of Congress would appear to meet them."[9] Vinson was also criticized for going much further than necessary to uphold the statute. Like Frankfurter and Jackson, he could have achieved the same result while still recognizing some limits imposed by the First Amendment.

The outcome of the *Douds* case signified that on most civil liberties issues, Frankfurter's and Jackson's professed self-restraint would result in their aligning with the Truman appointees, increasing the likelihood that the Court would tolerate more restrictions of individual rights than did the Stone Court. Had Rutledge and Murphy still been on the Court, the majority opinion could well have gone the other way on key points. The outcome also revealed that Black lacked support among his brethren for his absolutist position on the First Amendment freedoms. Douglas shared Black's view, but he did not participate in the *Douds* case. Starting with the 1949 term, Black and Douglas were increasingly in the minority, as more and more civil liberties cases reached the Court. In the first three terms with Vinson as chief justice, Black dissented on the average in 23 percent of the cases. In 1949 his dissent rate went up to 33 percent, and in the 1950 term it reached 38 percent. Douglas's rate of dissent increased over that same period from an average of 28 percent to an average of 38 percent. In contrast, Vinson's dissent rate decreased from 13 percent in his first three terms to a mere 4 percent in the 1949 and 1950 terms.[10]

As troubling as the *Douds* opinion was to civil libertarians, it was far overshadowed by another opinion, *Dennis* v. *United States* (1951).[11] This was the Court's response to the appeal of the Communist Party leaders who were convicted of violating the Smith Act in October 1949. The trial had lasted nine months, the longest criminal trial in American history at that time. Throughout the trial there were constant confrontations between the defendants and their lawyers and the presiding judge, Harold Medina. He exhibited little sympathy for the defendants and even less tolerance for their disruptive and dilatory tactics. The defendants appealed the verdicts to the Second Circuit Court of Appeals, which upheld the convictions.

The highly respected chief judge of the second circuit, Learned Hand, wrote the circuit court opinion. He reviewed several Supreme Court precedents in his opinion, beginning with the *Schenck* case, in which Holmes first enunciated the clear and present danger test, and ending with *Douds,* which he said "was in some ways the most important of all" because it had reaffirmed the court's role in weighing an infringement of free speech against the public interest in suppressing danger. In each case, Hand said, the courts "must ask whether the gravity of the 'evil,' discounted by its improbability, justifies such invasion of free speech as is necessary to avoid the danger."[12]

Hand justified the holding of a clear and present danger by reviewing the history of the Cold War. In particular, he assessed the situation in the summer of 1948 when the defendants were first indicted. Hand said that Dennis and his followers were acting in close concert with Communist factions in western Europe and that relations between the Soviet Union and the West were growing increasingly hostile. He noted that Communists had singled out the United States as the "chief enemy," and as a result "any border fray, any diplomatic incident, any difference in the construction of the modus vivendi—such as the Berlin Blockade . . . might prove a spark in the tinder-box, and lead to war." He asked "how one could ask for a more probable danger, unless we must wait until the actual eve of hostilities" (201, 213). Under these circumstances, Hand concluded, the United States was justified in prosecuting those who appeared to seek the overthrow of the government by force.

When the Supreme Court granted certiorari in October 1950, it limited its review to the questions of whether the Smith Act, either inherently or as construed and applied to the Communist Party officers, violated the First Amendment and whether the act violated the First and Fifth Amendments because of vagueness. Attorneys for the party officials sought to delay the oral arguments set for December 4, 1950, until January 22, 1951, purportedly to allow a British barrister to participate. The Court denied this request, and shortly thereafter Frankfurter circulated a memorandum to the members of the Court warning them that they were dealing with "extremely sophisticated tacticians" who were concerned not merely with legal issues but were "engaged in propaganda for extraneous ends." Frankfurter said he had "no appetite for debate with these men, and the Court should avoid giving them any opportunity for it."[13] Frankfurter's memorandum was in reference to the tactics being carried out by the Communist Party to generate public sympathy by "educating the masses" about the potential threat to constitutional freedom posed by the government's prosecutions.

Oral arguments were held on December 4, and the Court met in conference on December 9 to discuss the case. Douglas's conference notes provide a window on the Court's deliberations. His first entry was "C.J. affirms—practically no discussion." Vinson was followed by Black, who said the "clear and present danger test was not satisfied" and voted to reverse. Only Frankfurter and Jackson are reported as having discussed specific points at some length. Six justices at the outset voted to affirm the convictions. Clark did not participate. Only Black and Douglas voted to reverse. At the conclusion of his notes, Douglas added, "The amazing thing about the conference . . . was the brief nature of the discussion. Those wanting to affirm had [their] minds closed to argument and persuasion." There is nothing to indicate that Douglas was any more amenable persuasion than those he attacked. Clearly frustrated over his failure to sway more of the brethren to his point of view, he said the conference discussion was "largely *pro forma*," and he despaired that it signaled a "drastic return of the 'clear and present danger test' which [affirmation of convictions] required."[14]

For the next six months, the justices circulated copies of their opinions to each other. Even though a majority of six justices voted to affirm the convictions, those in the majority could not agree on a single opinion. Vinson assigned the majority opinion to himself, and Minton, Reed, and Burton joined him. Frankfurter and Jackson concurred with the majority, but each wrote separate concurring opinions. Black and Douglas each wrote separate dissenting opinions. Clark again did not participate in the case. While the justices debated in secret, some of those on the outside were hoping to influence their decisions through indirect means. In a statement carried over national airwaves, the Communist Party predicted protests and demonstrations in various cities if the convictions were not overturned. At the other end of the ideological spectrum, the American Bar Association (ABA) House of Delegates approved a resolution condemning the conduct of the defense attorneys at the trial of the Communist Party leaders and called for their disbarment. Frankfurter was so disturbed by these thinly veiled efforts to influence the Court that he thought the actions of both the ABA and the Communist Party deserved a judicial citation for contempt.[15]

In drafting the opinion for the majority, Vinson relied heavily on the circuit court opinion written by Hand. This proved to be a great benefit to Vinson, because Hand's opinion had provided legitimacy to views that Vinson held. The first issue that Vinson dealt with was the question of intent, because the structure and purpose of the Smith Act required proof of intent. "Congress was concerned with those who advocate and organize for the overthrow of the government," he said, and those "who recruit and combine for the purpose of advocating overthrow intend to bring that about."[16]

The crux of the problem was whether a criminal conviction could be sustained constitutionally merely by proving an intent to advocate the overthrow of the government by force and violence without proof that they actually intended to do so. Vinson thought that intent to advocate was enough. He equated advocacy with intent to follow through and declared that "the *power* of Congress to protect the Government of the United States from armed rebellion is a proposition that requires little discussion." He rejected the "right to rebellion" where the existing government structure provides for peaceful and orderly change. He said,

"We reject any principle of governmental helplessness in the face of preparation for revolution, which principle, carried to its logical conclusion, must lead to anarchy" (501).

Vinson defended the statute against the defendants' claims that it prohibited even academic discussion of the merits of Marxism-Leninism in violation of the Constitution's protection of free speech and free press. He said the very language of the Smith Act negated such a claim. The act, he declared, was "directed at advocacy not discussion. . . . Congress did not intend to eradicate the free discussion of political theories to destroy the traditional rights of Americans to discuss and evaluate ideas without fear of governmental sanction" (502). Rather, he argued that Congress was concerned with the kind of activity in which the party had engaged.

Vinson had to acknowledge, however, that advocacy of the overthrow of the government by force, even when coupled with intent to accomplish that overthrow, still contained an element of speech, and this forced Vinson to deal with the issue of what the boundaries of free speech were under the First Amendment. This led him to a discussion of the Court precedents relating to the clear and present danger test. He quoted a passage from Holmes's majority opinion in the 1918 *Schenck* case that enunciated the test in these words: "The question in every case is whether the words used are used in such circumstances and are of such a nature as to create a clear and present danger that they will bring about the substantive ills that Congress has a right to prevent."[17]

In *Gitlow* the Court majority had upheld the validity of the New York Criminal Anarchy Law and the conviction of a member of a left-wing section of the Socialist Party for violation of the law.[18] It also had ruled that *any statute* punishing advocacy of the overthrow of the government was constitutionally valid. Thus the precedent set by *Gitlow* limited the power of the Court to review such statutes. Vinson, however, disagreed with that aspect of the opinion. He did not believe that such convictions should automatically be sustained. Instead, he leaned in the direction of the dissent by Holmes and Brandeis, requiring proof of clear and present danger in each case. Holmes and Brandeis argued that when speech alone, separated from any action, was the evidence for the violation of a statute, then it was necessary to show that the speech itself created a clear and present danger. The two justices thought that Gitlow's speech did not pose such a threat. But Vinson did not go as far as Holmes and Brandeis did in their *Gitlow* dissent. It is unlikely that the Holmes-Brandeis version of clear and present danger, as enunciated in *Gitlow* and the subsequent case of *Whitney* v. *California,* would have sustained the convictions in the *Dennis* case.[19] What Vinson glossed over in his *Dennis* opinion was the belief of Holmes and Brandeis that the utterance or publication of a theory, separated from action, could be punished.

Vinson found a means to link the Holmes-Brandeis argument to the Court's opinion in *Douds,* where the Court pointed out that the Communist oath affidavits were not intended to punish belief but to regulate conduct of union affairs. He went on to argue again, as he had in *Douds,* that the clear and present danger test enunciated by Holmes and Brandeis was never intended to be "crystallized into a rigid rule to be applied inflexibly without regard to the circumstances of the case." "Speech," he declared, "is not an absolute," and the legislature can deem that "certain kinds of speech are so undesirable as to warrant criminal sanction."

Wading into a thicket about relativism, Vinson wrote, "Nothing is more certain in modern society than the principle that there are no absolutes, that a name, a phrase, a standard has meaning only when associated with the considerations which gave birth to the nomenclature. To those who would paralyze our Government in the face of impending threat by encasing it in a semantic straitjacket we must reply that all concepts are relative."[20] What Vinson intended by that statement was that the clear and present danger test produced no absolute standard for every case to determine the immediacy of threat. He went on to explain what the phrase meant in the context of the Communist beliefs.

Government, he said, had a "substantial enough interest" in protecting itself against violent overthrow. He declared this to be the "ultimate value" of any society, "for if a society cannot protect its very structure from armed attack, it must follow that no subordinate value can be protected." That is a succinct statement of Vinson's core belief. Order must come first if there is to be any other value, such as freedom. Thus, government is required to act. It need not "wait until the *putsch* is about to be executed, the plans have been laid and the signal is awaited" (509). An attempted overthrow, even if it is doomed to fail, "is a sufficient evil for Congress to prevent." Vinson then appropriated Hand's words: courts must "weigh whether the gravity of the evil, discounted by its probability, justifies the invasion of free speech." Adopting this as the Court's rule, Vinson said, "It is as succinct and inclusive as any other we might devise. . . . More we cannot expect from words" (510).

Even though no attempt to overthrow the government had actually occurred, Vinson said, the danger posed was real, for this was "a highly organized conspiracy with rigidly disciplined members subject to call when the leader felt that the time had come for action." Leaving no doubt as to the majority's position, Vinson rejected the argument of the minority that there is a distinction between a conspiracy to advocate and the advocacy itself, for "it is the existence of the conspiracy which creates the danger" (511).

Finally, Vinson dismissed the petitioners' claim that the language of the Smith Act violated the First and Fifth Amendments because the limits on speech were not sufficiently clear. He admitted that the standard set by the act was "not a neat mathematical formula," but he thought that the Court's attempts to clarify the scope of factors included in the standard adequately indicated "to those who would advocate constitutionally prohibited conduct that there is a line beyond which they may not go" (516). The fact that there might be "borderline cases" in the future involving the applicability of the standard did not warrant reversing the convictions because the petitioners were unaware that their activities were constitutionally proscribed by statute.

Frankfurter's concurring opinion, almost as long as the other four opinions combined, criticized the majority approach for its heavy reliance on the clear and present danger test and the preferred position doctrine with which Black and Douglas had enshrined freedom of speech. This, he said, had led to giving constitutional support to "uncritical libertarian generalities" (527). Instead, Frankfruter promoted his idea of a balancing test, which called for an "informed weighing of competing interests" (525). This responsibility, he said, falls primarily to the legislature, "and the balance they strike is a judgment not to be displaced by [the courts] unless outside the pale of fair judgment" (540). Frankfurter provided a lengthy discourse on precedents in which the Court had sought to resolve conflicts between speech and competing interests.

Jackson's concurring opinion offered a simpler and perhaps more logical way to uphold the convictions than the tortured reasoning that Vinson went through to apply the clear and present danger test or Frankfurter's weighty repudiation of it with the balancing test that severely restricted the Court's role. Jackson argued that the clear and present danger test was not the appropriate measure for dealing with the kind of activities in which the Communists engaged. Jackson maintained that the clear and present danger test should be applied "in the kind of cases for which it was devised, such as the threat posed by "hot-headed speech on the street corner, or a circulation of a few incendiary pamphlets, or parading of some zealots behind a red flag" (568).

Jackson thought the Court was on sounder legal ground to focus on the act of conspiracy, because there was no constitutional right to engage in conspiracy. He said, "Conspiracy may be an evil in itself, independently of other evil it seeks to accomplish, and no overt act is or need be required" (573–74). Jackson said the law of conspiracy was the "chief means" available to the government to deal with organizations like the Communist Party, albeit "an inept and awkward remedy," and government should not be deprived of it. He declared, "There is no constitutional right to 'gang up' on the government" (577).

Black's dissent is relatively brief, for he had agreed to allow Douglas to carry the burden of dissent.[21] Although both agreed that the Vinson opinion had not properly adhered to the Holmes-Brandeis formula for clear and present danger, each dissenter took a different thrust. Black began by clarifying that the defendants had not been charged with an attempt to overthrow the government nor any overt acts designed to overthrow the government. The charge was that they had "agreed to assemble and to talk and publish certain ideas at a later date." Black said that regardless of how the indictment was worded, it represented a "virulent form of prior censorship of speech and press, which I believe the First Amendment forbids."[22] Black essentially advocated an absolutist position on the First Amendment. He could not agree "that the First Amendment permits [the Court] to sustain laws suppressing freedom of speech and press on the basis of Congress' or our own notions of mere reasonableness." He said, "Such a doctrine waters down the First Amendment so that it amounts to little more than an admonition to Congress" (580). He concluded his opinion with the "hope that in calmer times, when present pressures passions and fears subside, this or some later Court will restore the First Amendment liberties to the high preferred place where they belong in a free society" (581).

Black's dissent revealed the sharp philosophical differences between himself and the Court's majority. These differences were captured even more vividly in some rather uncharitable comments that Black wrote on a February draft of the chief justice's opinion. When Vinson wrote that government did not have to wait "until the putsch is about to be executed," Black noted in the margin, "good semantic emotionalism and ghost conjuring." To Vinson's description of the imminent threat of the Communist conspiracy, Black added, "Emerging crisis, always the plea of those who would give dictatorial power to rulers." To other such references he said, "The goblins'll get you!" When Vinson referred to the "kind of activity" in which Dennis and his followers were engaged, Black asked, "What activity?" On another point he said, "These people were not convicted for their *acts*."[23] The mocking tone of Black's remarks reveals his lack of esteem for the chief justice, as well as a measure of intolerance of anyone who might take the Communist threat seriously.

Douglas, unlike Black, did not accept that freedom of speech is absolute. He conceded that "teaching methods of terror and other seditious conduct" would be beyond protection. However, the Communists were not charged with a "conspiracy to overthrow" but with forming a party to teach and advocate the overthrow of the government. He noted the paradox that books used by the Communists could legally remain on library shelves and be used in a class. That, he said, makes the crime "depend not on what is taught but on who the teacher is. That is to make freedom of speech turn not *on what is said* but on the *intent* with which it is said. Once we start down that road we enter territory dangerous to the liberties of every citizen."[24] Douglas did not think that the Communist Party in the United States posed such a threat. It is a "bogeyman," he declared, noting that it had been so thoroughly exposed in the United States that "it had been crippled as a political force." They are merely "miserable merchants of unwanted ideas; their wares remain unsold" (588–89).

The *Dennis* opinion came at the end of Vinson's fifth term as chief justice, and it stands as testimony to his inability to unite the Court. He was able to muster only a plurality to his position. The other two members of the majority supported the judgment of the Court to uphold the convictions of the Communist Party leaders, but they were as critical of his reasoning as the dissenters were. The muddled status of the clear and present danger test going into the case had contributed to the problems of crafting a majority opinion. Ambiguous precedents pointed in different directions. The multiple opinions in *Dennis,* rather than clarifying the matter, only muddied the waters. Four justices, Vinson, Reed, Burton, and Minton, sanctioned the validity of the clear and present danger test, albeit in a significantly modified version compared to the Court's direction prior to *Dennis.* Frankfurter repudiated it and substituted a balancing test. Jackson limited its applicability to a very narrow range of cases. Black essentially discounted clear and present danger or any test as an acceptable limit on free speech. Douglas thought "clear and present danger" could limit speech but not mere advocacy separated from action. In his historical analysis of free speech in the United States, David Rabban said that *Dennis* "marked both the apex and the turning point of the Court's reliance on the clear and present danger test [because] the phrase could no longer bear the pressure of the inconsistent interpretations placed upon it by different justices." Rabban noted that although subsequent decisions occasionally cited the test, it never recaptured the prominence it had before *Dennis*.[25]

Critics of the *Dennis* opinion, such as Melvin Urofsky, thought it had one redeeming aspect—that "the clear and present danger test never recovered from the beating it received from the hands of the majority."[26] Free speech scholar Harry Kalven blamed the problem on efforts by the Court's majority to adjust the test "to meet the political exigencies of the case . . . giving it the kiss of death."[27] The political exigencies to which Kalven was referring were the highly visible nature of the trial in Medina's court and the accompanying charges that the United States was indulging in political trials. Kalven said, given the importance of the occasion, the Court felt compelled to "reconcile the Government's anti-Communist strategy with the traditions of free speech and political tolerance." This is why Kalven said the Court had to "work so hard to confirm the convictions" in what otherwise should have been an open and shut case for reversal (195).

Michael R. Belknap, who has written extensively on political trials in the United States, blamed the Court for overreacting to anticommunist fever and participating in the political prosecution of the Communist Party leaders.[28] Belknap said such political prosecutions constituted "official abuse of dissenting minorities" and that in the United States they had most commonly occurred when the nation was under considerable stress.[29] In the *Dennis* case and other prosecutions of Communist Party leaders, the source of the stress was the Cold War. In Belknap's judgment, trials like *Dennis* represent an unjustified use of all the machinery of government, including the courts, to repress those whose views challenge the prevailing orthodoxy. In the case of the Communist Party leaders, Belknap said the methods used to debilitate "a small radical organization" were a high price for the country to pay because they "seriously endangered rights lying at the heart of the American constitutional system" (7). Views of legal commentators sounding similar themes appeared in such distinguished publications as the *Harvard Law Review,* the *Virginia Law Review,* the *Chicago Law Review,* the *Vanderbilt Law Review,* and the *American Political Science Review*.[30] These authors thought the actions of the Communist Party leaders did not constitute a sufficient threat and that therefore the infringement of their free speech was not justified.

There were, however, a number of scholars who defended *Dennis* as a reasonable response to a potential threat and not just a response to public opinion. They took more seriously the dangers of the Communists' "clandestine speech" and their "conspiratorial nature." Sidney Hook, professor of philosophy at New York University, in a book entitled *Heresy Yes—Conspiracy No!* echoed Vinson's concerns that the survival of the United States was threatened by a conspiratorial movement with ties to Moscow, making the Communist Party in the United States in effect "a para-military fifth column."[31] Belknap identified a flaw in this reasoning. The Communists were dangerous not because of the ideas that they taught but because of the nature of their organization with its ties to Moscow. There in a nutshell was the great divide. Could the Communist Party's ideas and doctrine be separated from its organizational roots and connections? Those who thought so believed that their speech was protected by the First Amendment, but people like Vinson, who did not think so, believed that the CPUSA presented a clear and present danger. Political scientist James Bolner, defending Vinson's reasoning in *Dennis* and *Douds,* said it was "far from being the irrational ravings of contemporary caricatures" but rather reflected "his honest and sincere reading of our constitutional history."[32]

Press reaction to the *Dennis* opinion was mixed. The *New York Times* lauded the Court for establishing an important principle: "that liberty shall not be abused to its own destruction." The *Times* said there was little reason to fear a Communist uprising, but there was reason to fear the "harmful activities of Communist spies and traitors. The First Amendment was designed to preserve our freedom and not to serve the purposes of a furtive conspiracy allied with foreign Governments to overthrow all freedom."[33] The *Washington Post* called the decision "the most important reconciliation of security and liberty in our time." The *Post* argued that the opinion would not diminish free speech and predicted that "the cool reasoning of the majority opinion will strongly appeal to the good judgment of the present and future generation."[34]

Not surprisingly, criticism came from the more liberal publications. The *New Republic* said the Court "paid tyranny the tribute of imitation" and that "the great damage lies in the deterioration of the American spirit of freedom."[35] The *St. Louis Post-Dispatch* labeled the opinion "narrow, timid and confused," whereas the *New York Post* accused the Supreme Court justices of exhibiting the "timidity of scared politicians."[36] Although no one in the press mentioned the fact, it is of interest to note that three of the four justices in the *Dennis* plurality—Vinson, Burton, and Minton—had all served in Congress. In fact, as a senator, Minton had voted for the Smith Act. Perhaps this made them more attuned to the pressures faced by politicians from a fearful public. Black, the only other member of the Court with a legislative background, was so committed to the sanctity of freedom of speech that his previous congressional experience was not a factor.

One aspect of Vinson's opinion that created an unexpected uproar was his statement, "Nothing is more certain in modern society than the principle that there are no absolutes." Vinson had used this in conjunction with his view that a phrase like "clear and present danger" could not be construed the same in all situations. *Barron's,* which praised Vinson's opinion in general, chided the chief justice for including the "logically fallacious" statement. The author of the article wrote, "If there are no absolutes then there is no such thing as truth and consequently there are no principles, which are themselves applications of fundamental truths."[37] Religious publications such as the *Christian Century* took Vinson to task for his statement, but the more temperate *Catholic Standard* offered a more thoughtful response.

The public spotlight generated an avalanche of letters from the public. Vinson's standard reply to the letter-writers was to urge them to reserve judgment until they had read the full opinion. Sometimes he added other comments that revealed that he was stung by the vehement response to this statement. In one reply he wrote, "I do not believe that you can find anything in my *Dennis* opinion or any other statement made by me, written or spoken, that would even squint at the interpretation given in the statement to which you referred in your letter. . . . It was a real shock to me to know that anyone could draw such an inference from the actual words used."[38] In another letter he said, "After you have read [my opinion], I would be glad to have your views on the injustice done to me."[39]

In the end, the *Dennis* opinion, for all the passions it stirred up, proved to be less significant than either its critics or its admirers predicted. In the short term it resulted in the stepped-up prosecution of Communist Party members, but at nowhere near the level that civil libertarians feared. By 1955 a total of 129 party members had been prosecuted, a far cry from the 12,000 to 25,000 that were originally projected.[40] The long-term effect of *Dennis* was limited as well. In 1957, in the case of *Yates v. United States,* the Supreme Court reversed convictions under the Smith Act of several leaders of the California branch of the Communist Party.[41] The opinion, written by John Marshall Harlan, modified Vinson's *Dennis* opinion by making a distinction between the advocacy of the teaching of an abstract doctrine and adding a requirement for concreteness. His opinion makes no reference at all to the clear and present danger formula.

Much had changed in the six years since *Dennis* was decided. Stalin died in 1953, and an armistice was declared in Korea. In 1954 the Senate censured Sen. Joseph McCarthy, and the public fixation over Communism had given way to more temperate views, giving the Court more breathing room. Also, the composition of the Court underwent drastic changes. Three justices in the *Dennis* plurality, Vinson, Reed, and Minton, along with Jackson, were no longer on the Court. The changed composition of the Court "in calmer times" produced a different response from the Court, and *Dennis* was history. Harlan's interpretation of *Dennis* made it virtually impossible to apply Smith Act conspiracy provisions to the Communist Party, and there were no further prosecutions.

Of all the cases that the Court heard regarding members of the Communist Party, none riveted the attention of the nation as much as that of accused spies Julius and Ethel Rosenberg. Coming at the end of Vinson's final year on the Court, the *Rosenberg* case speaks volumes about the continuing conflicts among the justices. It may have been the single most contentious issue that the Court dealt with. Conference debates degenerated into screaming matches, and justices leveled behind-the-scenes accusations that other justices were acting out of ulterior motives. The fight was bitter, and the Court was bloodied by the turmoil.

On April 5, 1951, Julius and Ethel Rosenberg were convicted of espionage by a federal jury for sharing atomic secrets with the Soviet Union in 1944 and 1945. Seven times between October 13, 1952, and June 18, 1953, the Supreme Court denied petitions of certiorari to review the case. Each request for review turned on a different issue, but each was denied. Vinson, Reed, Clark, and Minton voted against every petition. Frankfurter and Black consistently voted to grant the requests, albeit for entirely different reasons. Black thought all along that the case presented serious constitutional questions, whereas Frankfurter was more concerned about the Court's responsibility to hear the case and to dispel public perceptions that the Rosenbergs were being treated unfairly. Burton, Jackson, and Douglas vacillated in their positions. Douglas's behavior seemed the most peculiar and brought the Court's long-simmering personal rivalries to the boiling point once again.

For the first three appeals filed by the Rosenbergs' lawyers, Douglas sided with the majority to deny the petitions for certiorari. The last of these was on April 11, 1953. The Court's denial of the third request was held up for more than a month while Frankfurter debated writing a dissent. On May 20 Frankfurter sent a memorandum to the conference specifying that he and Black would simply state that they adhered to their previous position on granting review. Then on May 22 Douglas sent his colleagues a surprise memorandum announcing his change of position. He explained that he had studied the record further and "reluctantly concluded that certiorari should be granted." He said the conduct of the U.S. district attorney, which had been a key issue for those sympathetic to the Rosenbergs, "probably prejudiced the defendants seriously."[42] After receiving Douglas's memorandum, Vinson decided to reopen the case at the Court's regular conference on May 23. It turned into a stormy session.

Douglas's memorandum infuriated both Frankfurter and Jackson, who believed that Douglas had written the dissent to protect his libertarian reputation, knowing that there was no chance of the Court's granting review, because only two other justices—Black and Frankfurter—supported it. Frankfurter used Douglas's changed position as an opportunity to lobby Burton and Jackson to drop their opposition to reviewing the case. He succeeded in convincing Jackson, who thought that Douglas's memorandum was an embarrassment to the Court. At the May 23 conference, Jackson strongly rebuked Douglas and announced that he would vote to grant certiorari. He made the fourth justice to do so, thus denying Douglas the opportunity to publish his dissent. Douglas then withdrew his memorandum, saying it was "badly drawn" and that he had not realized that it might embarrass anyone. With the offensive memorandum withdrawn, Jackson announced he would vote to deny certiorari after all. As he left the conference room, he said to Frankfurter, "That S.O.B's bluff was called."[43]

The Court's denial of certiorari was announced on May 25, 1953, but it was not the final chapter in the *Rosenberg* saga. In his detailed account of the case, Michael Parrish said the May 25 decision was "only a prelude to the tangled legal and political conflicts of the following month [in which] passion often triumphed over reason."[44] On two more occasions the Court was presented with petitions in behalf of the Rosenbergs, and on both occasions the Court turned them down. Douglas voted against both petitions. Then on June 16, one day after the Court had finished its regular term, Douglas was presented with a request for a stay of execution for the Rosenbergs by Fyke Farmer, a Nashville, Tennessee, lawyer, and Daniel Marshall of Los Angeles. Neither had any connection to the case or to the defendants but purported to act for Irwin Edelman, who described himself as "next friend" to the Rosenbergs but who also had no connection to them. The petition raised a new issue, namely that the Atomic Energy Act of 1946, which required a jury recommendation for the death penalty in espionage cases, had superseded the Espionage Act, under which the Rosenbergs had been convicted and sentenced.

Douglas agonized over how to respond to the new petition, which he thought raised significant new issues. Although accounts differ slightly as to the sequence of events, Douglas apparently consulted both Vinson and Frankfurter about his dilemma. Vinson told Douglas that the issue of the Atomic Energy Act had already been disposed of in the Court's opinion in November 1952 and that Farmer did not have standing to litigate the issue. Frankfurter said he urged Douglas to do what his conscience told him to and not what the chief justice told him. At one o'clock on the morning of June 17, Douglas drove to Vinson's apartment and told him that he had almost decided to issue the stay. According to Douglas, they discussed the case for an hour, while Vinson tried to dissuade him. He left telling the chief justice he would sleep on it.[45] On June 17 Douglas issued an order staying the execution of the Rosenbergs and promptly left town for the summer, thinking that the issue would not be considered again until the Court reconvened in October.

He was mistaken. At some point in the process—the exact date is in dispute—Attorney General Herbert Brownell and Acting Solicitor General of the United States Robert L. Stern met with Vinson to discuss the stay of execution. FBI memoranda suggest that the meeting was arranged at the request of Jackson and took place before Douglas issued his stay and that Jackson was present at the meeting. Stern, who has written his own account of the meeting, said he was not sure whether the meeting occurred before or after the stay order was issued but that, contrary to what many scholarly sources have reported, Jackson was definitely not present when they met with the chief justice.[46] Regardless of the timing of that meeting, the day immediately following Douglas's stay, Brownell filed a request asking the chief justice to reconvene the Court to vacate the stay. That same day, Vinson called a special session of the Court for June 18, as previously agreed with Brownell. Most of the justices had left town for the summer and had to return to Washington.

Douglas heard the report of the special session on the radio while driving in Pennsylvania. He returned immediately to Washington. Vinson maintained that he had enlisted Pennsylvania state troopers to locate Douglas but was unsuccessful. Douglas later learned about Vinson's meeting with Brownell and his agreement to call a special session if necessary. According to FBI files, the meeting occurred the day before Douglas issued his stay. If this was the case, Vinson would have had time to advise Douglas of this plan. Douglas remained convinced that Vinson had set him up. He maintained that the chief justice had obtained agreement of five justices to overturn the stay regardless of the merits of the arguments presented in the special session.[47]

The Court held three hours of oral arguments on the morning of June 18, followed by a lengthy conference that afternoon and the following morning. Those conferences proved to be the most heated of all the conferences in which the Rosenbergs' case was discussed. Vinson's law clerk, William Oliver, recalled that it was one of the few times he could hear voices raised in conference. He said, "We heard Frankfurter screaming in a loud voice—we couldn't articulate exactly what it was, but it was Frankfurter's voice."[48] The Court deliberations included several highly charged points. Black denounced the special session and the hastiness of the Court's proceedings. Frankfurter questioned whether the Court had the authority to vacate Douglas's order, which he claimed had never been done before. Burton also thought that the Court should take more time to consider whether there was a substantial question. Vinson, Jackson, and Minton were convinced that the Atomic Energy Act did not apply to the case.

The Court then voted on three separate issues. The first one was a motion to uphold Douglas's stay pending full review by the lower courts. It lost five to three, with Black, Douglas, and Burton dissenting. Curiously, according to conference notes by both Burton and Douglas, Frankfurter abstained on that vote. The second vote, on a motion to shorten the stay and schedule further arguments within three weeks, lost by five to four. This time Frankfurter joined the minority. Finally, the Court voted six to three to vacate the stay. On the final vote, Burton joined the majority. After the Supreme Court announced it would vacate the stay, President Eisenhower rejected the Rosenbergs' final plea for clemency, and they were executed on June 19, 1953.

The Court's opinions, published after the Rosenbergs' deaths, reveal how fractured the Court was over the case. Vinson, writing what proved to be his final opinion for the Court, provided a lengthy history of the case from beginning to end. In his discourse he noted that the Court had deliberated in conference for several hours before deciding how to dispose of the questions raised by Douglas's stay. On the proofs of his opinion that Vinson circulated to the Court, Frankfurter scribbled a bitter but lengthy notation about the Court's deliberations. He said, "The fact is that all minds were made up as soon as we left the Bench— indeed, I have no doubt . . . before we met on it." He also claimed that most of the deliberations were about whether the results should be announced that same day or delayed until the following day.[49]

Vinson defended the Court's decision to vacate the stay. He acknowledged that the full Court had no practice of vacating stays by single justices, but he argued that this did not "prove the nonexistence of the power; it only demonstrates that the circumstances must be unusual before the Court, in its discretion, will exercise the power." He argued that the power was derived from the Court's role as the "final forum to render the answer to the question" that had been urged in the defendant's behalf. In so doing, Vinson said that the Court had carried out the limited purpose for which Douglas issued the stay.[50] Vinson also sought to answer critics who thought the Court should have delayed consideration of the stay, saying that the Court had the responsibility to supervise the administration of the criminal justice system by the federal judiciary and that this included seeing that "punishments prescribed by law are enforced with a reasonable degree of promptness and certainty." Had the stay been allowed to stand, it would have entailed "many more months of litigation in a case which had otherwise run its full course" (287). As to the merits of the case, Vinson simply noted that the Court had determined that the Atomic Energy Act did not displace the Espionage Act. Vinson's opinion was followed by concurring opinions from Clark and Jackson, who explained the Court's rationale as to why the Atomic Energy Act did not apply to the Rosenbergs.

Not surprisingly, vehement dissents were registered by Frankfurter, Black, and Douglas. All three were convinced that the Atomic Energy Act, passed in 1946, could be applied to the Rosenbergs. Even though their main crimes occurred in 1944 and 1945, prior to passage of the act, others continued up until 1950, thus bringing them under the latter act. Douglas was adamant that he was right in his reading of the law—that after 1946 Congress intended that before anyone could be sentenced to death for disclosure of atomic sentences, a jury recommendation for such punishment was necessary.

Although public opinion overwhelmingly supported the Court's decision, the majority was taken to task by several observers for its haste in making a decision without fully considering the issues raised and for vacating Douglas's stay without any precedent for doing so. The majority was portrayed as being hell-bent on assuring that the sentence of the

Rosenbergs be carried out, even at the expense of the defendants' rights.[51] Michael Parrish, who relied heavily on Frankfurter's version of the case, is especially hard on Douglas, calling his inconsistency in voting "inexplicable." William Cohen, one of Douglas's law clerks, wrote a strong defense of Douglas, arguing that his votes were not inconsistent but rather were based on the issues raised in each case.[52] Douglas faced public censure as well in the form of an impeachment resolution by Sen. William M. Wheeler of Georgia. Perhaps more than anything else, the *Rosenberg* case revealed that during the seven years with Vinson at the helm, the doctrinal fissures of the Court were as deep and wide as ever, and the personal relations seemed to have grown more bitter.

In 1951, the same year that the Court decided the *Dennis* case, it was confronted with other issues arising from the anticommunist strategies. Prominent among these were appeals from government employees caught in the web of federal and state loyalty programs. Truman's Executive Order 9835, which established a loyalty program for the federal government in 1947, authorized the attorney general to create a list of suspect organizations that was to be used in screening government employees and applicants. The list consisted of various categories of organizations, including totalitarian, fascist, Communist, and subversive. Organizations on the list were not subject to legal sanctions, but employees and potential employees who belonged to listed organizations could be subject to investigations by the FBI and subsequent hearings before regional loyalty boards. A Loyalty Review Board was set up to hear appeals from employees and applicants. Procedures used by the attorney general to complete his list were very informal and made no provisions for the targeted organization to offer evidence in its behalf before being listed. The government employee or applicant who belonged to such a group was given no opportunity in a hearing to challenge the listing of the organization.

The Vinson Court had a mixed record in deciding challenges to the government's loyalty programs, but Vinson himself denied relief to the plaintiffs in every case. He wrote none of the loyalty program opinions. The first major challenge to the federal loyalty program came in *Bailey* v. *Richardson*.[53] The petitioner, Dorothy Bailey, a government employee, claimed that the loyalty program violated her constitutional guarantees of due process and First Amendment rights. The district court and the court of appeals had denied Bailey's claims. In its unsigned opinion, the Supreme Court split four to four, thus affirming the lower court's ruling denying Bailey's claim. Douglas's conference notes shed light on the contentious nature of the conference debate about Bailey that resulted in the four-to-four split. Vinson took an extremely hard-line position. He was adamant that no government employee "had a vested right" to a job. He argued forcefully that "the Court cannot run the executive branch of government," which was what it would be doing if it interfered in the case. Also voting to affirm the lower court decision were Reed, Minton, and Burton. Black, Douglas, Frankfurter, and Jackson were on the other side. Again, Clark did not participate.

Along with *Bailey,* the Court announced its ruling in *Joint Anti-Fascist Refugee Committee* v. *McGrath,*[54] which also concerned the federal loyalty program. The Joint Anti-Fascists and two other organizations challenged their inclusion as Communist organizations on the attorney general's list, and they sought legal remedies to have their names removed from the list. They claimed that they were not Communists and had been included on the list arbitrarily. The groups lost their cases in both the district court and the court of appeals; but in a surprise ruling, the Supreme Court reversed the lower court rulings. Five justices—Burton, Black, Douglas, Frankfurter, and Jackson—voted to grant the relief sought by the Joint Anti-Fascists, but there was no majority opinion for the Court. Every one of the five justices filed a separate opinion, thereby undermining any coherent rationale behind the Court's actions. Kalven called *Joint Anti-Fascists* "a singularly frustrating and unhelpful precedent."[55]

The change in the Court's opinion from *Bailey* to *Joint Anti-Fascists* turned on Burton, who wrote the opinion for the Court. Burton's majority opinion, joined by Douglas, said it was not necessary to satisfy the rule on the constitutional issues, and it ruled against the government on procedural grounds. He thought that the attorney general had acted arbitrarily in failing to satisfy the requirement of the executive order for an "appropriate determination" before designating an organization as subversive. He must, Burton said, at least provide some indication as to why an organization was put on the list.

All of the other justices in the majority, including Douglas, wrote concurring opinions, and all raised constitutional questions about the loyalty program. Black said it violated the First Amendment and due process requirements and created a bill of attainder, punishing the plaintiffs without benefit of a trial. Frankfurter and Jackson thought due process had been denied, and Douglas thought the system of administrative loyalty trials as a whole was unconstitutional. Reed wrote the dissenting opinion, in which Vinson and Minton joined. Reed argued that the organizations had not been harmed by the government program because of their designation on the attorney general's list. The organizations had not been prohibited from conducting any business, nor had they been punished or deprived of any freedoms. In language reminiscent of *Douds* and *Dennis,* Reed said that under the Constitution the government was endowed with "the right and duty to protect it against any force that seeks its overthrow [by force]. Surely the government must not await an employee's conviction of a crime of disloyalty before separating him from public service."[56] As to the claim that the attorney general had infringed on the plaintiff's First Amendment rights, Reed noted, "This Court has never hesitated to deny the individual's right to use privileges for the overturn of law and order." There is not even a hint that the three dissenters thought constitutional rights were threatened.

In 1951 the Court gave its blessing to loyalty programs in several states. These typically took the form of loyalty oaths that public employees and applicants were required to take. In *Gerende* v. *Board of Supervisors of Elections,*[57] the Court unanimously upheld a loyalty oath requirement established by Maryland for candidates seeking public office. The same day it announced the *Dennis* opinion, the Court issued *Garner* v. *Board of Public Works,*[58] which sanctioned a loyalty oath required of all municipal employees in Los Angeles, regardless of the sensitivity of their jobs. In 1952, in *Adler* v. *Board of Education,*[59] the Court endorsed a loyalty program in New York barring persons belonging to subversive organizations from working in the state's school system. *Adler* upheld the constitutionality of the Feinberg law, which made membership in any organization listed as subversive by the State Board of Regents prima facie evidence of unsuitability for any job within the school system. It was the first case that dealt with screening the loyalty of schoolteachers. Vinson joined the majority opinion written by Minton, who argued that there was no right to work for a public school system on one's own terms.

Douds, Gerende, Garner, and *Adler* left no doubt where the Court's majority stood on the permissibility of loyalty oaths as a means of barring subversives from public employment, but even so there were signs that such tests were becoming increasingly suspect to a growing plurality of the Court. Four justices—Black, Douglas, Frankfurter, and Burton—dissented in *Garner.* The same group, with the exception of Burton, dissented in *Adler.*

The doubts of the dissenters finally bore fruit in 1953, shortly before Vinson's death. In *Wieman* v. *Updegraff* the Court unanimously invalidated an Oklahoma loyalty oath for state employees.[60] *Wieman* proved that there were limits of acceptability of loyalty programs even among the justices who had previously supported them. The Oklahoma loyalty oath was much broader than any of the ones previously reviewed by the Court. It excluded from state employment anyone who had been a member of any organization on the U.S. attorney general's list, regardless of their knowledge concerning the organizations to which they belonged. The case was brought by a group of faculty and staff members of an Oklahoma state college. Clark, who wrote for the Court, said, "Indiscriminate classification of innocent with knowing activity must fall as an assertion of arbitrary power. The oath offends due process" (191). Clark's opinion did not go so far as to overturn *Gerende, Garner,* and *Adler.* What distinguished the Oklahoma oath was the fact that it made no provision for those who might have innocently joined an organization designated as subversive.

Even though *Wieman* was a unanimous opinion, there were the usual multiple opinions filed by the justices. All agreed with the reasoning of the majority opinion, but some wanted to go further. Black wrote a separate concurrence, which Douglas joined, declaring that the Oklahoma statute was unconstitutional because it violated constitutional guarantees of thought, speech, and press. Frankfurter wrote a separate concurrence "to add a word by way of emphasis to the Court's opinion." In the field of education, from which the plaintiffs came, Frankfurter said the Oklahoma oath represented "an unwarranted inhibition upon the free spirit of teachers." Burton was listed separately as concurring, but he wrote no opinion. Jackson did not participate in the opinion. *Wieman,* coming in Vinson's last term on the Court, offers a glimmer of light as to the future legality of loyalty programs. The justices were not all singing from the same page, but on this one issue they were in the same choir.

The road to *Wieman* was long and winding, as evidenced by the Court's shifting position on other procedural rights of those accused of subversion. Issues about the Fifth Amendment privilege against self-incrimination for Communist Party members were good examples. In *Blau* v. *United States* (1950),[61] Black spoke for a unanimous Court in ruling that Patricia Blau, a witness before a federal grand jury, could refuse to answer questions about her affiliation with the Communist Party of Colorado. Black said she could invoke her Fifth Amendment privilege against self-incrimination because to admit her party activities could result in prosecution under the Smith Act. The Court reached a similar conclusion in a case involving Blau's husband in a decision announced on January 15, 1951.[62] The Court, speaking again through Black, unanimously upheld the husband's right not to divulge information about the activities and records of the Communist Party.[63] Originally, Minton had written a dissent, which Jackson had planned to join, but for the sake of unity, they abandoned the dissent.[64]

The two *Blau* opinions were only a temporary reprieve for broadening the protection against self-incrimination. Within six weeks of the second *Blau* opinion, the Court announced a third case that greatly impaired the protection, *Rogers* v. *United States*.[65] That case involved Jane Rogers, a cohort of Blau, who admitted to a Colorado grand jury that she had been the treasurer of the Colorado Communist Party and that in that capacity she had possessed membership lists and dues records. By the time of the inquiry, however, she was no longer treasurer and refused to tell the grand jury the name of her successor because she said she did not want to subject another person to what she was going through. Two days later, she was brought to court on contempt charges, and there, having heard a defendant in another case refuse to answer on the grounds of self-incrimination, she did the same. The trial court denied her claim and sentenced her to four months for contempt. Originally the Court majority was in favor of upholding Rogers's claim, and Vinson and Minton had both prepared dissents. However, Vinson's dissent was persuasive enough to convince Jackson to change his mind, and the chief justice's opinion became the opinion for the Court.[66]

Instead of using the *Rogers* case to expand upon the privilege of self-incrimination, Vinson, speaking for the Court, significantly narrowed the protection. His opinion upheld the trial court's contempt sentence on three grounds. First, Rogers had not specifically invoked her privilege against self-incrimination in her initial appearance before the grand jury. Instead, she had refused on the grounds of not subjecting her successor to what she had experienced. Vinson said, "The petitioner's claim of the privilege against self-incrimination was pure afterthought." Second, he argued that even if she had claimed the privilege initially, it would not justify her refusal to supply the name of the person to whom she had given the Party records. There was "no privilege with respect to the books of the Party." Finally, Vinson said that Rogers had waived her privilege of silence when she had freely admitted her own Communist Party membership and that she would not have further incriminated herself by answering other questions put by the grand jury.[67]

Black wrote a vigorous dissent, which was joined by Frankfurter and Douglas. He implied that the majority saw the privilege against self-incrimination "as more or less a constitutional nuisance which the Court should abate whenever or however possible" (376). He argued that the waiver of the privilege of self-incrimination is not to be inferred lightly and that in Rogers's case she had sought to avoid answering the questions on any grounds available until she became aware that she could assert the privilege against self-incrimination.

Other groups besides Communists were also affected by government policies aimed at subversive activities. Numerous cases pertained to the constitutionality of the procedures and methods of the House Un-American Activities Committee (HUAC). Members of certain groups, called to testify before HUAC, were convicted for failure to cooperate with the committee. From 1947 to 1949, the Supreme Court was asked five times to review the convictions of people who had failed to comply with HUAC investigations. The Court denied review in all but one of the cases. In the fifth case the Court was prevented from ruling on the merits of the case because the appellant had fled the country.

Starting with the October 1949 term, the Supreme Court finally began accepting appeals from HUAC-related cases. Two of the cases were appeals by leaders of the Joint Anti-Fascist Committee, an organization that claimed to be a charity providing aid to victims of the Spanish Civil War but which HUAC and the attorney general's office considered to be a subversive organization. In *United States* v. *Bryan,*[68] the executive secretary of the organization, who had custody of the group's records, had been subpoenaed by HUAC to produce specified records of the association to the committee. She refused to do so on the grounds that the committee lacked constitutional authority to demand them. She was then indicted, tried, and convicted for contempt of Congress. The court of appeals reversed her conviction on the grounds claimed by the defendant that the committee lacked a quorum at the time of her testimony and was not duly constituted, which justified not turning over the required documents.

Vinson's majority opinion dealt with two major issues. The first was whether the lack of a quorum of the committee nullified the defendant's obligation to testify. Vinson concluded that it did not. He noted that the defect in the composition of the committee was one that could have been easily remedied but that the defendant did not raise the issue of the committee composition until two years later at her trial. Further, Vinson noted that the defendant did not deny that she would not have complied with the subpoenas regardless of the composition of the committee. Vinson thought she was merely using the lack of a quorum as a vehicle of escape.

When the Court refused to accept Bryan's argument about the lack of a quorum, it reversed a precedent set the previous term in an almost identical case. In *Christoffel* v. *United States*,[69] the Court had invalidated a conviction for perjury before a House committee because of a failure to show that a quorum of the committee was actually in the room at the time that the perjured testimony was given, even though there had been a quorum when the session began. The Court's abrupt turnaround can be explained in part by the change in the Court's composition. *Christoffel* was decided by a five-to-four majority that included Murphy, Rutledge, and Douglas. Two members of the *Christoffel* majority—Rutledge and Murphy—were no longer on the Court. Douglas, who was recuperating in Arizona from major injuries suffered when he fell from a horse, and Clark, who had been attorney general when many Communist cases were prosecuted, did not vote in the *Bryan* case. Black and Frankfurter, who had apparently been in the majority in *Christoffel,* joined their colleagues on the quorum question to make the *Bryan* decision unanimous.

The second question in the *Bryan* case was whether excerpts from the defendant's testimony could be read to the jury that convicted her of contempt in view of an immunity statute that stipulated that "no testimony given by a witness before any committee of either House shall be used as evidence in any criminal proceeding . . . except in a prosecution for perjury." Bryan was tried for contempt, not perjury. Vinson conceded that her "testimony comes within the literal language of the statute," but he said that to interpret the statute in that manner led to "absurd conclusions" and ignored the legislative purpose, which was to obtain information through the granting of immunity. He argued that it would be unreasonable to assume that Congress also intended to grant immunity for failure to provide information. Congress, he said, intended the immunity only for "past criminal acts," and not for refusal to comply. There is no doctrine of "anticipatory contempt," he said.[70] Vinson's opinion in *Bryan* is somewhat inconsistent with his usual inclination to follow precedent and the language of the statute. In fact, both Black and Frankfurter dissented from the Court's interpretation of the statute. Black called the majority's refusal to read the statute literally "judicial lawmaking [that] is particularly questionable when used to restrict safeguards accorded defendants in criminal cases" (346).

A companion to the *Bryan* case handed down the same day was

United States v. *Fleischman,*[71] which involved a member of the board of the Joint Anti-Fascist Committee who refused to produce requested records and was subsequently convicted for contempt, even though the records were not in her possession or under her control. Virtually the same issues were presented in the *Fleischman* case, with the important distinction that Fleischman, unlike Bryan, did not have the documents in her possession. Vinson, again writing for the majority, dismissed this line of defense. Although Fleischman was only one member of the board, Vinson noted that she took no action to get the board to direct Bryan to produce the records, to transfer custody of the documents to someone else, or to remove Bryan from office. As a member of the board, Vinson said, Fleischman assumed an individual responsibility to act within the limits of her power to bring about compliance with the order. Instead, she had assumed no personal duty to do anything. To absolve her of such a responsibility would effectively remove the organization "beyond the realm of legislative or judicial commands," he said.

Further, Vinson said that the burden of proof was on Fleischman to show why she had failed to comply with the subpoena, instead of its being the responsibility of the government to show why she had taken so long to comply with the committee subpoena. This, Vinson said, was equivalent to proving a "negative proposition." Vinson recognized in his opinion that many people inside and outside of Congress were "vigorously demanding" reforms in the practices and procedures of certain committees and said that the Court's opinion should not be interpreted as "expressing either approval or disapproval of those practices." The remedy for reform, he said, "is certainly not to destroy the effective operation of all committees" (365). As in the *Bryan* case, Douglas and Clark did not participate, and Black and Frankfurter dissented. Black's opinion was highly critical of the majority view. He said that the refusal to comply could be punished only if the witness had the power to produce, and in this case the defendant did not have the power to produce the records.

Those who were dismayed by the Court's treatment of domestic subversives were even more distressed by the Court's decisions affecting aliens and naturalized citizens. Vinson, like the majority of the Court, was not inclined to support claims by aliens or naturalized citizens against the government. Yet he wrote one of his most libertarian opinions supporting the claim of a Japanese alien against the California Alien Land Law, which forbade aliens ineligible for American citizenship to acquire land.[72] That act provided that any property bought by "ineligible aliens" in violation of the statute would revert to the state. The law also contained a provision that property would revert to the state if transfers of property were made with the intent to prevent or avoid forfeiture. In 1934 Kajira Oyama, an ineligible alien, bought several acres of agricultural land in the name of his son Fred, a six-year-old American citizen. In 1944 the state sought to gain control of the land on the grounds that Oyama had conveyed the land to his son in violation of the statute.

In 1948 the Court, speaking through Vinson, upheld Oyama's claim. This required some creativity on Vinson's part, because there were Supreme Court precedents upholding the California act and similar acts in other states. To overcome the problem presented by precedents, Vinson accepted the argument presented by Oyama's attorney, Dean Acheson, later to become secretary of state, that the act was a discrimination against Oyama's citizen son. Vinson said, "The State has discriminated against Fred Oyama; the discrimination is based solely on his parents' country of origin; and there is absent the compelling justification which would be needed to sustain discrimination of that nature" (640). Typically, Vinson chose not to examine the validity of the California statute, but he said that assuming for the sake of argument that the law was constitutional, "it [did] not follow that there [was] no constitutional limit to the means which may be used to enforce it." He saw a conflict between two rights. One was the right of the state to formulate landholding rights within its jurisdiction and the right of American citizens to own property anywhere in the United States. "When these two rights clash," Vinson said, "the rights of a citizen may not be subordinated merely because of his father's country of origin" (646–47).

Even though *Oyama* commanded a majority of six, the Court's four most liberal justices wrote or joined in concurring opinions that went further than Vinson's. Black, in an opinion joined by Douglas, and Murphy, in an opinion joined by Rutledge, thought that the entire California statute was unconstitutional. Reed, writing for himself and Burton, dissented. Jackson wrote a separate dissent, challenging the logic of Vinson's opinion in setting aside the state's actions without invalidating the statute. He said, "If [the state's action] seems harsh as to the Oyamas, it is only because it faithfully carries out a legislative policy, the validity of which this Court does not question" (684).

Civil libertarians would have preferred that Vinson's majority opinion had gone one more step and invalidated the California statute, but even so they applauded the result. In upholding *Oyama,* Vinson had invalidated the only effective means of enforcement available to the state.

As a result of the ruling, the California attorney general immediately gave up trying to enforce the act and canceled all actions already initiated in pursuit of the act.[73]

In cases pertaining to aliens, Vinson's *Oyama* opinion was an aberration. Although he did not write any other opinions regarding aliens while he was on the Court, he joined the Court's majority to deny alien rights in each case. Most of the other cases involved decisions about entry or deportation, and in these matters aliens lacked the same constitutional rights as natural-born citizens. The rights to which they were entitled were a function of how far the Court was willing to go in interpreting constitutional protections and statutory law affecting their status. In 1949 the Court made a highly controversial decision in *United States ex rel Knauff* v. *Shaughnessy.*[74] The Immigration Service had denied Ellen Knauff, a German war bride, entry to the United States on the ground that it would be "prejudicial to the interests of the United States." The Supreme Court, in an opinion written by Minton, upheld the authority of the Immigration Service to deny her entry without giving her a hearing. The Immigration Service said it was following an administrative regulation established by the attorney general that allowed aliens to be excluded without a hearing. The authority for this regulation was a congressional statute that permitted the president to issue "reasonable rules, regulations and orders" governing the entrance of aliens during periods of national emergency. Minton, in upholding the Immigration Service, said that "whatever the procedure authorized by Congress is, it is due process as far as an alien denied entry is concerned." He added, "We are dealing here with a matter of *privilege*. Petitioner has no vested *right* of entry" (544). Minton was joined in his opinion by Vinson, Reed, and Burton. They were convinced that the attorney general and immigration officials were following the intent of Congress and that they should not intervene even if the results were harsh. Jackson wrote a strong dissent that Black and Frankfurter joined. Jackson said, "Congress will have to use more explicit language than any yet cited before I will agree that it has authorized an administrative official to break up the family of an American citizen or force him to keep his wife by becoming an exile" (551–52). Frankfurter wrote a separate dissent in which he charged that the majority had misconstrued congressional intent by interpreting the War Brides Act too narrowly.

The year after the *Knauff* decision, the Court continued its narrow construction of alien rights. In *Carlson* v. *Landon,*[75] the Court ruled that an alien could be committed to jail without bail while awaiting deportation hearings simply because the attorney general alleged that he was a Communist who, left at large, would pose a threat to national security. Denying Carlson and his fellow defendants bail meant that they could be incarcerated indefinitely, possibly for years, because deportation hearings were notoriously lengthy proceedings. Critics of the *Carlson* opinion were quick to point out the inconsistency between it and *Stack* v. *Boyle*,[76] an opinion announced only four months earlier. In *Stack*, Vinson, speaking for a rare unanimous Court, had ruled that bail set at fifty thousand dollars each for second-tier leaders of the Communist Party was a violation of the Eighth Amendment protection against excessive bail. Vinson's opinion was short and succinct. He began by noting that the only evidence offered by the government to justify such high bail was the forfeiture of bail by four other Communists, unrelated to these defendants, who had been convicted under the Smith Act. He also noted that federal law "unequivocally" provided that in cases of a noncapital offense a person *"shall* be admitted to bail." In a statement that for him was unusually critical of the government, Vinson said, "The Government asks the courts to depart from the norm by assuming, without prior introduction of evidence, that each petitioner is a pawn in a conspiracy and will, in obedience to a superior, flee the jurisdiction." He declared this to be "an arbitrary act," stating that "such conduct would inject into our own system of government the very principles of totalitarianism which Congress was seeking to guard against in passing the statute under which petitioners have been indicted" (5–6). In order to protect the constitutional rights of each petitioner, Vinson said, evidence must be presented to justify bail in excess of the amount usually set for serious charges of crime.

Despite his views in *Stack,* Vinson voted with the Court's majority in *Carlson* to deny bail in a noncriminal case to aliens subject to deportation hearings. The main difference was that the Carlson defendants were aliens. Reed, who wrote for the five-man *Carlson* majority, said that aliens were "denizens of the country" and were not entitled to release on bail, that detention without bail was not an abuse of the attorney general's discretion under the statute, and that the statute conferring such discretionary power was not an invalid delegation of legislative power. Reed made no effort to reconcile the *Carlson* opinion with *Stack,* which he simply ignored. He concluded that the Eighth Amendment against excessive bail was not applicable because "deportation is not a criminal proceeding and has never been held to be a punishment."[77] Black, Douglas, Frankfurter, and even Burton each wrote vigorous dissents deploring the government's actions as violations of the Constitution or statutory authority.

As harsh as the judgment of the Court was in *Carlson,* it was eclipsed the following year by the *Mezei* case.[78] Decided on March 16, 1953, it was the last alien case in which Vinson participated.[79] It epitomized the Court's view of aliens during his term as chief justice. It upheld the exclusion of Ignatz Mezei, an alien who had lived in the United States for twenty-eight years and who left the country to visit his dying mother in Romania, his homeland. Upon returning to the United States, he was excluded as an alien entering the country for the first time "on the basis of information of a confidential nature." Mezei was detained on Ellis Island pending efforts by the Immigration Service to return him to some suitable country, but no other country would accept him. After another twenty-one months of detention on Ellis Island, he brought a *habeas corpus* proceeding to obtain his release on bail. Clark wrote the opinion of the Court denying Mezei the right to a hearing because his exclusion was grounded on national security concerns. In effect the Court's ruling condemned Mezei to a life on Ellis Island because he literally had nowhere else to go.

The majority opinion generated vehement dissents by Black, with Douglas concurring, and Jackson, with Frankfurter concurring. Jackson could hardly contain his indignation. His angry dissent chided the Court for the harshness of its decision. To the government's claim that Mezei was free to leave the United States for any country of his choice, Jackson said, "that might mean freedom if only he were an amphibian." He concluded: "It is inconceivable to me that this measure of simple justice and fair dealing would menace the security of this country. No one can make me believe we are that far gone" (220, 228).

The judgment in *Mezei* seems especially harsh when compared to a decision announced only one month before in a case with strikingly similar circumstances. In *Kwong Hai Chew* v. *Colding,*[80] the Court afforded due process protection to another alien subjected to deportation after he left the country by categorizing him as a "resident alien." Chew, Chinese by birth, after living in the United States as a permanent resident, joined the Merchant Marine and left the country on an American vessel. When his ship returned to the United States, he was denied entry without a hearing. Unlike the unfortunate Mezei, Chew's petition to the Court received a more favorable response. Burton, who proved to be the most lenient of Truman's appointees toward the rights of aliens, wrote the majority opinion. The only dissent was cast by Minton. The majority opinion held that as a "resident alien" Chew was entitled to Fifth Amendment protections of due process. Granted, he could be deported for security reasons, but not without a hearing. Mezei, classified as a "returning alien," was not even entitled to a modicum of due process. Mezei's sin appears to be that he spent his absence from the United States "behind the Iron Curtain." The distinction between *Mezei* and *Kwong Hai Chew* can only be understood in terms of Cold War hysteria. As Kalven observed about Mezei, it belongs aside other cases "where homely and trivial facts are seen by the justices, in their endless dialogue about freedom under the law, to embody large principles."[81]

Although the decisions about subversives took center stage while Vinson was chief justice, the Court was confronted with other cases in which it had to wrestle with sharply contrasting views about the limits of free speech. Whereas national laws and practices were the objects of constitutional challenges in cases dealing with subversives, most of the other free speech cases dealt with challenges to local government regulations to maintain public order and prevent unwarranted disruptions to the community tranquility. Vinson's record in these cases was less clearcut than in those dealing with subversives. More often than not, he was inclined to uphold the local government, but on occasion he supported individual speech.

One means that local communities used to maintain order was ordinances against the use of sound trucks to deliver a message. The first such case to reach the Court after Vinson became chief justice was *Saia v. New York,*[82] decided in 1948. It involved a Lockport, New York, ordinance that prohibited the use of sound-amplification devices except with the permission of the chief of police. Saia, a Jehovah's Witness minister, gave sermons in a public park on designated Sundays using sound equipment mounted on top of his car. He had obtained a permit, but the police chief refused to renew it because there had been complaints about the noise. Saia used his equipment without a permit, and for this he was tried and convicted. In a five-to-four decision, which Vinson joined, the Court held the ordinance unconstitutional as a prior restraint on free speech because it prescribed no standards to be followed by the police chief. Douglas spoke for the Court, and his opinion relied on a precedent set in 1940 in *Cantwell* v. *Connecticut.*[83] In *Cantwell* the Court had invalidated a Connecticut statute that prohibited door-to-door canvassing for religious or philanthropic purposes without prior approval of a county welfare official. *Cantwell* set the rule that although a state could regulate such things as the time, places, and manner of soliciting contributions or holding meetings on its streets, it could not forbid them altogether. *Cantwell* affirmed the "preferred position" for free speech and established the principle that ordinances constituting prior restraint were constitutionally impermissible.

From 1948 to 1953, the Court began to modify *Cantwell,* moving away from the preferred position given to freedom of speech and giving more leeway to public officials concerned about public order. Vinson's own position about the validity of prior restraint laws fluctuated, depending on how reasonable he thought the restrictions were. In the year following *Saia* case, he voted with the majority to validate another local ordinance regulating sound trucks. In *Kovacs* v. *Cooper,*[84] the Court upheld a Trenton, New Jersey, statute prohibiting all sound trucks or similar amplifying devices that emitted "loud and raucous" noises on public streets. Even though eight of the justices agreed that sound amplification in public places could be subject to reasonable regulation and that prohibiting "loud and raucous" noises fell within reasonable bounds, the multiplicity of opinions created some confusion.

Vinson's switch in position from *Saia* created a majority of five justices who agreed to affirm the convictions in *Kovacs,* but there were three separate opinions among the majority justices. Vinson and Burton joined Reed, who spoke for the Court. He pronounced the Trenton ordinance constitutional by giving it a narrow interpretation—that it prohibited only "loud and raucous" sound trucks. He said "absolute prohibition" of all sound amplification devices would probably be unconstitutional. Both Frankfurter and Jackson indicated in separate opinions that sound trucks could be absolutely prohibited. Douglas and Rutledge joined the dissent by Black, arguing that the conviction should be overturned because no proof had been offered that the sound truck operated by Kovacs was emitting "loud and raucous noises." Rutledge found the ordinance to be an unconstitutional breach of the First Amendment, because he thought an accurate interpretation was that it would have prohibited all sound trucks. Murphy dissented but wrote no separate opinion.

An important difference between *Saia* and *Kovacs* that may explain Vinson's change of heart is that *Saia* involved people who were espousing religious views. The following term, Vinson wrote the majority opinion in two cases that invalidated licensing schemes for religious groups. Both opinions were decided on January 15, 1951, a time when the Court was embroiled in the *Dennis* case and a host of other cases affecting the rights of people labeled as subversive. *Niemotko* v. *Maryland* was a unanimous decision that reversed the convictions of two Jehovah's Witnesses who had been found guilty of disorderly conduct after attempting to hold a peaceful religious meeting in a public park without obtaining a permit.[85] There was no ordinance regulating the use of the park, but by "local custom" organizations wanting to hold a meeting there obtained a permit from the park commissioner. The Jehovah's Witnesses were denied a permit and appealed to the city council. The council rejected their appeal after asking them questions about their refusal to salute the flag and their views on the Bible. Vinson's opinion was short and succinct. The city's practices were a blatant denial of the rights of the plaintiffs. He noted that there was no ordinance or statute, just an "amorphous" practice that vested authority in the parks commissioner and the city council without any standards or limitations as to their decisions. This made the local practice an unconstitutional "prior restraint" of free speech. Vinson said it was inescapable that the plaintiffs were denied use of the park because the city council did not like their views. He declared, "The right to equal protection of the laws, in the exercise of those freedoms of speech and religion protected by the First and Fourteenth Amendments, has a firmer foundation than the whims or personal opinions of a local governing body" (272). Even though Frankfurter concurred in the judgment, he indulged the Court with an unnecessarily lengthy review of the Court's precedents regarding prior restraint, leading him to conclude the obvious—that free speech had to be balanced against other interests. He also used his concurrence to distinguish *Niemotko* from the other licensing case announced the same day, *Kunz v. New York*.[86]

Niemotko and *Kunz* were similar in that both dealt with licensing permits for groups that wished to use public streets or parks to spread their views. In *Kunz* a Baptist minister had run afoul of a New York City law that required a permit to hold religious meetings on city streets. Kunz had received such a permit, only to have it revoked by the police commissioner because he had ridiculed and denounced other religious views in violation of a criminal provision of the ordinance under which the permit was issued. Subsequent efforts to obtain a permit were denied by the police commissioner, but Kunz continued to preach his gospel on the city streets. For this he was arrested and fined ten dollars. Vinson wrote the majority opinion, which was barely five pages. He wasted no words in declaring the New York ordinance invalid as a prior restraint on First Amendment freedoms. He said the ordinance lacked "appropriate standards" to guide the police commissioner's discretion, but he was careful to note that the Court's ruling was directed only at attempts to suppress speech and not the power to punish, leaving open the question of what consequences the city could impose if the speech actually provoked disorder.

Frankfurter wrote a concurring opinion suggesting that a carefully drafted licensing system proscribing speech that would "outrage the religious sensibilities of others" might be valid, but only if the criteria for denying a permit based on predictive violence were clearly delineated. Even this, Frankfurter admitted, might convey too much discretion. Jackson filed the only dissent, a lengthy discourse on why communities should be allowed to deny permits to those who used speech to malign other religious believers. Unlike Vinson, Jackson included examples of Kunz's epithets, such as: "The Catholic Church makes merchandise out of souls," "Catholicism is a religion of the devil," and the Pope is "the anti-Christ." He also attacked Jews as "Christ-killers" and said, "All garbage that didn't believe in Christ should have been burnt in incinerators" (296).

Jackson noted that these utterances had in fact provoked some violence, and therefore were "fighting words," which the Court had placed beyond the protection of the First Amendment.[87] The presence of many Catholics and Jews on the streets of New York created a potential for violence that the city had a right to try to avoid. Jackson also took a swipe at the majority opinion for failing to mention the "clear and present danger" test, which figured so prominently in the *Douds* case and, he might have added, the *Dennis* case that the Court would soon announce. Vinson's willingness to bar local communities from protecting their streets from likely disorder does seem to be inconsistent with his willingness to let the national government take extreme measures to protect against subversive activities. The difference may be explained by his experience in the administrative branch, where he had to be vigilant about employees who might be subversives, as well as a sympathy for Truman, who in 1951 was fending off charges of Wisconsin senator Joseph McCarthy and other right-wingers of the Republican Party that he was soft on Communism. Perhaps the turmoil caused by the Harry Dexter White affair was still fresh in his memory.

Vinson reaffirmed his opposition to licensing schemes in his dissent in *Breard v. City of Alexandria,*[88] a case decided the same year as *Niemotko* and *Kunz.* The *Breard* case is interesting because of the way in which the justices aligned. A majority of six voted to uphold a city ordinance in Alexandria, Louisiana, that prohibited door-to-door solicitation without prior consent of the householder. Breard, who solicited subscriptions for a major magazine publisher, was convicted for violating the act. Reed wrote the majority opinion holding that the ordinance represented a reasonable balance between "the householder's desire for privacy and the publisher's right to distribute publications [in the way they] thought brought the best results." Reed argued that the city had acted reasonably in promoting a public interest—the right of privacy of those being solicited. He also rejected the argument that such ordinances were prohibited by the First Amendment, which he said applied only to the press or to "oral advocates," not to "solicitors for gadgets and brushes" (644).

In dissent, Vinson found himself in rare company on free speech issues. Both Vinson and Black wrote dissents, and each was joined by Douglas. However, even though they were in agreement on invalidating the law, Black and the chief justice were far apart in their reasoning. Consistent with his philosophy of restraint, Vinson chose to avoid the First Amendment issues and argued that the ordinance was unconstitutional because it constituted "an undue and discriminatory burden on interstate commerce." He said only Congress had the power to regulate interstate commerce, citing numerous precedents in which the Court had invalidated state and local laws infringing on interstate commerce. Black's dissent stood in sharp contrast to Vinson's. He used the opportunity once again to advance his "preferred position" view about First Amendment freedoms. He argued that the "constitutional sanctuary for the press must necessarily include liberty to publish and circulate [and] it must include freedom to solicit paying subscribers" (648).

As the Court contemplated the validity of local ordinances in cases like *Saia, Kovacs, Niemotko, Kunz,* and *Breard,* it was dealing primarily with issues of prior restraint. In these cases the Court had to work within the context of precedents under which prior restraint was deemed suspect because it constituted a form of censorship. A different set of issues was raised by speech that was deemed to be a threat to public order after that speech was uttered. In these cases, the questions were how and when law enforcement officials could intervene to protect the public in cases of a public disturbance and under what circumstances those whose speech threatened public order could be punished. As in the cases of prior restraint, bitter conflicts resulted from the Court's doctrinal differences. These differences were vividly reflected in *Terminiello* v. *Chicago* (1949),[89] especially in the sharp dissents by Vinson, Frankfurter, and Reed.

Terminiello, a defrocked priest, delivered an anti-Semitic and racially inflammatory message to his adherents in a Chicago auditorium.

His speech aroused his enemies outside the auditorium to violence. They hurled stones through windows and tried to force open the doors. These actions incited the people inside the auditorium, although they took no physical action against those outside, whom Terminiello called "slimy scum." Police were called and they were barely able to usher the speaker and his party safely out of the building. Terminiello was tried and convicted for causing a breach of the peace. At the trial the judge had instructed the jury that a breach of the peace consists of any behavior that "violates the public peace and decorum" and that such behavior constitutes a breach of the peace if it "stirs the public to anger, invites dispute, brings about a condition of unrest or creates a disturbance" (3). The counsel for the defendant did not specifically object to the judge's instructions to the jury at the time, even though they altered the language of the ordinance under which Terminiello was convicted.

In another five-to-four decision, the Court overturned Terminiello's conviction. Douglas spoke for the majority, which included Black, Reed, Murphy, and Rutledge. In an ironic twist, Douglas followed a restraint position by avoiding the larger constitutional issue of whether Terminiello's words were in fact protected by the First Amendment. He declared the conviction void because the judge had improperly construed the ordinance in his charge to the jury in such a way that the ordinance as applied was too broadly restrictive of speech. The majority opinion turned on the judge's instruction to the jury, even though the defense attorney had never raised that issue at the trial nor in two subsequent appeals in Illinois state courts. Neither had it been specifically raised in the certiorari petition to the Supreme Court.

Vinson objected strongly to the majority opinion, because it "discover[ed] in the record one sentence in the trial court's instructions which permitted the jury to convict on an unconstitutional basis." He pointed out that this "offending sentence" had gone completely unnoticed. In fact, he said, it was not part of the case "until this Court's independent research ferreted it out of a lengthy and somewhat confused record." His pique with the majority clearly showing, Vinson said: "I think it too plain an argument that a reversal on such a basis does not accord with any principle governing review of state court decisions heretofore announced by this Court" (7). Vinson said that had the petitioner's attorney raised the issue of jury instructions at the trial, he too would have supported the majority's opinion. Like Douglas, Vinson failed to address the question of whether a conviction by a properly instructed jury could have been upheld, but his communications with the justices during deliberations suggest he probably would have voted to reverse the conviction.

The *Terminiello* case caused Vinson a great deal of anguish, and he remained ambivalent about his position until the end. At the conference on February 5, 1949, he had indicated that he would have been inclined to reverse if the issue of the judge's charge to the jury had been raised earlier, but since it was not, he thought the case should be dismissed as "improvidently granted."[90] His reasons for thinking that the case should not have been accepted were clarified in a memorandum Vinson intended to be published with the opinion. It revealed how indecisive he was about the case. He said he found himself in agreement with aspects of both the majority opinion and the dissents. Specifically, Vinson said he agreed that the judge's instructions to the jury regarding what constituted breach of the peace had to be treated as if those words were actually written into the ordinance. He believed that such language made the ordinance as applied unconstitutional. The problem, however, was that the question put before the Court was one it could not reach. Did Terminiello's speech, based on the evidence in the record, constitute "fighting words"? Vinson said that if the jury had found that the speech belonged in that category, then the Court could properly review the jury's findings, but he noted, "The jury made no such finding because no such question was put to it." Given the record, Vinson said, the Court was left with only one question to decide, which was whether the definition of breach of the peace given to the jury was constitutionally valid. The majority opinion rested on that basis.

As sympathetic as Vinson was to that position, he understood the argument of the dissent, which was that the Court could not reverse the conviction on the "constitutional infirmity" of the instructions to the jury because that objection had not been raised in any of the lower courts and because it was "specifically and unequivocally waived" before the Supreme Court. This led Vinson to conclude that there was no question that the Court could properly answer and that therefore the case should be dismissed.[91] In another memorandum Vinson clarified even further what he found troubling about the majority's opinion in *Terminiello*. Given his practical bent, he was concerned about the impact that the decision would have on the state courts. He said that in order to avoid being overruled, state appellate courts would have to examine for all errors of application of criminal law in any case involving a constitutional attack of any sort. He concluded, "Since I do not believe that this is, or should be the law, I do not think that we may properly consider the infirmity of the instructions in this case."[92] In the end his concern about the burden placed on state courts led Vinson to write one of his few dissenting opinions. Oddly, it is less eloquent and forceful than the earlier memorandum he had written about the case.

Frankfurter's dissent, joined by Burton and Jackson, also forcefully decried the Court's overturning of the conviction on a procedural flaw that had never been raised by the defense or considered by any of the state appellate courts. The most noteworthy opinion was the twenty-five-page dissent written by Jackson. He took nine pages to recreate the unruly nature of the mob outside the auditorium and to quote verbatim the inflammatory remarks made by Terminiello. With the same passion he showed in his dissent in the *Kunz* case, Jackson equated the behavior of Terminiello and his enemies with a "world-wide and standing conflict between two organized groups of revolutionary fanatics" that had imported to the United States "the strong-arm technique" developed in the struggle that had devastated Europe. He conjured up images of Hitler's Germany, fresh in his memory from the Nuremberg trials.[93] Jackson classified Terminiello's remarks as "fighting words," and he said the majority opinion could endanger freedom of speech by destroying the order necessary to maintain it. In one of his more memorable statements, he wrote, "The choice is not between order and liberty. It is between liberty with order and anarchy without either" (37). Jackson later penned a bit of doggerel that summed up his view of the Court's opinions in *Terminiello:*

> If a special size street riot puts you flat on your back,
> Be philosophical with Douglas, Murphy, Rutledge, Reed, and Black;
> As you lie there bashed and bleeding, with your muscles badly hurt'n
> Say a little prayer for Vinson, Jackson, Frankfurter, and Burton.[94]

Douglas's majority opinion in *Terminiello* presented problems as far as precedent was concerned. He was criticized for avoiding the constitutional question of whether the speech of the defrocked priest was constitutionally protected. Indeed, the Court was forced to revisit the issue a year and a half later in *Feiner* v. *New York.*[95] The facts in *Feiner* were strikingly similar to *Terminiello* in that both involved provocative speech in a setting fraught with the potential for violence. Feiner was a university student who used a loudspeaker on a Syracuse street corner to publicize a meeting of the Young Progressives of America. He called Truman and the mayors of Syracuse and New York City "bums" and said the "American Legion is a Nazi Gestapo." He also said that "Negroes don't have equal rights; they should rise up in arms and fight for their rights." About seventy-five people, both black and white, blocked the sidewalk. Some jeered the speaker while others applauded. Police officers trying to relieve traffic tied up by the crowd heard members of the audience muttering angrily and saw "shoving" and "restlessness." One member of the audience told the police officers, "If you don't get that son of a bitch off, I will go over and get him off there myself." At that point the police told Feiner to stop speaking. He continued, and after three attempts to get him to stop they arrested him.

In a six-to-three decision, the Court affirmed Feiner's conviction. Vinson wrote the majority opinion. The libertarian tendency Vinson had shown in *Kunz* and *Niemotko* did not carry over to *Feiner*. Whereas Vinson may have had doubts about Terminiello's case, he had none about *Feiner*. In conference he said that the police "need not wait until an explosion took place," which is the same idea he incorporated into his *Dennis* opinion later that term when he said that "government need not wait for the putsch to occur." Vinson told his colleagues that it was a "simple breach of the peace case." He said, "the speaker had a right to be protected but he overstepped."[96]

Kalven suggested that *Feiner* "can best be understood as a reaction against *Terminiello*,"[97] which left doubt about when communities were justified in silencing speech to protect citizens against public disorder. It can also be explained by the change in the court membership. *Terminiello* was decided when Rutledge and Murphy were still on the Court, but when *Feiner* was decided, the two libertarian justices had been replaced by Clark and Minton. Clark voted with the chief justice, giving him a majority of six. Minton, in a move highly unusual for him, deserted his chief and joined Black and Douglas in dissent.

Vinson's opinion in *Feiner* rested on two main points. One was his complete acceptance of the trial judge's conclusion that the police officers were justified in taking action to prevent a breach of the peace. The other was that the police officers were motivated "solely by a proper concern for preservation of order and protection of the general welfare" and that there was no evidence to suggest that their actions were "a cover for suppression of petitioner's views and opinions."[98] Vinson acknowledged that "ordinary murmurings and objections of a hostile audience" were not a justification for limiting speech and that there was danger in giving "overzealous police" too much discretion to disband lawful public meetings. However, he could not accept that police were powerless to prevent a breach of the peace when a speaker "passes the bounds of argument or persuasion and undertakes incitement to riot" (315).

Black and Douglas each wrote separate dissents. In an opinion brimming with indignation, Black took exception to Vinson's reliance on the trial judges' determination that the unruliness of the crowd justified the police action in arresting Feiner. He asserted that the Court had the right to examine the evidence "to determine whether federally protected rights had been denied." To abandon that rule, Black said, would mark "a dark day for civil liberties." He declared that the convictions made a "mockery of the free speech guarantees" of the Constitution and that the Court's opinion was a "long step toward a totalitarian authority" (323). Unlike Vinson, who thought the police had an obligation to protect the public, Black thought the police had a responsibility to protect the speaker in the exercise of his constitutional rights. In an ironic twist, Black cited the opinions in *Kunz* and *Niemotko,* both written by Vinson and handed down the same day, where he said the Court "in obedience to past decisions" provided a "theoretical safeguard for free speech" (329). Whatever those cases had guaranteed, Black said, was taken away by *Feiner.*

Vinson's opinion in *Feiner* was criticized by the libertarian Court scholars. The primary criticism was that the Court opinion permitted the punishment of a public speaker simply because some members of the audience were annoyed by the message and threatened violence. Kalven said the Court had endorsed the "heckler's veto" by transferring the power of censorship to the crowd. He called *Feiner* "one of the Court's least satisfactory efforts—a decision which endorses conduct deeply offensive to free speech values. The man who has his way and emerges unscathed is the one who calls the defendant a 'son of a bitch' and threatens to hit him."[99] As Kalven noted, *Feiner,* in legitimating broad censorship of street-corner speech, established precedents with which the Court today still reckons. It clearly snuffed out the libertarian trend on the Court that had been entertained in *Terminiello,* which was not mentioned in the majority opinion or, surprisingly, in the dissent by Douglas, who wrote that opinion.

Feiner, Niemotko, and *Kunz* provide an excellent prism to view the Court's decision-making processes over the thorny issue of free speech versus community order. Frankfurter voiced his concerns about the Court's handling of the cases in several memorandums to Vinson. Although he was in agreement with Vinson in all three opinions that the chief justice authored, he once again felt compelled to justify his decision to write separate opinions, a practice that was a constant bone of contention between the two men. "You and I differ," he wrote, "in the importance we attach generally to a Court opinion for an agreed result." Frankfurter said that opinions not only resolved cases but also served as "progenitors" of future cases. He added that the Court would not be in the "mess" regarding "clear and present danger" if justices who had not subscribed to the majority view had not acquiesced to the pressure for unanimous decisions.[100] He cited examples of previous cases where he wished he had concurred instead of acquiescing. One is left to wonder how having multiple opinions in free speech cases could have made the "clear and present danger mess" any better. They do not seem to have contributed much clarity to the rule of law in the various free speech cases handed down in 1951, including *Douds* and *Dennis*.

One explanation for the "clear and present danger mess" is revealed in the shifting positions among the justices on each case. From November 25, 1950, through January 13, 1951, Vinson recorded different sets of votes for each case. At the outset of each case, there was a surprising number of justices whose votes were "unreported." This indecision was followed by some justices' shifting their positions, usually either to or from concurrence. The behavior of the justices in these cases resembled a story with which Vinson liked to delight Truman and his friends about the Court. The story originated with a comment made by Desha Breckinridge, Vinson's friend and newspaper publisher in Lexington, Kentucky. A reporter who worked for Breckinridge went to him while a local campaign was in process to get guidance in how to handle his stories. Asked what position the publisher planned to take in the campaign, Breckinridge replied that he had yet not made up his mind, but when he did he was going to be "damned bitter." Vinson said that when he became chief justice he told that story to members of the Court, and he used it on several occasions when they were deliberating a decision. Some justices, who were wavering about how to vote in a case, would use the expression that they had not decided, but when they did they would be "damned bitter."[101]

The numerous cases involving First Amendment freedoms that the Court heard between 1946 and 1953 presented frequent opportunities for the justices to become "damned bitter" with each other. Black and Douglas, whose views on freedom of speech had been in the ascendancy when Vinson became chief justice, were now in a minority, having been overwhelmed by the four Truman justices plus Reed and sometimes Frankfurter and Jackson. The latter often agreed with Vinson's disposition of a case but frequently felt the need to write separate opinions. In cases where members of the Communist Party challenged deprivation of their rights, Vinson always sided with the government. For all the divisiveness that these cases caused on the Court, their influence was short-lived. In the cases where individuals challenged state and local laws, Vinson did not always side with the government, particularly if the issue involved a licensing scheme administered with too much discretion for officials. Nonetheless, when street-corner speakers were getting other citizens riled up with inflammatory messages, Vinson was inclined to go with the judgment of the local officials that the threat of violence was real. These opinions have had more lasting influence as courts continue to wrestle with deciding where to draw the line between the right of individuals to express views that are highly offensive to others and the right of local governments to keep the peace in their communities. The Court under Vinson found that arriving at agreement on these issues was no easy matter. More than any other group of cases, the Court's ruling in this area underscores Vinson's inability to forge consistent and coherent Supreme Court majorities. Perhaps Frankfurter put it best when he wrote to Vinson in 1947 strongly objecting the chief justice's vote in a case. In the end, he said, "each man must tread the wine-press of doubt alone."[102]

CHAPTER 10

The Dilemma of Due Process and the Promise of Equality

Two of Fred Vinson's most notable traits as a justice, his commitment to judicial restraint and his adherence to precedent, exerted a strong influence on how he responded to the thorny constitutional issues about the requirements of due process and equal protection of the law. Although both issues had important ramifications for state governments, each one presented a different set of considerations. Vinson's role on the Court, and in particular his leadership of the Court, varied in the two areas. In Court debates about due process questions, Vinson was not the pivotal player. The main battle was between the Court's most visible and vocal protagonists, Hugo Black and Felix Frankfurter. Their strong views on these issues cast a long shadow over the Court's decisions. Although Vinson was almost always in the majority when the Court decided the rights of the accused, he wrote only a few majority opinions in this area and authored two notable dissents.

The extent of Vinson's role in the equal protection debate has generated a lengthy scholarly debate. Although he authored three of the Court's most important decisions overturning discriminatory practices by state governments, Court scholars are divided over whether he was a reluctant soldier in the drive for equal rights or a cautious leader who took significant steps that paved the way for the Court's landmark case on equal rights, *Brown* v. *Board of Education,* which was finally decided after his death.

There were a variety of issues about what exactly were the rights of the accused under the Constitution. One of the most contentious due process issues during Vinson's tenure as chief justice was how far to extend Fourth Amendment protections against unreasonable searches and seizures. An equally divisive issue was the fundamental question of which procedural guarantees of the Bill of Rights were incorporated in the Fourteenth Amendment due process clause and thus served to restrict the power of state governments as well as the power of the federal government. Both of these vexing questions represented to Vinson the necessity of balancing society's concern for order with the rights of the individual. As in civil liberties cases, he usually sided with government and opted for order. During Vinson's tenure as chief justice, the Court began to deal with these issues in earnest in 1947.

The Fourth Amendment protects citizens against unreasonable searches and seizures by requiring that before a search can be conducted, law enforcement officials must usually secure a warrant, issued by a judge, if there is sufficient evidence that the items sought are likely to be found on the premises to be searched. Simple as the words sound, there was no ready agreement among the justices about their application. Their debates were shaped by two important developments that occurred prior to Vinson's arrival on the Court. The earliest of these developments happened in 1914 in the case of *Weeks* v. *United States,*[1] when the Supreme Court determined that evidence obtained without a search warrant was not admissible in federal criminal trials. *Weeks* marked the birth of the "exclusionary rule" for federal prosecutions. The second development was the trend begun under Vinson's predecessor, Chief Justice Harlan Stone, toward liberalizing the rules about search and seizure by imposing strict standards on law enforcement practices. This process had exposed some sharp doctrinal differences among the justices about the application the Fourth Amendment. Thus, most justices already had established views about these issues when Vinson arrived in 1946.

Frankfurter, in particular, considered himself to be the Court's leading scholar on Fourth Amendment issues. In questions involving federal law enforcement practices, Frankfurter was adamant about strictly enforcing the exclusionary rule in federal cases. In 1947 his position clashed sharply with Vinson's in the case of *Harris* v. *United States,*[2] when the Court overturned the established precedent that a search without a warrant incidental to arrest could extend only to objects in plain view of the arresting officers. In *Harris,* FBI agents, in the course of carrying out an arrest warrant for mail fraud, had conducted a five-hour search of the defendant's four-room apartment. They expected to find evidence of check-forging operations but instead found some classification cards and registration cards for the Selective Service that were unlawfully in Harris's possession. He was tried and convicted on the basis of this evidence. By a five-to-four majority, the Court upheld the conviction.

Vinson wrote the majority opinion, which was supported by an unusual alignment of justices that included Black, Douglas, Reed, and Burton. Drawing upon his interpretation of precedents and the meaning of "reasonableness," Vinson gave wide latitude to law enforcement officials who conduct a search incident to an arrest but without a search warrant. At the outset he noted that the Constitution prohibited "only unreasonable searches and seizures" and that "the test of reasonableness cannot be stated in rigid and absolute terms." Vinson derived this position from his interpretation of the precedent set in *Go-Bart Importing Company* v. *United States* (1931), which held that "each case is to be decided on its own facts and circumstances."[3] In that case, however, the evidence seized was in plain view of the arresting officers.

Vinson offered several other precedents to support his contention that the law enforcement officers had acted "reasonably" in seizing the evidence. First, he said that search and seizure incident to a lawful arrest was a long-established practice of both the United States and the states. Moreover, he noted, earlier rulings had held that "under appropriate circumstances" searches incident to arrest could extend beyond the person of the one arrested and could include the premises under his immediate control. Vinson argued that the law enforcement officers had authority to enter the dwelling to effect the arrest, and this entitled them to search the premises for the canceled checks. The fact that these items could be easily hidden in some secluded spot justified the lengthy and intensive search. Although such a search was "reasonable" in these circumstances, Vinson said it would not be reasonable in a search for a "stolen automobile or an illegal still." He thought the law enforcement agents' search had been conducted in "good faith" that they would find the evidence they sought. When they found the stolen draft cards instead, they acted within the law to seize them because their mere possession provided evidence that a crime was thus being committed in their presence. Vinson declared that no previous Court decisions would "support the suggestion that under the circumstances the law-enforcement officials must impotently stand aside and refrain from seizing such contraband material." The premise that government officials should not be helpless to respond to threats against order was a frequent theme in Vinson's opinions and was featured prominently in the *Dennis* case and the steel seizure case.

Although Vinson acknowledged that excesses of law-enforcement officials could endanger the fundamental personal rights, he argued that the Court would always be "alert to protect against such abuses." He concluded, however, that the Court should not permit the "knowledge that abuses sometimes occur to give sinister coloration to procedures which are basically reasonable."[4]

Frankfurter, Murphy, and Jackson all wrote vociferous dissents. An early draft of Frankfurter's opinions alluded to the sharpness of the debate that occurred in conference. "If during our discussion of this case I spoke with too much vehemence and intensity," he said, "I apologize."[5] In an opinion twice as long as Vinson's, Frankfurter roundly condemned the tactics of the law enforcement agents and the majority opinion, which he said posed "serious threats to basic liberties." In his pedantic style, Frankfurter launched into a lengthy historical discourse on the Fourth Amendment, beginning with the debate among the framers of the Constitution and including a recitation of the Court's precedents. Frankfurter's chief argument was that "searches are 'unreasonable' unless authorized by a warrant, and a warrant hedged about by adequate safeguards."[6]

The dissents by Murphy and Jackson were equally forceful, although Jackson thought the Court's previous opinions might have created enough ambiguity that it was understandable that the law enforcement agents felt justified in conducting their search. However, in the end Jackson said that a search "with no practical limits on premises and for things which no one describes in advance" would be "unreasonable" and the kind of search the Constitution intended to prohibit.[7]

Among legal scholars the minority opinions in the Harris case were viewed much more favorably than Vinson's majority opinion. Even his strong supporters could provide only a qualified approval. Francis A. Allen, a former Vinson law clerk who later became a professor of law at Harvard, said it would be "difficult to resist the conclusion that the *Harris* case makes serious inroads into the rights secured by the Fourth Amendment." Allowing an exception for a search without a warrant as incident to arrest, Allen said, "virtually swallows the rule." He explained that Vinson was averse to situations like *Harris* where "an obviously guilty criminal" sought to overturn a conviction on "otherwise competent evidence" because it was illegally seized. He noted that Vinson rejected all such claims based on the Fourth Amendment. This included eleven cases involving federal law enforcement agents and three cases involving state prosecutions.[8] Ironically, on the circuit court of appeals, Vinson had written one of his strongest defenses of individual rights in a case involving unreasonable searches and seizures. In that case Vinson said "the public interest did not call for the rough and speedy conduct of officers tracking down a felon."[9]

James J. Bolner, whose doctoral dissertation analyzed Vinson's opinions in depth, called *Harris* "perhaps the most bizarre opinion ever handed down in a search and seizure case."[10] In his comprehensive analysis of the Vinson Court, Herman Pritchett identified the extent of the protections afforded by the Fourth Amendment as the primary problem facing the Court in the area of criminal prosecutions. Before Vinson's arrival on the Court, the law regarding searches and seizures was fairly clear. *Harris* changed all of that. "It got the Court into the most trouble in this field," Pritchett said.[11]

The very next year, the Court changed course again. So tenuous was the majority in the *Harris* case that at the first opportunity to do so, Douglas deserted to the other side. His shift in position in a trilogy of cases created a new, but short-lived, majority that reasserted some restrictions on searches and seizures incidental to arrest. In *Di Re* v. *United States,*[12] the Court ruled that a search of a companion of a suspect validly arrested for a federal offense was "unauthorized and exploratory" and therefore a violation of the Fourth Amendment. In that case only Black and Vinson dissented, but neither wrote an opinion. In a five-to-four decision a month later, the Court ruled that if law enforcement agents had adequate opportunity prior to an arrest to obtain a search warrant and failed to do so, the arrest, search, and seizure would be unreasonable. The slim majority in that case, *Johnson* v. *United States,*[13] consisted of Jackson, Frankfurter, Douglas, Murphy, and Rutledge. This same majority prevailed in the third case, *Trupiano* v. *United States,*[14] leaving Vinson in the position of having to write his first dissenting opinion as chief justice.

In *Trupiano,* police officers had known for at least three weeks that a building on a farm was being used for illicit distilling. They made a nighttime raid on the distillery without a warrant for arrest or a search warrant. An agent, seeing one of the petitioners in the case engaged in illicit distilling through an open door, entered the premises, arrested the petitioner, and seized the equipment. Justice Murphy, one of the Court's two most ardent libertarians, wrote the majority opinion. Even though the Court determined that the arrest itself was lawful, it held that the search was not justified because the agents had had "more than adequate opportunity" (703) to obtain search warrants before the raid occurred. Furthermore, Murphy maintained that the proximity of the contraband property to the person of the petitioner at the moment of his arrest was a "fortuitous circumstance which was inadequate to legalize the seizure" (707). He explained that if the defendant had been outside the building and arrested in the farmyard, the government's argument supporting seizure would collapse.

The majority opinion carefully avoided overruling *Harris.* That case, Murphy argued, dealt with evidence the law enforcement officials did not know in advance they would find. Even with this qualification, the majority's argument was too extreme for Vinson. Unlike the two other search and seizure cases in which he dissented, Vinson felt compelled to write a dissenting opinion in *Trupiano.* His frustration with the majority rested on his strong conviction that Court precedents clearly supported a search incident to a lawful arrest. He argued that there was no doubt that the petitioners "were in flagrant violation of the laws" and that the possession of the materials seized constituted a crime and thus "were the type subject to a lawful procedure." Clearly, Vinson's sympathies were on the side of order. He said that insisting on a search warrant where the issuance of such would contribute nothing to the preservation of rights under the Fourth Amendment would only serve "to open an avenue of escape for those guilty of crime and to menace the effective operation of government which is an essential precondition to the existence of all civil liberties" (715).

Vinson objected strongly to the majority's position that the petitioner's presence in the building where the contraband materials were located was a "fortuitous circumstance" and not adequate to legalize the seizure. To this, Vinson quipped: "Criminals do not normally choose to engage in felonious enterprises before an audience of police officials." Perhaps influenced by his own experiences as a prosecutor, Vinson was concerned about the practical implications of the ruling. He said the Court in effect had conditioned the right of seizure incident to a valid arrest "upon an *ex post facto* judicial judgment of whether the arresting officers might have obtained a search warrant." He predicted that the rule enunciated by the Court could be "expected to confound confusion in a field already replete with complexities" (715–16).

Vinson's prediction was prophetic. Two years later, in 1950, the Court added to the confusion. In *United States* v. *Rabinowitz,* [15] the Court returned to the *Harris* principle of allowing warrantless searches incident to arrest and specifically overturned *Trupiano* by upholding the search even though law enforcement agents had time to secure a warrant in advance. Vinson was again in the majority, but the change in the Court's position resulted not from his own leadership but from the untimely

Vinson at the funeral of Justice Frank Murphy on July 22, 1949, at Harbor Beach, Michigan. On Vinson's left are justices Hugo L. Black, Felix Frankfurter, and Wiley B. Rutledge. (Courtesy of Special Collections, University of Kentucky Library.)

deaths of Justices Rutledge and Murphy in 1949 and their replacement with Tom Clark and Sherman Minton. The *Rabinowitz* majority consisted of the four Truman appointees plus Stanley Reed. Vinson assigned the majority opinion to Minton, who was in his first term on the Court and who became Vinson's most loyal ally there. Even Black, who had strongly objected to the *Trupiano* ruling, wrote a dissenting opinion in the *Rabinowitz* case, but he did so mainly on the grounds that it would add "new confusions 'in a field already replete with complexities'" (68), ironically citing words from Vinson's *Trupiano* dissent.

Rabinowitz signaled a new hard-line approach to search and seizure issues as well as other criminal procedure issues that prevailed throughout Vinson's term as chief justice. As Pritchett observed, the net effect of the search and seizure rulings under Vinson's tenure was "unquestionably to give federal law enforcement lawyers greater leeway in making searches without warrants and to leave reviewing courts with rather vague notions as to the grounds on which searches might be declared unreasonable."[16] The uncertainty of the law in the field of searches and seizures, which could not have pleased the practical-minded Vinson, was a product of the divided Court that he inherited as well as his own inability to provide leadership to a Court where many of the members considered him to be their intellectual inferior.

The Court's erratic efforts to determine the extent of protections guaranteed by the Fourth Amendment in federal cases were matched in full measure when it came to cases pertaining to state prosecutions. The *Weeks* ruling had established that the exclusionary rule applied only to federal trials. The issue of what was required in criminal prosecutions in state courts was part of a contentious debate on the Court extending back to the case of *Palko* v. *Connecticut* (1937).[17] That case centered on the fundamental question of whether the Fourteenth Amendment due process clause incorporated procedural guarantees in the Bill of Rights that protected individual rights in criminal investigations and prosecutions. In the decade before the *Palko* case, the Supreme Court had determined that key provisions of the First Amendment, such as freedom of speech and freedom of the press, were absorbed into the due process clause of the Fourteenth Amendment.[18] As a result of such rulings, states were not allowed to interfere with these fundamental freedoms.

Palko raised a different question—whether a state was barred by the Fifth Amendment prohibition from subjecting a defendant to double jeopardy. Although in 1897 the Supreme Court had held that the just compensation requirement of the Fifth Amendment was applicable to the states, none of the criminal procedural protections of the Bill of Rights had been deemed to have similar status. In the *Palko* case the Supreme Court refused to incorporate other procedural rights into the Fourteenth Amendment. In this landmark ruling, written by Justice Benjamin Cardozo, the Supreme Court held that only those rights considered essential to "a scheme of ordered liberty" were absorbed into the Fourteenth Amendment.[19] Procedural protections like double jeopardy were not deemed essential and thus did not restrict the states in the same way that they limited federal power.

Justice Black had just joined the Court when *Palko* was decided, and although he voted with the majority, he had lingering doubts about the soundness of making such distinctions among the rights guaranteed in the first eight amendments. Black's concerns slowly led him to develop his doctrine of "total incorporation," which emerged full-blown in the case of *Adamson* v. *California* (1948).[20] That case raised the question of whether defendants in state court proceedings were entitled to the Fifth Amendment protection against self-incrimination. The debate in the *Adamson* case, decided in Vinson's first year as chief justice, exposed the sharp fissures on the Court about the nationalization of the Bill of Rights for criminal defendants. This was one of the most important constitutional issues the Court would debate during Vinson's tenure, but the chief justice himself was not in the forefront of the battle. The intensity of the debate no doubt served as a clear signal to Vinson of the monumental hurdles he would have to leap if he was to bring some harmony to the bench. At the same time, the nature of the debate between Black and Frankfurter must have made him aware that his leadership on the Court would have to rest on something other than intellectual prowess and that the issue of incorporation was not an area where he was likely to have much impact.

In the *Adamson* case, Black argued passionately that the framers of the Fourteenth Amendment intended for all of the first eight amendments to be incorporated into the due process clause. He convinced three other justices of his point of view—Douglas, Rutledge, and Murphy. Although Reed wrote for the majority, which included Vinson, it was Frankfurter's concurring opinion that provided the strongest counterpoint to Black's view. He rejected the rigidity of Black's position and argued that although judges were bound to ascertain "whether the criminal proceedings which resulted in conviction deprived the accused of due process of law, they were not required to define due process according to any specific provision of the first eight amendments." Judges, Frankfurter said, should judge criminal proceedings by whether they offended the accepted "canons of decency and fairness." To curb the "idiosyncrasies of personal judgment," Frankfurter argued that judges must show deference to the state court under review (67).

Even though they were at odds over many other matters, Vinson was in strong consensus with Frankfurter's philosophy regarding procedural rights, which remained the dominant view throughout Vinson's tenure on the Court. Not only was that position in keeping with precedent, but he also found common agreement in Frankfurter's fair-trial interpretation of the Fourteenth Amendment. Like Frankfurter, Vinson was uncomfortable with rigid positions such as Black's total incorporation theory. It was this aversion to doctrinaire views that got him into trouble in the *Dennis* case when he declared that "there were no absolutes." Under fair-trial jurisprudence, judges sought to determine whether a defendant had been accorded fundamental fairness based on the record of the trial. As David Bodenhamer observed, "the fair-trial test meant that the Court would decide case by case which rights of the accused enjoyed constitutional protection."[21] A ruling would be based not on one specific aspect of the proceedings but on the whole record of the case. The notion that each case was unique and would be decided on its own merits was consistent with Vinson's more pragmatic and nonideological approach to decision making.

"It soon became clear," Melvin Urofsky noted, "that *Adamson* had not resolved the issue but was merely the opening scene of what would be an ongoing debate within the Court."[22] A notable example was the case of *Wolf* v. *Colorado* (1949).[23] In that case the Court visited the issue of whether the Fourth Amendment protection against unreasonable searches and seizures was incorporated under the due process clause of the Fourteenth Amendment. The Court majority concluded that the Fourth Amendment was not specifically incorporated into the Fourteenth Amendment, but by applying the fair-trial test, it ruled unanimously that "the security of one's privacy against arbitrary intrusion by the police—which is at the core of the Fourth Amendment—is basic to a free society" (28). Thus the core principle of the Fourth Amendment, forbidding warrantless searches, was made applicable to the states. However, on the question of whether this meant that evidence seized without a warrant must be excluded from the state court trial, the Court ruled six to three that it did not. Oddly, the opinion protected a right but denied a remedy, which is tantamount to not having the right at all. Frankfurter, writing for the majority of six, including Vinson, argued that the Fourth Amendment did not require the exclusion of evidence in state trials. He reached this conclusion based on the fact that at the time thirty states did not apply the *Weeks* rule, and consequently the failure to apply it was not sufficiently arbitrary or unfair to require states to comply. Other remedies besides exclusion could be used to overturn evidence obtained in a warrantless search. The *Wolf* precedent of not extending the exclusionary rule to states stood until 1961, when it was overturned in the case of *Mapp* v. *Ohio*.[24]

The application of the fair-trial concept did not always result in a ruling favorable to the state. A case in point was the unanimous ruling in *Rochin* v. *California* (1952).[25] The defendant in the case had been convicted on the basis of two capsules of morphine that doctors had forcibly pumped from his stomach against his will at the direction of law enforcement agents. The Court overturned Rochin's conviction on the grounds that the stomach-pumping method violated the due process clause of the Fourteenth Amendment. In conference almost all the justices expressed dismay at the manner in which the evidence had been obtained. Vinson called it a "shocking case," although he said that the rule of confessions was not applicable because the capsules were seen and known. Others were more colorful in their language. Both Reed and Frankfurter said that the case made them "puke."[26]

Vinson acquiesced to Frankfurter's eagerness to write the opinion so that he could show how the due process clause could be used to rein in abusive practices by the state without having to acknowledge that the clause was a "handbag for the eight original amendments."[27] Frankfurter wrote that the use of stomach pumping without the consent of the accused "shocks the conscience" and constituted "methods too close to the rack and screw to permit constitutional differentiation."[28] He was careful not to abandon the Court's stand on incorporation. Black and Douglas wrote concurring opinions in which they argued that the basis for overturning the decision should have been the Fifth Amendment protection against self-incrimination. Their view that the Fifth Amendment was incorporated into the Fourteenth Amendment did not prevail until 1964, more than a decade after Vinson's death. Until that time the Court muddled along with fair-trial jurisprudence, leaving wide latitude to the states in their law enforcement practices and trial proceedings.

Consistent with his philosophy of restraint, Vinson's record on issues pertaining to rights of the accused was decidedly progovernment, whether it was a matter of federal or state procedures. When Vinson became chief justice, defendants in federal cases were guaranteed the right to have an attorney through the Sixth Amendment even if they could not afford one. At the state level, however, the Court had extended that guarantee only to capital offenses.[29] Beyond that, whether a defendant who could not afford an attorney was guaranteed the right to counsel depended on the circumstances. In 1942 the Court had ruled in *Betts* v. *Brady* that the right to counsel was not required by the Fourteenth Amendment absent any proof that some special injustice had been done.[30] *Betts* meant that the Court would have to decide on a case-by-case basis whether denial of counsel resulted in an unfair trial.

The Court ruled in twelve right-to-counsel cases while Vinson was chief justice. In six of those cases, the Court determined that absence of counsel had not denied the defendant a fair trial.[31] Vinson voted with the majority in each of these. The first five of those cases were decided before the deaths of Rutledge and Murphy, who along with Black and Douglas vehemently objected to the majority rulings. For example, in *Bute* v. *Illinois* (1948), the Court upheld the denial of counsel in a trial in which the defendant was charged with taking indecent liberties with children. Given the strong emotions such a crime was likely to produce, the four usual dissenters thought that a skilled lawyer was essential to a fair trial. The majority did not see it that way. By 1950, when the Court ruled in *Quicksall* v. *Michigan* that counsel was not constitutionally required where there was no fundamental unfairness, Black and Douglas were the only dissenters in cases where lack of counsel was condoned.

When the Court reversed convictions on the grounds that the defendant had been denied right to counsel, Vinson was usually in agreement with the dissenters. An example is *Townsend* v. *Burke* (1948),[32] where the Court overturned a conviction because the defendant had been sentenced on the basis of false assumptions conveyed to the jury by the judge. In *Townsend,* Vinson joined in dissent. He also dissented in a Pennsylvania case, *Palmer* v. *Ashe* (1951),[33] when the Court overturned the conviction of a defendant with diminished mental capacity. The Court held that the absence of counsel had prevented the defendant's plea of guilty from being an "understanding" one. Vinson joined the unanimous Court in *Gibbs* v. *Burke* (1949) in overturning a conviction where inadmissible hearsay and otherwise incompetent evidence had been presented at the trial without objection from the defendant, who was acting as his own counsel.[34] Although the Court was unanimous in overturning that case, Black and Douglas wanted the Court to go further and overturn *Betts.* It was not until *Gideon* v. *Wainwright* in 1963 that the Black-Douglas view that indigent defendants in state courts were entitled to counsel in all felony cases prevailed.[35]

Vinson's position on the right to counsel was mirrored in his record on issues of coerced confessions. He usually voted with the minority when confessions were invalidated on the basis that the methods used to obtain them violated standards of due process. For example, he dissented in *Haley* v. *Ohio* (1948) when the Court overturned the murder conviction of a fifteen-year-old African American who had been questioned by police for five hours without an attorney or any other adult present.[36] For three days he was held incommunicado, and a lawyer was denied access to him. The majority opinion, written by Black, determined that the defendant's treatment constituted "a disregard of the standards of decency." Vinson, along with Reed and Jackson, joined the dissent written by Burton. The same four justices dissented in *Upshaw* v. *United States* when a majority of the Court ruled that a confession obtained after the accused had been detained for thirty hours solely because the police lacked sufficient evidence to charge him was inadmissible.[37] The quartet of Vinson, Reed, Burton, and Jackson dissented again in three cases in 1949 when the Court ruled that confessions obtained through intense psychological pressure violated due process.[38]

To classify Vinson as a strict law-and-order judge based on his positions on right to counsel and coerced confessions is justified. However, in some respects his record actually affords a more complex view. His position on cases involving habeas corpus proceedings from state courts indicates that he was not indifferent when claims of denial of due process reached the court. Petitions for habeas corpus are requests from convicted defendants who believe that they were deprived of rights in the course of their trial and that therefore they are being unlawfully detained. Such petitions are usually filed by indigent defendants through in forma pauperis applications. The Supreme Court had a long-standing rule that all appropriate state remedies must be exhausted before prisoners could appeal their convictions with a writ of certiorari to the U.S. Supreme Court or a petition of habeas corpus to a federal district court. Such petitions were becoming particularly burdensome to the Supreme Court when Vinson became chief justice. How and when to dispose of these petitions presented thorny issues for the Court, and especially for Vinson, who as chief justice had the responsibility for overseeing the fair and uniform disposition of appeals.

The state of Illinois was by far the chief offender in failing to provide adequate postconviction appeals, as evidenced by the fact that in the 1946 term nearly half of the petitions for postconviction review originated from that state. So troublesome was this flood of petitions from Illinois that Rutledge, in a 1947 case,[39] complained that the state's procedures were so complex that they worked against the defendants, who frequently were told that they had pursued the wrong remedy and thus denied a hearing of their claims.

A 1949 case, *Young* v. *Ragen*,[40] gave Vinson the opportunity to address this recurring problem with Illinois courts. The petitioner in the case, who had been convicted and sentenced to prison in an Illinois circuit court, petitioned that same court for habeas corpus, claiming denial of due process under the Fourteenth Amendment. His petition was denied by the circuit court without a hearing on the ground that it was "insufficient in law and substance." In the Supreme Court review of the case, the attorney general representing Illinois acknowledged that although the petition raised substantial federal questions, habeas corpus was not a proper remedy under state law at the time that the petition was denied. He also acknowledged that subsequent rulings of the Illinois Supreme Court indicated that habeas corpus would now be an appropriate procedure in the case under review, but he maintained that the decisions regarding procedures were solely a question of Illinois law and did not warrant intervention by the Supreme Court.

Vinson, speaking for a unanimous court, said, "It is not simply a question of state procedure when a state court of last resort closes the door to *any* consideration of a claim of denial of a federal right. . . . Unless habeas corpus is available we are led to believe that Illinois offers no post-trial remedy in cases of this kind" (238). Vinson acknowledged the difficulties that the Illinois Supreme Court faced in adapting state procedures to requirements for adequate postconviction review when prisoners raised claims of denial of federal rights, but he forcefully asserted, "That requirement must be met." He warned that if the state lacked such a posttrial procedure, "we wish to be advised of that fact upon remand of the case" (239).

The problems of adequate postconviction procedures troubled Vinson, and he spoke of this concern in an address before the American Bar Association in September of 1949. He emphasized that "the right of a prisoner who claims the denial of a federally protected right to petition is an extremely important one." At the same time, Vinson said he was concerned about the large volume of these petitions, averaging more than six hundred a year. Vinson said that ninety-six out of every one hundred had little or no legal merit and that something should be done "to stem the flow."

Despite his obvious frustration with the number of these cases, Vinson said, "I firmly believe, despite the burden, that the right to petition the Supreme Court should remain and should not be made more difficult."[41] Instead, Vinson said, the solution lay in the post-conviction remedies adopted by the states. If states would provide a well-defined method by which prisoners could challenge their convictions in open hearings, most of the cases could be disposed of at the state level. Vinson noted that the problem of appropriate postconviction remedies had been most acute in Illinois, but he expressed optimism that a newly adopted state statute providing a definite, comprehensive posttrial remedy would result in a marked decline in the number of petitions from that state.

His optimism proved to be unfounded. Within the next two years, twenty-five cases under the new act had come to the Supreme Court. In 1951 Vinson again addressed the problem in the case of *Jennings* v. *Illinois*,[42] one of a trio of cases pertaining to posttrial petitions from the state of Illinois. The petitioner in the case had filed a petition in the court in which he had been convicted alleging a violation of his rights under the U.S. Constitution through the admission of a coerced confession. The circuit court dismissed the petition without a hearing or any other means of determining the factual issues presented. The state supreme court, without argument and without opinion, dismissed the case through a form order, stating merely that it had examined the record and found no violation of the petitioner's constitutional rights.

Vinson's opinion reflected his impatience with the Illinois system, which in effect deprived indigent defendants of any appropriate remedy for determining their claims that their federal rights had been infringed. "Petitioners are entitled to their day in court for resolution," he said. One matter of concern to Vinson in the *Jennings* case was that the petitioner's right of appeal under Illinois law was contingent on paying for transcripts, which, as an indigent, he was unable to do. Vinson concluded that this amounted to no appeal at all. Vinson's sensitivity to the plight of indigent defendants was not a passing one. He was the honorary president of the National Association of Legal Aid Organizations, and he told that group in 1947 that it was "the only organization with which I am similarly connected other than as required by law by reasons of my office as Chief Justice."[43] Vinson had also emphasized the importance of in forma pauperis applications in 1949 in his address to the American Bar Association when he noted that "most of the cases in which the Court has spelled out the requirements of a fair trial under the due process clause of the Constitution have come as *in forma pauperis* petitions."[44]

The *Jennings* case was remanded to the Illinois Supreme Court so that it could be "permitted to provide definite answers to the questions raised by these cases." If the state court could resolve it through an inquiry into the truth of the allegations or a finding that the defendant had waived his rights, then there would be no further intervention by the federal bench. However, if Illinois failed to provide an appropriate remedy for determining these questions, Vinson said the petitioners could file petitions of habeas corpus with the U.S. district court.

In the *Young* case in 1949, Vinson had been able to gain unanimous support for his opinion, but in *Jennings* he could not do so. Both Frankfurter and Minton, the two justices who were most deferential to state courts, dissented. Frankfurter used the opportunity to find fault with the Court's majority for failing to make clear exactly what issues it expected the Illinois court to address. He thought the Supreme Court had failed to clarify what was the substantial federal question before it, because that issue, he said, had never been properly presented to the Court in the petition. Vinson's failure to gain the support of Minton, his most faithful ally on the Court, suggests that the chief justice, although he highly valued unanimity on the Court, was not inclined to use his powers of persuasion as chief justice, even among his friends, to achieve unity. As a result the matter of posttrial procedures continued to be a source of confusion for the Court, although it should be noted that the state of Illinois did develop a much more effective set of procedures for postconviction review.

On occasion Vinson could be very passionate about protecting the rights of defendants. He demonstrated this in a forceful dissent in the case of *Brock* v. *North Carolina* (1953) during his final year on the Court.[45] In this case the defendant claimed that he had been denied his protection against double jeopardy when the trial judge declared a mistrial at the request of the prosecution. In the first trial, two accomplices, who had been separately convicted, refused to testify on the grounds that they might incriminate themselves with respect to their pending appeals. The trial judge, on a motion of the state, withdrew a juror from the panel and declared a mistrial. After the accomplices' convictions were affirmed, their testimony was admitted in the second trial, at which the defendant was convicted.

The issue before the court was whether the second trial for the same offense violated the due process clause of the Fourteenth Amendment. In conference, only Vinson and Black voted to reverse, and only Vinson is recorded as having spoken about the issue. He said it was shocking "to say you can try a man, put on all this evidence, and then for the sole reason that there may be a chance of getting better evidence get a mistrial and try him again."[46] Minton, ever sensitive to the prerogatives of the states, wrote the majority opinion affirming the conviction. He relied on previous decisions favoring the discretion of the trial judge to declare a mistrial and to require a new panel to try the defendant "if the ends of justice" would be served. Minton was a strong adherent of the fair-trial concept and argued that no hard and fast rule could be laid down to determine what constituted due process. Instead, he said, "the pattern of due process is picked out in the facts and circumstances of each case."[47]

The chief shortcoming of the fair-trial concept is that the subjectivity of the individual justices can result in uncertainty about the law. Vinson's lengthy dissent in *Brock* illustrates how individual justices can reach opposite conclusions. In Vinson's view, allowing the second trial was contrary to due process. He wrote that "orderly justice could not be secured if the rules allowed the defendant to ask for a mistrial at the conclusion of testimony because the state had done well and the defense had done poorly. The same limitation applies to the prosecution if the scales of justice are to be kept in equal balance" (432). In the remainder of the dissent, Vinson provided one of his most well-written and well-reasoned opinions. A thorough review of existing practices in other states revealed that North Carolina was the only state that did not allow a plea of double jeopardy and that even in that state earlier court rulings had held it to be an essential right. He rejected the idea put forth by North Carolina that the state's practice fell within the *Palko* guidelines. In that case, Vinson said, the state had asked for a second trial to obtain a trial free from error by the court prejudicial to the state. Here, the state asked for its second trial in order to "suit the convenience of the Solicitor" to strengthen the state's case, when the defendant had done nothing to bring about trial errors (438).

Having distinguished the *Brock* case from *Palko,* Vinson went on to argue that some of the language in the *Palko* opinion actually supported his position. He quoted from Cardozo's opinion that the Court was not asked in *Palko* to consider the question of whether the state would be permitted to appeal a trial that was free from error. Vinson could not resist an opportunity to tweak Frankfurter, who had written a concurring opinion siding with the majority. He noted that in his concurring opinion, Frankfurter had acknowledged that a state would fail to provide due process if it prevented a trial from proceeding to a termination that would favor the accused merely to allow a prosecutor who has been incompetent or ineffective to see if he could do better a second time.

In Vinson's final year on the Court, the justices heard three cases pertaining to racial discrimination in the selection of jurors. Up to that point the Court had a fairly consistent record of overturning convictions if systematic discrimination in the jury selection could be proven. Most of these decisions were unanimous. In the 1952 term, however, the Court's consensus broke down. In two cases from North Carolina, the Court upheld the convictions by a six-to-three majority despite evidence of discrimination in jury selection. In one case the Court upheld the validity of selecting a jury panel from a list of payers of county property and poll taxes.[48] In a companion case the Court upheld the validity of drawing jurors from a list of taxpayers who had the "most property."[49] In both cases the jury selection process had resulted in a disproportionate number of whites on the jury. The Court dismissed the fact that in the second case the cards with the names of blacks were marked with a dot because a child of five had drawn the names, and all persons on the list, including blacks, had been called.

Vinson voted with the six-man majority to uphold the state procedures in both of the above cases, but in a third case involving racially biased jury selection he voted to overturn the conviction, and a unanimous majority of the Court agreed. In the case of *Avery* v. *Georgia*,[50] a defendant, who had been convicted of rape and sentenced to death, objected to the jury selection for two reasons. One was that the jury panel contained no blacks, and the other was that the cards from which the names were drawn were different colors for each race. The judge in the case had drawn the names of potential jurors from both races and had turned the cards over to the court clerk to "arrange" the tickets and type up the list for jury selection. The state supreme court had found a prima facie case of discrimination because the panel of jurors contained no blacks, but it affirmed the conviction after concluding that the defendant had not presented evidence of any particular act of discrimination by any particular state official. The state court's position was that the burden fell on the defendant to prove a specific act of discrimination.

Vinson did not agree. It was up to the state to provide sufficient evidence "to dispel the prima facie case of discrimination." Vinson said the practice of using different-colored tickets for members of each race in the jury pool made it easier for "those who are of a mind to discriminate" to do so. Vinson found support in a 1942 precedent that those responsible for jury selection had a constitutional duty to follow procedures that did not discriminate in the selection of jurors. He said: "If they fail in that duty, then this conviction must be reversed—no matter how strong the evidence of the petitioner's guilt. That is the law established by decisions of this Court spanning more than seventy years of interpretation of the meaning of 'equal protection'" (561).

The cases that raised questions about the constitutionality of discrimination in jury selection were distinct from the other issues of fair trials because they were brought to the Court under the equal protection clause of the Fourteenth Amendment, rather than the due process clause. The Court's efforts to wrestle with the meaning of equal protection were most prominent in Vinson's final year on the Court. He clearly made a more significant contribution to that debate than to the deliberations about due process. Although he authored three of the Court's main civil rights decisions, scholars of the Court remain divided about how much credit the chief justice deserves for moving the court in the direction of overturning the separate-but-equal doctrine established in *Plessy* v. *Ferguson* in 1896.[51]

A careful reading of multiple commentaries about the extensive court deliberations of segregation cases leading up to the *Brown* v. *Board of Education* decision in 1954 indicates that Vinson deserves more credit for laying the groundwork to overturn the separate-but-equal doctrine than his most ardent critics give him. However, there is no doubt that he moved cautiously and, for some, too slowly in his considerations about whether and how the Court should proceed to overturn a practice strongly embedded in the fabric of society and sanctioned by the Court for fifty years. Although his sense of fairness led him to believe segregation was wrong, his pragmatism led him to consider the consequences for the Court and the country of moving too quickly.

Just as in other issues deliberated by the Court, actions by President Truman cast a shadow over the discussion of desegregation cases, and his policies formed a backdrop as the Court began its long journey toward ending segregation in public facilities, public transportation, and, most important, public education. Truman's contribution stemmed from a commission that he established in December 1946 called the President's Committee on Civil Rights. This body submitted a report on October 29, 1947, entitled *To Secure These Rights,* which claimed that a "pervasive gap" existed between American ideals and practices. This gap, the committee wrote, created "a kind of moral dry rot" that was eating away "at the emotional and rational bases of democratic beliefs."[52] The President's Committee declared that it was time to create a permanent, nationwide system of guardianship for civil rights, and it recommended thirty-five measures to protect the rights of minorities. Among these was the creation of a permanent federal commission on civil rights, a standing committee of Congress on civil rights, and a reorganization and enlargement of the civil rights section of the Department of Justice. The committee recommended ending segregation in American life in the areas of employment, education, housing, health services, and public services.

Truman promised to study the report with great care, and he was true to his word. In February 1948 he urged Congress to pass a fair employment practices act and legislation to outlaw the poll tax, lynching, and segregation in interstate commerce. Unsuccessful in getting Congress to act, he acted on his own. He ordered an end to racial segregation in the armed services and reorganized the Department of Justice civil rights section and directed it to assist private litigants in civil rights cases. While Truman was pushing stringent measures to end segregated practices in all facets of American life, his friend Fred Vinson was in a position to further the president's objectives through the judicial branch.

The first cases that the Court dealt with were about discrimination in transportation, and these practices were challenged via the interstate commerce clause. Precedents established by the Stone Court were important in how the Vinson Court responded to these cases. In 1946, just before Vinson took his seat as chief justice, the Court had ruled in the case of *Morgan* v. *Virginia* that a woman traveling on a Greyhound bus from Baltimore to Virginia could not be ordered to the back of the bus because of a state law requiring segregation of the races.[53] The basis of the Court's ruling was that the state law posed an undue burden on the necessity of uniformity in interstate travel. Justice Burton, the lone dissenter in the case, warned the Court about the problems of overturning state laws on the grounds that they created a burden on interstate commerce without actually assessing the extent of that burden.

Two years later, when Vinson was chief justice, the Court was forced to contemplate the consequences of the Morgan decision. In *Bob Lo Excursions* v. *Michigan*,[54] the Court was confronted with a situation in which the commerce clause was invoked as a way to thwart the protection of equal rights rather than enforcing them. A Michigan civil rights law forbidding discrimination was invoked against an amusement park company that conducted steamboat excursions to an island on the Canadian side of the Detroit River. The company had refused to allow a young black girl, who was with forty white girls, to ride on the steamboat. The firm claimed that it operated in foreign commerce, which was not subject to state laws. The Court's majority, led by Justice Rutledge, got around this dilemma by declaring that the commerce in question was more local in nature than foreign. Even though the destination was politically under the jurisdiction of another country, it was "economically and socially" an adjunct of the city of Detroit. This logic was too much for Vinson and Jackson, who thought that the Court had expanded state police powers over foreign commerce on the ground that it was "not very foreign" (44). Vinson's opposition to the *Bob Lo* majority was no indication of his lack of support for civil rights. Rather, it was consistent with his view of how the Constitution had allocated state and national powers. In Vinson's view, Congress had exclusive power over foreign commerce, and this could not be transgressed even in the name of individual rights.

As Herman Pritchett noted, the *Bob Lo* case illustrated the difficulty of "attempting to achieve egalitarian goals through the cold-blooded and clumsy constitutional concept of commerce."[55] Despite these problems, the Court resisted efforts to attack the practice of separate-but-equal in public transportation as an outright violation of the Constitution. In 1950, in the case of *Henderson* v. *United States,*[56] the Court was confronted with the same kind of issue. Elmer Henderson, an employee of the federal Fair Employment Commission, was traveling by rail from Washington to Birmingham to investigate discrimination in war production. The railroad usually set aside two tables in the dining car near the kitchen for African Americans, reserving the rest of the tables for whites. However, if all of the white tables were filled, then whites could be seated in the seats set aside for African Americans. When Henderson arrived for dinner, whites had filled all but one of the seats designated for African Americans, but he was not allowed to have that seat. Instead, the railroad offered to serve him at his Pullman car seat, but he refused and insisted on sitting in the dining car. No seats opened up before the dinner ended at 9:00 P.M.

Henderson complained to the Interstate Commerce Commission (ICC) and then, dissatisfied with its handling of the matter, appealed to a lower federal court. It sided with the ICC, so he appealed to the Supreme Court. In an unusual move that reflected the impact of Truman's civil rights policies, the Justice Department, which had defended the ICC in the lower courts, reversed its position and submitted an amicus curiae brief on behalf of Henderson. Dennis Hutchinson, professor of law at the University of Chicago, said that the brief submitted by the Justice Department was significant in three ways. First, it asserted for the first time that segregated facilities were unlawful; second, it argued for the very first time that the *Plessy* doctrine should be overruled; and third, it sought to explain that segregation itself, not the resulting inequality of facilities, violated the Interstate Commerce Act and the Constitution by creating a "badge of inferiority" for those who were excluded. Hutchinson said: "The importance of this argument cannot be overstated. By emphasizing the actual harm to the individual black experiencing segregation, the Government was expanding the focus of the constitutional inquiry from the nature of the separate facilities to the nature and impact of racial classification."[57]

Although the Justice Department wanted the Court to overturn *Plessy,* the Court majority was not yet ready to go that far. Douglas was the lone member of the Court who thought that segregated facilities were a violation of the Constitution. From the outset, Vinson thought the segregated practices were illegal, but he argued that they violated the Interstate Commerce Act, which prohibited "any undue or unreasonable prejudice" by interstate carriers. He thought the case should be resolved on the basis of the statute and not the Constitution. In conference Black and Reed agreed with this position, as did Burton, who was assigned to write the opinion. Clark did not participate because the case had been heard in a lower court while he was attorney general. Eventually, all of the participating justices, except Frankfurter and Douglas, agreed to Burton's draft opinion that segregated dining tables based on race violated the Interstate Commerce Act. Burton had been careful to explain that the Court's opinion was rooted in a precedent established in a 1941 case,[58] which ruled that the Interstate Commerce Act prohibited the denial of equal access on the basis of race to interstate rail passengers.

Frankfurter, who throughout the Court's consideration of the segregation cases was reticent to move too fast in ending discriminatory practices, lobbied Burton for more narrow language than what he originally wrote and was instrumental in getting him to limit the wording to refer only to the unequal access to the dining car and not include language that might be construed as outlawing discrimination in general. Douglas wrote an opinion concurring in the result but arguing that segregated facilities violated the Constitution, but at the last hour he dropped his concurrence and agreed with the majority.[59]

The *Henderson* decision was one of three desegregation decisions announced on June 5, 1950. The other two were about segregation in higher education, *Sweatt* v. *Painter* and *McLaurin* v. *Oklahoma*.[60] Vinson played a minimal role in negotiations over *Henderson* because, as the author of the majority opinion in *Sweatt* and *McLaurin,* he was busy trying to secure unanimous agreement for those opinions. Those two opinions, along with his earlier opinion in the landmark restrictive-covenant case of *Shelley* v. *Kraemer,*[61] helped to establish Vinson's role in facilitating the eventual demise of the separate-but-equal doctrine.

The *Shelley* case offered Vinson an opportunity to advance the cause of civil rights in a way that was consistent with Truman's commitment to end discriminatory practices. The report of the President's Committee had specifically recommended the abolition of restrictive covenants. *Shelley* raised the question of whether state courts could enforce racially restrictive covenants when they were breached. This case was heard together with a similar case from Michigan, *McGhee* v. *Sipes*.[62] In both cases state courts had issued injunctions, at the request of white homeowners, to prevent African Americans from moving into homes purchased in violation of racially restrictive covenants. The petitioners claimed that state court enforcement of the covenants violated their rights under the equal protection clause of the Fourteenth Amendment. Oral arguments in these two cases were heard simultaneously with the arguments for two restrictive-covenant cases from the District of Columbia, *Hurd* v. *Hodge* and *Urciolo* v. *Hodge*.[63] The latter two raised a different constitutional issue, because the Fourteenth Amendment equal protection clause only restricts the power of states. The *Hurd* and *Urciolo* cases challenged restrictive covenants under a federal statute and the due process clause of the Fifth Amendment.

In accepting these cases for review, the Vinson Court deviated sharply from the Stone Court, which three years earlier had denied certiorari in a restrictive-covenant case. Adding to the drama of the Shelley case was that the Justice Department, spurred by Truman's civil rights initiatives and intense lobbying from liberal organizations, submitted a brief on behalf of the petitioners. This was not the first time that the government had intervened in a civil rights case, but it was the first time it had submitted a brief in a case outside the more traditional issues like the interpretation of a federal statute. Underlying the import of the government's action was the fact that both Attorney General Tom Clark and Solicitor General Phillip Perlman signed the document.[64] Another unusual aspect of the case was that three justices—Reed, Jackson, and Rutledge—withdrew from the case. In keeping with customary practice, they gave no reasons for withdrawing, but later investigations by the news media revealed that both Jackson and Rutledge owned property covered by racially restrictive covenants. Although Justice Reed never acknowledged his reason for withdrawing from the case, he did own property in Mason County, Kentucky, where many of the deeds contained racial covenants.[65]

The restrictive-covenant cases were accepted by the Court for review in June 1947. One of Vinson's law clerks, Francis A. Allen, recalled that he was "uneasy" about Vinson's commitment to reverse the lower court rulings on the subject. His concern stemmed from his knowledge of how Vinson made decisions. He said that Vinson's thought processes relied more on oral exchange than on reading and private meditation. "He possessed a remarkable talent for absorbing complex ideas by ear, an attribute no doubt sharpened by his years in Congress," Allen said. What worried Allen about Vinson's commitment to reversing the lower court was "that he had not gone through his characteristic process of spoken language, so important to his decision making." Allen labored "long hours" over the summer to prepare a memo to the chief justice that would persuade him to vote for reversal. He said that "by summer's end the memo had grown impressively in size," along with his "pride of authorship." He delivered the memo to Vinson when he returned to Washington in September, and a couple of days later had "one of the most deflating experiences of my professional life." Vinson said to him, "You know when I left here in June I thought I was going to vote to reverse in the covenant cases. After reading your memo, I'm not so sure."[66]

Oral arguments in all four of the restrictive-covenant cases were heard on January 15 and 16, 1948. Arguments for the petitioners were presented by attorneys for the NAACP and Solicitor General Perlman, who spoke for the government. Although oral arguments do not always influence the final outcome of a decision, Allen thought they might have "strengthened the Chief's resolve to reverse the lower court decisions."[67] Mark Tushnet also said that these arguments actually "sharpened the issues in the cases somewhat." Thurgood Marshall's response to a question from Chief Justice Vinson may have hit its mark. Marshall argued that restrictive covenants were not just a matter of agreement among private parties. They had to have the assistance of the state. "The essence of the contract," he said, "is its ability to be enforced. . . . The parties cannot enforce the agreement against a recalcitrant promissor without state aid." According to Tushnet, "Marshall's rhetorically powerful argument cut away most of the analytic complexities of the case."[68]

Whether it was the force of Marshall's argument or his own sense of fair play, or perhaps both, Vinson was convinced from the outset that state court enforcement of restrictive covenants violated the Fourteenth Amendment provision that no state could deny anyone within its jurisdiction equal protection of the law. He initiated the conference debate by stating that he would reverse the lower court rulings upholding the injunctions; he declared unequivocally that according to "the letter of the Fourteenth Amendment," the injunctions issued by state courts constituted state action. These petitioners, he said, "have been deprived of their constitutional rights."[69] Most of the justices at the conference agreed, and Vinson drafted an opinion, which several of his colleagues strongly endorsed. One of the most poignant notes was from Harold Burton, who wrote, "If you can get unanimous action it will be a major contribution to the vitality of the 14th Amendment, the Civil Rights Act, the general subject of interracial justice, and the strength of this Court as the 'living voice of the Constitution' (Bryce)."[70]

Vinson's opinion, delivered on May 3, 1948, was one of his longer and more eloquent opinions. Before he delivered it, he received a handwritten note from Justice Murphy saying that the opinion was "as important as Dred Scott and other epoch making decisions." Murphy counseled his colleague to "take his time."[71] Vinson heeded that advice and delivered a deliberate and verbatim reading of the full opinion. Allen, his law clerk at the time, said Vinson thought that reading the full opinion was justified, "given the portentous nature of the decision."[72]

Although Vinson's opinion might have lacked the flair of decisions written by some of his more scholarly brethren, it contained some moving and imaginative phrases. It also bore his familiar characteristic of relying on precedent to justify a decision. Given the potential impact of the Court's opinion on a practice widely in use, Vinson thought it important to show that the ruling did not represent a significant departure from long-standing precedents, even though arguably it was just that. First he noted that the ruling did not invalidate racial restrictive covenants per se. Consistent with previous Court rulings, it left them squarely intact. In these earlier cases involving restrictive covenants, Vinson said, the court had never been asked to consider whether the equal protection clause of the Fourteenth Amendment inhibited judicial enforcement by state courts of racially restrictive covenants. He concluded that the equal protection clause did prohibit such enforcement. He pointed to previous court rulings that invalidated city ordinances that denied African Americans the right to occupy houses in blocks where there were mostly white-occupied residences because they were contrary to the equal protection clause.[73] To Vinson the distinction between a city ordinance and court action was immaterial. He said, "That action of state courts and judicial officers in their official capacities is to be regarded as action of the State within the meaning of the Fourteenth Amendment, is a proposition which has long been established by decisions of this Court." According to Vinson, there could be no doubt that there had been state action in these cases "in the full and complete sense of the phrase."[74]

With a fervor not often found in Vinson's opinions, he wrote that these were not cases in which the states had merely abstained from interference in the decisions by private individuals to impose discriminations as they saw fit. Echoing Marshall's point in oral argument, he said that in these cases states had made available to such individuals "the full coercive power of government to deny petitioners, on the grounds of race or color, the enjoyment of property rights. The difference between judicial enforcement and nonenforcement of the restrictive covenants is the difference to petitioners between being denied rights of property available to other members of the community and being accorded full enjoyment of those rights on an equal footing" (19).

Vinson was not persuaded by the argument of the respondents that "state courts stand ready to enforce restrictive covenants excluding white persons from the ownership and occupancy of property." He dismissed this argument by noting that the parties had failed to cite a single case in which a state or federal court had been asked "to enforce a covenant excluding members of the white majority from ownership or occupancy of real property on the grounds of race or color." What was more important, he asserted, was that the petitioners were claiming a "personal right"; to argue that "courts may also be induced to deny white persons rights of ownership and occupancy on the grounds of race or color" is not a satisfactory response. He said that "equal protection of the laws is not achieved through indiscriminate imposition of inequalities." Driving home his main point, he concluded, "The Constitution confers upon no individual the right to demand action by the State which results in the denial of equal protection to other individuals" (22).

In his opinions in *Hodge* and *Urciolo,* Vinson invalidated restrictive covenants in the District of Columbia on the basis of a statute rather than the Constitution. Showing his inclination toward judicial restraint, he wrote, "It is a well-established principle that this Court will not decide constitutional questions where other grounds are available and dispositive of the issues of the case."[75] He argued that the Civil Rights Act of 1866 and its subsequent amendments had provided "all citizens" of the United States the same rights as whites to "inherit, purchase, lease, sell, hold and convey real and personal property" in every state and territory. The Fourteenth Amendment had made African Americans citizens of the United States, and the District of Columbia was included in the phrase "every state and territory." Given these facts, Vinson concluded, judicial enforcement of restrictive covenants by courts in the District of Columbia was prohibited by the Civil Rights Act. Although he could have stopped with that point, Vinson went a step further by relating the *Hodge* case to the *Shelley* case, decided at the same time. He said: "It is not consistent with the public policy of the United States to permit federal courts in the Nation's capital . . . to compel action denied state courts where such state action has been held to be violative of the guaranty of the equal protection of laws. We cannot presume that the public policy of the United States manifests a lesser concern for the protection of such basic rights against discriminatory action of federal court than against such action taken by the courts of the States" (35).

Vinson took great care to distinguish his opinion in the *Hurd* case from one that he had written in 1942 in a restrictive-covenant case on the circuit court of appeals in which he had ruled that racial restrictive covenants were not only valid but also enforceable.[76] However, the court majority, consisting of Vinson and Chief Judge Lawrence Groner, had refused to issue the injunction, because African Americans were the only buyers in a neighborhood that was already partially black. Vinson and Groner determined that white property owners would be disadvantaged by a court order preventing them from selling to the only potential buyers. In his *Hurd* opinion, Vinson said that in the earlier case the circuit court had "refused enforcement of a restrictive agreement where changes in the character of the neighborhood would have rendered enforcement inequitable." What explains Vinson's change of heart is a matter of speculation, but it was more than mere circumstance. Vinson was an astute politician, and he could sense that Washington in 1948 was a different place than it was in 1942. Attitudes of the average citizen may not have changed significantly during those six years, but official Washington had signaled that discrimination was no longer to be tolerated. In *To Secure These Rights,* the President's Committee on Civil Rights maintained that not only did American ideals require an end to segregation, but also America's reputation in the eyes of the world necessitated that the nation set a good example in the area of civil rights. This argument was highlighted in the brief submitted by Attorney General Clark and Solicitor General Perlman, which stated that "the United States has been embarrassed in the conduct of foreign policy by acts of discrimination taking place in the country."[77]

Several scholars have devoted considerable attention to the influence of the Cold War on the battle against racism in the United States. Mary L. Dudziak, a scholar whose work is prominent in this area,[78] argued that as the United States emerged from World War II, it confronted a dilemma. The rhetoric of the country's leaders was that the victory over Hitler represented a victory over racism, but in fact life in American society was divided along racial lines, and government laws and practices sanctioned the division. This aspect of American life received increasing attention by other countries and proved embarrassing to the nation's leaders who were trying to promote democracy and to contain Communism. The contradiction between ideology and practice created problems in American relations with countries in Asia, Africa, and Latin America—nations that were seen as crucial to our efforts to contain Communist influence.[79] Linking discrimination to the battle against

Communism had a likely influence on Vinson's thinking about civil rights issues.

The initial response to Vinson's restrictive-covenant opinions was positive. He must have been gratified by the notes he received from his colleagues. Murphy's was especially effusive. He wrote, "You will receive many blows for your covenant cases . . . but with time the cases will make you immortal. It took not only wisdom about the law but also vast courage for a Chief Justice from Kentucky to hold fast to his beliefs."[80] Walter White, secretary for the NAACP, sent a telegram thanking Vinson "most warmly for not only that magnificent decision today but for the conviction with which you delivered the opinion."[81] A former Kentuckian, transplanted to Chicago, wrote Vinson that his "fearless action has placed you along side Abraham Lincoln, Justice Harlan, Theodore Roosevelt and the unforgettable Franklin Delano Roosevelt and had liquidated a previous decision which asserted that the Negro has no rights which a white man need respect."[82]

The scholarly community was more mixed in its reactions to Vinson's restrictive-covenant opinions. One criticism of the opinion was that in the short run the practical consequence would be small. The broad use of the covenants, not confined to the deep South, coupled with extralegal sanctions, meant that little would change in the way of segregated housing. John Frank, a frequent Vinson critic, regretted the way that the Court went out of its way to reaffirm the *civil rights* cases that limited the application of the Fourteenth Amendment to state action and to conclude that the Fourteenth Amendment could not be used to protect against private conduct that was discriminatory. Frank thought the Court should have addressed more squarely Justice John Marshall Harlan's dissent in the *Plessy* case in which he declared that segregation was a "badge of slavery" and therefore a violation of the Thirteenth Amendment's prohibition against slavery.[83] Another critic, Irving Lefberg, claimed that the emphasis on the concept of "state action" meant that *Shelley* would be "an obstacle, rather than a spur, to future efforts at open housing legislation." Lefberg agreed with others that the decision was not "likely to upset customary patterns of racial segregation [or] elicit widespread political opposition."[84] Yet any Supreme Court decision could be attacked on the same ground, as Gerald N. Rosenberg argued persuasively in *The Hollow Hope,* where he examined the question of whether courts could be effective agents of social reform. Using the school desegregation cases as one example, Rosenberg concluded that other factors, such as economic and political change, are more important in facilitating societal change.[85]

The merit of an opinion is always in the eye of the beholder, and where critics like Lefberg took issue with the narrowness of the opinion, others saw that as its virtue. Vinson's former law clerk Allen, speaking about the *Shelley* case four decades later, explained the narrow nature of the opinion in terms of the convictions and attributes of the chief justice. As a man of strong institutional loyalties, Vinson was concerned about how the divisions on the court had damaged its authority and prestige, and one of his main objectives was to strive for a unanimous opinion so that the Court could speak with one voice. This concern contributed to *Shelley*'s "minimalist posture." Allen said that was why "one may find in the opinion an effort to limit what was said to the prevailing consensus on the Court, to accomplish the reversal of judgments in the instant cases, leaving for another day, when division and controversy might be less damaging, the difficult problems of application to different facts."[86] Allen claimed that it was important to Vinson "that the opinion not 'reach' for its result, [and] that the argument of the Court, in so far as possible, rely on familiar and established assumptions of constitutional law" (722).

Shelley was perhaps a more significant shift in the law than is commonly assumed. In his classic article "Toward Neutral Principles of Constitutional Law," Herbert Wechsler argued that *Shelley* emphasized results over principle by failing to clarify why the state court enforcement of a private covenant became state enforcement of discrimination rather than a legal recognition of an individual right.[87] Although *Shelley* did declare, as Vinson emphasized, that the decision by a state court constituted state action, what was not obvious, according to Wechsler, was "that the state may be properly charged with the discrimination when it does no more than give effect to an agreement that the individual involved is, by hypothesis, entirely free to make" (29). Seen through this lens, *Shelley* represented a sharp departure from existing law, despite Vinson's attempt to claim continuity with the past. The traditional role of the state court as the enforcer of private contracts entered into freely by the individual had been redefined as the agent of discrimination. The problem, Wechsler said, was determining the principle for application to other situations where the state perpetuated segregation initiated through private action, for example, the state enforcement of a will that draws a racial line.

The argument that *Shelley* represented a significant departure from existing law is buttressed in an analysis by Michael J. Klarman of the case of *Buchanan* v. *Warley* (1917),[88] cited by Vinson in *Shelley*. In *Buchanan* the Court had invalidated a Louisville ordinance providing that houses sold on city blocks that were owned by a majority of a given race (e.g., white or black) could be occupied only by members of that race. The Court had overturned the ordinance on substantive due process grounds, namely, that in effect it deprived African Americans of their individual right to own private property in accordance with their choice. Klarman argued, however, that as a property rights case it could not advance the cause of civil rights to any large extent.[89] The *Shelley* opinion, by placing the emphasis on the Court's role in enforcing the equal protection clause rather than the protection of property rights, represented an important shift in the Court's thinking about what priority to assign competing constitutional rights.

Those who argued that Vinson's opinion did not go far enough to end racial segregation in housing failed to take note of several things. First, the main thrust of the argument put forth by the petitioners themselves was that judicial intervention constituted state action. Whereas the *McGhee* case put much more emphasis on the sociological and economic aspects of the practice of restrictive covenants, in *Shelley* the "sociological claims were subordinate to the legal and constitutional claims."[90] Second, no recorded conference notes indicated that any justice was pushing for the Court to go further than it did. Lefberg mistakenly presumed in his criticism of Vinson that it was he, along with Burton and Frankfurter, who "took the most pains to limit the scope and impact of *Shelley*" and that "plausibly the Justices Douglas and Murphy argued for reconsideration of the Civil Rights cases."[91] In fact, none of the justices were observed to have made such an argument. As Allen has pointed out, "*Shelley* was litigated before the civil rights movement entered the phase of public protest . . . and the civil rights legislation was more than a decade away."[92] No public outcry propelled the Court to go further than necessary.

As Klarman and others have maintained, the importance of the social and political context in which a case is decided cannot be overlooked. Supreme Court justices are influenced by their contemporary culture, and, Klarman argued, they are not likely to "coerce the nation into adopting policies that such a substantial majority oppose." This is partially because their values reflect the majority and partially because of the possibility of inciting determined resistance. Klarman used as an example the southern white resistance to the Court's decisions in *Brown*.[93] Just as *Buchanan*'s emphasis on property rights was consistent with the progressive ideology of the early part of the twentieth century, *Shelley* can be seen as advancing the cause of civil rights in a manner that was consistent with the changing social and political climate at midcentury. It may have been slightly in advance of broad public support for equal rights, but it did not go so far as to incite popular protest.

In all of the debates about whether *Shelley* was a minimal step or a significant departure from existing law, it should not be forgotten that the opinion did bring relief to the families of the four petitioners who brought the suits and to others in their neighborhoods and similar neighborhoods across the country who were allowed at last to move into their homes. Orsel McGhee of Detroit said he was "mighty happy. . . . We've tried to be good neighbors. If some of them don't like us, we just can't help it." A neighbor of James Hurd's in Washington, D.C., said: "Well, what do you know? That is a great thing. I knew it couldn't stay that way. This is America."[94] Thurgood Marshall said the 1948 opinion gave "thousands of prospective home buyers throughout the United States new courage and hope in the American form of government."[95]

In the final analysis, the most significant impact of the decision was its symbolic effect. It is easy, viewing the case from a distance of several decades, to overlook the intangible effects of the case. *Shelley* was one of many small but necessary steps toward overturning the separate-but-equal doctrine. In removing the only legal means of enforcing restrictive-covenants, *Shelley* "marked a turning point in the Court's position on racial discrimination."[96] Lefberg agreed that "the theoretical significance of the Shelley decision should not be understated, for Vinson upset a long held judicial attitude that had clearly favored the interests of the white property owners."[97] Most important, perhaps, was the impact on the nascent civil rights movement. As Allen noted, it is easy, "looking back over the last forty years, to believe that the destruction of legal supports sustaining racial segregation in the United States was inevitable and foreordained. Not only does this easy assumption distort the experiences by those participating in the case, but it also overlooks the crucial importance of *Shelley* in bolstering the morale and providing impetus for the civil rights struggles in the following decades."[98] The *Shelley* opinion gave those who were working in the trenches to advance the cause of civil rights a ray of hope. White, of the NAACP, acknowledged that "the fight was not over" because "vast interests" were attempting to maintain segregation, but, he said, "we have moved forward a long way through this decision and those who believe in democracy are now on the offensive and have put the enemies of decency on the defensive as they have never been before."[99] Allen, framing a rhetorical question, put *Shelley* into historical perspective. He asked: "What would the history of human rights in the United States have been had the Court announced in 1948 that the great moral imperatives of the Fourteenth Amendment were irrelevant to the system of racial discrimination created and sustained by restrictive agreements? In short, what if *Shelley* had been decided the other way?"[100]

The *Shelley* opinion came four months after the Supreme Court had ruled in the case of *Sipuel* v. *Oklahoma,*[101] which was the opening round in the NAACP's salvo against the separate-but-equal doctrine in public education. Ada Sipuel, who was qualified for admission in every way, was denied entry to the University of Oklahoma law school because state law barred African Americans from attending the all-white university. She appealed the school's refusal to accept her to the Oklahoma courts, but she lost before the lower court and the state supreme court. The U.S. Supreme Court granted her petition for certiorari in the fall of 1947, and the Court heard oral arguments on January 7 and 8. Within four days of hearing the arguments, the Court reached a unanimous decision that the state law violated the equal protection clause of the Fourteenth Amendment and handed down a per curiam decision declaring that the state had to provide her with a legal education "in conformity with the equal protection clause of the Fourteenth Amendment and provide it as soon as it does for applicants of any other group" (633). The opinion cited as precedent *Missouri ex rel Gaines* v. *Canada* (1938),[102] which upheld the validity of separate-but-equal practices in higher education but declared that the Missouri practice of sending qualified black applicants to out-of-state schools failed to meet the test of equality.

What happened next in *Sipuel* revealed the fragility of the Court's facade of unanimity. In response to the Court's initial ruling, Oklahoma hastily set up a separate law school for African Americans in the state capitol. It consisted of three rooms and was staffed by three local attorneys. Sipuel and the NAACP found this unacceptable and filed a motion with the Supreme Court requesting that it order that Sipuel be admitted to the existing white law school. As the justices debated the motion, the underlying tensions rose to the surface. Vinson, hoping to avoid a nonunanimous decision, wanted to dispose of the case as quickly and simply as possible and sought to avoid the question of whether separate law schools met the test of separate-but-equal. In a memorandum to the conference, he argued that the only question before the Court was whether the Court's order to Oklahoma had been followed, and he insisted that it had.[103] He circulated a per curiam opinion denying the motion requested, stating that the petitioners had not presented the issue of whether a state might not satisfy the equal protection clause by creating a separate law school for blacks.

Although Vinson succeeded in keeping the opinion as narrow as possible, even acceding to changes suggested by Frankfurter that helped achieve that objective, he was not able to achieve a unanimous decision. Murphy dissented because he thought there should have been a hearing on the issue and Rutledge because he thought it was impossible to create equality with separate schools. The *Sipuel* case was only a temporary setback for the NAACP's strategy of overturning the separate-but-equal doctrine. Within four months it achieved a major victory in the *Shelley* case, and at the same time it was working on two other cases involving segregation in higher education that would lead the Court far beyond its reticence in *Sipuel* to declare that separate schools failed to provide equality. *Sweatt* v. *Painter* pertained to separate law schools in the state of Texas, and *McLaurin* v. *Oklahoma* concerned separate treatment in graduate education.

Herman Marion "Bill" Sweatt was a postal worker in Texas who first became involved in civil rights by challenging a policy of the postmaster barring African Americans from being clerks. From this experience he developed an appreciation for the role of lawyers in helping to remedy discrimination and decided to go to law school. He also became active in the local chapter of the NAACP. His decision to pursue a legal education coincided with the NAACP's quest for test cases to challenge segregation in education, and he was happy to accommodate them. In 1946 he applied to the University of Texas Law School at Austin and was rejected. Then, backed by the NAACP, he sued in state court to be admitted to the law school. The state trial judge denied Sweatt's request and gave the state six months to come up with a "substantially equal" law school. After a couple of false starts, the state legislature established Texas State University for Negroes in Houston. In the interim the state set up a temporary law school in Austin, in the basement of a building near the state capitol. Three law professors from the University of Texas were assigned to teach the courses. The school opened in March of 1947, but as a result of efforts by the NAACP to discourage enrollments, no students applied.

Perhaps unknowingly, the state of Texas had played into the hands of the NAACP. By creating a separate school, the state had made the *Gaines* precedent, based on a situation in which no school for blacks existed in the state, irrelevant. This opened the way to challenge the *Plessy* doctrine of separate but equal. Marshall knew he was on solid ground in challenging the equality of separate law schools. He once told his supporters, "It is easier to prove that a law school is unequal than it is to prove a primary school is unequal." Having been trained in the law, he understood what factors contributed to the quality of a legal education, and he was certain he could find in his network of acquaintances expert witnesses who would explain why it was not possible for a new and segregated law school to be equal to an existing one, regardless of the quality of the physical facilities.[104]

As the *Sweatt* case was taking form in Texas, another case was developing in the neighboring state of Oklahoma, which had just finished litigating the *Sipuel* case. In January 1948 six African Americans sought admission to several graduate programs at the University of Oklahoma. The university chose not to create separate programs at the state university for African Americans. George McLaurin, who wished to pursue a doctoral degree in education, successfully sued to obtain admission. He registered for four courses, all of which were promptly rescheduled for a single classroom that contained an alcove, where McLaurin was required to sit so that he would be separated from the white students. Marshall saw in this situation a good opportunity to show that separate arrangements were humiliating and degrading. He decided that *McLaurin* would be a good companion to *Sweatt* (130).

The NAACP filed petitions in the *McLaurin* and *Sweatt* cases in March of 1949, but it was not until the fall of 1949 that the Court agreed to hear the two cases, an unusually long period for the Court to wait before responding. Tushnet suggested that the reason for the delay was that the justices understood "that they were being asked to reconsider and overrule *Plessy* v. *Ferguson* and needed time to decide how to respond" (135). Another possible explanation might have been the lack of time. As late as May, four weeks before the end of the term, the Court was still receiving amicus curiae briefs in the *Sweatt* case.[105] When the Court finally agreed to hear the two cases, there had been significant changes in its membership. Tom Clark and Sherman Minton had replaced Murphy and Rutledge, who had died within months of each other. The latter two could be counted on to support the NAACP, but there was uncertainty about how Clark and Minton would vote. In the end, all nine justices voted in November of 1949 to grant certiorari, and oral arguments in the two cases, along with the *Henderson* case, were set for April 3 and 4, 1950.

Marshall, the lead attorney in the *Sweatt* case, decided the time had come to make the Court confront *Plessy,* saying that the "issue of separate but equal was raised right from the beginning of the case."[106] He noted that the NAACP had been trying to get the basic question of segregation before the Court for thirty years and that it was time for the Court to decide the question. He also dealt with what had become a real conundrum for the justices as well as the NAACP when wrestling with the Fourteenth Amendment. Did the framers of that amendment intend it to prohibit segregated schools? Marshall conceded in his presentation that the history of the amendment "afforded arguments for both sides and that it was not possible to make a clear-cut demonstration that the framers . . . intended either to permit or forbid segregation" (141). In their oral presentation, lawyers for the Justice Department argued that *Plessy* should be overturned. They focused on the intangible inequalities that result from separate schools, regardless of whether the facilities are equal.

When the justices met in conference to discuss the two cases, unanimity in *McLaurin* developed rather quickly. All of the justices agreed that the Oklahoma practice of segregating African Americans in the classroom constituted unequal treatment. Vinson said that "Negroes were entitled to enter the university without restriction if they are admitted at all." In *Sweatt* the central point of discussion was the intent of the framers of the Fourteenth Amendment. Vinson spoke at length on the subject. He started by noting that there was clearly separate treatment in the *Sweatt* case and that in the professional field that would not be equal, but he was uncertain whether it was prohibited by the Fourteenth Amendment. Given the history surrounding the adoption of the Fourteenth Amendment and the Civil Rights Act of 1866, he said, it was not conceivable that Congress "did not have the problem [of public schools] in front of them." The District of Columbia and the states in both the North and the South had separate schools. Vinson also commented on a proposal circulated by Clark that the Court could apply the Fourteenth Amendment to graduate education but not elementary and secondary education. Vinson said he did not think it was possible to make that distinction under the Constitution. At the end of his comments, Vinson said he was leaning toward affirming the state court's ruling; he was the only one of the justices to take that position. Vinson's initial reticence to strike down the separate schools in the *Sweatt* case appeared to arise from his concern about its possible application to elementary and secondary education. He said that all of the Court's decisions regarding equal protection had "assumed that schools were different," and he referred to it as a "bothersome problem."

Black offered up a long discussion of the Fourteenth Amendment. He said he did not think the "Fourteenth Amendment was designed to perpetuate a caste system [that was] a hangover from days when Negroes were slaves." Frankfurter, who agreed that the separate schools were not equal, thought that it was possible to limit the decision to graduate education. He argued that the Court "should abstain from saying anything about segregation as such."[107] He cautioned that no one could say with certainty what was the original intent of the equal protection clause. Jackson argued that there was no basis for finding that Fourteenth Amendment applied to schools. "In effect," he said, "we would be amending the Constitution."[108] He agreed with Vinson that it was impossible under the Constitution to distinguish between graduate and elementary education. Nonetheless, he favored reversing the state courts in both cases because the state practices in question were clearly unequal.

At the end of the conference, the Court was unanimous that *McLaurin* should be reversed, but only seven justices were solidly in favor of reversing in *Sweatt*. Vinson, who spoke in conference before hearing the other justices, was leaning toward affirming, and Reed had indicated that he could affirm or support remanding the case for "further findings." Black was the senior justice in the majority, and he assigned both cases to himself. However, in early April, Vinson changed his position in *Sweatt* and assigned both cases to himself. On May 17 he circulated draft opinions in both cases. They were relatively short. Each explained that separate educational programs at the graduate level failed to provide the equal protection guaranteed in the Fourteenth Amendment. In *Sweatt,* Vinson wrote that the Court did not agree with the petitioners that *Plessy* should be overturned. All justices except for Douglas indicated support for the draft opinions. Black, who had relinquished writing the drafts at Vinson's behest, wrote a gracious note saying, "This is written in beautiful style and I sincerely hope it can obtain a unanimous approval. . . . Full acceptance of this would add force to the holdings."[109] There was no doubt that Vinson wanted to achieve a unanimous opinion, and he was amenable to most of the suggestions for changes in wording. Both Reed and Frankfurter suggested revisions that would limit the scope of the opinion. In the *Sweatt* draft, Vinson wrote that "no one who has practiced law would choose to study in an academic vacuum, removed from the interplay of ideas and the human relationships with which the law is concerned." Reed asked him to change "human relationships" to "exchange of views."[110] Frankfurter agreed that Reed's wording was preferable but thought that the paragraph should be dropped altogether. Vinson agreed to adopt Reed's recommended wording but not to drop the entire paragraph. Where Reed had recommended the wording "these are handicaps to an effective education," Frankfurter asked that it read "these are handicaps to a graduate education." Vinson agreed to that change.

Vinson also agreed, with some reluctance, to change one other phrase suggested by Frankfurter. Vinson had characterized state practices of separate education as "expanding inequalities." Frankfurter thought that "expanding" should be dropped. Such changes would "accomplish the desired result without needlessly stirring the kind of feelings that are felt even by truly liberal and high minded Southerners like Jonathan Daniels."[111] Vinson drafted a response to Frankfurter that apparently was never sent, but it showed his pique at Frankfurter's badgering. He said he "would not want to have anything in the opinion which would stir up feelings of anger and resentment in any portion of the country." He acknowledged that much progress had been made in the South's recognition that the Fourteenth Amendment is part of the Constitution, but he said "the devices used by Oklahoma, and the Texas action here are in the nature of circumventions, and I would not be surprised but what there are other techniques which are or might be used. It was this thought that caused me to use the word 'expanding.'" Then, in reference to two other sentences that Frankfurter wanted deleted, he said, "I have always endeavored to meet the suggestions of my Brethren, and if the Court desires to delete the two sentences, they will be stricken."[112] Shortly after these changes were made, Douglas agreed to join the majority opinion in each case, making the opinions unanimous.

On June 5 the Court announced the opinions in *Sweatt, McLaurin,* and *Henderson.* Vinson read the *Sweatt* opinion first. In the first paragraph he made it clear that the Court had chosen not to decide whether *Plessy* should be overturned. He said that even though the petitioners had urged the Court to consider "broader issues," the Court would adhere to its principle of deciding "constitutional questions only when necessary to the disposition of the case at hand, and that such decisions were drawn as narrowly as possible." Almost apologetically, he added that the Court's "traditional reluctance" to extend constitutional interpretations to situations or facts that are not before it made "much of the excellent research and detailed arguments presented in these cases . . . unnecessary to their disposition."[113]

To answer the narrower question of whether the separate law schools provided the equality required by the Fourteenth Amendment, Vinson compared the two institutions. He said that the University of Texas Law School was superior in every respect, including the number of faculty, the variety of courses and opportunity for specialization, the scope of the library, and the availability of law review and similar activities. Then Vinson turned to the most significant aspect of the opinion, which was the reference to intangible factors. "What is more important," he wrote, "the University of Texas Law School possesses to a far greater extent those qualities which are incapable of objective measurement but which make for greatness in a law school." These include the reputation of the faculty, the experience of the administration, the position and influence of the alumni, the standing in the community, and the school's traditions and prestige. Vinson said, "It is difficult to believe that one who had a free choice between these law schools would consider the question close" (634). In dealing with the "qualities incapable of objective measurement," Vinson opened the door for the consideration of intangible factors that would become a key aspect of the Court's 1954 *Brown* decision overturning the *Plessy* separate-but-equal doctrine.

Then Vinson addressed other ways in which separate law programs would affect students. He argued that the profession of law "is an intensely practical one [and] the law school, the proving ground for legal learning and practice, cannot be effective in isolation from the individuals and institutions with which the law interacts. . . . No one who has practiced law would choose to study in an academic vacuum, removed from the interplay of ideas and the exchange of views with which the law is concerned." Vinson noted that the law school that Texas would have allowed Sweatt to attend "excludes from its student body 85% of the population of the state that includes most of the lawyers, witnesses, jurors, judges and other officials with whom the petitioner will inevitably be dealing when he becomes a member of the Texas Bar."

In response to the state's claim that excluding Sweatt from the University of Texas Law School was no different from excluding whites from the new law school, Vinson said such a contention "overlooks realities [for] it is unlikely that a member of a group so decisively in the majority, attending a school with rich traditions and prestige . . . would claim that the opportunities afforded him for legal education were unequal to those held open to the petitioner." He cited from his *Shelley* opinion: "Equal protection of the laws is not achieved through indiscriminate imposition of inequalities" (635).

Vinson said that the rights claimed by Sweatt were "personal and present," which meant according to the precedent set in *Sipuel* that the state had to provide him with a legal education "in conformity with the equal protection clause of the Fourteenth Amendment and provide it as soon as it does for applicants of any other group." Having established that Sweatt had a constitutional right to a legal education equivalent to that offered to whites, Vinson said "such education is not available to him in a separate law school." Thus, he said, the Court did not agree with the state that the *Plessy* doctrine required an affirmation of the state court's ruling upholding the separate law school. "Nor," he added, did the Court need to reach "the petitioner's contention that *Plessy* v. *Ferguson* should be reexamined in the light of contemporary knowledge respecting the purposes of the Fourteenth Amendment and the effects of racial segregation" (636). With those words he dashed the hopes of the NAACP that *Sweatt* would be the vehicle for overturning the separate-but-equal doctrine.

The *McLaurin* opinion was shorter and even more succinct than *Sweatt*'s. Vinson said that setting McLaurin apart from other students "handicapped his pursuit of an effective graduate education. "Such restrictions," Vinson said, "impair and inhibit his ability to study, engage in discussion and exchange views with other students, and in general, to learn his profession." He argued that an increasingly complex society created a corresponding need for trained leaders. McLaurin's case, he wrote, "represents the epitome of that need." Vinson said that denying him an equal educational opportunity meant that the education of those who came under his influence would "necessarily suffer." Following this was the line that he narrowed at Frankfurter's request: "State imposed restrictions which produce such inequalities cannot be sustained."

The state had argued that even if the restrictions were removed, McLaurin would still be set apart by his fellow students. This argument carried no weight with the chief justice. He said, "There is a vast difference—a Constitutional difference—between restrictions imposed by the state which prohibit the intellectual commingling of students, and the refusal of individuals to commingle where the state presents no such bar." As in *Sweatt,* Vinson declared that the conditions under which McLaurin was required to receive his education deprived him of "his personal and present right to the equal protection of the laws."[114]

Assessments of the significance of *Sweatt* and *McLaurin* fall into two categories. One group holds that the opinions were a very significant step in overturning the practice of separate but equal even if they did not do so explicitly. The second group argues that the Court's ruling was too narrow and had limited impact. In the first category are scholars like Tushnet, whose 1987 work attributed significance to Vinson's references to the intangible dimensions of education. He said: "Invoking the intangibles committed the justices as much as any doctrine could to the position that equality could not be achieved in separate graduate schools. And [this] opened the way to the adoption of the sociological argument."[115] The *New Republic* at the time agreed. It said that the rulings bore "directly on segregated primary and secondary schools, since it is impossible for them adequately to prepare the Negro for life in a predominantly white society."[116] Another observed that the rulings left "separate but equal a meaningless phrase" and that the opinions were "broad enough to undermine all racial discrimination in public education."[117]

Erwin Griswold, dean of the Harvard Law School, wrote Marshall the day after the opinions were announced that the NAACP "came out pretty well, yesterday." Griswold told Marshall that even though he probably "would have liked to have the school decisions go further," it was "more important that the decisions were unanimous." Marshall wrote to friends and supporters that although he would have preferred the Court to overturn *Plessy,* he still thought the opinions were "replete with road markings," that *Plessy* "has been gutted," that "the end is in sight," and that "we have at least obtained an opening wedge."[118]

Dennis Hutchinson strongly endorsed the view that *Sweatt, McLaurin,* and *Henderson,* all announced on the same day, played a key role in eventually overturning *Plessy.* Hutchinson said that to understand how the Court reached its unanimous decision in *Brown* v. *Board of Education* in 1954, it is necessary to look at the "1950 Trilogy." He said, "It was there, not with Brown, that the Supreme Court developed its attitude to statutorily imposed racial segregation and came to value addressing the issue with one voice." Hutchinson said that although the eventual outcome in *Brown* was not a foregone conclusion in 1950, the cases decided then played "an enormous part in shaping the Court's thinking about more broad-scaled attacks on segregation." Even though the Court avoided ruling on the constitutionality of segregation per se, Hutchinson said the Court's deliberations were far-reaching in scope and began the internal process that culminated in the segregation cases of 1954.[119]

Other scholars have been less laudatory about Vinson's opinions in *Sweatt* and *McLaurin.* In their view the opinions were written in such a way that they would have limited impact or could be construed in various ways, leading to disparate results. For example, Pritchett has argued that by failing "to come to grips with the essential principle of segregation by reconsideration of *Plessy v. Ferguson* . . . the Court would continue to be besieged with cases in this area." The result, Pritchett said, was that the constitutionality of any segregated practice would hinge on the equality or inequality of educational facilities for each race, and lower courts were bound to produce conflicting determinations, which they did.[120]

Lefberg was highly critical of the opinions for similar reasons. He attacked the "ambiguity of the Chief Justice's words." It was not clear, Lefberg said, whether Vinson was saying that "separate law school facilities were presumptively unequal" or that the legal education in "*the particular* Negro law school in Texas" was unequal because its tangible facilities were factually inferior to its white counterpart.[121] If Vinson meant the former, Lefberg said, then clearly the *Plessy* doctrine was weakened, but if it meant the latter, then Vinson had merely reaffirmed cases like *Gaines* and *Sipuel.* Lefberg pointed to subsequent cases in which both federal courts and state courts, and even the Supreme Court itself, interpreted *Sweatt* and *McLaurin* "as merely a refinement of the *Plessy* v. *Ferguson* doctrine." Lefberg argued that in none of the cases he cited "were Vinson's opinions afforded a construction even remotely anticipating the Court's revolutionary invalidation of elementary and secondary segregation" (277).

Vinson himself, no doubt, would have agreed in large part with Lefberg's assessment. Vinson's son Fred junior once said of his father that he was "an evolutionary as opposed to a revolutionary."[122] Allen, his law clerk, offered a similar assessment. He said that in approaching issues like the equal protection clause, Vinson "revealed no disposition to attempt a revolutionary reconstruction of the constitutional law in this area. He tended to move so far, and only so far, as required to achieve the immediate objective." Despite this caution, Allen thought there could be no doubt that the equal protection clause of the Fourteenth Amendment was significantly broadened during his tenure as chief justice. Vinson sought to achieve this, Allen said, "insofar as possible, within the traditional framework."[123]

The Court opinions in *Sweatt* and *McLaurin* were an important factor, although not the only factor, influencing Marshall to launch the next phase of the NAACP's strategy—an all-out attack on segregation. Three weeks after the opinions were announced, he convened a conference of NAACP attorneys to plot the legal strategy that would end legally imposed segregation at the elementary and secondary level. Two cases that would become the major vehicles for challenging segregation in public education were already brewing at the lower court level, *Briggs* v. *Elliott* in South Carolina and *Brown* v. *Board of Education of Topeka* in Kansas. On June 9, 1952, the Supreme Court noted probable jurisdiction in the two cases. Tom Clark recalled that the vote to note jurisdiction was unanimous, but Burton's conference votes recorded that there were seven justices who voted to "note" and one, Justice Jackson, who voted to "hold." Lefberg saw something "mysterious" in the absence of a recorded vote for Vinson and concluded, without any corroborating evidence, that the chief justice must have abstained or voted negatively on the jurisdiction question. Richard Kluger, author of *Simple Justice,* a detailed analysis of the *Brown* case, suggested, however, that not much should be made of any justice's vote, because only four votes were needed to grant jurisdiction. Moreover, Kluger cautioned against assuming that a justice's disposition in a case could be predicted on the basis of his vote on jurisdiction.[124]

During the 1952 October term, the Court became more and more immersed in cases relating to segregation and discrimination. In October the Court consolidated a case from Virginia, *Davis* v. *County School Board,* and a case from Delaware, *Gebhart* v. *Belton,* with the *Brown* and *Briggs* cases and also invited petitioners in *Bolling* v. *Sharp,* a case involving segregated schools in the District of Columbia, to file for certiorari. On December 9, 10, and 11, the Court heard oral arguments in all of the school segregation cases. Vinson's questions revealed his cautious nature and his concern about the potential effects of ruling that segregation itself was unconstitutional. It is also evident that he would have preferred to rely on precedents to address the demands for equality. To that end, Vinson's questions focused mainly on the issue of equal facilities. In the *Brown* case he pressed Robert L. Carter, who argued the case for the NAACP, on whether the physical facilities were the same in the two Topeka school systems. Carter admitted that they were but said that the heart of the case was that "segregation made educational opportunities inferior." To this Vinson replied, "That is all that you have to base your segregation issue upon,"[125] suggesting that the chief justice was leery of addressing that issue.

In the Virginia case, he again pressed the counsel for the petitioners about the issue of equal facilities. In that case the attorney for the petitioner, Spottswood W. Robinson, claimed that the state had actually not provided tangible equal educational opportunities and that it would be some time before the schools were equal in this regard; he added that even if they were equal, that would not be acceptable. Instead, he argued, the segregation was the real issue, but the petitioners understood that it would take time for administrative problems to be worked out to end it. Vinson asked why he was willing to allow "reasonable time" to be granted if segregation was held unconstitutional but not to allow the state time to achieve equal facilities. Robinson replied that even though there had been a violation of a legal right, it might be necessary for there to be a delay "incidental to the affording of that remedy." He equated it with a court order to tear down a house: "The man has got to have a reasonable opportunity to get the house down." Vinson responded, "A man might have to have a reasonable opportunity to get out of the house before it is torn down" (105). In oral argument and in conference, he kept returning to the idea of the "time factor" as an important consideration in how to approach the question of school desegregation.

The conference on the school desegregation cases was held on December 13, 1952. Various efforts to document what transpired in the conference have produced some conflicting stories, but some aspects of the conference deliberations seem clear. The first attempt to document the conference debate was Kluger's extensive work on the *Brown* case, but since publication of that work, more data have become available and subsequent investigations have provided different interpretations. Generally, the more recent interpretations by scholars, such as Hutchinson's and Tushnet's, have been more generous in their treatment of Vinson's role than Kluger's was.

One thing that is certain about the December 13 conference is that there was no clear consensus among the justices about the issues raised in the desegregation cases; had the justices been asked to decide that day, odds are good that there would not have been a unanimous decision. However, the extent of disagreement among the justices is in dispute. Black wrote later that had a vote been taken that day, the decision would have been five to four to uphold segregation. Frankfurter thought the Court would have reversed *Plessy* by a vote of four to five. Burton and Jackson thought that if *Plessy* had been reversed, there would have been between two and four dissenters.[126] Another thing that was clear was Vinson's concern about the impact of a decision declaring segregation to be unconstitutional. His presentation to the conference focused on points that he had made in the 1950 graduate education cases. In the District of Columbia case, Vinson pointed out that segregation had been imposed there by a Congress of men who had also supported the Fourteenth Amendment, leading him to believe that they did not consider segregated schools to be a violation of the Constitution. Two accounts show that Vinson attached significance to the facts that Justice John Marshall Harlan had failed to mention school segregation in his famous dissent in *Plessy* and that Harlan had written for a unanimous Court three years later in a case that inferentially upheld a Georgia state policy classifying students by race.[127] Recently some scholars have stressed that Harlan's *Plessy* dissent was driven by the status of the railroads as common carriers, not by concern for other forms of segregation.[128]

Vinson thought that Congress could abolish segregation in the District of Columbia but not in the states, but he did not "think much of the idea," suggested by Jackson in oral arguments, that the Court should wait for Congress to act. In the state cases, Vinson argued that schools would have to be made equal and noted that in South Carolina the schools had been made equal, but it had taken a long time. The problem for Vinson was reconciling the university cases, where the Court had determined that the right was "personal." He said applying that doctrine to the public schools would be more difficult because of the "large numbers" involved. He said the Court could not close its eyes "to problems in various parts of the country" or to the seriousness of the time problem. Vinson noted that they were not supposed to take the possible reaction into account, but he said, "I can't throw it all off. When you face the complete abolition of public schools in some areas then it is most serious." Then, in a sentence often overlooked, but documented in at least three accounts, Vinson said, "Boldness is essential but wisdom is indispensable."[129]

At the end of the conference, at least four of the justices—Black, Douglas, Burton, and Minton—had indicated a willingness to overturn segregation, although each had some reservations about the speed with which such a decision should be implemented. Reed was recorded as saying that he would vote to uphold segregation. That left Vinson, Frankfurter, Jackson, and Clark with reservations but no firm stand. Tushnet concluded that there was in fact more unanimity than appeared, that those who would have voted to overturn *Plessy* were not overly enthusiastic and that the rest were ambivalent. "If push had come to shove," Tushnet wrote, "a majority probably would have overruled Plessy. But . . . no one was willing to push hard enough." Vinson, who as chief justice was a likely candidate to assume such a role, was too ambivalent, as was Frankfurter, the other likely justice to assume the leadership role. Frankfurter's ambivalence stemmed from his concern about whether a "legally satisfactory opinion overruling *Plessy* could be written."[130]

Of all the justices with doubts, Jackson's views appeared to be the closest to Vinson's, especially in terms of the intent of the Fourteenth Amendment and how the Court had interpreted the equal protection clause over a long span of time. They both saw the issue as more a question of politics than of law.[131] As a lawyer, Jackson could not bring himself to conclude that segregation was unconstitutional, even though he doubted the fairness and wisdom of maintaining such a policy. He was troubled by the petitioners' reliance on sociological and psychological arguments to make the case that segregation was inherently unequal, which did not seem to bother Vinson; but like Vinson, Jackson was concerned about the effects of overturning a precedent of nearly sixty years. Whereas Vinson agonized about the social turmoil that might result, Jackson worried about the "the nation's respect for 'a supposedly stable organic law'" (604). Like Vinson, Jackson was concerned about the differences among the justices. Both men are reported to have asked that no formal vote be taken at the conference.[132]

Frankfurter, who was Jackson's closest ally on the Court, was caught in a dilemma. He personally thought that segregation was wrong and that in the District of Columbia, the Court could outlaw it as a matter of due process. The issue of segregation in the states was more problematic. He also questioned how it was possible to say with certainty, as Black did, that the Fourteenth Amendment intended to abolish segregation, and he too thought it would be a mistake to decide the issue on the basis of sociological arguments.[133] Frankfurter's biggest problem was coming to grips with Jackson's arguments that segregation could not be overturned as a matter of law and that thus the decision would be more political than constitutional. Frankfurter, avowedly against the idea of reaching a decision not based on the law, was unable to resolve his dilemma and suggested the idea that the cases be set for reargument.

Despite the reservations of these various justices, Tushnet concluded after a careful analysis of the Court's discussion that all of the justices except Reed were willing to "go along" with a desegregation decision if it was based on gradual compliance and that even Reed's views would have allowed him to join in that result. What stood in the way of unanimity was not differences over merits, "but division over how to justify the results." Mainly the discussions were the justices "talking through their concerns about what they knew they were going to do" (194). The justices were aware that whatever they decided would have to be a united vote and that it would take time to find a course they could all agree upon. As the term was coming to an end, in May 1953, Frankfurter per-

Vinson at a luncheon on February 6, 1953, with President Eisenhower and other members of the Court. (Courtesy of Special Collections, University of Kentucky Library.)

suaded his colleagues to set the cases for reargument in the next term. He proposed to the conference a list of five questions for discussion at reargument that would be submitted to both parties. On June 8, 1953, the Court assigned all five segregation cases to the docket for argument on October 12, 1953.

In the interim between the December conference on the segregation cases and the announcement that the cases would be set for reargument in October, the Court wrestled with two other highly visible issues of racial discrimination—voting and housing. In *Terry* v. *Adams* (1953),[134] the Court declared unconstitutional the all-white primary held by the Jaybird Association, a county political organization in Texas. The Jaybird primary, held before the Democratic Party primary, allowed only whites to vote. The nominees chosen by the association were automatically put on the ballot for the party primary without any indication that they had been nominated by the organization. The petitioners challenged the Jaybird primary as a violation of the Fifteenth Amendment, which prohibited states from denying the right to vote on the basis of race. They determined that the actions of the Jaybird Association did constitute state action and ruled that the primary held by the organization was unconstitutional. Vinson agreed with the majority.

Far more problematic for Vinson was the case of *Barrows* v. *Jackson*.[135] This was a restrictive-covenant case that represented the fallout from the *Shelley* ruling. In *Barrows* one white property owner sued another for damages because she violated the terms of a restrictive covenant by selling her property to a non-Caucasian. In her defense the second property owner claimed that it would be a violation of the Fourteenth Amendment for the state to award damages against her, because in doing so they were upholding a policy that discriminated against nonwhites. For the petitioner to make a claim in behalf of a third party not immediately embroiled in the suit raised the issue of standing, a rule that allows only those persons directly affected by a situation to have their concerns addressed by the Court. Unless the issue of standing could be addressed, discrimination resulting from restrictive covenants would continue. The Court's opinion in *Shelley* had held only that a state court could not enforce a restrictive covenant. It had not prohibited a suit for damages in a state court.

Minton, the lone dissenter in *Terry,* wrote the majority opinion in *Barrows,* which concluded that the petitioner could invoke the rights of a third party. Minton solved the problem of standing by relying on a precedent from a previous case, in which private schools were allowed to challenge a state statute requiring all parents to send their children to public schools as a violation of the parents' constitutional rights, even though no parent affected by the statute sought redress from the Court. Minton drew the support of all the participating justices except Vinson. Reed and Jackson did not participate.

The chief justice wrote a forceful and bitter dissent. He took exception to several aspects of the majority opinion. First, he said it had misconstrued the *Shelley* decision, and he proceeded to distinguish between the two cases. In *Shelley,* he said, the Court did not strike down restrictive covenants but rather the judicial enforcement of them to deny rights based on race. In *Barrows* Vinson charged that the majority had identified no non-Caucasian who had been injured or could be injured if damages were assessed against the person who violated the covenant. He accused the Court of reaching its decision in the case and then contriving a vehicle for hearing the case, which he thought the Court should not have heard. Vinson was clearly irritated that the Court had violated what he considered the long-standing principle that the Court should refrain "from imposing a novel constitutional limitation" upon the power of the state courts to enforce contract laws as they chose. He chided the Court for cavalierly abandoning its principle of "self-restraint," saying he could not "assent to a manner of vindicating constitutional rights of persons unknown which puts personal predisposition in a paramount position over well-established positions of power" (267). He reiterated in the conclusion of his dissent the idea that the majority had given in to their personal predilections. He said, "We must rest our decision on the Constitution alone, we must set aside predilections on social policy and adhere to the settled rules which restrict the exercise of our power of judicial review—remembering that the only restraint upon this power is our own sense of self-restraint" (269).

Vinson's critics point to his dissent in *Barrows* as strong evidence that he was not truly committed to the cause of equal rights. Lefberg, for example, described Vinson's dissent in *Barrows* as a "product of a conservative judicial mind. It is the decision of a Justice for whom 'racial equality' occupied a lower position on the hierarchy of human values than 'judicial restraint.'" In Lefberg's view, Vinson's behavior puts in doubt any civil libertarian reputation he might have earned as the result of *Shelley*. Lefberg concluded that Vinson "occupied the most conservative position on the Court among those deciding Shelley."[136] It is ironic that Lefberg took Vinson to task for defending the property rights of those who form restrictive covenants by adhering to judicial restraint, for only two decades earlier it was the liberals who attacked the Court for judicial activism. Once the liberals gained control of the Court, however, they abandoned their animosity to judicial activism and began to pursue an agenda that promoted activism in behalf of "personal rights." Property rights, once considered the bastion of individual freedom, were relegated to a lower rung on the hierarchy on individual rights.[137]

The *Barrows* opinion was handed down on June 15, one week after the Court announced the school desegregation cases for reargument. On the heels of these pronouncements, the Court became embroiled in the numerous appeals over the pending execution of the Rosenbergs. The bitterness generated by that dispute did not bode well for the coming term of the Court, when it would have to take up once again the segregation cases. Fate intervened, however, to change forever the Court's course of action. Chief Justice Vinson died of a massive heart attack at his home on the morning of September 8, 1953.

The reaction among the justices varied. Sherman Minton was devastated and had nothing but words of praise for his friend and colleague. He said: "Fred Vinson was a great Chief Justice because he was a great lawyer with a background of experience in government unexcelled by anyone. He was a prodigious worker with a capacity for friendship which gave him leadership. He was ever kind and considerate, which endeared him to all. His death is a great loss to the Court and the country and I grieve for the death of a great friend."[138] Minton wrote to Vinson's widow, Roberta, that "outside of his family, no one loved him more than I."[139]

Harold Burton also wrote kind words about the chief justice. In his diary for September 8, 1953, he wrote, "He was a great friend to me [and] he contributed much not only to the stability of the court but to the development and strengthening of the Conference of the U.S. (of Chief Judges of the 11 Circuits)."[140] The most widely reported response of any of the justices, and without doubt the most uncharitable, was a statement Frankfurter made to his former law clerk, Philip Elman, who met Frankfurter at the train station when he returned to the capital for Vinson's funeral service. "Phil," Frankfurter said, "this is the first solid piece of evidence I've ever had that there really is a God." Elman at the time was working in the Solicitor General's Office, and Frankfurter had kept him apprised of how the justices were responding to the civil rights cases. Elman, even less charitable than his mentor, said three decades later that Frankfurter was right. "Without God," Elman said, "we never would have had *Brown,* a unanimous decision that racial segregation is unconstitutional. Without God, the Court would have remained bitterly divided, fragmented, unable to decide the issue forthrightly. . . . God won *Brown* v. *Board of Education,* not Thurgood Marshall, or any other lawyer or any other mortal. God intervened. . . . He took care of the American people and little children and *Brown* by taking Fred Vinson when he did."[141]

Elman's zeal in promoting God as the force behind *Brown* was almost matched in his praise of the role Frankfurter played in helping the Court to reach a unanimous decision. The tenor of his remarks serves as an example of why Vinson's role in expanding civil rights tended to be denigrated in many of the earlier historical accounts of the *Brown* decision. Tushnet wrote a detailed analysis of what went on behind the scenes at the Court as the justices struggled with how to respond to the cases brought by the NAACP. Tushnet's interpretation examined the roles of the key justices from two perspectives, the "standard version," which favored Frankfurter's contributions, and the "alternative version" constructed by himself, which is more favorable to Vinson. According to Tushnet, the standard interpretation relied heavily on Frankfurter's own accounts and became the accepted version because Frankfurter produced through numerous memoranda and letters more evidence than any of the other justices. Although there was other evidence, it tended to be overlooked by those writing the standard version, many of whom were Frankfurter's former clerks, with whom he maintained close personal ties. Many of his clerks became academics and played an important role in "conveying to the legal academy the sense that Frankfurter was a wise and insightful man."[142]

Tushnet argued that Frankfurter's role is overblown in the standard version and that what it failed to account for is that starting in 1952 and continuing until 1954, Frankfurter was largely responsible for the Court's delaying a decision. In the alternative version constructed by Tushnet, Vinson is shown to be far less opposed to overturning segregation than is usually assumed. For example, Tushnet pointed out that nowhere in his conference statement did Vinson commit himself either to reaffirming or to overruling the separate-but-equal doctrine, "but on balance the tone of his comments suggests that he would go along with a decision by a majority of the Court to hold segregation unconstitutional, as he had gone along in the university cases despite his initial inclination the other way" (1903–4). Tushnet said Vinson's line that "boldness is essential but wisdom is indispensable" was a good indication that he understood that the Court had to invalidate segregation.[143]

Following the *Brown* decision, several of the justices claimed that if the decision had been made while Vinson was chief justice, it would not have been unanimous, and possibly the Court would have upheld segregation. Among those making such a claim was Frankfurter, who wrote to his longtime friend Learned Hand that the road to unanimity in Brown was long, but that "it would not have come to pass with Vinson." He wrote similar statements to other colleagues.[144] Tushnet suggested that such conclusions were overstated because they failed to take into account the ambivalence shown by both Frankfurter and Jackson and to recognize the possibility that potential dissenters might have been persuaded to go along with the majority. Tushnet saw Frankfurter as the crux of the problem in reaching a decision. He could not be swayed by the argument put forth by Jackson, who was willing to approach the decision as a political one because he was convinced that overturning segregation could not be grounded in the law. Frankfurter could not go along unless he could be convinced that the ruling was based in law. Caught between his desire to see segregation ended and his need to render a decision justified by law, Frankfurter wanted more time. His proposal to reargue the cases was designed to stall for time, mainly so that he could find a course that was satisfactory to him. In pursuit of that objective, he had his clerk, Alexander Bickel, conduct extensive research on the origins and intent of the Fourteenth Amendment. Bickel started his research in the 1952 term but did not complete it until the summer of 1953. He reported to Frankfurter that the legislative history provided "no evidence" that the framers of the Fourteenth Amendment intended to outlaw school segregation. At the same time, Bickel said, the legislative history "did not foreclose future generations from acting on the question either by congressional statute or by judicial review."[145] Bickel's memo proved critical to the eventual result in Brown, for it allowed Frankfurter to see a way out of his dilemma. It allowed him to claim that the decision to overturn desegregation would be a judicial decision rather than a political one.

Although Vinson fared better in Tushnet's account, he does not come off as one who played a leadership role in helping the justices find a resolution for their dilemma. Nevertheless, it is difficult to say with certainty how the Court would have decided *Brown* under his tenure. The available evidence does suggest that he was amenable to the idea of overturning segregation if it could be done on a gradual basis. It was not his intent, but Lefberg, one of Vinson's harshest critics, provided evidence that Vinson eventually would have agreed to end segregation. He classified Vinson as a conservative who was philosophically opposed to expanding civil rights, and he sought to explain why Vinson voted as he did in *Shelley, Sweatt,* and *McLaurin.* Finding nothing in Vinson's own philosophy that would explain such votes, he offered two other explanations. One was that Vinson voted out of loyalty to Truman, who pushed for desegregation through the executive branch, and the other was Vinson's strong stance against Communism. Lefberg thought that Vinson, with his strong animosity toward Communism, was influenced by the argument promoted by the President's Committee on Civil Rights as well as others that the treatment of African Americans by the United States was the key to our success in the battle against Communism.[146] If these were Vinson's reasons for ending segregation in higher education, Lefberg offers no reason why they would have been less significant in his decision in *Brown.*

If Vinson did finally conclude that segregation must end, then it is reasonable to conclude that he would have worked, as he did in *Sweatt* and *McLaurin,* to bring about a unanimous decision. After all, one of Vinson's most strongly held convictions was the importance of unanimity to the institutional integrity of the Court. Though he failed miserably in unifying the Court on so many other issues, he deserves some credit for working to achieve unanimity in the civil rights cases. Hutchinson argued that unanimity in the 1950 Trilogy "exercised a kind of hydraulic pressure on the reservations expressed in 1950 by Reed and Clark—two of the justices most uncomfortable with broad based challenges to segregation." Hutchinson also concluded that "if Vinson could have overcome his concern with the timing and scope of relief in *Brown* and its companion cases, it is probable . . . that Vinson—not Warren—could have authored the unanimous decisions in 1954."[147] Certainly there could be no doubt that the result in *Brown* would have been a far less likely outcome in 1954 if *Sweatt* and *Painter* had not been unanimous or, worse yet, if the decision had gone the other way.

Assessments of Vinson's brief tenure as chief justice, especially from the scholarly community, have generally been more negative than favorable. Some of his harshest critics have branded him "a failure," a label that has taken hold and frequently been perpetuated without more thorough and objective analysis. Those who have examined his record with more diligence have provided accounts that portray Vinson more fairly and with greater balance.[148] In important respects, he did not provide the kind of leadership that the divided court needed, but at the same time he did leave an imprint on the institution at a crucial time in its history.

Vinson's most visible failures were his inability to unite the Court and his limited contribution to the ongoing philosophical debates among the justices over the proper role of the Court in the political system and the questions about incorporation of the Bill of Rights into the due process clause of the Fourteenth Amendment. Vinson inherited a Court wracked with personal rivalries and a reputation for divisiveness, as evidenced by the large number of nonunanimous opinions. Although Vinson cannot be credited with ending the personal animosities altogether, they at least receded into the background and ceased to be the subject of journalistic fodder. Bolner observed that Vinson "engendered a healthier atmosphere among the Court members [and] this made it possible for the Court to carry on the discussion of the proper limits of judicial power."[149] However, if measured by the number of nonunanimous opinions, the Court became even more divided under Vinson than under his predecessor, Stone: The number of concurring and dissenting opinions increased, from 64 per cent of all opinions written in Stone's last term to 81 per cent in Vinson's last term.[150] He was continually troubled by the lack of unity because he thought it damaged the reputation of the Court. Vinson tried to lead by example, writing only three concurring opinions and thirteen dissenting opinions during his seven years on the bench.

However, he was unable to convince some of his colleagues to follow his lead.

Vinson proved no more capable of effecting compromise among the Brethren in the all-important debates over the proper extent of judicial power in a democratic society and the fundamental issue of the extent to which the specific provisions of the Bill of Rights were incorporated into the due process clause of the Fourteenth Amendment. In this task, Vinson's role was hampered by the intellectual prowess of the protagonists, Frankfurter and Black and their allies Jackson and Douglas, and the absence of a consistent judicial philosophy of his own. Vinson was by nature a pragmatist, a problem solver, "a man of action," and these traits that had served him so well in his previous experiences in government did not fit so congruently with the intellectual sparring of the other justices over constitutional interpretation and nuances in wording. He was good at negotiating solutions to problems and was not given to speculating about long-term consequences. To him a good decision was one that could generate enough consensus to be acceptable. He was not interested in breaking new ground. His opinions were narrowly drawn to fit a specific situation, and he was not concerned with setting precedents for the future. This trait is reflected clearly in three of his most famous opinions—*United Mine Workers, Dennis,* and *Youngstown.* In each of these cases, Vinson saw an urgent need and found a way to address it. He was much more concerned with the practical consequences of the decision than with long-term implications. As his law clerk Allen said, "he was reluctant to sacrifice a clear present advantage in the interest of a remote and speculative future gain."[151]

Vinson's pragmatism clashed, sometimes bitterly, with the inclination of his more intellectual colleagues to define issues in broader terms even if it meant overturning an existing precedent or moving the Court in new directions. Vinson liked to resolve cases whenever possible on the basis of precedent, and reliance on precedent meant a cautious approach in determining the law. This trait antagonized some liberals who wanted him to move more quickly to overturn the separate-but-equal doctrine in public education. His adherence to precedent was prominent in his rebuke to his colleagues in his dissent in *Barrows,* the only time he ever dissented alone. It is also present in the *Dennis* decision, where he struggled to fit his opinion into the Holmes-Brandeis "clear and present danger" legacy.

Vinson's problem-solving approach led him to side with the government in most cases. He had a strong faith in the power of government to develop solutions to society's problems, and this belief was most pronounced in cases where he thought social order was threatened. Vinson had an unqualified belief that the only way to promote freedom was to have order and security in society. Without order, there could be no freedom, and to this end Vinson thought that the first task of the Court was to uphold the rule of law. This belief led him to support the government in cases like the *United Mine Workers,* where he was incensed that Lewis and the UMW had tried to defy a court order; in *Dennis,* where he thought the nation's security was at risk from Communist activities; in *Youngstown,* where he thought the president should have the power to protect our national interest during a war; and in search and seizure cases like *Harris,* where he thought law enforcement agents, acting on "good faith," were entitled to take evidence obtained incident to an arrest.

Vinson's strong support of the government was in large part a function of his philosophy of judicial restraint and the belief that in a democratic society judges were obligated to show deference to legislatures. Given his own experiences, Vinson thought the legislative branch was the best place for the resolution of society's conflict, and he was reluctant to upset a consensus reached by representatives of the people. This approach produced sharp conflicts with his more libertarian colleagues like Black and Douglas in cases involving civil liberties and with Frankfurter in the search and seizure cases. In all of these cases, Vinson tried to balance the needs of government against the rights of the individual, and he almost always came down on the side of government. It is in this area of the law, more than any other, that Vinson's record generates the harshest criticism. His decisions upholding government restrictions on political speech of nonconformists such as *Douds* and *Dennis* have been targeted as his worst decisions because of their antilibertarianism. Even his supporters have found it hard to defend them. Yet, as it turned out, Vinson's perceptions about the threat of Communist subversion in the United States was not as far-fetched as his critics maintained. More recent scholarship has shown that Communist infiltration of the government was far more extensive than many liberals at the time believed to be the case.[152]

Vinson has been criticized by some Court scholars for interrupting the Stone Court's efforts to expand individual rights, but in reality the picture is more complex. Urofsky described both the Stone and Vinson Courts as transitional courts, caught in the changing perspectives among conservatives and liberals about the virtues of judicial restraint and judicial activism. Before 1937 conservatives applauded judicial activism when the Court struck down economic regulations imposed by government as violations of property rights protected under the Constitution. Liberals decried this activism. Under Stone and then Vinson, the views of activism began to shift. Activism in striking down legislative restriction on civil liberties met with approval by liberals but not by conservatives. Although Vinson himself was more inclined to follow restraint in issues involving civil liberties, the Court under his tenure continued the trend toward elevating civil liberties, such as speech and press, to a preferred position over economic rights.[153] With the exception of *Barrows,* Vinson showed no strong interest in defending the rights of property owners.

Although Vinson was an advocate of relying on precedent and adhering to judicial restraint and was favorably disposed to the government's exercise of power, he was not completely rigid in his approach. He stated many times in his opinions that he was leery of broad generalizations and absolutist positions. Thus, he did not always follow judicial restraint, adhere to precedent, or side with government. Further, Vinson recognized that there were certain cases that required a different approach, a political approach. According to Paul Kelley, who served as Vinson's confidential secretary and aid for approximately seventeen years, the chief justice distinguished between two types of cases—political cases and ordinary cases. Political cases were those whose issues were the topic of widespread public discussion and required the application of different standards. As a result they "had to be decided with an eye to the total situation or to as much of the situation as the judges could grasp."[154] *Dennis, United Mine Workers,* and the steel seizure case would fall into the category of political cases.

What Vinson brought to the Court during his tenure as chief justice was the mind of a politician. In that respect it was important to him that the Court maintain the respect and support of the average citizen. That is why he tried to nudge the Court toward greater unanimity in its opinions, and it also explains in part the brevity and succinctness of his opinions. Willard Pedrick, Vinson's law clerk on the circuit court of appeals, recalled his boss's admonition that the court's opinions should not be "too fancy. . . . We're trying to communicate so the folks back home can understand it."[155] In the end, Vinson's political instincts may have served the Court well as it tried to steer a course through some of the most politically charged issues ever to confront the Court. To the extent that his cautious and pragmatic approach kept the Court from veering too far from the realm of public acceptability, he helped to insulate it from public censure that might have undermined its effectiveness by generating disobedience or outright resistance to its pronouncements. His goal of maintaining continuity with the past through relying on precedent, while inching forward in areas like equal protection, helped establish the legitimacy for the Warren Court to overturn the separate-but-equal doctrine.

Consistent with his view of how a democracy ought to work, Vinson sought to balance the competing interests of society and the individual and to weigh the benefits of an immediate solution against a long-term advantage. Although his critics on and off the Court thought his scales were weighted too often toward the government and short-term necessities, he himself believed that democracy was better served through a moderate course than one of extremism. In Vinson's political view, legislatures, with the give-and-take of competing interests, were better suited to adopt social reforms, but that did not mean that the Court could avoid the responsibility for resolving social problems in the proper circumstances. When those circumstances presented themselves, the Court had to act, as it did in the cases involving equal protection. It is in those areas of the law where Vinson's legacy was more long-term.

Why was Vinson less willing to show deference to the legislative will in the matter of equal rights than in other areas of policy? A plausible explanation is that Vinson sensed that the time had come, that there was a certain inevitability about social reform that the Court had to accommodate. Following World War II, the United States began to experience significant social, economic, and political changes that affected the attitudes of Americans about race. Some of the influences on both black and white attitudes during that period were the contradiction of racial discrimination following a war fought against a country whose leaders espoused racial superiority; the demands on American foreign policy to demonstrate a commitment to egalitarianism at the height of the Cold War; and the expansion of urbanization and industrialization of the country that led to increased social and economic integration of the nation, enhanced economic opportunity, and eroded southern insularity. Klarman and Rosenberg, in separate works, examined these changes and theorized that they offer the best explanation as to why the Supreme Court could render its unanimous *Brown* decision in 1954, when a decade earlier it would have been considered unthinkable.[156] During Vinson's tenure as chief justice, these forces translated into a political imperative that drove the Truman administration's policies aimed at dismantling segregation and ultimately influenced Vinson.

Epilogue

Baseball Commissioner Fred M. Vinson? President Fred M. Vinson? At the midway point of the twentieth century, it seemed altogether possible that yet another position of power and prestige, even the highest office in the land, was in store for the folksy, bushy-browed man from eastern Kentucky. Fred M. Vinson had been, after all, a man for all seasons during the decade of the forties, frequently and effortlessly moving from one job of importance to the next with calm and confidence. If a vacuum on the national scene existed, the public had come to expect that it would be filled by Vinson. He joked at one time, "If I were to be assigned to all the jobs that the press had indicated I am to be appointed to, I would have to be more than a single individual."[1] Although he might have been tempted by the prospect of becoming czar of the game he loved so passionately and flattered to be widely and prominently mentioned as a possible Democratic presidential candidate in 1952, he declined to pursue either venture, choosing instead to remain in the last office he would ever hold—chief justice of the United States.

When Happy Chandler lost his job as commissioner of baseball in 1951, Vinson was on the list of possible replacements. To someone as crazy about baseball as Vinson, the chance to while away lazy summer afternoons in a box seat at the ballpark must have been alluring. It sure had to beat presiding over long and contentious Saturday conferences at the Supreme Court or listening to Felix Frankfurter drone on ad nauseam. The handsome salary, double what he made as chief justice, also had to be appealing to Vinson, who was never very far removed from indebtedness. In the end, though, he followed his mind and not his heart, deciding that it would defile the dignity of the judiciary if its top officer left to take a position in the slightly soiled and frivolous world of baseball.

Resigning from the Court to run for president, something Harry Truman fervently tried to get Vinson to do, would have been more understandable and more palatable to the public. But Vinson resisted his friend's overtures and those of others, explaining that his wife was adamantly opposed to the idea. She was concerned about his health, and rightly so. Vinson was an old sixty-two in the election year of 1952. He was overweight, devoured unfiltered Camels, disdained exercise, and heartily ate high-fat meals that would sound the alarms by today's standards. Vinson himself was not all that keen on the notion of getting into the race. As he explained to an old colleague from Congress who was touting him as presidential material, "There is none of the virus of that type in my blood. My sole desire and ambition is to assist in maintaining and securing the respect of the country for the Court and its product."[2]

Whether another Democratic candidate would have fared any better against the wildly popular war hero Gen. Dwight Eisenhower than did Adlai Stevenson is, of course, unknown. Still, there was a certain logic to a Vinson candidacy. He was the stuff of American legends: born in a small town to parents of meager means; became a scholar and star athlete at an elite, private college through raw intelligence, hard work, and determination; married his hometown sweetheart; won election after election with the support of Republicans as well as Democrats; sat at the right hand of presidents to help them in times of war and peace; and took on the job as chief justice to restore respect for a fractured Supreme Court. A modern-day campaign strategist would have had a field day extolling, without needing to resort to embellishment, the values and virtues of Vinson, a man without enemies. He was the genuine article. He had been near or at the throttle of power in Washington for almost three decades, but he remained humble, unassuming, and approachable. The essence of Vinson was captured by a photograph in a *Life* magazine spread shortly after he was named chief justice. There on a Louisa street corner stands the newly appointed head of the judiciary branch of the federal government—in suit and tie, hat in one hand, cigarette in the other—shooting the breeze with four just plain folks. His idea of a good time was staying home in his hotel apartment on a Sunday evening to play bridge with his son Fred and a few of Fred's friends.

"Ike" versus "Fred" would have been an interesting race, pitting two men who were good friends and who had much in common. Both were born in 1890 and both were imbued with the character, discipline, and sense of purpose that came from being raised amid struggle in America's heartland at the turn of the century. It is hard to conceive that these two dignified and reserved men would have engaged in anything approaching negative campaigning, although Eisenhower's running mate, Richard Nixon, might well have dredged up Harry Dexter White to tar Vinson for not dismissing his former Treasury Department assistant over allegations of Communist activities.

But by 1952, Vinson had not run in an election for sixteen years, and it is highly unlikely that he would have had the energy and stamina to wage a national campaign over the course of many months. Wisely, he remained on the sidelines during the presidential season, content to restrict his participation to the swearing in of Dwight David Eisenhower as the nation's thirty-fourth president on January 20, 1953. Inauguration Day was a bittersweet one for the Vinsons. They were thrilled to be with the new president on the reviewing stand during the inaugural parade, but then they had to dash off to Union Station to say good-bye to their friends Harry and Bess Truman. Writing about the day to her son Jimmy, then in army basic training, Roberta said, "We were heartbroken to see the Trumans leave, and I wept a little after the train pulled out. It is the end of an era for us."[3] Still, she said, it had been quite a day for her. "The new President called me darling, and the outgoing President kissed me before some thousand people." Although Vinson's relationship with the new occupant of the White House obviously was not to be on par with the one he had enjoyed with Truman, he did occasionally go to the White House to play bridge with Eisenhower.

No sooner had the exuberance of the inauguration subsided when another cause for celebration graced the Vinson household. The news came that Jimmy's wife, Peggy, was pregnant. And when a baby boy arrived in early August, the Vinsons were elated to have "entered the circle of grandparents," as the proud grandfather wrote in a letter to his daughter-in-law. He noted that Roberta had "cried and cried with joy" at hearing the news. "They have a saying down Kentucky-way," he continued, "that the Vinsons are wild about their children." He said he had talked about wanting a girl, but, "Frankly, I always wanted a boy. I would love it just as much if it hadn't been a boy, but I am particularly proud to know that my name will be carried on."[4]

Sherman Minton, Vinson's colleague on the Court and friend, wrote to welcome him into "the Ancient and Decrepit Order of Grandfathers," adding, "I can assure you there is nothing more satisfying than a grandchild."[5] In his reply of thanks, Vinson said he and Roberta "try to be convinced that he is the only grandchild. However, in recalling the seraphic smiles which I have seen on the faces of Grandpas Black, Reed,

Douglas, Jackson, Burton, Clark, and yourself, I realize that those of us who are only Grandpa once must take a back seat."[6]

In late August the Vinsons went to Kentucky to see their grandson, James Robert Vinson Jr. They returned to Washington a few days later armed with glowing accounts of the baby and a stack of photographs of the newest member of the Vinson clan. The joy that blessed event brought to the family would soon be overshadowed by the devastating blow that struck in the early morning hours of September 8, 1953.

Vinson, who had not been seriously ill, went to bed at his home in Washington the night before, complaining of a slight attack of indigestion. He woke at 2:30 the following morning in considerable pain and breathing with difficulty. Roberta and Fred junior, who was staying with his parents at their hotel apartment, called the family physician. But before he could arrive, Fred M. Vinson, the thirteenth chief justice of the United States, had died of a heart attack at age sixty-three.

As word spread of Vinson's unexpected death, heartfelt expressions of shock and grief began pouring forth. His only surviving sibling, his sister Miss Lou, was in seclusion at home in Louisa and was "torn all to pieces," a relative said. In his statement, President Eisenhower, who was vacationing at the summer White House in Denver, called Vinson an outstanding citizen who had served "with efficiency, dignity and integrity" in all three branches of national government.[7] He proclaimed a thirty-day period of mourning and directed that the national flag be flown at half-staff. From his home in Independence, former president Truman, shaken by the news that his intimate friend had died, hailed Vinson as "a great man and a great justice as well as a great citizen of the country."[8] Vice President Nixon, Cabinet members, fellow justices, and congressional Republicans and Democrats added their tributes to Vinson. Secretary of State John Foster Dulles said, "The whole nation will rightly mourn his passing," adding that his was also a personal loss, "because I was honored to have the Chief Justice include me among his friends." Republican senator Alexander Wiley of Wisconsin said that although many might have differed with Vinson, including members of his own Court, "I haven't ever met an American who didn't like Fred personally or who didn't respect him for his personal integrity, his warm genial disposition, his love of country." Justice Robert H. Jackson said Vinson brought to the court "the practical viewpoint of the country lawyer, the legislative experience of long service in Congress and the teaching of several important posts in the executive branch." Senate Democratic leader Lyndon Johnson said Vinson's concept of public service "should serve as a standard for all time to come."

To honor his personal traits of modesty, simplicity, and humility, Vinson's family decided that he would lie in state in the unpretentious surroundings of a Washington funeral home rather than having the pomp and ceremony of a state funeral in the Capitol rotunda to which he was entitled. Hundreds filed past the open plain mahogany casket, which was devoid of flowers, candles, or a flag, to pay their last respects. Services followed in Washington Cathedral and then the next day in the Louisa Methodist Church. Eisenhower, interrupting his vacation, flew in from Colorado for the Washington funeral, and Truman came by train from Missouri. It was their first face-to-face meeting since Inauguration Day in January. Eisenhower, who had spent many hours playing bridge with Vinson, was described as "grave but dry-eyed during the ceremony." Truman, his face drawn and gray, stood silently as others in the cathedral sang "Abide with Me," one of Vinson's favorite hymns. A newspaper account said that behind his gold-rimmed glasses, "Truman appeared to be blinking back the tears."

A special train carried the body back to Louisa for a brief, simple service at the small red brick church that was located across the town square from where Vinson was born. Just two years before at the dedication of a monolith to him in the square, Vinson had said: "From where I stand, I see my birthplace. I see my school and its playground, where my education began. Over there is the temple of justice [the courthouse] where my career in law began. And there is the temple of my faith," pointing to the church.[9] On the afternoon of the funeral, schools were closed and all businesses shut down. Supreme Court justices; Kentucky governor Lawrence Wetherby; Kentucky's U.S. senators, John Sherman Cooper and Earle Clements; House Speaker Sam Rayburn; and Alben Barkley, former vice president and U.S. senator from Kentucky, were among those who filled the three hundred seats in the tiny church for the funeral. Hundreds of others stood outside on the square listening to the service over loudspeakers. Kentucky congressman Noble Gregory, describing the services in a letter to Vinson's longtime House colleague Robert Doughton of North Carolina, said, "I have never seen a tribute more genuine or more American than that demonstrated by his friends in Kentucky and elsewhere who gathered for the final rites. These people represented all walks of life, all avocations, and all creeds." Besides the dignitaries, the mourners were "farmers, laborers and plain citizens, men in overalls and working clothes, but all with the same thought and objective—to pay tribute to a great man," Gregory said.

The minister officiating, a part-time preacher and part-time schoolteacher, selected for his reading the first chapter of Joshua and its reference to Moses as servant and leader. Gregory said he "paraphrased this biblical reference and compared it to Fred with the exhortation that even though our leader is gone, we should move forward—that we should go ahead." The trek to the local cemetery and the family plot on a hill overlooking Louisa followed. "The grave side service was simple with hundreds of people there paying tribute to one they loved, to a local boy buried in judicial robe and one who started there sixty-three years ago and who had reached the highest pinnacle in his profession, but still a local boy," Gregory wrote. "This to me was and is America."[10]

A year after Vinson's death, according to tradition, the Supreme Court and members of its bar held memorial services to honor him. A host of prominent figures from the nation's legal fraternity, including Chief Justice Earl Warren, Attorney General Herbert Brownell, and Solicitor General Simon Sobeloff, paid tribute to Vinson's government service and personal virtues. Warren said, "Although he rose from humble beginnings to the highest offices in all three branches of our government, he never lost his understanding of people—that common touch and good judgment so essential in one who attains such heights."[11] He noted that Vinson "had devoted practically all of his mature years to rendering valuable service for his country." In discussing Vinson's time on the District of Columbia court of appeals, Brownell said that Vinson "was a stickler for facts and studied each record with great care. Lacking pretense and despising sham, he would not hesitate to pierce the armor of any attorney who dared advance an untenable argument or one not based on the record." Yet, he continued, Vinson was also so considerate, gentle, and courteous that off the bench, "in meeting a young attorney, the 'Chief' did not permit the occasion to pass without offering a kind word of encouragement." Brownell said Vinson's most outstanding quality was his complete devotion to duty. "When the country called upon him to render service to it he responded without the slightest hesitation or thought of personal sacrifice. The circumstances surrounding his resignation from the Court of Appeals testify to the high sense of duty which actuated him."[12] Sobeloff, who traced Vinson's life from beginning to end, said Vinson graced every role he held. "To each task he gave his best with genial spirit, confident of the promise of the future. A man of good will, friendly, approachable, genuinely interested in 'folks,' he has left behind him friends literally without number," Sobeloff said.[13]

As evidence of the kind of respect and affection that Vinson could engender, the Vinson Club, an elaborate annual dinner that District of Columbia lawyers started in 1943 as a way of honoring the achievements of their colleague, continued in existence long after Vinson's death.

A further tribute to Vinson came when the *Northwestern University Law Review* devoted its entire March–April 1954 issue to a review and an assessment of Vinson's thirty-year career in public service. The dean of the law school, Harold C. Havighurst, said that since "most of his law clerks were Northwestern graduates, it seems especially appropriate that this Law Review should publish a commemorative issue." During his time as chief justice, nine Northwestern graduates served as Vinson law clerks, including Newton Minow and Howard Trienens. Vinson's connection with the law school actually began earlier on the court of appeals when he selected Willard Pedrick and Wilbur Lester, Northwestern graduates, as his law clerks. Both later served as personal assistants to Vinson in the Office of Economic Stabilization. Lester, in assessing Vinson's three years in the executive branch, said Vinson was above all else "a practical politician. He was a politician in that he thought it important to know—and he did know—how government works. He was practical in that he had little interest in any abstract study of the art or science of government, but he had great concern as to how the government was run on behalf of the people."[14]

Amid the thousands of words of praise justly accorded Vinson upon his death, perhaps a succinct two-paragraph tribute in the *New York Times* captured as well as any the most salient point about his life. With his knowledge of the law and tax matters and his personal connections, Vinson probably could have made a fortune, "had he cared to leave the small rewards of public life and turn his hand to business," the editorial said. "Probably he could have been a millionaire more than once." That he did not make that choice, the writer concluded, was "simply another shining mark on the record of a fine American statesman and jurist."[15]

Notes

Introduction

1. "The Cover . . . ," *Parade,* Dec. 7, 1947. Bob Burchette was a *Washington Post* staff photographer.
2. FMV to Garland R. Farmer, Jan. 11, 1946, box 400, VCUK.
3. FMV to Brooklyn-Queens Political Society, Oct. 13, 1947, box 326, VCUK.
4. Willard H. Pedrick, interview by Terry L. Birdwhistell, Oct. 22, 1976.

1. A Long Journey from "Jail"

1. Truman, *Memoirs,* 2:215.
2. Bendiner, "Available Vinson," 18.
3. Pringle, "Sitter-on-the-Lid," 98.
4. Truman, *Memoirs,* 2:214.
5. Ely, *Big Sandy Valley,* 157–58.
6. The genealogy portion of this chapter is based on various correspondence Vinson had with relatives and others seeking to learn of his ancestors; Hatcher's Ph.D. dissertation, "Fred Vinson, pt. 1"; W.E. Connelley and E.M. Coulter, *History of Kentucky* (Chicago: The American History Society, 1922); Ely's *Big Sandy Valley;* Wolfford's *Lawrence County;* and entries on Vinson in the *National Cyclopedia of American Biography* (New York: J.T. White, 1956) and George Lee Willis's *Kentucky Democracy,* vol. 2 (Louisville: Democratic Historical Society, 1935).
7. Kornitzer, *American Fathers,* 173.
8. Stewart, "Presidential Timber."
9. Bendiner, "Available Vinson," 19.
10. Fred M. Vinson to Billy Bagby, Mar. 4, 1927, box 2, VCUK.
11. Hatcher, "Fred Vinson," 61.
12. Ibid., 65.
13. FMV to Mrs. Gertrude Haney, Dec. 23, 1923, box 72, VCUK.
14. Kornitzer, *American Fathers,* 175.

15. Hatcher, "Fred Vinson," 79.

16. Bendiner, "Available Vinson," 19.

17. FMV to Judge W.L. Watson, Apr. 19, 1924, box 17, VCUK.

18. George L. Alley, "An Error in Prophecy," newspaper article in box 325, VCUK.

19. Speech by John Diederich, date unknown, in Vinson file in the Alumni Office, Centre College, Danville, Ky.

20. "Centre Vinson Memorial Foundation," 1.

21. Hatcher, "Fred Vinson," 90.

22. *Cardinal and Blue*, 47.

23. FMV to J. Barbour Russell Jr., Sept. 27, 1924, box 12, VCUK.

24. Diederich speech.

25. The law school at Centre suspended operations three years after Vinson graduated.

26. Kornitzer, *American Fathers*, 186.

27. FMV to R.A. Chiles, Oct. 8, 1938, box 307, VCUK.

28. "Portrait of Late Justice Vinson."

29. W.E. Crutcher, interview by Terry L. Birdwhistell, Jan. 8, 1975, VOHP.

30. Judge Chesley A. Lycan, interview by Terry L. Birdwhistell, Jan. 9, 1975, VOHP.

31. Crutcher interview, VOHP.

32. Connelley and Coulter, *History of Kentucky*, 564.

33. Harry E. Ritter to FMV, Oct. 12, 1927, box 19, VCUK.

34. Kornitzer, *American Fathers*, 183.

35. Crutcher interview, VOHP.

36. Stewart, "Presidential Timber," 23.

37. Leonard Lyons, "Cracking the Self-Defense Chestnut," Apr. 14, 1947, box 330, VCUK.

38. *Biggs v. Commonwealth*, 196 *Kentucky Reports* 655 (1922) 658, 659.

39. Rodell, "Chief Justice," 108.

40. Stewart, "Presidential Timber," 25.

41. Welcome address by Vinson, Sept. 1927, Fair and Home-Coming, Louisa, box 389, VCUK.

2. The Capitol as His Oyster

1. Mrs. Althea Swinford Hutton, interview by Terry L. Birdwhistell, Mar. 28, 1975, VOHP.

2. Galloway, *History of the House of Representatives* (1961), 256.

3. Hatcher, "Fred Vinson," 171, 172.

4. FMV to John and Mary Bahan, Mar. 3, 1924, box 2, VCUK.

5. Klotter, *Portrait in Paradox*, 274.

6. From a campaign speech Vinson made in support of Democratic gubernatorial candidate J.C.W. Beckham in 1927, box 389, VCUK.

7. FMV to Grannis Bach, Nov. 24, 1923, box 72, VCUK.

8. Jewell, *Kentucky Votes*, 10.

9. FMV to M.F. Conley, Feb. 18, 1924, box 3, VCUK. The other counties in

the Ninth District were Bath, Bracken, Breathitt, Boyd, Carter, Elliott, Fleming, Greenup, Harrison, Lewis, Mason, Menifee, Montgomery, Morgan, Nicholas, Robertson, Rowan, and Wolfe.

10. FMV to E.E. Shannon, Feb. 15, 1924, box 20, VCUK.

11. FMV to J.A. Moneyhon, Feb. 27, 1924, box 8, VCUK.

12. Galloway, *History of the U.S. House of Representatives* (1965), 127.

13. FMV to J.H. Testor, Mar. 24, 1924, box 3, VCUK.

14. FMV to Shannon, Feb. 1, 1924, box 20, VCUK.

15. Donald R. McCoy, *Calvin Coolidge: The Quiet President* (Lawrence: Univ. Press of Kansas, 1988), 223.

16. Vinson campaign speech for Beckham in 1927, box 389, VCUK.

17. Abels, *In The Time of Silent Cal,* 215.

18. *Congressional Record,* 68th Cong., 1st sess., 1924, vol. 65, pt. 3, 2602–19.

19. Mooney, *Roosevelt and Rayburn,* 15.

20. Testor to FMV, Mar. 19, 1924, box 3, VCUK.

21. *Congressional Record,* 68th Cong., 1st sess., 1924, vol. 65, pt. 6, 6117, 6130–35.

22. J. Franklin Reynolds Jr. to FMV, June 6, 1924, box 12, VCUK.

23. Charles M. Cooper to FMV, Apr. 17, 1924, box 5, VCUK.

24. FMV to Dr. S.D. Laughlin, Apr. 23, 1924, box 7, VCUK.

25. Form letter from Ex-Service Men's Anti-Bonus League to FMV, box 68, VCUK.

26. Vinson to Ex-Service Men's Anti-Bonus League, Feb. 9, 1924, box 68, VCUK.

27. *Congressional Record,* 68th Cong., 1st sess., 1924, vol. 65, pt. 5, 4298.

28. In 1924 Congress passed pension increases for veterans of earlier wars and the adjusted compensation bill for World War I soldiers. President Coolidge vetoed the pension bill and it was upheld, but his veto of the compensation measure was overridden.

29. FMV to J.T. Mercer, Apr. 19, 1924, box 2, VCUK.

30. FMV to George H. Geahart, Jan. 2, 1925, box 3, VCUK. In 1926 Congress passed and President Coolidge signed a bill similar to Howell-Barkley, although it was by then known as the Watson-Parker Railroad Labor Act.

31. G.R. McGuire to FMV, May 29, 1924, box 3, VCUK.

32. FMV to Charles M. Cooper, Mar. 3, 1924, box 5, VCUK.

33. FMV to Shannon, Mar. 12, 1924, box 20, VCUK.

34. FMV to W.E. Coleman, Mar. 25, 1924, box 4, VCUK.

35. FMV to Dr. T.D. Burgess, Feb. 8, 1926, box 2, VCUK.

36. Stanley Reed to FMV, Feb. 10, 1927, box 12, VCUK.

37. FMV to Clay W. Stamper, Apr. 19, 1924, box 16, VCUK.

38. FMV to Mrs. Elizabeth Sebastian, Mar. 6, 1926, box 12, VCUK.

39. FMV to Rev. John Cheap, Mar. 4, 1924, box 4, VCUK.

40. FMV to Mary Land Brunner, Dec. 6, 1924, box 2, VCUK.

41. John W. Langley to FMV, June 4, 1924, box 7, VCUK.

42. FMV to Virginia Vinson, Mar. 1, 1924, box 306, VCUK.

43. FMV to Joseph W. Morris, May 14, 1925, box 8, VCUK.

44. FMV to Virginia Vinson, Feb. 3, 1927, box 306, VCUK.
45. FMV to Robert Dixon, Apr. 1, 1924, box 5, VCUK.
46. FMV to Virginia Vinson, Mar. 22, 1924, box 306, VCUK.
47. FMV to Chiles, June 9, 1924, box 4, VCUK.
48. Chiles to FMV, May 28, 1924, box 4, VCUK.
49. FMV to Chiles, June 2, 1924, box 4, VCUK.
50. FMV to Dixon, Apr. 1, 1924, box 5, VCUK.
51. FMV to J.T. Rees, May 22, 1924, box 12, VCUK.
52. FMV campaign letter, undated, box 69, VCUK.
53. Crutcher interview, VOHP.
54. FMV to Rees, Dec. 15, 1924, box 12, VCUK.
55. Cooper to FMV, Nov. 20, 1924, box 5, VCUK.
56. Octave P. Beauvais to FMV, Feb. 14, 1925, box 304, VCUK.
57. C.L. Kilburn to FMV, Feb. 14, 1925, box 304, VCUK.
58. Howard Gumm to FMV, Feb. 26, 1925, box 70, VCUK.
59. Van Antwerp to FMV, Feb. 14, 1925, box 304, VCUK.
60. FMV to Van Antwerp, Feb. 16, 1925, box 304, VCUK.
61. *Congressional Record,* 69th Cong., 1st sess., 1926, vol. 67, pt. 11, 12421.
62. Howard E. Coffin to FMV, July 19, 1926, box 13, VCUK.
63. Vinson to Dr. S.C. Smith, Jan. 13, 1928, box 3, VCUK.
64. *Congressional Record,* 70th Cong., 2nd sess., 1929, vol. 70, pt. 5, 4923.
65. FMV to Martin R. Rice, Apr. 7, 1928, box 3, VCUK.
66. Smith to FMV, Jan. 7, 1928, box 3, VCUK.
67. FMV to Smith, Jan. 23, 1928, box 20, VCUK.
68. *Congressional Record,* 70th Cong., 2nd sess., 1929, vol. 70, pt. 5, 5130–33.
69. J.H. Meek to Ben Williamson, Mar. 12, 1926, box 3, VCUK.
70. FMV to the U.S. Corps of Engineers Office, Huntington, W.Va., Sept. 30, 1925, box 12, VCUK.
71. Johnson, *Illustrated History,* 202.
72. *Congressional Record,* 70th Cong., 2nd sess., 1929, vol. 70, pt. 5, 5131–32.
73. Klotter, *Portrait in Paradox,* 284.
74. Campaign speech for Beckham in 1927, box 389, VCUK.
75. Klotter, *Portrait in Paradox,* 286.
76. Bailey to FMV, Feb. 6, 1928, box 19, VCUK.
77. Ibid., Aug. 6, 1928, box 72, VCUK.
78. Underwood to FMV, Sept. 8, 1928, box 71, VCUK.
79. Howerton to FMV, Sept. 12, 1928, box 71, VCUK.
80. Pierce to FMV, Sept. 8, 1928, box 71, VCUK.
81. Michelson to FMV, Aug. 30, 1928, box 73, VCUK.
82. FMV to the *Western Recorder,* Sept. 13, 1928, box 73, VCUK.
83. "Chief Justice–Nominee Vinson."

3. Rapid Recovery and Rise

1. *Congressional Record,* 70th Cong., 2nd sess., 1929, vol. 70, pt. 5, 5130–33.
2. FMV to J.A. Thompson, Oct. 30, 1929, box 73, VCUK.

3. FMV to Courtney Combs, May 15, 1930, box 73, VCUK.

4. "Vinson Makes Statement," *Mt. Sterling (Ky.) Gazette,* May 2, 1930, box 74, VCUK.

5. "Fields' Opening Address," box 73, VCUK.

6. Garner to FMV, Nov. 7, 1930, box 73, VCUK.

7. FMV to Garner, Nov. 10, 1930, box 73, VCUK.

8. The long gap between elections and the time the president, vice president, senators, and representatives actually assumed office was shortened considerably by the Twentieth Amendment to the Constitution, the so-called Lame Duck Amendment, which was ratified in January 1933.

9. FMV to Leonidas Y. Redwine, Mar. 8, 1927, box 12, VCUK.

10. FMV to Thompson, Nov. 10, 1930, box 75, VCUK.

11. FMV to Johnson, Dec. 3, 1930, box 74, VCUK.

12. FMV to Shouse, Jan. 17, 1931, box 76, VCUK.

13. Shouse to FMV, Jan. 20, 1931, box 76, VCUK.

14. FMV to Eudaley, Jan. 27, 1931, box 76, VCUK.

15. FMV to Thompson, Feb. 19, 1931, box 76, VCUK.

16. Pearce, *Divide and Dissent,* 33, 34.

17. *Congressional Record,* 72nd Congress, 1st sess., 1932, vol. 75, pt. 2, 12208.

18. J.N. Camden to FMV, Apr. 25, 1932, box 78, VCUK.

19. FMV to Camden, Apr. 30, 1932, box 78, VCUK.

20. *Congressional Record,* 72nd Cong., 1st sess., 1932, vol. 75, pt. 7, 7306.

21. Ibid., pt. 9, 9495.

22. Vinson's radio address is reproduced in *Congressional Record,* 72nd Cong., 1st sess., 1932, vol. 75, pt. 8, 9082.

23. Newell to FMV, Apr. 5, 1932, box 34, VCUK.

24. Vinson's radio address is reproduced in *Congressional Record,* 72nd Cong., 1st sess., 1932, vol. 75, pt. 14, 15049, 15050.

25. Mrs. L.B. Carrick to FMV, July 3, 1932, box 30, VCUK.

26. FMV to Carrick, July 19, 1932, box 30, VCUK.

27. Vinson press release, undated, box 29, VCUK.

28. "Find Double Taxes Weigh on Business," 21.

29. According to the Tax Foundation, total tax collections in the United States in the late 1990s reached $2.7 trillion, with the federal government collecting $1,805.8 billion of the total, or 67.7%, and state and local governments taking $861.4 billion. The tax bill for every household in the country averaged $26,434 in 1998, and for every U.S. resident it averaged $9,881.

30. Logan Caldwell to FMV, Jan. 5, 1933, box 34, VCUK.

31. FMV to Caldwell, Jan. 10, 1933, box 34, VCUK.

32. *Congressional Record,* 72nd Cong., 1st sess., 1932, vol. 75, pt. 2, 1534.

33. House Committee on Ways and Means, "Payment of Adjusted-Compensation Certificates," 72nd Cong., 1st sess., 1932, report no. 1252, 2.

34. Ibid., 3.

35. Ibid., 4.

36. *Congressional Record,* 72nd Cong., 1st sess., 1932, vol. 75, pt. 12, 12912.

37. Dixon to FMV, July 13, 1932, box 78, VCUK.

38. Campaign letter, Aug. 1, 1932, box 78, VCUK.
39. "Remember Vinson," *Cynthiana (Ky.) Democrat,* Aug. 4, 1932.
40. "Vote First for Vinson for Congress," *Carlisle (Ky.) Mercury,* Aug. 4, 1932.
41. "Has Earned the Support of All Loyal Democrats," *Bracken (Ky.) Chronicle,* Aug. 4, 1932.
42. G.L. Drury to FMV, July 28, 1932, box 78, VCUK.
43. Ed. L. Weathers to FMV, Aug. 2, 1932, box 79, VCUK; FMV to Weathers, Aug. 4, 1932, box 79, VCUK.
44. W.M. Caudill to FMV, Aug. 17, 1932, box 78, VCUK.
45. FMV to Garner, Nov. 6, 1932, box 78, VCUK.
46. The others were John Y. Brown, A.J. May, Brent Spence, Virgil Chapman, Glover H. Clay, W.V. Gregory, C.R. Carden, and Finley Hamilton.
47. FMV to Henry H. Curran, Sept. 9, 1930, box 73, VCUK.
48. FMV to Rev. W.C. Pierce, Oct. 10, 1930, box 74, VCUK.
49. FMV to Pierce, July 30, 1932, box 79, VCUK.
50. FMV to R.M. Bagby, June 18, 1932, box 78, VCUK.

4. The Loyal Lieutenant

1. Schlesinger, *New Deal,* 1.
2. Edsforth, *New Deal,* 121.
3. Herring, "First Session of the 73rd Congress," 65.
4. Schlesinger, *New Deal,* 23.
5. Stewart, "Presidential Timber."
6. "Assassin's Bullets," 4.
7. Walter Mayo to FMV, Mar. 15, 1933, box 24, VCUK.
8. FMV to Mayo, Mar. 24, 1933, box 24, VCUK.
9. Mayo to FMV, Mar. 27, 1933, box 24, VCUK.
10. Edmon Burgher to FMV, Mar. 14, 1933, box 23, VCUK.
11. V.V. Adkins to FMV, Mar. 27, 1933, box 23, VCUK.
12. Desha Breckinridge to FMV, Mar. 16, 1933, box 23, VCUK.
13. J.C. Courtenay to FMV, Mar. 13, 1933, box 23, VCUK.
14. Paul M. Ferguson to FMV, Mar. 12, 1933, box 24, VCUK.
15. FMV to Ferguson, Mar. 16, 1933, box 24, VCUK.
16. John C. Hatcher to FMV, Mar. 28, 1933, box 24, VCUK.
17. Joe T. Lovett to FMV, undated, box 24, VCUK.
18. FMV to Lovett, Mar. 24, 1933, box 24, VCUK.
19. Lovett to FMV, Mar. 28, 1933, box 24, VCUK.
20. FMV to Lovett, Apr. 3, 1933, box 24, VCUK.
21. FMV to J.T. Rees, Mar. 14, 1933, box 24, VCUK.
22. FMV to Howard E. Gumm, Apr. 3, 1933, box 24, VCUK.
23. FMV to Rees, Mar. 14, 1933, box 24, VCUK.
24. FMV to Breckinridge, Mar. 28, 1933, box 23, VCUK.
25. J.Q. Lackey to FMV, Mar. 14, 1933, box 24, VCUK.
26. Zeno F. Fisher to FMV, Mar. 21, 1933, box 24, VCUK.
27. Henry W. Sullivan to FMV, Mar. 13, 1933, box 24, VCUK.

28. *Congressional Record,* 73rd Cong., 1st sess., 1933, vol. 77, pt. 1, 837.

29. Ibid., 841. Bingham was confirmed in 1933 as U.S. ambassador to the Court of St. James, where he served until his death in 1937.

30. *Congressional Record,* 73rd Cong., 1st sess., 1933, vol. 77, pt. 1, 882, 883.

31. FMV to Perry B. Gaines, Jan. 25, 1934, box 85, VCUK.

32. D. Bernard Coughlin to FMV, Mar. 16, 1934, box 85, VCUK.

33. A.B. Rosen to FMV, Mar. 16, 1934, box 85, VCUK.

34. Campaign letter dated Oct. 22, 1934, box 85, VCUK.

35. FMV to D.N. Rees, Aug. 13, 1935, box 86, VCUK.

36. FMV to Lindsey Douglas, July 8, 1935, box 86, VCUK.

37. Speech for 1935 gubernatorial general election, box 389, VCUK.

38. FMV to J.H. Armstrong, July 13, 1936, box 87, VCUK.

39. Ray Murphy to FMV, Feb. 11, 1936, box 88, VCUK.

40. Frank N. Belgrano Jr. to FMV, Feb. 7, 1936, box 88, VCUK.

41. John L. Lewis to FMV, July 1, 1936, box 88, VCUK.

42. "President Signs Coal Mining Bill," 8.

43. Blakey, *Hard Times and New Deal in Kentucky,* 8, 113.

44. Joseph A. Fagan to FMV, Jan. 29, 1934, box 34, VCUK.

45. FMV to Fagan, Feb. 13, 1934, box 34, VCUK.

46. Primary campaign press release from Vinson, July 18, 1936, box 88, VCUK.

47. FMV to Frank C. Taylor, Jan. 26, 1935, box 34, VCUK.

48. Keen Johnson to FMV, Apr. 2, 1934, box 34, VCUK.

49. FMV to James A. Farley, May 16, 1934, box 34, VCUK.

50. "Service the Farmers Do Not Need."

51. "Why Farmers Are against the Flannagan Bill."

52. FMV to Underwood, June 3, 1935, box 35, VCUK.

53. FMV to Nette McClanahan, Jan. 23, 1934, box 82, VCUK.

54. FMV to William C. Fox, July 7, 1934, box 82, VCUK.

55. William Johnson to FMV, June 13, 1934, box 82, VCUK.

56. FMV to Johnson, July 12, 1934, box 82, VCUK.

57. FMV to Evelyn R. Payne, May 1, 1934, box 82, VCUK.

58. FMV to J.B. Fannin, Jan. 31, 1934, box 82, VCUK.

59. M.J. Allen to FMV, July 23, 1934, box 84, VCUK.

60. FMV to Allen, July 26, 1934, box 84, VCUK.

61. FMV to Anna L. Bartlett, Oct. 27, 1938, box 307, VCUK.

62. A newspaper reporter, Tom Stokes, charged that Barkley was using WPA workers in his campaign against Kentucky governor Happy Chandler, who opposed him in the 1938 Democratic primary for the Senate. A Senate investigation into the matter found improper use of public employees in both campaigns but concluded that neither candidate had been aware of such activities.

63. Hatcher, "Fred Vinson," 449.

64. "Disappointing Veto."

65. Roosevelt to FMV, Oct. 6, 1937, Official File no. 41, container 1, Roosevelt Library.

66. Hatcher, "Fred Vinson," 351.

67. Fred M. Vinson Jr., interview by Charles L. Atcher, May 22, 1973, VOHP.

68. Eliot, "25 Years After," 72–75.

69. "See Vast Loan Use for Security Fund," 2.

70. Arthur Altmeyer, interview no. 2, Mar. 23, 1966, Oral History Research Office, Columbia University.

71. Edwin E. Witte to FMV, Apr. 10, 1935, box 28, VCUK.

72. "Reflections on the Beginnings of Social Security," by Edwin E. Witte, Aug. 15, 1955, remarks delivered at the observance of the twentieth anniversary of the Social Security Act, Washington, D.C. Social Security Adminstration website, <http://www.ssa.gov/history/witte4.html>.

73. The principle eventually became part of the Internal Revenue Code and today is known as the accumulated earnings tax. Retained earnings above a specified limit, set fairly high to benefit small companies, are taxed at the highest individual tax rate.

74. *Congressional Record,* 74th Cong., 2nd sess., 1936, vol. 80, pt. 8, 10337.

75. "Conservative Democrats Were Tax Bill Framers," 22.

76. Graham and Wander, *Franklin D. Roosevelt,* 416.

77. "Profit Tax Relief Put at Top of List," 4.

78. Wesley Winans Stout to FMV, Aug. 17, 1937, box 30, VCUK.

79. FMV to Stout, Aug. 28, 1937, box 30, VCUK.

80. *Philadelphia Record,* Nov. 22, 1937, box 30, VCUK.

81. FMV to Harry T. Saylor, Nov. 25, 1937, box 30, VCUK.

82. Ballard and Ballard actually was acquired by the giant Pillsbury Mills in 1951.

83. Thruston Ballard Morton to FMV, Feb. 18, 1938, box 33, VCUK.

84. Thomas J. Davis to FMV, Dec. 6, 1937, box 32, VCUK.

85. Myron A. Loewen to FMV, Feb. 23, 1938, box 33, VCUK.

86. Fred Schrey to FMV, Oct. 22, 1937, box 30, VCUK.

87. John B. Berryman to FMV, Nov. 17, 1937, box 31, VCUK.

88. J.H. Long to FMV, Feb. 18, 1938, box 33, VCUK.

89. FMV to Long, Feb. 22, 1938, box 33, VCUK.

90. Herbert M. Goldsmith to FMV, Jan. 14, 1938, box 32, VCUK.

91. Paul H. Schollenberg to FMV, Nov. 17, 1937, box 31, VCUK.

92. Robert C. Clothier to FMV, Feb. 15, 1938, box 33, VCUK.

93. Mrs. Morton Prince to FMV, Dec. 3, 1937, box 32, VCUK.

94. Howard Van Antwerp Jr. to FMV, Nov. 24, 1937, box 31, VCUK.

95. FMV to Van Antwerp, Nov. 24, 1937, box 31, VCUK.

96. *Congressional Record,* 75th Cong., 3rd sess., 1938, vol. 78, pt. 6, 6692-98.

5. Vinson's Transition from Legislator to Jurist

1. Today members of the circuit court are called judges, but in 1938 they were called associate justices. The head of the circuit court was called the chief justice.

2. Memorandum from Bell to Attorney General Cummings, Nov. 23, 1937, OF-51S, Court of Appeals for D.C., 1933–1945, Franklin D. Roosevelt Library.

3. Goldman, *Picking Federal Judges,* 26.

4. Stephens to Groner, Aug. 27, 1940, private papers of Harold Stephens, box 125, Library of Congress.

5. Goldman, *Picking Federal Judges,* 57.

6. Hatcher, "Fred M. Vinson," 495.

7. Goldman, *Picking Federal Judges,* 61.

8. Cited in Goldman, *Picking Federal Judges,* 34. Original source is Cummings to Roosevelt, October 9, 1937, OF 51 s END, U.S. Court of Appeals for District of Columbia 1933–1945, Franklin D. Roosevelt Library.

9. Goldman, *Picking Federal Judges,* 27. The original source is OF 51 s, Court of Appeals for the District of Columbia 1933–1945, Franklin D. Roosevelt Library.

10. Stephens to D. Lawrence Groner, Aug. 9, 1937, box 125, HSCLC.

11. Stephens to Henry W. Edgerton, Feb. 16, 1937, box 134, HSCLC.

12. Taken from an article published in the *Cornell Law Quarterly* and sent by Edgerton to Stephens, Mar. 16, 1937, box 125, HSCLC.

13. Stephens to Groner, Aug. 11, 1945, box 125, HSCLC.

14. *Maysville (Ky.) Daily Independent,* Nov. n.d., 1939, box 401, VCUK.

15. Crawford and Stewart, "Fred M. Vinson," 407.

16. Bolner, "Mr. Chief Justice Vinson," 19.

17. *Congressional Record,* 75th Congress, 3rd sess., vol. 83, 6675.

18. FMV to Coleman Taylor, Aug. 27, 1938, box 308, VCUK.

19. FMV to Mrs. Robert Dixon, Jan. 12, 1940, box 308, VCUK.

20. FMV to Rev. J.S. Thompson, July 7, 1938, box 308, VCUK.

21. Pedrick, "From Congress to the Court of Appeals," 59.

22. Draft of tribute to Rutledge for a joint publication of the *Indiana Law Journal* and the *Iowa Law Review,* ca. 1950, box 399, VCUK.

23. Stephens to Groner, Aug. 9, 1937, box 125, HSCLC.

24. Goldman, *Picking Federal Judges,* 27. Original source is OF 51 s, Court of Appeals for the District of Columbia 1933–1945, Franklin D. Roosevelt Library.

25. Groner to the associate justices, Nov. 13, 1942, box 90, WBRCLC.

26. FMV to Stephens, May 14, 1941, box 90, WBRCLC.

27. Stephens to Rutledge, June 12, 1941, box 132, WBRCLC.

28. Rutledge to Stephens, June 13, 1941, box 132, WBRCLC.

29. *Scharfield* v. *Richardson,* 133 F2d 340 (1942).

30. *Evans* v. *Ockerhausen,* 100 F2d 695 (1938).

31. Groner to FMV, July 19, 1938, box 89, VCUK.

32. FMV to Groner, July 21, 1938, box 89, VCUK.

33. Miller to FMV, July 26, 1938, box 89, VCUK.

34. Stephens to FMV, Dec. 23, 1941, box 9, VCUK.

35. Pedrick, "From Congress to the Circuit Court of Appeals," 57.

36. Stephens, "The Chief Justice," 388.

37. Pedrick, "From Congress to the Court of Appeals," 58.

38. Stephens, "The Chief Justice," 388.

39. *Washington Evening Star,* May 12, 1938.

40. David J. Lewis to FMV, Feb. 27, 1939, box 90, VCUK.

41. Pedrick, "From Congress to the Court of Appeals," 56.

42. *Railroad Retirement Board* v. *Bates,* 126 F2d 642 (1942).

43. *Railroad Retirement Board* v. *Bates,* 126 F2d 642 (1942), 645.

44. Rutledge to FMV, Feb. 17, 1942, box 95, VCUK.

45. *National Association of Wool Manufacturers* v. *Fleming,* 122 F2d 617 (1941).

46. The other two cases involving the power to establish wages were *Southern Garment Mfrs. Association, Inc. et al.* v. *Fleming, Administrator, Wage and Hour Division,* 122 F2d 622 (1941); and *Andree Seedman, Inc. et al.* v. *Administrator of Wage and Hour Division, U.S. Department of Labor,* 122 F2d 634 (1941).

47. *National Association of Wool Manufacturers* v. *Fleming,* 122 F2d 617 (941), 622.

48. *Switchmen's Union of North America et al.* v. *National Mediation Board et al.,* 135 F2d 785 (1943).

49. *Switchmen's Union of North America et al.* v. *National Mediation Board et al.,* 320 U.S. 297 (1943).

50. *Prevost* v. *Morgenthau, U.S. Secretary of the Treasury,* 106 F2d 330 (1939).

51. Lewis Deschler to FMV, Nov. 15, 1939, box 90, VCUK.

52. *McCord* v. *Commissioner of Internal Revenue,* 123 F2d 164 (1941).

53. Groner to FMV, Oct. 21, 1941, box 94, VCUK.

54. Edgerton to FMV, Oct. 21, 1941, box 94, VCUK.

55. Stephens to FMV, Oct. 21, 1941, box 94, VCUK.

56. *United States ex rel Denholm & McKay Co.* v. *United States Board of Tax Appeals,* 125 F2d 557 (1942).

57. Rutledge to FMV, Feb. 2, 1942, box 95, VCUK.

58. Miller to FMV, Feb. 2, 1942, box 95, VCUK.

59. *John Hancock Mut. Life Ins. Co.* v. *Helvering, Com'r of Revenue,* 128 F2d 745 (1942). The other cases were *The Northwestern Mutual Life Insurance Company, Petitioner,* v. *Guy T. Helvering, Commissioner of Internal Revenue,* 128 F2d 752 (1942); *Connecticut General Insurance Company, Petitioner,* v. *Guy T. Helvering, Commissioner of Internal Revenue,* 128 F2d 752 (1942); *State Mutual Life Insurance Company* v. *Guy T. Helvering, Commissioner of Internal Revenue,* 128 F2d 753 (1942); *Equitable Life Insurance Company of Iowa* v. *Guy T. Helvering,* 128 F2d 753 (1942).

60. Bolner, "Mr. Chief Justice Vinson," 25.

61. *John Hancock Mutual Life Ins.* v. *Helvering,* 128 F2d 745 (1942), 747.

62. *National Federation of Railway Workers* v. *National Mediation Board,* 110 F2d 529 (1940).

63. Ibid., 538.

64. *Civil Rights Cases,* 109 U.S. 3 (1883).

65. *Shelley* v. *Kraemer,* 334 U.S. 1 (1948).

66. *Terry* v. *Adams,* 345 U.S. 461 (1953).

67. *Viereck* v. *United States,* 130 F2d 945 (1942).

68. *History of the U.S. Court of Appeals.*

69. *Viereck* v. *United States,* 130 F2d 945 (1942), 950.

70. *Viereck* v. *United States,* 318 U.S. 236 (1943).

71. *Viereck* v. *United States,* 139 F2d 847 (1944).

72. *Nueslein* v. *District of Columbia,* 115 F2d 690 (1940).

73. *Weeks* v. *United States,* 232 U.S. 383 (1914). For an excellent discussion of the history of Fourth Amendment rights, see Bodenhamer, *Fair Trial,* esp. 76–80.

74. *Nueslein* v. *District of Columbia,* 115 F2d 690 (1940) 695.

75. *Warring* v. *Colpoys,* 122 F2d 642 (1941).

76. Ibid., 646.

77. *Warring* v. *Colpoys,* 122 F2d 642 (1941) 646.

78. *United States* v. *Offutt,* 127 F2d 336 (1942).

79. Ibid., 340.

80. Hatcher, "Fred Vinson," 110–12.

81. Rutledge to FMV, Apr. 4, 1942, box 95, VCUK.

82. *Parmelee* v. *United States,* 113 F2d 729 (1940).

83. *Parmelee* v. *United States,* 113 F2d 729 (1940) 741.

84. Rutledge to FMV, May 6, 1940, box 92, VCUK.

85. Edgerton to FMV, May 6, 1940, box 92, VCUK.

86. Frank Crowther to FMV, May 17, 1940, box 92, VCUK.

87. Speech to the District of Columbia Bar Association, Jan. 12, 1943, box 391, VCUK.

88. Speech by Judge Bolitha J. Laws to the District of Columbia Bar Association, Jan. 1944, box 391, VCUK.

89. Ely, "Property Rights and the Supreme Court," 20.

90. *Davies Warehouse Co.* v. *Brown, Price Administrator,* 137 F2d 201 (1943).

91. Pedrick, "From Congress to the Court of Appeals," 60.

92. Stephens, "The Chief Justice," 388.

6. Available Vinson

1. Kefauver to FMV, Jan. 1, 1945, box 319, VCUK.

2. Proctor to FMV, Jan. 1, 1945, box 320, VCUK.

3. FMV to Proctor, Jan. 11, 1945, box 320, VCUK.

4. Robertson, *Sly and Able,* 326.

5. "O.W.M. Expected to Consult Roosevelt Soon."

6. "Man Who Does Not Make Promises He Cannot Keep."

7. "Vinson's New Job Thrills His Spouse."

8. "Vinson: Senate's 'Businessman,'" 17.

9. Copy of speech found in Harold M. Stephens Manuscript Collection, box 40, Library of Congress.

10. Bendiner, "Available Vinson," 56.

11. Rodell, "The Chief Justice," 113.

12. "Another Progress Report," Jan. 12, 1945, box 319, VCUK.

13. FMV to Jacobs, Jan. 30, 1945, box 319, VCUK.

14. Willard Pedrick, interview by Terry L. Birdwhistell, Oct. 22, 1976, VOHP.

15. Crawford and Stewart, "Fred M. Vinson," 409.

16. Judge Marvin Jones, interviews, Apr. 3, 20, 24, May 8, 14, 1970, Truman Library.

17. Prichard to FMV, Apr. 28, 1944, box 354, VCUK.

18. Campbell, *Short of the Glory,* 93.

19. In late 1947 Porter joined with Thurman Arnold, a former U.S. court of appeals judge, and Abe Fortas, later a Supreme Court justice, to form Arnold and Porter, which became one of Washington's most influential law firms.

20. "Senate Votes Rise of 8C in Rail Pay," 1.

21. Press release from the Office of War Information, Oct. 2, 1943, box 109, VCUK.

22. FMV to President Roosevelt, Mar. 8, 1945, box 108, VCUK.

23. "Heat on Textiles," 80.

24. "Vinson Hits Subsidy Foes," 28.

25. "President Upheld by House," 1.

26. Paul Porter, interview by Terry L. Birdwhistell, Mar. 19, 1975, VOHP.

27. Ibid.

28. Bowles, *Promises to Keep,* 89.

29. FMV to Dr. A.M. Lyon, Aug. 10, 1944, box 316, VCUK.

30. FMV to Lou Urban, Dec. 23, 1944, box 316, VCUK.

31. Harrod, *Life of John Maynard Keynes,* 579.

32. Van Dormael, *Bretton Woods,* 218.

33. Weil and Davidson, *Gold War,* 10.

34. "Loan Rumors Raised by Wolcott," 10.

35. FMV to Roosevelt, Mar. 8, 1945, box 108, VCUK.

36. H.G. Hoffman to FMV, Feb. 19, 1945, box 319, VCUK.

37. Sgt. Robert Sikes to FMV, Mar. 6, 1945, box 321, VCUK.

38. Lt. (jg) Byron B. Berry to FMV, Mar. 11, 1945, box 317, VCUK.

39. Porter to FMV, Mar. 5, 1945, box 320, VCUK.

40. "Jesse Jones's Successor," 114.

41. "Vinson: Senate's 'Businessman,'" 17–19.

42. "Judge Vinson Never Met a Pay Roll."

43. "Vinson's Executive Talent."

44. Somers, *Presidential Agency,* 87.

45. "Vinson Tells U.S. What It Faces," 17.

46. Peggy Crowther to FMV, May 26, 1945, box 317, VCUK.

47. FMV to Crowther, June 11, 1945, box 317, VCUK.

48. Bendiner, "Available Vinson," 61.

49. "The Road to Tokyo and Beyond," July 1, 1945, box 320, VCUK.

50. "Charter for Postwar America," 90.

51. "Economic Charter for America."

52. "Declaration of Our Interdependence."

53. "Jacob's Voice, Esau's Hands."

54. "Fostering a Cruel Illusion."

55. "We'll Appeal to Uncle."

56. Rodell, "The Chief Justice," 114.

57. "Friends Praise Vinson."

58. "Vinson Becomes Head of Treasury," 13.

59. FMV to Robert L. Doughton, July 26, 1945, box 318, VCUK.

60. Truman, *Memoirs,* 1:327.

61. FMV to Crowther, June 11, 1945, box 317, VCUK.

62. Paul, *Taxation in the United States,* 410.

63. Edward F. Prichard, interview by Paul E. Fuller, Oct. 11, 1974, VOHP.

64. "Vinson Has Trouble Explaining Tax Cuts."

65. Hamby, *Man of the People,* 367.

66. Crawford and Stewart, "Fred M. Vinson," 410.

67. Ibid.

68. "Vinson Campaigns for British Loan," 13.

69. "Vinson, Acheson Urge British Loan," 25.

70. "Vinson Calls Loan to Britain a 'Must,'" 8.

71. Truman to FMV, June 6, 1946, President's Secretary's Files, Truman Library.

72. Harrod, *Life of John Maynard Keynes,* 630.

73. Gardner, *Sterling Dollar Diplomacy,* 265.

74. "Harry Dexter White."

75. Rees, *Harry Dexter White,* 411. Recent books by scholars Harvey Klehr and John Earl Haynes provide convincing evidence that despite White's protestations, he did assist Communist espionage against the United States by passing information to the Soviet Union and by using his position to promote a number of KGB sources within the federal government.

76. FMV to Truman, May 7, 1946, President's Secretary's Files, box 327, Truman Library.

77. "Secretary Vinson Urges Granting of Loan to Britain," 1.

7. The Chief Justice and His Court

1. *Louisville Times,* June 24, 1946.

2. Gerhart, *America's Advocate,* 280–81.

3. This excerpt is quoted in a letter from Merlo J. Pusey, associate editor of the *Washington Post* and author of a biography of Chief Justice Hughes, to Truman, Apr. 24, 1952, WHCF, Official File, box 328, Truman Library.

4. *Jewell Ridge Coal Corp.* v. *Local 6167, United Mine Workers,* 325 U.S. 161 (1945), 137.

5. *Washington Evening Star,* May 16, 1946.

6. Gerhart, *America's Advocate,* 260.

7. "Supreme Court Postscript," 5.

8. *New York Times,* June 7, 1946, 15.

9. Personal interviews with Jackson reported by Gerhart, *America's Advocate,* 498 n. 8.

10. Jackson to Truman, June 8, 1946, box 216, VCUK.

11. Truman to Jackson, June 8, 1946, box 216, VCUK.

12. Jackson to Truman, June 11, 1946, box 216, VCUK.

13. Short to Pusey, Apr. 29, 1952, WHCF, Official File, box 268, Truman Library.

14. Gerhart to Truman, Nov. 30, 1951, WHCF, Official File, box 268, Truman Library.

15. Hutchinson, "Black-Jackson Feud," 203, 216–17.

16. Tom Clark, interview by Jerry N. Hess, Oct. 17, 1972, OHPTL, 54.

17. Groner to Stephens, June 11, 1946, box 128, HSCLC.

18. Stephens to Groner, June 13, 1946, box 128, HSCLC.

19. Newman, *Hugo Black,* 344.

20. Kirkendall, "Fred M. Vinson," 2639.

21. McCullough, *Truman,* 507.

22. Abraham, *Justices and Presidents,* 238.

23. Matthew J. Connelly, interview by Jerry N. Hess, Nov. 28–30, 1967, OHPTL.

24. Ferrell, *Off the Record,* 46.

25. Corcoran to FMV, June 11, 1946, TGCCLC.

26. Riggs, "Vinson Hates to Go Up."

27. Riggs, "Senate Group Gives Its Okay to Vinson."

28. *New York Times,* Oct. 6, 1946, E4.

29. Ibid., Oct. 8, 1946, 1.

30. Diary of Harold H. Burton (microfilm), Oct. 10, 1946, HHBCLC.

31. Mason, *Harlan Fiske Stone,* 769.

32. Frankfurter to Murphy, June 10, 1946, box 28, FFCLC.

33. Urofsky, *Division and Discord,* 151.

34. Ely, *The Guardian of Every Other Right,* 102–5. Ely provides an excellent review of the history of the Supreme Court's decisions about property rights.

35. Urofsky, *Division and Discord,* 3.

36. *West Coast Hotel Company* v. *Parrish,* 300 U.S. 379 (1937).

37. *NLRB* v. *Jones and Laughlin Steel Corp.,* 301 U.S. 128 (1937).

38. One of Roosevelt's appointees, James Byrnes, left the Court to serve as director of economic stabilization, and less than a year later he was appointed to head the War Mobilization Board.

39. *Schenck* v. *United States,* 249 U.S. 47 (1919).

40. *Dennis* v. *United States,* 341 U.S. 494 (1951).

41. Diary of Harold Burton (microfilm), Sept. 17, 1945, HHBCLC.

42. Allen, "Vinson and the Theory of Constitutional Government," 6.

43. *Brandenburg* v. *Ohio,* 395 U.S. 454 (1969).

44. Hugo L. Black to Fred Rodell, Sept. 5, 1962, box 47, HLBCLC.

45. Allen, "Vinson and the Theory of Constitutional Government," 7.

46. Frankfurter, "Twenty Years of Holmes' Constitutional Opinions," 909.

47. Allen, "Vinson and the Theory of Constitutional Government," 4.

48. Danelski, "Influence of the Chief Justice," 497–508. Also see Robert J. Steamer, *Chief Justice: Leadership and the Supreme Court* (Columbia: Univ. of South Carolina Press, 1986).

49. Steamer, *Chief Justice,* xi.

50. Danelski, "Influence of the Chief Justice," 497.

51. Lash, *Diaries of Felix Frankfurter,* 270–71.

52. Douglas, *The Court Years,* 248–49.

53. Lash, *Diaries of Felix Frankfurter,* 274.

54. Edward F. Prichard Jr., interview by Paul E. Fuller, Oct. 11, 1971, VOHP, 55–56.

55. FMV to Felix Frankfurter, June 26, 1946, as cited in Hirsch, *Enigma of Felix Frankfurter,* 189.

56. Lash, *Diaries of Felix Frankfurter,* 300.

57. See Hirsch, *Enigma of Felix Frankfurter,* 188–91.

58. Tom Clark, interview by Robert Ireland, May 8, 1973, VOHP.

59. Newton Minow and Howard Trienens, interview by Terry L. Birdwhistell, Feb. 27, 1975, VOHP, 38–39.

60. Minow and Trienens interview, VOHP, 13, 33.

61. Clark interview, VOHP, 50.

62. Douglas, *The Court Years,* 226.

63. Frankfurter, memorandum to Court, Nov. 23, 1951, box 209, VCUK.

64. Ibid., Jan. 24, 1950, box 198, WODCLC.

65. FMV, memorandum to Court, Jan. 30, 1950, box 198, WODCLC.

66. Frankfurter, memorandums to Court, Feb. 1, 3, 1950, box 198, WODCLC.

67. Frankfurter to FMV, Dec. 12, 1947, box 215, VCUK.

68. Handwritten note from Frankfurter to FMV, date not known, box 215, VCUK.

69. Handwritten note from Frankfurter to FMV, dated 1946, box 215, VCUK.

70. Frankfurter, memorandum to Court, Oct. 10, 1950, box 198, WODCLC.

71. Frankfurter, memorandum for the conference, June 1, 1951, box 306, HLBCLC.

72. FMV to Frankfurter, Oct. 11, 1951, box 209, WODCLC.

73. Fassett, *New Deal Justice,* 507.

74. Steamer, *Chief Justice,* 275.

75. Danelski, "Influence of the Chief Justice," 503.

76. Minow and Trienens interview, VOHP, 10–11.

77. Frank, "Fred Vinson and the Chief Justiceship," 212–13, 241.

78. Brenner and Palmer, "Time Taken to Write Opinions," 179–84.

79. *Securities & Exchange Commission* v. *Chenery Corporation,* 332 U.S. 194 (1947).

80. Memorandum from Wiley B. Rutledge to Frankfurter, June 18, 1947, box 55, WBRCLC.

81. *Securities & Exchange Commission* v. *Chenery,* 332 U.S. 194 (1947,) 210.

82. Rodell, "The Supreme Court Is Standing Pat," 11.

83. Palmer and Brenner, "Determinants of the Amount of Time Taken," 147.

84. Frank, "Fred Vinson and the Chief Justiceship," 212–13.

85. Rodell, "The Supreme Court Is Standing Pat," 11.

86. Palmer and Brenner, 144.

87. James A. Thomson. "Frederick Moore Vinson," in Urofsky, *Supreme Court Justices,* 492.

88. Minow and Trienens interview, VOHP, 24–25.

89. Lash, *Diaries of Felix Frankfurter,* Nov. 6, 1946, 288.

90. *United States* v. *Alcea Band of Tillamooks,* 329 U.S. 40 (1946).

91. Lash, *Diaries of Felix Frankfurter,* Nov. 23, 1946, 304.

92. Stanley F. Reed, interview by Terry L. Birdwhistell, Nov. 12, 1975, VOHP, 5–6.

93. Kirkendall, "Fred M. Vinson," 2642.

94. Schwartz, *History of the Supreme Court,* 254.

95. *Francis* v. *Resweber,* 329 U.S. 459 (1947).

96. Fassett, *New Deal Justice,* 422.

97. Rudko, *Truman's Court,* 66.

98. *Kovacs* v. *Cooper,* 366 U.S. 77 (1949).

99. Frankfurter to FMV, Nov. 29, 1948, box 215, VCUK.

100. FMV to Frankfurter, Dec. 1, 1948, box 215, VCUK.

101. Frankfurter to FMV, Dec. 2, 1948, box 215, VCUK.

102. FMV to Frankfurter, Dec. 3, 1948, box 215, VCUK.

103. Frankfurter to FMV, Dec. 3, 1948, box 215, VCUK.

104. Frank, "United States Supreme Court, 1948–49," 54–55.

105. Frank, "United States Supreme Court: 1949–50," 49–50; Frank, "United States Supreme Court: 1950–51," 165, 216; Frank, "United States Supreme Court: 1951–52," 57.

106. Frank, "United States Supreme Court: 1949–50; Jaffe, "The Supreme Court, 1950 Term," 108; Harper and Rosenthal, "What the Supreme Court Did Not Do," 293–325.

107. "Chief Justice Vinson and His Law Clerks," 28.

108. Frank, "United States Supreme Court: 1950–51," 216.

109. Jaffe, "The Supreme Court, 1950 Term," 108.

110. Frank, "Fred Vinson and the Chief Justiceship," 214.

111. William Oliver, interview by Terry L. Birdwhistell, Feb. 26, 1975, VOHP, 6.

112. Jaffe, "The Supreme Court, 1950 Term," 114.

8. The Chief Justice, the President, and the Politics Of Economic Stabilization

1. Hechler, *Working with Truman,* 23.

2. *United Mine Workers of America* v. *United States* 330 U.S. 258 (1947); and *Youngstown Sheet and Tube* v. *Sawyer* 343 U.S. 579 (1952). In another case, *California* v. *United States* 332 U.S. 19 (1947), Vinson wrote the majority opinion upholding Truman's 1945 Continental Shelf Proclamation, which asserted federal jurisdiction over all mineral resources in the lands beneath the ocean, out to the end of the continental shelf of the United States. Vinson's ruling was a victory for the federal government over the states, which had fought a vigorous legal battle to defend land that historically had been in their domain. Some questioned whether Vinson, who typically sided with state powers, was unduly influenced by his loyalty to Truman in this matter.

3. Truman, *Memoirs,* 1:327–28.

4. Clark Clifford, interview by Roger K. Newman, cited in Newman, *Hugo Black,* 344.

5. Information derived from FBI wiretap of Corcoran, cited in Newman, *Hugo Black,* 344.

6. Murphy, *Brandeis/Frankfurter Connection,* 7.

7. Hamby, *Man of the People,* 600.

8. Donald J. MacDonald, interview by Jerry N. Hess, August 3, 1970, OHPTL, 24–25.

9. Clifford, *Counsel to the President,* 720.

10. Truman, *Bess,* 259.

11. McCullough, *Truman,* 11.

12. Truman, *Bess,* 349.

13. Hechler, *Working with Truman,* 113. Hechler said Roberta Vinson was the only person he ever saw at Key West and that she did not stay very long.

14. Belair, "Mr. Truman's Friend."

15. Clifford, *Counsel to the President,* 215.

16. Truman, *Memoirs,* 2:213–14.

17. Truman, *Bess,* 352.

18. *New York Times,* Mar. 21, 1950.

19. Ibid., Dec. 10, 1950.

20. Diary of Harold Burton (microfilm), Dec. 13, 1950, HHBCLC.

21. Truman, *Memoirs,* 2:488.

22. Charles S. Murphy, interview by Jerry N. Hess, May 3, 1971, OHPTL, 341–42.

23. Truman, M*emoirs,* 2:490.

24. Truman's personal notes; Hechler, *Working with Truman,* 246 n. 13.

25. Hechler, *Working with Truman,* 246–47.

26. Truman, *Memoirs,* 2:489.

27. Truman, *Bess,* 351.

28. Truman, *Memoirs,* 1:502.

29. *New York Times,* May 5, 1946.

30. Ibid., May 10, 1946.

31. Ibid., Oct. 23, 1946.

32. Truman, *Memoirs,* 1:505.

33. *New York Times,* Nov. 18, 1946.

34. Ibid., Nov. 19, 1946.

35. Ibid., Dec. 8, 1946.

36. Transcript of Pearson broadcast, Dec. 8, 1946, box 228, VCUK.

37. Ibid., Dec. 15, 1946.

38. Pearson, "Washington Merry-Go-Round."

39. Ibid.

40. Fine, *Frank Murphy,* 528.

41. *New York Times,* Dec. 17, 1946.

42. Ibid., Jan. 15, 1947.

43. Douglas conference notes, Jan. 20 1947, box 139, WODCLC.

44. Fine, *Frank Murphy,* 529; Douglas, *The Court Years,* 139.

45. John E. Lewis to FMV, July 1, 1936, box 88, VCUK.

46. *New York Times,* Oct. 21, 1946.

47. Douglas to FMV, Feb. 11, 1947, box 128, WODCLC.

48. Harper, *Justice Rutledge,* 221–22.

49. *New York Times,* Mar. 7, 1947.

50. Fassett, *New Deal Justice,* 429.

51. Frankfurter to FMV, Feb. 3, 1947, box 106, RCUK.

52. Douglas to FMV, Feb. 11, 1947, box 138, WODCLC.

53. Reed, memorandum to conference, Feb. 15, 1947, box 106, RCUK.

54. Undated handwritten memo from Frankfurter to FMV, box 228, VCUK.

55. Reed, memorandum to conference, Feb. 15, 1947, box 106, RCUK.

56. Undated document, Feb. 24, 1947, box 106, RCUK.

57. Frankfurter, memorandum to Burton, undated, and Burton's handwritten reply, Feb. 24, 1947, box 102, RCUK.

58. Frankfurter, note to Reed, undated, box 102, RCUK.

59. Diary of Harold Burton (microfilm), Feb. 8, 17, 25, 26, 27, 1946, HHBCLC.

60. *New York Times,* Mar. 7, 1947.

61. Diary of Harold Burton (microfilm), Mar. 6, 1947, HHBCLC.

62. Undated, unsigned memorandum, box 228, VCUK.

63. *Time,* Mar. 17, 1947, 21.

64. *United States* v. *United Mine Workers of America,* 330 U.S. 258 (1947), 270.

65. *Time,* Mar. 17, 1947, 22.

66. *United States* v. *United Mine Workers of America,* 330 U.S. 258 (1947), 286–87.

67. *United States* v. *Shipp,* 203 U.S. 563 (1906).

68. *United States* v. *United Mine Workers of America,* 330 U.S. 258 (1947), 293.

69. Bolner, "Mr. Chief Justice Vinson," 113.

70. Urofsky, *Division and Discord,* 194.

71. Fine, *Frank Murphy,* 532.

72. Gregory, "Government by Injunction Again," 368.

73. Bolner, "Mr. Chief Justice Vinson," 117.

74. Cited in Fine, *Frank Murphy,* 531.

75. Lester, "Vinson in the Executive Branch," 47–48.

76. *Washington Post,* Mar. 8, 1947, 8.

77. *New York Times* editorial, Mar. 7, 1946.

78. McClure, *The Truman Administration,* 152–53. McClure's work provides an excellent treatment of efforts to control labor disputes in the mid-1940s.

79. Marcus, *Truman and the Steel Seizure Case,* 19.

80. Ferrell, *Harry S. Truman,* 282.

81. Marcus, *Truman and the Steel Seizure,* 59–60.

82. Ibid., 76.

83. Donovan, *Tumultuous Years,* 386.

84. Ferrell, *Harry S. Truman,* 374; Truman, *Bess,* 385.

85. John W. Snyder, interview by Jerry N. Hess, Nov. 8, 1967, OHPTL, 1072.

86. Howard Trienens and Newton Minow, personal interview by authors, Aug. 23, 1994, Chicago, Ill.

87. *New York Times,* Aug. 24, 1982.

88. Tom Clark to Elbert D. Thomas, Feb. 2, 1949, box 277, VCUK.

89. Truman's radio and television address, Apr. 8, 1952, 257, as cited in Marcus, *Truman and the Steel Seizure,* 81.

90. Donovan, *Tumultuous Years,* 387.

91. *New York Times,* Apr. 30, 1952.

92. *New York Times,* May 3, 1952.

93. Diary of Harold Burton (microfilm), May 3, 1952, HHBCLC.

94. Ibid., May 10, 1952.

95. *New York Times,* May 13, 1952.

96. *U.S. News and World Report,* May 23, 1952, 25.

97. *New York Times,* May 13, 1952.

98. Story told to David N. Atkinson by Justice Minton's secretary in an interview, Jan. 30, 1968, cited in Atkinson, "Minton and the Supreme Court."

99. *New York Times,* May 13, 1952.

100. FMV, memorandum to justices, May 16, 1952, box 10, WODCLC.

101. Douglas conference notes, May 16, 1952, WODCLC. Except where noted, all information about what was said in the conference is based on Douglas's handwritten notes.

102. Trienens and Minow, interview by authors.

103. Tom C. Clark, interview by Robert Ireland, May 8, 1973, VOHP.

104. Rehnquist, *The Supreme Court,* 91.

105. Fassett, *New Deal Justice,* 521.

106. *Youngstown Sheet and Tube* v. *Sawyer,* 343 U.S. 579 (1952), 887.

107. Ibid., 635–39.

108. *New York Times,* June 3, 1952.

109. *Youngstown Sheet and Tube* v. *Sawyer,* 343 U.S. 579 (1952), 695.

110. *New York Times,* June 3, 1952.

111. *Youngstown Sheet and Tube* v. *Sawyer,* 343 U.S. 579 (1952), 701.

112. Truman, *Memoirs,* 2:477.

113. *New York Times,* June 3, 1952.

114. Marcus, *Truman and the Steel Seizure Case,* provides an excellent review of the published scholarly opinions of the *Youngstown* opinions.

115. Frank, "United States Supreme Court: 1951–1952," 12.

116. Freund, "The Supreme Court, 1951 Term," 104.

117. Frank, "United States Supreme Court: 1951–1952," 2.

118. Freund, "U.S. Supreme Court, 1951 Term," 104.

119. Marcus, *Truman and the Steel Seizure Case,* 228–31.

120. Frank, "Fred Vinson and the Chief Justiceship," 217.

121. Howard Trienens and Newton Minow, interview by Terry L. Birdwhistell, Feb. 27, 1975, VOHP, 22.

122. Marcus, *Truman and the Steel Seizure Case,* 228–31.

9. Individual Rights in the Cold War Climate

1. Speech before the American Bar Association, Sept. 22, 1947, box 395, VCUK.

2. Klehr, Haynes, and Firsov, *Secret World of American Communism,* 16.

3. Klehr, Haynes, and Anderson, *Soviet World of American Communism.*

4. Weinstein and Vassiliev, *The Haunted Wood,* is a good example of this scholarship.

5. Memorandum from J. Edgar Hoover, dated Feb. 1, 1946, forwarded by

Harry Truman to FMV, Feb. 6, 1946. President's Secretary's File, box 140, Truman Library.

6. Haynes and Klehr, *Venona.*

7. *American Communications Association* v. *Douds,* 339 U.S. 382 (1950).

8. Ibid., 388–89.

9. Frank, "United States Supreme Court: 1949–1950," 33.

10. Based on data presented in Pritchett, *Civil Liberties and the Vinson Court,* 184–85.

11. *Dennis* v. *United States,* 341 U.S. 494 (1951).

12. *Dennis* v. *United States,* 183 F2d 201 (1950), 211–12.

13. Memorandum on "Motion to Postpone Argument," circulated Nov. 24, 1950, cited in O'Brien, *"Dennis* v. *United States,"* 617.

14. Douglas conference notes, Dec. 9, 1950, box 207, WODCLC.

15. Frankfurter, "Memorandum for Conference," box 215, VCUK.

16. *Dennis* v. *United States,* 341 U.S. 494 (1951), 499.

17. *Schenck* v. *United States,* 249 U.S. 47 (1919), 52.

18. *Gitlow* v. *New York,* 268 U.S. 652 (1925).

19. *Whitney* v. *California,* 274 U.S. 357 (1927).

20. *Dennis* v. *United States,* 341 U.S. 494 (1951), 508.

21. Ball and Cooper, *Of Power and Right,* 144.

22. *Dennis* v. *United States,* 341 U.S. 494 (1951), 579.

23. Black notations on draft of Vinson opinion, n.d., Feb. 1951, box 306, HLBCLC.

24. *Dennis* v. *United States,* 341 U.S. 494 (1951), 583.

25. Rabban, *Free Speech in Its Forgotten Years,* 377.

26. Urofsky, *Division and Discord,* 175.

27. Kalven, *A Worthy Tradition,* 191.

28. Michal R. Belknap, "Cold War in the Court Room: The Foley Square Communist Trial," in *American Political Trials,* ed. Michal R. Belknap, 208.

29. Belknap, *Cold War Political Justice,* 4.

30. Belknap reviews the scholarly assessments of *Dennis* in ibid., 142–43.

31. Hook, *Heresy Yes—Conspiracy No!* 105–6, as cited in Belknap, *Cold War Political Justice,* 143.

32. Bolner, "Vinson and the Communist Controversy," 389–90.

33. *New York Times,* June 5, 1951.

34. *Washington Post,* June 6, 1951.

35. *New Republic,* June 18, 1951, 5.

36. Press clippings cited in O'Brien, *"Dennis* v. *United States,"* 651–52.

37. Morley, "Affirmation of Materialism," 3.

38. FMV to Rev. Wilfred Savard, Jan. 28, 1952, box 270, VCUK.

39. FMV to Raymond R. Cameron, Aug. 7, 1952, box 270, VCUK.

40. Sabin, *In Calmer Times,* 91.

41. *Yates* v. *United States,* 354 U.S. 298 (1957).

42. Douglas, "Memorandum to the Conference," May 22, 1953, box 284, VCUK.

43. Frankfurter, "Rosenberg Memorandum," June 4, 1953, box 65, file 1, Frankfurter Papers, Harvard Law School Library, as cited in Parrish, "Cold War

Justice," 825. Parrish provides a detailed account of the justice's responses to each of the petitions presented in behalf of the Rosenbergs.

44. Parrish, "Cold War Justice," 827.

45. Douglas, *The Court Years,* 80.

46. Stern, "Rosenberg Case in Perspective," 83.

47. Radosh and Milton, *Rosenberg File,* 403–4.

48. William Oliver, interview by Terry L. Birdwhistell, Feb. 26, 1975, VOHP, 15.

49. Frankfurter's handwritten remarks can be found in his file of the Rosenberg case, box 85, file 4, Frankfurter papers, Harvard Law School, cited in Parrish, "Cold War Justice," 837.

50. *Rosenberg et al.* v. *United States,* 346 U.S. 273 (1953), 286.

51. See Parrish, "Cold War Justice," 839–40; Cohen, "Justice Douglas and the Rosenberg Case," 211. Urofsky, *Division and Discord,* 183; and Radosh and Milton, *Rosenberg File,* 453.

52. Cohen, "Justice Douglas and the Rosenberg Case," 211–52.

53. *Bailey* v. *Richardson,* 341 U.S. 918 (1951).

54. *Joint Anti-Fascist Refugee Committee* v. *McGrath,* 341 U.S. 123 (1951).

55. Kalven, *A Worthy Tradition,* 289.

56. *Bailey* v. *Richardson,* 341 U.S. 918 (1951), 193.

57. *Gerende* v. *Board of Supervisors of Elections,* 341 U.S. 56 (1951).

58. *Garner* v. *Board of Public Works,* 341 U.S. 716 (1951).

59. *Adler* v. *Board of Education,* 342 U.S. 485 (1952).

60. *Wieman* v. *Updegraff,* 344 U.S. 183 (1952).

61. *Blau* [Patricia] v. *United States,* 340 U.S. 159 (1950).

62. *Blau* [Irving] v. *United States,* 340 U.S. 332 (1951).

63. Another issue in the second *Blau* case concerned Irving Blau's refusal to provide the grand jury with information about his wife's whereabouts on the grounds that such information between husband and wife was confidential. The Court upheld his right to withhold the information of his wife's whereabouts, although Minton and Jackson dissented on this point.

64. Draft of Minton dissent, box 272, VCUK.

65. *Rogers* v. *United States,* 340 U.S. 367 (1951).

66. Jackson, memorandum to Vinson, switching his position, Dec. 21, 1951, box 272, VCUK.

67. *Rogers* v. *United States,* 340 U.S. 367 (1951), 371.

68. *United States* v. *Bryan,* 339 U.S. 323 (1950).

69. *Christoffel* v. *United States,* 338 U.S. 84 (1949).

70. *United States* v. *Bryan,* 339 U.S. 323 (1950), 341.

71. *United States* v. *Fleischman,* 339 U.S. 349 (1950).

72. *Oyama* v. *California,* 332 U.S. 633 (1948).

73. Pritchett, *Civil Liberties and the Vinson Court,* 120.

74. *United States ex rel Knauff* v. *Shaughnessy,* 338 U.S. 537 (1950).

75. *Carlson* v. *Landon,* 342 U.S. 524 (1952).

76. *Stack* v. *Boyle,* 342 U.S. 1 (1951).

77. *Carlson* v. *Landon,* 342 U.S. 524 (1952) 533.

78. *Shaughnessy* v. *United States ex rel. Mezei,* 345 U.S. 206 (1953).

79. One other alien case was handed down the same day. In *Heikkila* v. *Barber,* 345 U.S. 229 (1953), Clark wrote for a seven-man majority denying an alien the right to a hearing before being deported.

80. *Kwong Hai Chew* v. *Colding,* 344 U.S. 590 (1953).

81. Kalven, *A Worthy Tradition,* 444.

82. *Saia* v. *New York,* 334 U.S. 558 (1948).

83. *Cantwell* v. *Connecticut,* 310 U.S. 296 (1940).

84. *Kovacs* v. *Cooper,* 336 U.S. 77 (1949).

85. *Niemotko* v. *Maryland,* 340 U.S. 268 (1951).

86. *Kunz* v. *New York,* 340 U.S. 290 (1951).

87. The Court declared in *Chaplinsky* v. *New Hampshire* 315 U.S. 568 (1942) that "fighting words" fell outside the bounds of constitutional protection.

88. *Breard* v. *City of Alexandria,* 341 U.S. 622 (1951).

89. *Terminiello* v. *Chicago,* 337 U.S. 1 (1949).

90. Douglas conference notes, Feb. 5, 1949, box 186, WODCLC.

91. Memorandum by the chief justice, Apr. n.d., 1949 (hand stamped April 8, 1949), box 269, VCUK.

92. Draft of memorandum by the chief justice, Apr. n.d., 1949, box 269, VCUK.

93. *Terminiello* v. *Chicago,* 337 U.S. 1 (1949), 23.

94. Jackson doggerel, undated, Robert H. Jackson papers, in possession of Philip B. Kurland, cited in Fine, *Frank Murphy,* 582.

95. *Feiner* v. *New York,* 340 U.S. 315 (1951).

96. Douglas conference notes, Oct. 21, 1950, box 204, WODCLC.

97. Kalven, *A Worthy Tradition,* 89.

98. *Feiner* v. *New York,* 340 U.S. 315 (1951), 319.

99. Kalven, *A Worthy Tradition,* 89–90.

100. Frankfurter to FMV, Dec. 26, 1950, box 271, VCUK.

101. Ayres, *Truman in the White House,* 299.

102. Memorandum from Frankfurter to FMV about his vote in *Winters* v. *New York,* 333 U.S. 507 (1948), box 252. VCUK.

10. The Dilemma of Due Process and the Promise of Equality

1. *Weeks* v. *United States,* 232 U.S. 383 (1914).

2. *Harris* v. *United States,* 331 U.S. 145 (1947).

3. *Go-Bart Importing Company* v. *United States,* 282 U.S. 344 (1931), 357.

4. *Harris* v. *United States,* 331 U.S. 145 (1947), 153–55.

5. Draft of Frankfurter's *Harris* opinion, Apr. (n.d.) 1947, box 227, VCUK.

6. *Harris* v. *United States,* 331 U.S. 145 (1947) 161–162.

7. *Harris* v. *United States,* 331 U.S. 145 (1947) 198.

8. Allen, "Vinson and the Theory of Constitutional Government," 14.

9. *Nueslein* v. *District of Columbia,* 115 F2d 690 (1940). This case is discussed in chapter 5.

10. Bolner, "Mr. Chief Justice Vinson," 187.

11. Pritchett, *Civil Liberties and the Vinson Court*, 147.

12. *Di Re* v. *United States*, 332 U.S. 581 (1948)

13. *Johnson* v. *United States*, 333 U.S. 10 (1948).

14. *Trupiano* v. *United States*, 334 U.S. 700 (1948).

15. *United States* v. *Rabinowitz*, 339 U.S. 56 (1950).

16. Pritchett, *Civil Liberties and the Vinson Court*, 152.

17. *Palko* v. *Connecticut*, 302 U.S. 319 (1937).

18. In 1925, in *Gitlow* v. *New York* (268 U.S. 652), the Court extended the protection of free speech to the states; and in 1931, in *Near* v. *Minnesota* (231 U.S. 697), the Court ruled that freedom of the press was also protected against state encroachment.

19. *Palko* v. *Connecticut*, 302 U.S. 319 (1937) 326.

20. *Adamson* v. *California*, 332 U.S. 46 (1948).

21. Bodenhamer, *Fair Trial*, 98.

22. Urofsky, *Division and Discord*, 219.

23. *Wolf* v. *Colorado*, 338 U.S. 25 (1949).

24. *Mapp* v. *Ohio*, 367 U.S. 643 (1961).

25. *Rochin* v. *California*, 342 U.S. 165 (1952).

26. Douglas conference notes, box 228, WODCLC.

27. Newman, *Hugo Black*, 357.

28. *Rochin* v. *California*, 342 U.S. 165 (1952) 173.

29. *Powell* v. *Alabama*, 287 U.S. 45 (1932).

30. *Betts* v. *Brady*, 316 U.S. 455 (1942).

31. *Carter* v. *Illinois*, 329 U.S. 173 (1946); *Foster* v. *Illinois*, 332 U.S. 134 (1947); *Gayes* v. *New York*, 332 U.S. 145 (1947); *Bute* v. *Illinois*, 333 U.S. 640 (1948); *Gryger* v. *Burke*, 334 U.S. 728 (1948); and *Quicksall* v. *Michigan*, 339 U.S. 660 (1950).

32. *Townsend* v. *Burke*, 334 U.S. 736 (1948).

33. *Palmer* v. *Ashe*, 342 U.S. 134 (1951).

34. *Gibbs* v. *Burke*, 337 U.S. 773 (1949).

35. *Gideon* v. *Wainwright*, 372 U.S. 335 (1963).

36. *Haley* v. *Ohio*, 332 U.S. 596 (1948).

37. *Upshaw* v. *United States*, 335 U.S. 410 (1948).

38. *Watts* v. *Indiana*, 338 U.S. 49 (1949); *Turner* v. *Pennsylvania*, 338 U.S. 62 (1949); and *Harris* v. *South Carolina*, 338 U.S. 68 (1949).

39. *Marino* v. *Ragen*, 332 U.S. 561 (1947).

40. *Young* v. *Ragen*, 337 U.S. 235 (1949)

41. Speech before the American Bar Association, Sept. 9, 1949, box 395, VCUK.

42. *Jennings* v. *Illinois*, 342 U.S. 104 (1951).

43. Remarks to the Standing Committee on Legal Aid Work at the American Bar Association Convention at Cleveland, Ohio, Sept. 22, 1947, Speech File, box 395, VCUK.

44. Address to American Bar Association, Speech File, box 39, VCUK.

45. *Brock* v. *North Carolina*, 344 U.S. 424 (1953).

46. Douglas conference notes, box 228, WODCLC.

47. *Brock* v. *North Carolina*, 344 U.S. 424 (1953), 432.

48. *Brown* v. *Allen*, 344 U.S. 443 (1953).

49. *Speller* v. *Allen,* 344 U.S. 443 (1955).

50. *Avery* v. *Georgia,* 345 U.S. 559 (1953).

51. *Plessy* v. *Ferguson,* 163 U.S. 537 (1896).

52. *New York Times,* Oct. 30, 1947, 14.

53. *Morgan* v. *Virginia,* 328 U.S. 373 (1946).

54. *Bob Lo Excursions* v. *Michigan,* 333 U.S. 28 (1948).

55. Pritchett, *Civil Liberties and the Vinson Court,* 128.

56. *Henderson* v. *United States,* 339 U.S. 816 (1950).

57. Hutchinson, "Unanimity and Desegregation," 18–19.

58. *Mitchell* v. *United States,* 313 U.S. 80 (1941).

59. Hutchinson, "Unanimity and Desegregation," 27–30.

60. *Sweatt* v. *Painter,* 339 U.S. 629 (1950); *McLaurin* v. *Oklahoma,* 339 U.S. 637 (1950).

61. *Shelley* v. *Kraemer,* 334 U.S. 1 (1948).

62. This case had been decided by the Michigan Supreme Court on Jan. 7, 1947, and accepted by review by the U.S. Supreme Court on June 23, 1947.

63. *Hurd* v. *Hodge,* 334 U.S. 24 (1948).

64. Hutchinson, "Unanimity and Desegregation," 13.

65. Fassett, *New Deal Justice,* 444–47.

66. Allen, "Remembering *Shelley* v. *Kraemer,*" 720.

67. Ibid.

68. Tushnet, *Making Civil Rights Law,* 94.

69. Douglas conference notes, Feb. 2, 1948, box 160, WODCLC.

70. Burton to FMV, Apr. 25, 1948, box 241, VCUK. Burton's parenthetical citation of Bryce was a reference to James Bryce, a British politician, historian, and diplomat who was best known in the United States for his classic study of the U.S. Constitution, *The American Commonwealth* (1888).

71. Murphy to FMV, May 3, 1948 (no date actually shown), box 216, VCUK.

72. Allen, "Remembering *Shelley* v. *Kraemer,*" 734.

73. *Buchanan* v. *Warley,* 245 U.S. 60 (1917).

74. *Shelley* v. *Kraemer,* 334 U.S. 1 (1948), 14–15.

75. *Hurd* v. *Hodge,* 334 U.S. 24 (1948), 30.

76. *Hundley* v. *Gorewitz,* 132 F2d 23 (1942).

77. Hutchinson, "Unanimity and Desegregation," 13.

78. Dudziak, *Cold War Civil Rights.* Other scholars writing on this theme include Rosenberg, *Hollow Hope,* 162–67; Klarman, "*Brown,* Racial Change, and the Civil Rights Movement," 26–30; and Lefberg, "Vinson and the Politics of Desegregation," 297–304.

79. Dudziak, *Cold War Civil Rights,* 9–14.

80. Murphy to FMV, May 3, 1948 (no date actually shown), box 216, VCUK.

81. White to FMV, May 3, 1948, box 205, VCUK.

82. James A. Mundy to FMV, May 12, 1948, box 205, VCUK.

83. Frank, "United States Supreme Court: 1947–1948," 24.

84. Lefberg, "Vinson and the Politics of Desegregation," 260.

85. Rosenberg, *Hollow Hope.* Klarman makes a similar argument in "*Brown,* Racial Change, and the Civil Rights Movement," 7–150.

86. Allen, "Remembering *Shelley* v. *Kraemer,*" 721.

87. Wechsler, "Toward Neutral Principles," 1–35.
88. *Buchanan* v. *Warley,* 245 U.S. 60 (1917).
89. Klarman, "Race and the Court," 881–952.
90. Vose, *Caucasians Only,* 186.
91. Lefberg, "Vinson and the Politics of Desegregation," 267.
92. Allen, "Remembering Shelley v. Kraemer," 714.
93. Klarman, "Race and the Court," 883–84.
94. Reactions of petitioners and neighbors cited in Vose, *Caucasians Only,* 211.
95. Higginbotham, "45 Years in Civil Rights Law," 84.
96. Bolner, "Mr. Chief Justice Vinson," 343
97. Lefberg, "Vinson and the Politics of Desegregation," 256. An exception would be the Court's 1917 opinion in *Buchanan* v. *Warley.*
98. Allen, "Remembering *Shelley* v. *Kraemer,*" 714.
99. White's comments are from his newspaper column, cited in Tushnet, *Making Civil Rights Law,* 96.
100. Allen, "Remembering Shelley v. Kraemer," 735.
101. *Sipuel* v. *Oklahoma,* 332 U.S. 631 (1948).
102. *Missouri ex rel Gaines* v. *Canada,* 305 U.S. 337 (1938).
103. Vinson, memorandum to the conference, Feb. 13, 1948, Jackson papers, Library of Congress, cited in Urofsky, *Division and Discord,* 252.
104. Tushnet, *Making Civil Rights Law,* 131.
105. Hutchinson, "Unanimity and Desegregation," 15.
106. Tushnet, *Making Civil Rights Law,* 140.
107. Douglas conference notes, Apr. 8, 1950, box 191, WODCLC.
108. Quote taken from notes of Justices Burton and Clark, as cited in Hutchinson, "Unanimity and Desegregation," 24.
109. Black to FMV, May 18, 1950, box 262, VCUK.
110. Reed to FMV, May 18, 1950, box 262, VCUK.
111. Frankfurter to FMV, May 19, 1950, and draft memo, FMV to Frankfurter, May 24, 1950, box 262, VCUK. Daniels was a newspaper editor from North Carolina.
112. Draft memo, FMV to Frankfurter, May 24, 1950, box 262, VCUK.
113. *Sweatt* v. *Painter,* 339 U.S. 629 (1950), 630.
114. *McLaurin* v. *Oklahoma,* 339 U.S. 637 (1950), 641–42.
115. Tushnet, *The NAACP's Legal Strategy,* 132.
116. "Jim Crow in Handcuffs," *New Republic,* June 19, 1950, as cited in Tushnet, *The NAACP's Legal Strategy,* 133.
117. Bolner, "Mr. Chief Justice Vinson," 330.
118. Correspondence found in NAACP papers, as cited in Tushnet, *Making Civil Rights Law,* 147.
119. Hutchinson, "Unanimity and Desegregation," 3.
120. Pritchett, *Civil Liberties and the Vinson Court,* 136.
121. Lefberg, "Vinson and the Politics of Desegregation," 273.
122. Fred M. Vinson Jr., interview by Charles L. Atcher, May 22, 1973, VOHP.
123. Allen, "Vinson and the Theory of Constitutional Government," 8.
124. Kluger, *Simple Justice,* 538.

125. Friedman, *Argument,* 18–19.

126. Tushnet, *Making Civil Rights Law,* 187.

127. Kluger, *Simple Justice,* 590.

128. For example, see Przybyszewski, *Republic according to Harlan,* esp. 90–102; and Maltz, "Only Partially Color Blind," 973–1016.

129. Conference notes of Justice Tom Clark, Dec. 13, 1952, included as an appendix in Hutchinson, "Unanimity and Desegregation," 91.

130. Tushnet, *Making Civil Rights Law,* 188.

131. Kluger, *Simple Justice,* 591, 604.

132. Tushnet, *Making Civil Rights Law,* 187; Kluger, *Simple Justice,* 608.

133. Tushnet, *Making Civil Rights Law,* 193.

134. *Terry* v. *Adams,* 345 U.S. 461 (1953).

135. *Barrows* v. *Jackson,* 346 U.S. 249 (1953).

136. Lefberg, "Vinson and the Politics of Desegregation," 266.

137. James W. Ely Jr. provides an excellent discussion of the Court's shift, starting in 1937, from protecting economic rights to protecting personal rights. See Ely, *The Guardian of Every Other Right;* and Ely, "Reflections on *Buchanan* v. *Warley,*" 953–73.

138. *New Albany Tribune,* Sept. 8, 1953.

139. Minton to Roberta Vinson, Sept. 13, 1953, VCUK.

140. Diary of Harold Burton (microfilm), Sept. 8, 1953, HHBCLC.

141. Elman, "Solicitor General's Office," 840.

142. Tushnet, "What Really Happened in Brown," 1883.

143. Tushnet, *Making Civil Rights Law,* 194.

144. Hutchinson, "Unanimity and Desegregation," 35.

145. Tushnet, "What Really Happened in Brown," 1874.

146. Lefberg, "Vinson and the Politics of Segregation," 301.

147. Hutchinson, "Unanimity and Desegregation," 87.

148. Included in these more in-depth analyses are Bolner, "Mr. Chief Justice Vinson" (1962); Urofsky, *Division and Discord* (1997); Hutchinson, "Unanimity and Desegregation" (1979); and Tushnet, "What Really Happened in Brown" (1991).

149. Bolner, "Mr. Chief Justice Vinson," 362.

150. Pritchett, *Civil Liberties and the Vinson Court,* 21.

151. Allen, "Vinson and the Theory of Constitutional Government," 4.

152. See chapter 9, notes 2, 3, and 4, for a discussion of these works.

153. Urofsky, *Division and Discord,* 7.

154. Bolner, "Mr. Chief Justice Vinson." 355.

155. Willard H. Pedrick, interview by Terry L. Birdwhistell, Oct. 22, 1976, VHOP.

156. Rosenberg, *Hollow Hope,* 157–69; Klarman, "*Brown,* Racial Change, and the Civil Rights Movement."

Epilogue

1. FMV to Thomas Graham, Jan. 11, 1945, box 318, VCUK.

2. FMV to Edgar Howard, Aug. 8, 1949, box 332, VCUK.

3. Roberta Vinson to James Vinson, Jan. 21, 1953, box 358, VCUK.

4. FMV to Mrs. James R. Vinson, Aug. 6, 1953, box 358, VCUK.

5. Minton to FMV, Aug. 22, 1953, box 56, VCUK.

6. FMV to Minton, Aug. 24, 1953, Minton Papers, Lilly Library, Indiana University.

7. "Eisenhower Leads Tributes to Vinson," *New York Times,* Sept. 9, 1953, 1.

8. Truman's comments and the others that follow are from *New York Times,* Sept. 9, 1953, 22.

9. "Final Tribute to Chief Justice Vinson to Be Paid at Louisa Church," *Lexington Herald,* Sept. 11, 1953.

10. Gregory to Doughton, Sept. 21, 1953, box 358, VCUK.

11. "Proceedings of the Bar and Officers of the Supreme Court of the United States," Oct. 25, 1954, 58.

12. Ibid., 54.

13. Ibid., 52.

14. Lester, "Vinson in the Executive Branch," 36.

15. "A Man's Estate," *New York Times,* Sept. 25, 1953, 20.

Bibliography

Manuscript Collections

Margaret I. King Library, Univ. of Kentucky

Papers of Stanley F. Reed (RCUK)
Papers of Fred Vinson (VCUK)

Manuscript Division, Library of Congress

Papers of Hugo L. Black (HLBCLC)
Papers of Harold H. Burton (HHBCLC)
Papers of Thomas G. Corcoran (TGCCLC)
Papers of William O. Douglas (WODCLC)
Papers of Felix Frankfurter (FFCLC)
Papers of Wiley B. Rutledge (WBRCLC)
Papers of Harold M. Stephens (HSCLC)

Franklin D. Roosevelt Presidential Library, Hyde Park, N.Y.

Papers of Franklin D. Roosevelt

Harry S. Truman Library, Independence, Mo.

Papers of Harry S. Truman

Fred M. Vinson, Oral History Project, Univ. of Kentucky (VOHP)

Tom C. Clark
W.E. Crutcher
Althea Swinford Hutton
Chesley A. Lycan
Newton Minow
William Oliver
Willard H. Pedrick

Paul Porter
Edward L. Prichard
Stanley F. Reed
Howard J. Trienens
Fred M. Vinson Jr.
James R. Vinson

Oral History Project, Harry S. Truman Library (OHPTL)
Tom C. Clark
Matthew J. Connelly
Marvin Jones
Donald J. McDonald
Charles S. Murphy
John M. Snyder

Newspapers and Magazines

American Political Science Review, Atlantic Monthly, Big Sandy News, Business Week, Collier's, Finance & Development, Lexington Herald, Life, Louisville Courier-Journal, Louisville Herald-Post, Louisville Times, New Republic, New York Times, PM Sunday Picture News, Washington Evening Star, Washington Post

Books

Abels, Jules, *In the Time of Silent Cal.* New York: Putnam's, 1969.
Abraham, Henry J. *Justices and Presidents, a Political History of Appointments to the Supreme Court.* New York: Oxford Univ. Press, 1985.
Ayres, Eben. *Truman in the White House: The Diary of Eben A. Ayres.* Columbia: Univ. of Missouri Press, 1991.
Ball, Howard, and Phillip J. Cooper. *Of Power and Right: Hugo Black, William O. Douglas, and America's Constitutional Revolution.* New York: Oxford Univ. Press, 1992.
Belknap, Michal. *Cold War Political Justice: The Smith Act, the Communist Party, and American Civil Liberties.* Westport, Conn.: Greenwood Press, 1977.
————, ed. *American Political Trials.* Revised, expanded ed. Westport, Conn.: Greenwood Press, 1994.
Berry, Mary Francis. *Stability, Security, and Continuity: Mr. Justice Burton and Decision-Making in the Supreme Court.* Westport, Conn.: Greenwood Press, 1978.
Blakey, George T. *Hard Times and New Deal in Kentucky, 1929–1939.* Lexington: Univ. Press of Kentucky, 1986.
Bodenhamer, David. *Fair Trial: Rights of the Accused in American History.* New York: Oxford Univ. Press, 1992.

Bowles, Chester. *Promises to Keep: My Years in Public Life 1941–1969*. New York: Harper and Row, 1971.

Campbell, Tracy. *Short of the Glory*. Lexington: Univ. Press of Kentucky, 1998.

Cardinal and Blue, Centre College Yearbook, Danville, Ky., 1909.

Clifford, Clark. *Counsel to the President: A Memoir.* New York: Random House, 1991.

Donovan, Robert J. *Tumultuous Years: The Presidency of Harry S. Truman, 1949–1953*. New York: W.W. Norton, 1982.

Douglas, William O. *The Court Years, 1937–1975*. New York: Random House, 1980.

Dudziak, Mary L. *Cold War Civil Rights: Race and the Image of American Democracy*. Princeton, N.J.: Princeton Univ. Press, 2000.

Edsforth, Ronald. *The New Deal: America's Response to the Great Depression*. Malden, Mass.: Blackwell, 2000.

Ely, James W. *The Guardian of Every Other Right: A Constitutional History of Property Rights, 2nd ed.* New York: Oxford Univ. Press, 1998.

Ely, William. *The Big Sandy Valley*. Catlettsburg, Ky.: Central Methodist Press, 1887.

Fassett, John D. *New Deal Justice: The Life of Stanley Reed*. New York: Vantage Press, 1994.

Ferrell, Robert H. *Harry S. Truman: A Life*. Columbia: Univ. of Missouri Press, 1994.

———, ed. *Off the Record: The Private Papers of Harry Truman*. New York: Harper and Row, 1980.

Fine, Sidney. *Frank Murphy: The Washington Years*. Ann Arbor: Univ. of Michigan Press, 1984.

Friedman, Leon, ed. *Argument: The Oral Argument before the Supreme Court in Brown v. Board of Education of Topeka, 1952–1955*. New York: Chelsea House, 1969.

Galloway, George B. *History of the House of Representatives*. New York: Thomas Y. Crowell, 1961.

———. *History of the United States House of Representatives*. Washington, D.C.: U.S. Government Printing Office, 1965.

Gardner, Richard N. *Sterling Dollar Diplomacy*. New York: McGraw-Hill, 1956.

Gerhart, Eugene C. *America's Advocate: Robert H. Jackson*. Indianapolis: Bobbs-Merrill, 1958.

Goldman, Sheldon. *Picking Federal Judges: Lower Court Selection from Roosevelt through Reagan*. New Haven, Conn.: Yale Univ. Press, 1997.

Graham, Otis L., Jr., and Meghan Robinson Wander. *Franklin D. Roosevelt: His Life and Times, an Encyclopedic View*. Boston: G.K. Hall, 1985.

Hamby, Alonzo. *Man of the People: A Life of Harry S. Truman*. New York: Oxford Univ. Press, 1995.

Harper, Fowler V. *Justice Rutledge: The Bright Constellation*. Indianapolis: Bobbs-Merrill, 1965.

Harrod, Roy F. *The Life of John Maynard Keynes.* New York: Augustus M. Kelley, 1969.

Haynes, John Earl, and Harvey Klehr. *Venona: Decoding Soviet Espionage in America.* New Haven, Conn.: Yale Univ. Press, 1999.

Hechler, Ken. *Working with Truman: A Personal Memoir of the White House Years.* New York: Putnam's, 1982.

Hirsch, H.N. *The Enigma of Felix Frankfurter.* New York: Basic Books, 1981.

History of the United States Court of Appeals for the District of Columbia Circuit in the Country's Bicentennial Year. U.S. Court of Appeals for the District of Columbia, 1976.

Hook, Sidney. *Heresy Yes—Conspiracy No!* Garden City, N.J.: Doubleday, 1953.

Jewell, Malcolm E. *Kentucky Votes: Presidential Elections, 1952–1960; U.S. House Primary and General Elections, 1920–1960.* Lexington: Univ. Press of Kentucky, 1963.

Johnson, Leland R. *An Illustrated History of the Huntington District, U.S. Army Corps of Engineers, 1754–1974.* Washington, D.C.: U.S. Government Printing Office, 1977.

Kalven, Harry, Jr. *A Worthy Tradition: Freedom of Speech in America.* New York: Harper and Row, 1988.

Klehr, Harvey, John Earl Haynes, and Fridrikh Igorevich Firsov. *The Secret World of American Communism.* New Haven, Conn.: Yale Univ. Press, 1995.

Klehr, Harvey, John Earl Haynes, and Kyrill M. Anderson. *The Soviet World of American Communism.* New Haven, Conn.: Yale Univ. Press, 1998.

Klotter, James C. *Kentucky Portrait in Paradox, 1900–1950.* Frankfort: Kentucky Historical Society, 1996.

Kluger, Richard. *Simple Justice: The History of Brown v. Board of Education and Black America's Struggle for Equality.* New York: Alfred A. Knopf, 1976.

Kornitzer, Bela. *American Fathers and Sons.* N.p.: Hermitage House, 1952.

Lash, Joseph P. *From the Diaries of Felix Frankfurter.* New York: W.W. Norton, 1975.

Marcus, Maeva. *Truman and the Steel Seizure Case: The Limits of Presidential Power.* New York: Columbia Univ. Press, 1977.

Mason, Alpheus T. *Harlan Fiske Stone: Pillar of the Law.* New York: Viking Press, 1956.

McClure, Arthur F. *The Truman Administration and the Problems of Postwar Labor, 1945–1948.* Rutherford, N.J.: Farleigh Dickinson Univ. Press, 1969.

McCullough, David. *Truman.* New York: Simon and Schuster, 1992.

McCune, Wesley. *The Nine Young Men.* New York: Harper, 1947.

Mooney, Booth. *Roosevelt and Rayburn: A Political Partnership.* Philadelphia: Lippincott, 1971.

Murphy, Bruce A. *The Brandeis/Frankfurter Connection: The Secret Political Activities of Two Supreme Court Justices.* New York: Oxford Univ. Press, 1982.

Murphy, Walter, and Herman Pritchett. *Courts, Judges, and Politics: An Introduction to the Judicial Process.* New York: Random House, 1961.

Newman, Roger K. *Hugo Black: A Biography.* New York: Pantheon Books, 1994.

Paul, Randolph E. *Taxation in the United States.* Boston: Little, Brown, 1954.

Pearce, John Ed. *Divide and Dissent: Kentucky Politics 1930–1963.* Lexington: Univ. Press of Kentucky, 1987.

Pritchett, C. Herman. *Civil Liberties and the Vinson Court.* Chicago: Univ. of Chicago Press, 1954.

Przybyszewski, Linda. *The Republic according to John Marshall Harlan.* Chapel Hill: Univ. of North Carolina Press, 1999.

Rabban, David. *Free Speech in Its Forgotten Years.* Cambridge Univ. Press, 1997.

Radosh, Ronald, and Joyce Milton. *The Rosenberg File.* New York: Holt, Rinehart, and Winston, 1983.

Rees, David. *Harry Dexter White, A Study in Paradox.* New York: Coward, McCann, and Geoghegan, 1973.

Rehnquist, William O. *The Supreme Court: How It Was, How It Is.* New York: William Morrow, 1987.

Robertson, David. *Sly and Able.* New York: W.W. Norton, 1994.

Rosenberg, Gerald N. *The Hollow Hope: Can Courts Bring About Social Change?* Chicago: Univ. of Chicago Press, 1991.

Rudko, Frances. *Truman's Court: A Study in Judicial Restraint.* Westport, Conn.: Greenwood Press, 1988.

Sabin, Arthur J. *In Calmer Times: The Supreme Court and Red Monday.* Philadelphia: Univ. of Pennsylvania Press, 1999.

Schlesinger, Arthur M., Jr. *The Coming of the New Deal.* Boston: Houghton Mifflin, 1958.

Schwartz, Bernard. *A History of the Supreme Court.* New York: Oxford Univ. Press, 1993.

Somers, Herman M. *Presidential Agency, the Office of War Mobilization and Reconversion.* Cambridge, Mass.: Harvard Univ. Press, 1950.

Truman, Harry S. *Memoirs.* 2 vols. Garden City, N.Y.: Doubleday, 1955–1956.

Truman, Margaret. *Bess W. Truman.* New York: Macmillan, 1986.

Tushnet, Mark. *Making Civil Rights Law: Thurgood Marshall and the Supreme Court, 1936–1961.* New York: Oxford Univ. Press, 1994.

———. *The NAACP's Legal Strategy against Segregated Education, 1925–1950.* Chapel Hill: Univ. of North Carolina Press, 1987.

Urofsky, Melvin. *Division and Discord: The Supreme Court under Stone and Vinson, 1941–1953.* Columbia: Univ. of South Carolina Press, 1997.

———, ed. *The Supreme Court Justices: A Biographical Dictionary.* New York: Garland, 1994.

Van Dormael, Armand. *Bretton Woods, Birth of a Monetary System.* New York: Holmes and Meier, 1978.

Vose, Clement. *Caucasians Only: The Supreme Court, the NAACP, and the Restrictive Covenant Cases.* Berkeley: Univ. of California Press, 1959.

Weil, Gordon, and Ian Davidson. *The Gold War.* New York: Holt, Rinehart, and Winston, 1970.

Weinstein, Allen, and Alexander Vassiliev. *The Haunted Wood: Soviet Espionage in America—The Stalin Era.* New York: Random House, 1999.

Wolfford, George. *Lawrence County: A Pictorial History.* Ashland, Ky.: WWW Co., 1972.

Articles

Allen, Francis A. "Chief Justice Vinson and the Theory of Constitutional Government: A Tentative Appraisal." *Northwestern University Law Review* 49 (Mar.–Apr. 1954): 3–25.

———. "Remembering *Shelley* v. *Kraemer:* Of Public and Private Worlds." *Washington University Law Quarterly* 67 (1989): 709–35.

"Assassin's Bullets." *Louisville Courier-Journal,* Mar. 13, 1933.

Belair, Felix, Jr. "Mr. Truman's Friend—And His Nominee?" New York Times, Dec. 16, 1951.

Bendiner, Robert. "Available Vinson." *Collier's,* Mar. 22, 1952.

Bolner, James J. "Mr. Chief Justice Vinson and the Communist Conspiracy: A Reassessment." *Register of the Kentucky Historical Society* 66 (1968): 378–91.

Brenner, Saul, and Jan Palmer. "The Time Taken to Write Opinions as a Determinant of Opinion Assignment." Judicature 72 (1988): 179–84.

"Centre Vinson Memorial Foundation to Be Tribute to Late Chief Justice." *Lexington Herald,* Feb. 19, 1956.

"Charter for Postwar America." *Collier's,* Sept. 15, 1945, 90.

"Chief Justice–Nominee Vinson, in Lexington to Address U.K. Graduates, Sees Old Friends." *Louisville Courier-Journal,* June 8, 1946.

"Chief Justice Vinson and His Law Clerks." *Northwestern University Law Review* 49 (1954): 26–35.

Cohen, William. "Justice Douglas and the Rosenberg Case." *Cornell Law Review* 70 (1985): 211–52.

"Conservative Democrats Were Tax Bill Framers." *New York Times,* Apr. 23, 1936.

Crawford, Kenneth G., and Gilbert W. Stewart. "Fred M. Vinson." *American Mercury,* Apr. 1946, 409.

Danelski, David. "The Influence of the Chief Justice in the Decisional Process." In *Courts, Judges, and Politics: An Introduction to the Judicial Process,* ed. Walter F. Murphy and C. Herman Pritchett, 497–508. New York: Random House, 1961.

"A Declaration of Our Interdependence." *Louisville Courier-Journal,* July 4, 1945.

"A Disappointing Veto." *Cincinnati Times-Star,* June 29, 1938.

"An Economic Charter for America." *Chicago Sun,* July 4, 1945.

Elman, Philip. "The Solicitor General's Office, Justice Frankfurter, and Civil Rights Legislation, 1946–1960: An Oral History." *Harvard Law Review* 100 (1987): 817–52.

Ely, James W., Jr. "Property Rights and the Supreme Court in World War II." *Journal of Supreme Court History* 1 (1996): 19–34.

———. "Reflections on *Buchanan* v. *Warley,* Property Rights and Race. *Vanderbilt Law Review* 51 (1998): 953–73.

"Find Double Taxes Weigh on Business." *New York Times,* Jan. 16, 1933.

"Fostering a Cruel Illusion." *Macon Telegraph,* July 3, 1945.

Frank, John P. "Fred Vinson and the Chief Justiceship." *University of Chicago Law Review* 21 (winter 1954): 212–46.

———. "The United States Supreme Court, 1946–47." *University of Chicago Law Review* 15 (1947): 1–50.

———. "The United States Supreme Court, 1947–48." *University of Chicago Law Review* 16 (1948): 1–55.

———. "The United States Supreme Court, 1948–49." *University of Chicago Law Review* 17 (1949): 1–55.

———. "United States Supreme Court: 1949–50." *University of Chicago Law Review* 18 (1950): 1–54.

———. "United States Supreme Court: 1950–51." *University of Chicago Law Review* 19 (1951): 165–236.

———. "United States Supreme Court: 1951–52." *University of Chicago Law Review* 20 (1952): 1–68.

Frankfurter, Felix. "Twenty Years of Mr. Justice Holmes' Constitutional Opinions." *Harvard Law Review* 36 (1923).

Freund, Paul A. "The Supreme Court, 1951 Term." *Harvard Law Review* (1952): 89–184.

"Friends Praise Vinson As He Enters Cabinet." *Courier-Journal,* July 24, 1945.

Gregory, Charles O. "Government by Injunction Again." *University of Chicago Law Review* 14 (1947): 363–69.

Harper, Fowler V., and Alan S. Rosenthal. "What the Supreme Court Did Not Do in the 1949 Term—An Appraisal of Certiorari." *University of Pennsylvania Law Review* 99 (Nov. 1950): 293–325.

"Harry Dexter White and the International Monetary Fund." *Finance and Development,* Sept. 1998.

"Heat on Textiles." *Business Week,* Dec. 2, 1944, 80.

Herring, E. Pendleton. "First Session of the 73rd Congress," *American Political Science Review* 28 (Feb. 1934): 65–83.

Higginbotham, A. Leon. "45 Years in Civil Rights Law." *Ebony,* Nov. 1990, 80–86.

Hutchinson, Dennis J. "The Black-Jackson Feud." *Supreme Court Review* (1988): 203–43.

———. "Unanimity and Desegregation: Decision Making in the Supreme Court." *Georgetown Law Journal* 68 (1979): 1–87.

"Jacob's Voice, Esau's Hands." *Arkansas Democrat,* July 3, 1945.

Jaffe, Louis L. "The Supreme Court, 1950 Term." *Harvard Law Review* 65 (1951): 107–83.

"Jesse Jones's Successor." *New Republic,* Mar. 19, 1945, 114.

"Judge Vinson Never Met a Pay Roll." *Louisville Courier-Journal,* Mar. 7, 1945.

Kirkendall, Richard. "Fred M. Vinson." In *The Justices of the United States Supreme Court: Their Lives and Major Opinions,* ed. Leon Friedman and Fred L. Israel. 2639–2649. New York: R.R. Bowker and Chelsea House, 1969.

Klarman, Michael J. "*Brown,* Racial Change, and the Civil Rights Movement." *University of Virginia Law Review* 80 (1994): 7–150.

———. "Race and the Court in the Progressive Era." *Vanderbilt Law Review* 51 (1998): 881–953.

Lefberg, Irving. "Chief Justice Vinson and the Politics of Desegregation." *Emory Law Journal* 24 (1975): 243–312.

Lester, Wilbur R. "Fred M. Vinson in the Executive Branch." *Northwestern University Law Review* 49 (1954): 36–53.

"Loan Rumors Raised by Wolcott at Hearing on World Fund Bill." *New York Times,* Mar. 17, 1945, 10.

Maltz, Eric. "Only Partially Color Blind: John Marshall Harlan's View of Race and the Constitution." *Georgia State Law Review* 12 (1996): 973–1016.

"A Man Who Does Not Make Promises He Cannot Keep." *Boston Daily Globe,* Sept. 14, 1945.

Morley, Felix. "Affirmation of Materialism: Chief Justice Vinson Questions the Reality of Moral Standards." *Barrons,* June 18, 1951.

"O.W.M. Expected to Consult Roosevelt Soon; Vinson, Sworn In, Smiles 'For Last Time.'" *Louisville Courier-Journal,* May 30, 1943.

Palmer, Jan, and Saul Brenner. "Determinants of the Amount of Time Taken by the Vinson Court to Process Its Full Opinion Cases." *Journal of Supreme Court History* (1990) 142–51.

Parrish, Michael. "Cold War Justice: The Supreme Court and the Rosenbergs." *American Historical Review* 82 (1977): 804–42.

Pearson, Drew. "Washington Merry-Go-Round." *Louisville Courier-Journal,* Dec. 16, 1946.

Pedrick, Willard. "From Congress to the Court of Appeals." *Northwestern University Law Review* 49 (Mar.–Apr. 1954): 54–61.

"Portrait of Late Justice Vinson Is Presented to Centre College." *Lexington Herald,* Jan. 8, 1954.

"President Signs Coal Mining Bill." *New York Times,* Apr. 27, 1937.

"President Upheld by House in Veto of Subsidies Ban." *New York Times,* Feb. 19, 1944, 1.

Pringle, Henry F. "Sitter-on-the-Lid." *Saturday Evening Post,* Mar. 18, 1944.

"Profit Tax Relief Put at Top of List." *New York Times,* Dec. 2, 1937.

Riggs, Robert L. "Senate Group Gives Its Okay to Vinson." *Louisville Courier-Journal,* June 20, 1946.

————. "Vinson Hates to Go Up and Let Man He Fought Get the Treasury Post." *Louisville Courier-Journal,* June 7, 1946.

Rodell, Fred. "The Chief Justice." *Life,* June 24, 1946.

————. "The Supreme Court Is Standing Pat." *New Republic,* Dec. 19, 1949, 11–13.

"Secretary Vinson Urges Granting of Loan to Britain." *Louisville Courier-Journal,* Mar. 24, 1946, 1.

"See Vast Loan Use for Security Fund." *New York Times,* Feb. 9, 1935.

"Senate Votes Rise of 8C in Rail Pay, Overruling Vinson." *New York Times,* Dec. 10, 1943, 1.

"A Service the Farmers Do Not Need Is Proposed in the Flannagan Bill." *Lexington Herald,* May 22, 1935.

Stephens, Harold M. "The Chief Justice." *American Bar Association Journal* 32 (1946): 387–89.

Stern, Robert L. "The Rosenberg Case in Perspective—Its Present Significance." *Journal of Supreme Court History* (1990): 79–92.

Stewart, Kenneth. "Presidential Timber: Amiable 'Available' Vinson." *P.M. Sunday Picture News,* Sept. 14, 1947.

"Supreme Court Postscript." *Progressive,* May 27, 1956.

Tushnet, Mark, and Katya Lezin. "What Really Happened in Brown v. Board of Education." *Columbia Law Review* 91 (Dec. 1991): 1867–1930.

"Vinson: Senate's 'Businessman.'" *Business Week,* Mar. 17, 1945, 17–19.

"Vinson, Acheson Urge British Loan." *New York Times,* Jan. 13, 1946, 25.

"Vinson Becomes Head of Treasury." *New York Times,* July 24, 1945, 13.

"Vinson Calls Loan to Britain a 'Must.'" *New York Times,* Mar. 6, 1946, 8.

"Vinson Campaigns for British Loan." *New York Times,* Jan. 10, 1946, 13.

"Vinson Has Trouble Explaining Tax Cuts with Borrowed Specs." *Cincinnati Post,* Oct. 17, 1945.

"Vinson Hits Subsidy Foes." *New York Times,* Oct. 21, 1943, 28.

"Vinson Makes Statement." *Mt. Sterling (Ky.) Gazette,* May 2, 1930.

"Vinson's Executive Talent, Poker Playing Win Friends." *St. Louis Star-Times,* Apr. 4, 1945.

"Vinson's New Job Thrills His Spouse." *Washington Post,* May 30, 1943.

"Vinson Tells U.S. What It Faces against Japan, Eases Some Curbs." *New York Times,* May 10, 1945, 17.

"We'll Appeal to Uncle." *Ogden (Utah) Standard-Examiner,* July 6, 1945.

Wechsler, Herbert. "Toward Neutral Principles of Constitutional Law." *Harvard Law Review* 73 (1959): 1–35.

"Why Farmers Are against the Flannagan Bill." *Lexington Herald,* May 27, 1935.

Dissertations

Atkinson, David N. "Mr. Justice Minton and the Supreme Court, 1949–1956." Ph.D. diss., Univ. of Iowa, 1962.

Bolner, James J. "Mr. Chief Justice Vinson: His Politics and His Constitutional Law." Ph.D. diss., Univ. of Virginia, 1962.

Hatcher, John H. "Fred Vinson: Congressman from Kentucky, a Political Biography: 1890–1938." Ph.D. diss., Univ. of Cincinnati, 1967.

O'Brien, Kevin J. *"Dennis v. United States:* The Cold War, the Communist Conspiracy, and the F.B.I." Ph.D. diss., Cornell Univ., 1979.

Court Cases

Adamson v. *California,* 332 U.S. 46 (1948).

Adler v. *Board of Education,* 342 U.S. 485 (1952).

American Communications Assn. v. *Douds,* 339 U.S. 382 (1950).

Andree Seedman, Inc. et al. v. *Administrator of Wage and Hour Division, U.S. Department of Labor,* 122 F2d 634 (1941).

Avery v. *Georgia,* 345 U.S. 559 (1953).

Bailey v. *Richardson,* 341 U.S. 918 (1951).

Barrows v. *Jackson,* 346 U.S. 249 (1953).

Blau [Irving] v. *United States,* 340 U.S. 332 (1951).

Blau [Patricia] v. *United States,* 340 U.S. 159 (1950).

Bob Lo Excursions v. *Michigan,* 333 U.S. 28 (1948).

Bolling v. *Sharp,* 347 U.S. 497 (1954).

Brandenburg v. *Ohio,* 395 U.S. 454 (1969).

Breard v. *City of Alexandria,* 341 U.S. 622 (1951).

Briggs v. *Elliott,* 347 U.S. 483 (1954).

Brock v. *North Carolina,* 344 U.S. 424 (1953).

Brown v. *Allen,* 344 U.S. 443 (1953).

Brown v. *Board of Education,* 347 U.S. 483 (1954).

Buchanan v. *Warley,* 245 U.S. 60 (1917).

Bute v. *Illinois,* 333 U.S. 640 (1948).

California v. *United States,* 332 U.S. 19 (1947).

Cantwell v. *Connecticut,* 310 U.S. 296 (1940).

Carlson v. *Landon,* 342 U.S. 524 (1952).

Carter v. *Illinois,* 329 U.S. 173 (1946).

Chaplinsky v. *New Hampshire,* 315 U.S. 568 (1942).

Christoffel v. *United States,* 338 U.S. 84 (1949).

Davies Warehouse Co. v. *Brown, Price Administrator,* 137 F2d 201 (1943).

Davis v. *County School Board,* 347 U.S. 483 (1954).

Dennis v. *United States,* 183 F2d 201 (1950).

Dennis v. *United States,* 341 U.S. 494 (1951).

Di Re v. *United States,* 332 U.S. 581 (1948).

Evans v. *Ockerhausen,* 100 F2d 695 (1938).

Feiner v. *New York,* 340 U.S. 315 (1951).

Foster v. *Illinois,* 332 U.S. 134 (1947).

Francis v. *Resweber,* 329 U.S. 459 (1947).

Garner v. *Board of Public Works,* 341 U.S. 716 (1951).

Gayes v. *New York*, 332 U.S. 145 (1947).

Gebhart v. *Belton*, 347 U.S. 483 (1954).

Gerende v. *Board of Supervisors of Elections*, 341 U.S. 56 (1951).

Gibbs v. *Burke*, 337 U.S. 773 (1949).

Gideon v. *Wainwright*, 372 U.S. 335 (1963).

Gitlow v. *New York*, 268 U.S. 652 (1925).

Go-Bart Importing Company v. *United States*, 282 U.S. 344 (1931).

Gryger v. *Burke*, 334 U.S. 728 (1948).

Haley v. *Ohio*, 332 U.S. 596 (1948).

Harris v. *South Carolina*, 338 U.S. 68 (1949).

Harris v. *United States*, 331 U.S. 145 (1947).

Heikkila v. *Barber*, 345 U.S. 229 (1953).

Henderson v. *United States*, 339 U.S. 816 (1950).

Hurd v. *Hodge*, 334 U.S. 24 (1948).

Jennings v. *Illinois*, 342 U.S. 104 (1951).

Jewell Ridge Coal Corp. v. *Local 6167, United Mine Workers*, 325 U.S. 161 (1945).

John Hancock Mutual Life Insurance. Co. v. *Helvering, Com'r of Revenue*, 128 F2d 745 (1942).

Johnson v. *United States*, 333 U.S. 10 (1948).

Joint Anti-Fascist Refugee Committee v. *McGrath*, 341 U.S. 123 (1951).

Kovacs v. *Cooper*, 336 U.S. 77 (1949).

Kunz v. *New York*, 340 U.S. 290 (1951).

Kwong Hai Chew v. *Colding*, 344 U.S. 590 (1953).

McCord v. *Commissioner of Internal Revenue*, 123 F2d 164 (1941).

McLaurin v. *Oklahoma*, 339 U.S. 637 (1950).

Missouri ex rel Gaines v. *Canada*, 305 U.S. 337 (1938).

Morgan v. *Virginia*, 328 U.S. 373 (1946).

National Association of Wool Manufacturers v. *Fleming*, 122 F2d 617 (1941).

National Federation of Railway Workers v. *National Mediation Board*, 110 F2d 529 (1940).

Near v. *Minnesota*, 231 U.S. 697 (1931).

Nueslein v. *District of Columbia*, 115 F2d 690 (1940).

Niemotko v. *Maryland*, 340 U.S. 268 (1951).

NLRB v. *Jones and Laughlin Steel Corp.*, 301 U.S. 128 (1937).

Oyama v. *California*, 332 U.S. 633 (1948).

Palko v. *Connecticut*, 302 U.S. 319 (1937).

Palmer v. *Ashe*, 342 U.S. 134 (1951).

Parmelee v. *United States*, 113 F2d 729 (1940).

Plessy v. *Ferguson*, 163 U.S. 537 (1896).

Prevost v. *Morgenthau, U.S. Secretary of the Treasury*, 106 F2d 330 (1939).

Quicksall v. *Michigan*, 339 U.S. 660 (1950).

Railroad Retirement Board v. *Bates*, 126 F2d 642 (1942).

Rochin v. *California*, 342 U.S. 165 (1952).

Rogers v. *United States*, 340 U.S. 367 (1951).

Rosenberg et al. v. *United States,* 346 U.S. 273 (1953).

Saia v. *New York,* 334 U.S. 558 (1948).

Scharfield v. *Richardson,* 133 F2d 340 (1942).

Schenck v. *United States,* 249 U.S. 47 (1919).

Securities and Exchange Commission v. *Chenery Corporation,* 332 U.S. 194 (1947).

Shaughnessy v. *United States ex rel. Mezei,* 345 U.S. 206 (1953).

Shelley v. *Kraemer,* 334 U.S. 1 (1948).

Sipuel v. *Oklahoma,* 332 U.S. 631 (1948).

Southern Garment Mfrs. Association, Inc. et al v. *Fleming, Administrator, Wage and Hour Division,* 122 F2d 622 (1941).

Speller v. *Allen,* 344 U.S. 443 (1955).

Stack v. *Boyle,* 342 U.S. 1 (1951).

Sweatt v. *Painter,* 339 U.S. 629 (1950).

Switchmen's Union of North America et al. v. *National Mediation Board, et al.,* 135 F2d 785 (1943).

Switchmen's Union of North America et al. v. *National Mediation Board et al.,* 320 U.S. 297 (1943).

Terminiello v. *Chicago,* 337 U.S. 1 (1949).

Terry v. *Adams,* 345 U.S. 461 (1953).

Trupiano v. *United States,* 334 U.S. 700 (1948).

Turner v. *Pennsylvania,* 338 U.S. 62 (1949).

United Mine Workers of America v. *United States,* 330 U.S. 258 (1947).

United States v. *Alcea Band of Tillamooks,* 329 U.S. 40 (1946).

United States v. *Bryan,* 339 U.S. 323 (1950).

United States v. *Fleischman,* 339 U.S. 349 (1950).

United States v. *Offutt,* 127 F2d 337 (1942).

United States v. *Rabinowitz,* 339 U.S. 56 (1950).

United States v. *Shipp,* 203 U.S. 563 (1906).

United States v. *United Mine Workers of America,* 330 U.S. 270 (1947).

United States ex rel Denholm & McKay Co. v. *United States Board of Tax Appeals,* 125 F2d 557 (1942).

United States ex rel. Knauff v. *Shaughnessey,* 338 U.S. 537 (1950).

Upshaw v. *United States,* 335 U.S. 410 (1948).

Viereck v. *United States,* 130 F2d 945 (1942).

Viereck v. *United States,* 318 U.S. 236 (1943).

Viereck v. *United States,* 139 F2d 847 (1944).

Warring v. *Colpoys,* 122 F2d 642 (1941).

Watts v. *Indiana,* 338 U.S. 49 (1949).

Weeks v. *United States,* 232 U.S. 383 (1914).

West Coast Hotel Company v. *Parrish,* 300 U.S. 379 (1937).

Whitney v. *California,* 274 U.S. 357 (1927).

Wieman v. *Updegraff,* 344 U.S. 183 (1952).

Wolf v. *Colorado,* 338 U.S. 25 (1949).

Yates v. *United States,* 354 U.S. 298 (1957).

Youngstown Sheet and Tube v. *Sawyer,* 343 U.S. 579 (1952).

Index